Elmer A. Martens and Willard M. Swartley, Editors

Daniel

Paul M. Lederach

HERALD PRESS
Scottdale, Pennsylvania
Waterloo, Ontario

Library of Congress Cataloging-in-Publication Data
Lederach, Paul M.
Daniel / Paul M. Lederach.
p. cm.
Includes bibliographical references and index.
ISBN 0-8361-3663-2
1. Bible. O.T. Daniel—Commentaries. I. Bible. O.T. Daniel. English. New Revised Standard. 1994. II. Title.
BS1555.3.L43 1994
224'.5077—dc20 94-19516
CIP

The paper used in this publication is recycled and meets the minimum requirements of American National Standard for Information Sciences—Permanence of Paper for Printed Library Materials, ANSI Z39.48-1984.

BELIEVERS CHURCH BIBLE COMMENTARY: DANIEL

Library of Congress Catalog Card Number: 94-19516
International Standard Book Number: 0-8361-3663-2
Printed in the United States of America
Cover by Merrill R. Miller

03 02 01 00 99 98 97 96 95 94 10 9 8 7 6 5 4 3 2 1

To Mary,
my spouse of over forty years,
Proverbs 31:28-29

BELIEVERS CHURCH BIBLE COMMENTARY
VOLUMES AVAILABLE TO 1995

Old Testament
Genesis, by Eugene F. Roop
Jeremiah, by Elmer A. Martens
Daniel, by Paul M. Lederach

New Testament
Matthew, by Richard B. Gardner
Acts, by Chalmer E. Faw
Colossians, Philemon, by Ernest D. Martin
1 and 2 Thessalonians, by Jacob W. Elias

Other Volumes in Process

Contents

Part 3: Reading Scriptures and Receiving Visions, 8:1—12:13 (in Hebrew)

Series Foreword

The Believers Church Bible Commentary Series makes available a new tool for basic Bible study. It is published for all who seek more fully to understand the original message of Scripture and its meaning for today—Sunday school teachers, members of Bible study groups, students, pastors, and other seekers. The series is based on the conviction that God is still speaking to all who will listen, and that the Holy Spirit makes the Word a living and authoritative guide for all who want to know and do God's will.

The desire to help as wide a range of readers as possible has determined the approach of the writers. Since no blocks of biblical text are provided, readers may continue to use the translation with which they are most familiar. The writers of the series use the *New Revised Standard Version*, the *Revised Standard Version*, the *New International Version*, and the *New American Standard Bible* on a comparative basis. They indicate which text they follow most closely, as well as where they make their own translations. The writers have not worked alone, but in consultation with select counselors, the series' editors, and the Editorial Council.

Every volume illuminates the Scriptures; provides necessary theological, sociological, and ethical meanings; and in general, makes "the rough places plain." Critical issues are not avoided, but neither are they moved into the foreground as debates among scholars. Each section offers explanatory notes, followed by focused articles, "The Text in Biblical Context" and "The Text in the Life of the Church." This commentary aids the interpretive process but does not try to supersede the authority of the Word and Spirit as discerned in the gathered church.

The term *believers church* has often been used in the history of the church. Since the sixteenth century, it has frequently been applied to the Anabaptists and later the Mennonites, as well as to the Church of the Brethren and similar groups. As a descriptive term, it includes more than Mennonites and Brethren. *Believers church* now represents specific theological understandings, such as believers baptism, commitment to the Rule of Christ in Matthew 18:15-20 as crucial for church membership, belief in the power of love in all relationships, and willingness to follow Christ in the way of the cross. The writers chosen for the series stand in this tradition.

Believers church people have always been known for their emphasis on obedience to the simple meaning of Scripture. Because of this, they do not have a long history of deep historical-critical biblical scholarship. This series attempts to be faithful to the Scriptures while also taking archaeology and current biblical studies seriously. Doing this means that at many points the writers will not differ greatly from interpretations which can be found in many other good commentaries. Yet basic presuppositions about Christ, the church and its mission, God and history, human nature, the Christian life, and other doctrines do shape a writer's interpretation of Scripture. Thus this series, like all other commentaries, stands within a specific historical church tradition.

Many in this stream of the church have expressed a need for help in Bible study. This is justification enough to produce the Believers Church Bible Commentary. Nevertheless, the Holy Spirit is not bound to any tradition. May this series be an instrument in breaking down walls between Christians in North America and around the world, bringing new joy in obedience through a fuller understanding of the Word.

The Editorial Council

Author's Preface

When I was asked to prepare a commentary on the book of Daniel for the Believers Church Bible Commentary, I was hesitant to accept the invitation. The interpretation of Daniel is a matter of sharp controversy. I was aware that whatever I wrote would come under attack. Yet I am inclined to avoid criticism and controversy.

My life's work has been in Christian education publications. For a period of three decades, I have wrestled with the issues of communicating biblical truth to persons across the life span within the congregation. My goal has been to assist them to respond to Jesus Christ in love, faith, and obedience to the full extent of their ability at every age. I have planned church-school curriculum, guided writers, and edited teaching materials for children, youth, and adults. In addition to this, I have served as an ordained minister for fifty years, attempting in that role to communicate the gospel in preaching and in pastoral care. Thus in many respects, I was prepared to write this style of commentary.

To write a commentary is no small undertaking. I have been studying the book of Daniel over a period of years. This led to opportunities to preach, teach, and lecture in a variety of contexts. My interpretation of Daniel, while not ignoring traditional approaches, differs from many commonly held views. It is presented for further testing. So, after consulting with many persons, I accepted the invitation.

The Believers Church Bible Commentary attempts to address two important needs. First, to provide interpretations of the books of the Bible that will be useful to active lay persons in congregations such as Sunday school teachers. Second, to provide interpretations of the books of the Bible that lift up, support, and do not overlook the insights and commitments given to believers in the identifiable theological stream known as "Anabaptist."

For Lay Persons

What should a commentary written for congregational lay persons be like? Many commentary writers seem to address their comments to fellow members of the scholarly community. When writers comment on a particular verse or paragraph, they often do so by agreeing or disagreeing with another scholar's comments. This is important in scholarly work and helpful in expanding, amplifying, correcting, or supporting new interpretations. However, active lay persons may have difficulty finding their way through the thicket of scholarly conversations when looking for help to teach in the congregation.

Consequently, I have tried to write this commentary as though talking face to face with lay persons. I have attempted to distill from many sources and from personal study the essence of each segment of the book. References to other commentaries, to scholarly works, and to the positions of many scholars have been kept to a minimum. References to passages in Old and New Testament books that shed light or are relevant to the text under study have been included without hesitation. While this approach obviously has its limitations, the hope is that these comments will assist lay persons in grasping the sense and significance of Daniel in its historical context, within the Scripture, and in the light of competent and recent studies.

Anabaptist Perspective

To write a commentary giving attention to Anabaptist theological commitments is a challenge for at least two reasons. First, we do not go to the Scriptures to find support for preconceived notions. As one informed by and committed to Anabaptist thought, I have tried to allow the book of Daniel to speak for itself—insofar as possible for me, with a Western education, standing in the North American culture, with a Swiss-Mennonite background, and living in the twentieth century. I am surprised and gratified to see emerge in almost serendipitous fashion many themes central to the Anabaptist tradition: faithfulness in persecution, the way of nonresistance, in but not of the world, commitment to and participation in the faith community, faith commitments taking precedence over the demands of the state (theology of the two kingdoms), and the emphasis on discipleship.

Second, the articulation of themes of Anabaptist theology is in transition. In recent years tremendous strides have been made in understanding the roots and sixteenth-century milieu of Anabaptism. Also, as persons in modern times have joined the movement from many ethnic, cultural, and geographic backgrounds, they have broadened and deepened these themes and shown new implications of them. Fifty years ago the noted Anabaptist historian, theologian, and teacher Harold S. Bender delivered his presidential address to the American Society of Church History, "The Anabaptist Vision" (1943). This was a fresh interpretation of the main themes of Anabaptism and has served as a classic statement since it was first presented. But if contemporary scholars and theologians would attempt such a statement today, the "vision" likely would be stated differently. At the same time, churches that identify themselves as part of the Anabaptist family are constantly at work stating and restating their confessions of faith.

A decade ago when I began to study the book of Daniel, I soon was convinced that, whatever predictive elements are in the book, they must not overshadow the persistent call to endurance and faithfulness. This call comes in the midst of suffering, persecution, and alienation resulting from believers' allegiance to God and his kingdom. This kingdom is ever present and is moving to fullness and completeness in God's own time and way. In this context the great Anabaptist themes noted earlier emerge with clarity and power. The book of Daniel speaks to every generation of the faithful, telling in stories and visions of God's ultimate control of history and of the way his people must live and act in each crisis until the end.

There may indeed be some outrageously evil tyrant(s) before God brings to an end the time between Jesus Christ's ascension and his return (2 Thess. 2:3-6; 1 John 2:18-22). The final focus of Daniel, however, is not on the beasts of history, whose end will come, with none to help. Instead, it is on the Ancient of Days who is sovereign over all, one like a son of man who is given kingship, the holy ones [angels] of the Most High who protect the faithful, and God's everlasting dominion entrusted to the holy people (Dan. 7:9-27).

Many Thanks

I thank many persons for their help in writing this commentary.

First, I am grateful to the Franconia (Pa.) Mennonite Church for their cooperation while I served as a pastor and also tried to find time to write. I am grateful to the group of lay persons in the congregation who read parts of the manuscript and gave helpful suggestions. I want to thank the church council and the elders for granting me several weeks each year to get away to write and also for including in Geraldine Cassel's work as administrative assistant the large task of typing the manuscript, using the congregation's computer. She has been untiring in seeing the manuscript through a variety of revisions to its present form.

I am grateful to my sister and brother-in-law, Mary Jane and Hiram Hershey, for allowing me to use their house facing the Atlantic Ocean in Ocean Grove, New Jersey, as a place to write.

In recent years I enjoyed many invitations to teach the book of Daniel on a variety of levels, from seminary credit courses to conference studies for ministers and congregational programs. During these times of study, I have been challenged and enriched by participants and have been encouraged to keep writing as they became familiar with the views expressed in this commentary.

I am grateful to James C. Longacre, for many years coordinator for the Franconia Mennonite Conference (with offices at Souderton, Pa.) and now pastor of the historic Salford Mennonite Church, Harleysville (Pa.), and to Gerald C. Studer, Lansdale (Pa.), conference minister for the Atlantic Coast Mennonite Conference, for reading the manuscript. Their help was both encouraging and valuable, with strong support for the direction of the commentary and suggestions for improving the content and sharpening the focus.

I am grateful to the Believers Church Bible Commentary Editorial Council for its support. I am especially grateful to Elmer A. Martens, Old Testament editor, for his good guidance, careful editing, and many insightful and helpful suggestions for the organization and content of this commentary. I value his expertise in the Old Testament, and especially in Hebrew and Aramaic. I appreciate his help in assuring the accuracy of my references to words in the original languages. S. David Garber, book editor at Herald Press, must be included in this list of persons who have been of great help, as he made chronology consistent, improved the order of materials, and filled in gaps at important points along the way. Millard C. Lind, professor of Old Testament, Associated Mennonite Biblical Seminary, Elkhart, Indiana, has provided many helpful suggestions for improving the content of the commentary.

Finally, I am grateful to my wife, Mary, for her patience and support. Many days I spent in study and writing—days which we could have spent together doing things of interest to her. Nevertheless, she was unfailing in encouraging me to complete the task.

The writing of a commentary is never done. There is always another point to be made or another area to be explored. Nor is any commentary a final word. Some will disagree with what I have written. But I have tried to write with integrity and with a spirit of humility. Perhaps God's truth is like a rainbow, made up of many colors. I hope this commentary will contribute to that rainbow by providing some color, however dim or overlooked, that will contribute to the overall beauty of God's truth as revealed in Daniel.

Paul M. Lederach
Souderton, Pennsylvania

Becoming Acquainted

The Man Daniel

The book of Daniel takes its name from the leading character, a person called Daniel. The name means "God has judged." The name was common among the Hebrews. David had a son named Daniel (1 Chron. 3:1). Among the exiles returning from Babylon was a son of Ithamar with the name Daniel (Ezra 8:2). The name also appears in a list of priests setting their seal to "a firm agreement" (Neh. 9:38; 10:6).

Ezekiel links a man named Daniel with Noah and Job. This Daniel would likely have lived early in biblical history, between the flood and the patriarchs. He was noted for righteousness (Ezek. 14:14). The name Daniel is mentioned in the tirade against the prince of Tyre. The prince was condemned for pride in thinking himself divine. God's word came to the prince, "You are indeed wiser than Daniel" (Ezek. 28:3). This Daniel is characterized as wise. The relation of these shadowy figures to the central character in the book of Daniel is not clear. One suggestion, still debated, is that the Daniel mentioned in Ezekiel is the Daniel of the Ugaritic myths (ca. 14th century B.C.), known to us since 1930 from the Ras Shamra excavations in modern Syria, ancient Phoenicia. On this assumption, all three—Noah, Job, and an early Daniel—could be non-Israelites.

The hero of the book of Daniel, however, combines in himself the righteousness of the Hebrew faith and the wisdom of the Babylonian sages. Daniel is a person of unshakable faith and of courage in persecution. He also has ability to receive and interpret visions and dreams.

What is known about the person of Daniel comes from the book itself. He was among an early group of deportees to Babylon, taken by Nebuchadnezzar perhaps in late 604 B.C., more likely in 597 B.C. *[Nebuchadnezzar, p. 293.]* (See essays.) Daniel stays in Babylon until the first year of Cyrus, 539 B.C. (1:21), and one of his visions is reported to come in the third year of Cyrus (10:1). Thus Daniel's presence and service in Babylon span a period of sixty to seventy years.

Structure: Stories and Visions

On the surface, the book has a simple structure. There are six stories (Dan. 1–6) and four visions (Dan. 7–12). The stories, easily told, are filled with human interest. The visions are complicated, with many obscure references, and largely in apocalyptic form, to reveal hidden heavenly messages in relation to earthly events.

Part of the book Daniel is in the Hebrew language and part in Aramaic. In addition, some parts are written in the first person (*I*) while others are in third person. There is no common agreement among scholars as to how the book is best divided for purposes of interpretation. Nor is there agreement as to the authorship and the dating of the book. *[Daniel: Date and Authorship, p. 285.]*. Even the length of the book itself is not without discussion, since the Greek version is longer than the Hebrew version. *[Supplements to Daniel, p. 297.]*

In this commentary a three-part structure is recognized:

Part 1: Introduction

Chapter 1 provides introductory material for the book. It ties the book to history, citing specific persons, events, and dates. By verse 6, it presents Daniel and his companions Hananiah, Mishael, and Azariah. It sets the stage for the stories that follow by introducing such themes as those about a God who acts, allegiance to God in the face of competing allegiances, and faithful living in a hostile environment.

Part 2: A Tract to the Nations

Chapters 2:4b to 7:28 are in the Aramaic language. As the tongue of culture and commerce, it was the international language of the time, much like English is today. Though some feel the whole book was originally written in Aramaic, with 1:1—2:4a and 8:1—12:13 translated later into Hebrew, nevertheless the Aramaic section is treated as a unit. Not only is the language international, but also information about the God of Israel is addressed to *all peoples, nations, and languages* by the leading political figures of the times (4:2; cf. [compare] 3:29; 6:25). The stories of Daniel and his associates, the acts of God, and the testimonies of world rulers comprise a message to the nations about Israel's God. Yet this material addresses a dual audience. It speaks meaningfully to the dislocated and suffering people of God as well as to *all peoples, nations, and languages.*

The tract to the nations begins with the kingdom of God. Nebuchadnezzar dreams (Dan. 2) of a great image with head of gold, breast and arms of silver, middle and thighs of bronze, legs of iron, and feet of iron and clay (2:32). According to Daniel's interpretation, this image represents four earthly kingdoms. But these kingdoms give way to a *kingdom* that *the God of heaven will set up*, one *that shall never be destroyed* (2:44). This kingdom is inaugurated by a *stone . . . cut from the mountain not by hands*, which in the vision struck the image, broke it into pieces, and then *filled the whole earth* (2:45, 34-35).

The tract to the nations concludes with the kingship and kingdom of God. In Daniel's vision (chap. 7), one like a son of man (RSV; NRSV: human being) comes before the Ancient One (RSV: Ancient of Days). He is given dominion, glory, and kingship that *all peoples, nations, and languages should serve him* (7:14). This kingdom in turn *shall be given to the people of the holy ones of the Most High; their kingdom shall be an everlasting kingdom, and all dominions shall serve and obey them* (7:27).

Between these pictures of the kingdom of God at the beginning and at the end of the tract, kings and kingdoms are confronted by the God of Israel through his faithful servants. In chapter 3, Shadrach, Meshach, and Abednego (renamed, 1:7) refuse to bow to Nebuchadnezzar's image of gold. Their faithfulness and subsequent deliverance from the fiery furnace leads Nebuchadnezzar to issue a decree warning *any people, nation, or language* about disrespect, and affirming that *there is no other god who is able to deliver in this way* (3:29).

In chapter 6, Daniel refuses to cease praying to his God. After Daniel is delivered from the lions' den, Darius writes to *all peoples and nations of every language throughout the whole world*. He decrees that *all . . . should tremble and fear before the God of Daniel,* because *he is the living God, . . . his kingdom shall never be destroyed*, and *he delivers and rescues* and *works signs and wonders in heaven and on earth* (6:25-27).

In the middle two stories (Dan. 4–5), God confronts two kings directly. Nebuchadnezzar struts on the roof of his palace and gloats over the city of Babylon: *Is not this magnificent Babylon, which I have built as a royal capital by my mighty power and for my glorious majesty?* (4:30). He is struck with insanity until he has *learned that the Most High has sovereignty over the kingdom of mortals and gives it to whom he will* (4:32). The king's reason returns when he lifts his eyes to heaven. In a letter to *all peoples, nations and languages* (4:1), he not only speaks of the greatness of the Most High God but also confesses that *all his works are truth, and his ways are justice; and he is able to bring low those who walk in pride* (4:37).

Next, God confronts Belshazzar through a hand mysteriously writing on the wall of the great banquet hall (5:5). Belshazzar, unwilling to turn from his sacrilegious ways, meets death on the night of his revelry (5:30). That event speaks loudly enough. No further call is needed for all peoples, nations, and languages to learn about the God of Israel.

Chapter 7 completes the Aramaic section. The four metals of the image in chapter 2 (gold, silver, bronze, and iron) parallel the four beasts of chapter 7 (lion, bear, leopard, and the beast *terrifying and dreadful and exceedingly strong;* 7:4-7). In style and content, chapter 7 departs from the material in earlier chapters. This is a vision, not a human-interest story. Its apocalyptic style sets the stage for the visions that follow in the third part of the book, chapters 8 to 12. *[Apocalyptic Literature, p. 280.]* Though chapter 7 furthers the theme of the kingdom of God begun through Nebuchadnezzar's dream in chapter 2, it also introduces a terrible and dreadful figure, a fourth beast that makes war with the saints and prevails over them. This dreadful king keeps appearing in the visions that follow. But before the dreadful acts of this beastly king are unveiled, chapter 7 makes clear that his fate is sealed: *The beast was put to death, and its body destroyed and given over to be burned with fire* (7:11). *His dominion shall be taken away, to be consumed and totally destroyed* (7:26).

Chapter 7, therefore, serves a dual purpose. It completes the tract to the nations. It also introduces Daniel's visions, written in the first person, about the trials and tribulations that will come upon the people of God many years later when the dreadful king Antiochus IV Epiphanes (175-164 B.C.) comes on the scene. *[Antiochus Epiphanes, p. 279.]*

Part 3: Reading Scriptures and Receiving Visions

The third section, chapters 8:1—12:13, contains three visions of Daniel. Chapter 8 is of a ram and goat. This provides a brief review of secular history from the time of Alexander the Great to the emergence of a king of bold countenance who would destroy the people of the saints, who confronts God himself, but who will be broken by no human hand. The vision of the *ram* and *male goat* is interpreted by Gabriel.

The next vision comes to Daniel meditating on a prophecy of Jeremiah, after his lengthy, intercessory prayer (chap. 9). In his prayer, Daniel reviews sacred history, recalling God's power, righteousness, love, and faithfulness on behalf of his people in contrast to their sin, rebellion, and rejection of his commandments and ordinances. Daniel prays for forgiveness and mercy, and for the restoration of Jerusalem and its sanctuary.

Again Gabriel appears to Daniel. He does not speak of Israel's restoration to their homeland after the seventy years of Jeremiah. Instead, Gabriel speaks of great trouble coming 490 years later. As in the other visions, the focus is on a dreadful king to come. Again, the end of the king is assured, when *the decreed end is poured out upon the desolator* (9:27).

The third vision (chaps. 10–12) has a lengthy introduction followed by a veiled retelling or foretelling of history from Alexander the Great to the rise of Antiochus IV Epiphanes. *[Seleucids, p. 295.]* As in the previous visions, the dreadful king comes to his end, *with no one to help him* (11:45). The final part of the vision adds a significant dimension. Though the faithful have suffered and many have died at the hands of tyrants, and though kings and kingdoms are brought down, this is not the whole story for the faithful. There is resurrection. *Many of those who sleep in the dust of the earth shall awake, some to everlasting life, and some to shame and everlasting contempt. Those who are wise shall shine like the brightness of the sky, and those who lead many to righteousness, like the stars forever and ever* (12:2-3).

This final revelation completes the theme begun in chapter 2: *the God of heaven will set up a kingdom that shall never be destroyed* (2:44). That theme is further clarified in chapter 7: *the kingship . . . shall be given to the people of the holy ones of the Most High; their kingdom shall be an everlasting kingdom, and all dominions shall serve and obey them* (7:27). The same theme is then climaxed in the resurrection of the *wise*, who *shall shine . . . like the stars for ever and ever* (12:2-3).

INTRODUCTION

(HEBREW)

Ch. 1
Ties Book to History
Worldwide Acts of God
Introduces Daniel and Companions
Allegiance to God
Sets Stage for Events and Conflicts to Follow

TRACT TO THE NATIONS

(ARAMAIC)

	Ch. 2	Ch. 3	Ch. 4	Ch. 5	Ch. 6	Ch. 7
	Theme A KINGDOM	Theme B TEST OF FAITHFULNESS	Theme C RULE OF GOD	Theme C RULE OF GOD	Theme B TEST OF FAITHFULNESS	Theme A KINGDOM
	Nebuchadnezzar's Dream	Burning Fiery Furnace	Nebuchadnezzar's Madness	Writing on the Wall	Lions' Den	Earthly Turmoil Heavenly Court
	Statue—*Four Metals*					*Four Beasts*
ALL PEOPLES, NATIONS, AND LANGUAGES		3:29	4:1	5:19	6:25	7:14
TRUTH ABOUT GOD FOR THE WHOLE WORLD	God of Gods Is Revealer 2:47	Able to Deliver 3:29	Works Truth, Justice; Abases Proud. 4:37	Peril of Refusing to Honor God 5:26, 30	The Living God Works Signs & Wonders. 6:26-27	
	God Will Set Up a Kingdom 2:44					Kingdom Given to Holy Ones and People of the Most High 7:18, 22, 27

VISIONS — FUTURE OF DANIEL'S PEOPLE

(HEBREW)

Ch. 7	Ch. 8	Ch. 9	Ch. 10–12
Four Beasts	Charging Ram Flying Goat	Jeremiah's Prophecy	Great Conflict
7:14	Overview of History 8:3-14	Intercessory Prayer 9:3-19	Preparation for Vision, Ch. 10; Vision Ch. 11:2–12:4; Conclusion 12:5-13
RISE AND FALL OF THE DREADFUL KING *AS TOLD BY:*			
Heavenly Being 7:7-11, 23-26	Gabriel 8:23-25	Gabriel 9:26-27	Heavenly Being 11:21-45
Kingdom Given to Holy Ones and People of the Most High 7:18, 22, 27			The Wise Shall Shine Like Stars Forever and Ever 12:3

The book of Daniel both in its stories and apocalyptic visions emphasizes the sovereignty of God. It provides courage and hope for God's people in the midst of a hostile culture. At the same time, the Aramaic tract to the nations bears witness to all peoples, nations, and languages about the nature and work of Israel's God. This is an offer of grace to the world, a missionary motif. We do not know how widely this tract was circulated or what its impact was outside the Jewish community before it became part of the Hebrew canon. Yet we must give due recognition to its own explicit objective to speak universally.

In the Light of the New Testament

When interpreting Daniel, it is important to discern the meaning of the text among those who first received it, whether in the sixth or the second centuries B.C. *[Daniel: Date and Authorship, p. 285.]* It is also important to remember that the OT (Old Testament) writers themselves did not envision how their writings might be used and reinterpreted by later generations of readers. When Amos wrote about the restoration of David's reign (Amos 9:11-12), he did not foresee that James, under the direction of the Holy Spirit, would use that passage to support Gentiles entering Christ's kingdom by becoming part of the church (Acts 15:15-17). Hosea's prediction of the salvation of Israel (Hos. 1:10; 2:23) was used by Paul to demonstrate that the church made up of Jews and Gentiles had become God's people (Rom. 9:25-26).

The relationship of Daniel to the NT (New Testament) is clearly perceived in the great themes it anticipates. Daniel anticipates the words of Jesus, "Do not be afraid, little flock, for it is your Father's good pleasure to give you the kingdom" (Luke 12:32). It supports the words of Peter and the apostles, "We must obey God rather than any human authority" (Acts 5:29). It anticipates the preaching and example of the apostle Paul, who urges his hearers to "turn from these worthless things to the living God" (14:15). Paul exhorts them "to continue in the faith," saying, "It is through many persecutions that we must enter the kingdom of God" (14:22). And he "welcomed all who came to him, proclaiming the kingdom of God and teaching about the Lord Jesus Christ" (28:30-31). Supremely, Daniel anticipates resurrection. "If Christ has not been raised, your faith is futile. . . . Then those also who have died in Christ have perished. . . . But in fact Christ has been raised from the dead, the first fruits of those who have died" (1 Cor. 15:17-20).

In addition to the large themes, there are textual allusions to Daniel in the NT, especially in the book of Revelation. For example, the description of the Son of Man in Revelation 1 echoes the descriptions of celestial figures found in Daniel 7 and 10. Chapters 4 and 5 in the book of Revelation show a unified structure that corresponds to Daniel 7:9-27, as G. K. Beale has shown. Clear allusions to the beast described in Revelation 13 are found in Daniel 7. Beale (244) concludes that "about two-thirds (21) of all the OT references in chap. 13 come from Daniel." Revelation 17, describing the beast with the horns, is heavily dependent on Daniel. Beale (265) concludes that well over half the OT usages in Revelation 17 are from Daniel. Beyond his detailed investigation into the verbal relationship between Daniel and Revelation, Beale explores the possibility that "the book of Daniel may be more determinative on the overall *theology* and *structure* of the Apocalypse than any other traditional or O.T. source" (271; italics his).

On a broader base, the NT church took over and used OT patterns in new ways. Physical circumcision gave way to circumcision of the heart, spiritual not literal (Deut. 10:16; 30:6; Rom. 2:28-29). The church, so some interpret, became the "Israel of God" (Gal. 6:16). Mount Zion, the city of the living God, referred to those who have come to Jesus, the mediator of a new covenant (Heb. 12:22-24). Just as persons failed to recognize in OT passages predictions concerning the nature and work of Jesus' first coming, believers today do well not to try to arrange a sequence of events in connection with Christ's second coming, either from Daniel or other OT apocalyptic material. It is important to look for Christ's return. The understanding of this event is best drawn from and based upon explicit NT teaching.

The Way of Peace

There is yet another theme that dominates the book of Daniel. In the stories and the visions, the way of meekness, of defenselessness, of peace, and of nonresistance anticipates the way of Jesus and his teaching. If the book of Daniel was compiled in the second century during the time of Antiochus Epiphanes and the Maccabean resistance, the book offers an alternative way to resist evil. *[Maccabees, p. 290; Seleucids, p. 295.]* Daniel sides with those who endure persecution, rather than those who take up arms against the powers. It distances itself from the Maccabees and their policies. The book does not glory in the upsurge of human fortitude. It chooses rather to emphasize God's goals for history, and it trusts God to act.

There are a few clues that point to a pacifist community among the Jews during the days of Antiochus IV Epiphanes. Many stood firm to keep the covenant law at great cost and martyrdom. They felt bound to obey the Torah and not to revolt and would not even defend themselves on the Sabbath (1 Macc. 1:62-63; 2:29-38; Goldstein, 1976:5). Mattathias persuaded some of these pious folks to join him in striking down Jewish renegades, enforcing the law, and fighting against the Syrians. But after the temple was cleansed and rededicated, many Hasideans were content to live under Syrian rule if they were permitted to keep the Mosaic law (though 1 Maccabees portrays them as naive for believing Syrian words of peace: 1:30; 7:12-18). Second Maccabees goes further in honoring prayer, trust in God (rather than arms), nonresistance, martyrdom, and resurrection. *[Maccabees, p. 290.]*

The book of Daniel places itself in the peaceful stream that runs through the OT and finds its fulfillment in Jesus. From the days of the Exodus, God promised to make room for his people by driving out the nations before them with hornets or pestilence, not by sword or bow (Exod. 23:28, Deut. 7:20, Josh. 24:12; cf. RSV and NRSV). The ideal king (Deut. 17:14-20) would not "acquire more horses": he would not build up military might. Isaiah viewed even defensive military strategy as atheism (Isa. 22:8-11; 30:15-18) and longed for peaceful ways (2:2-4; 9:6-7; 11:9).

At no point in Daniel does God appear as a divine warrior or act like one. At times in the OT, God is seen as a soldier (Exod. 15:3; Isa. 42:13, 25; 59:15b-19; 63:1-6), and this imagery passed into apocalyptic material, but not in Daniel. In this book, warfare and commotion are characteristics of beastly kings that emerge from the sea of chaos and evil. Instead of an evolutionary upward movement, the kingdoms of humanity are declining and becoming ever more inhumane. In the midst of suffering and persecution, the faithful maintain integrity. Their behavior appears powerless and helpless as they pray and await the gift of the everlasting kingdom, from the Most High, who overcomes and judges the enemies with fire and with angels (Dan. 7:10-11; 10:20-21; 12:1).

The stories of Daniel and his friends illustrate meekness, peacemaking, and nonviolence. The visions depict violent, ruthless tyrants who oppress the people of God. The saints, however, endure with a nonresistant faith, self-giving even to death, renouncing claims and counterclaims in the struggle to live, aware that the militarism of the

Maccabees will not transform the world. That comes only with divine intervention.

The events of history that affect the people of God are supervised and directed from heaven. The presentation in the book of Daniel suggests that history is written ahead of time: what will happen has already been inscribed *in the book of truth* (10:21). Further, the events inscribed in the book of truth are carried out by heavenly figures: Gabriel, the angel-prince who speaks to Daniel (8:16; 10:13); the angel-prince of the kingdom of Persia (10:13); and Michael, the angel-prince of Israel (10:13, 21).

In 1 Maccabees, though God's action in history is acknowledged, the focus is upon humans who take action into their own hands. They use military methods to combat the armies of Antiochus. In 2 Maccabees, fighting is not as important as trust in God. Prayer and martyrdom are valued because they bring God's mercy and deliverance. But Daniel goes further in this direction. At no point in Daniel's visions are there suggestions that, as world powers dominate the Israelites and their land, they should use military power to protect themselves or overthrow the invaders. Instead, God's faithful people are called to be nonresistant, and those among them who are violent are disparaged as providing *little help* (Dan. 11:34). Thinking they can secure God's purpose with force, they fail (11:14).

In Daniel there is great disdain for worldly power. At best it is seen as short-lived. Themes like these occur: *The Most High is sovereign over the kingdom of mortals; he gives it to whom he will* (4:17, 25, 32; 5:21). *Dominion . . . shall be given* (7:27). *He shall be broken, and not by human hands* (8:25). *The decreed end is poured out* (9:27). Victory is seen even through death itself (11:33; 12:2-3).

Worldly powers use methods not in harmony with God's ways, and in the end they always fail. Chapter 11 provides a litany of the destinies of kings who rely on military might:

> *His kingdom shall be broken.* (11:4)
> *She shall not retain her power,*
> *and his offspring shall not endure.* (11:6)
> *He shall not prevail.* (11:12)
> *He shall stumble and fall,*
> *and shall not be found.* (11:19)
> *Within a few days he shall be broken.* (11:20)
> The last dreadful king *shall come to his end,*
> *with no one to help him.* (11:45)

The overthrow of tyrants is the work of God. They will not long succeed (11:36). God delivers the faithful. The holy people simply trust their God, not military power. The wise do not take up arms, because to follow the way of militarists is to suffer the fate of the militarists: *They shall fail* (11:14). The faithful ones endure sword, flame, captivity, and plunder (11:33), knowing that ultimately they shall shine like the stars forever (12:3).

Nonresistance for Christians today springs from loyalty to Jesus and following his teachings to love God, to love neighbor, to love self, and to love the enemy. The insights set forth in Daniel foreshadow, support, and provide illustrations of Jesus' teaching against the use of the sword. Themes supporting Jesus' way of life and teaching about peace include the following:

1. God is in ultimate control of history. He raises up and puts down kings and empires (4:17, 25, 32; 5:21).

2. Politicians and empires come and go; those who accept and do the will of God find the eternal kingdom, are given the kingdom, and/or form that kingdom (1:21; 2:44; 5:30—6:2; 7:27).

3. In the choice between the demands of God and the demands of the state, the faithful may lose liberty and life in obedience to God, but only things temporal and external are lost. The eternal kingdom in this life and that to come is gained (3:20-23; 6:16; 12:1-3).

4. Evil does not cease to be a problem for believers. Kings and kingdoms are unjust. God does not remove the faithful from distress, oppression, and injustice. Obedience and loyalty to God and his ways are of greater significance than prolongation of life, especially at the expense of compromise (7:25-27).

5. No matter how high a person may climb or how powerful a person may become, that person is not beyond the control of God. The world's love affair with privilege and power is ultimately a delusion (5:18-21).

6. God sides with those who endure persecution, not with those who violently resist. Believers can maintain integrity, rectitude, and communion with God even when oppressed (3:16-18; 6:10).

7. God's kingdom is neither inaugurated by nor maintained with military might (7:14, 27).

8. Political leaders often use religion to boost their power and to support their violent ways. The faithful must be alert not to be caught in such distortions and misuse of religion (3:14; 6:7-9).

9. Faithfulness is most effectively maintained in the context of a humble, nonviolent, prayerful community. Daniel *represents* the community at prayer (2:17-19; 6:10-11).

10. Militarism never delivers what it promises. It may provide *a little help*, but that is only temporary and fleeting when compared with God's ultimate victory (11:34).

11. The action of the faithful in times of crisis is to help persons understand the ways of God, knowing that in the process they may fall by the sword, flame, captivity, or plunder (11:33).

12. Times of violence and oppression are short-lived. The faithful who are oppressed take the long view, looking for God's intervention in his time and way (7:25-26; 8:14; 9:27).

The book of Daniel is a book for our time, giving its divine perspective on nations, its assessment of the workings of human government, its encouragement to the faithful, and its strong assertion of God's sovereignty.

Part 1

Introduction

Daniel 1:1-21 (in Hebrew)

Faithfulness in an Alien World

PREVIEW

In a skillful way, the first chapter of Daniel brings together an immense amount of material providing background information and theological insights necessary for understanding the stories to follow. Daniel 1 is in Hebrew, like chapters 8 through 12, while Daniel 2:4b—7:28 are in Aramaic. The two languages suggest that the book of Daniel is addressed both to Jews and to all peoples and nations of the world. Aramaic in the time of Daniel was the international language of commerce, much like Koine Greek in the time of Paul and English today. The Hebrew beginning and ending enabled the book to speak authoritatively to the Jewish community.

The first chapter makes these contributions:

1. It ties the book of Daniel to history. The names of rulers and specific dates are recorded. This suggests that the narratives to follow are not fairy tales, beginning with "once upon a time." They are to be considered as stories of real people in difficult situations.

2. The God of the Hebrews is more than a tribal deity. God oversees history; this prepares for the later teaching that even though evil has sway for a time, God's reign will ultimately prevail. God's activity is not limited to Palestine, and his concern is broader than the Israelites. Thus God *let* Jehoiakim *fall into* the *power* of Nebuchadnezzar at Jerusalem. In Babylon, God *allowed* Daniel to receive official favor and *gave knowledge and*

skill to Daniel and his companions.

3. Daniel 1 explains how the vessels from the temple in Jerusalem came to Babylon. This is important for the story in chapter 5.

4. It tells how Daniel and his companions arrived in Babylon.

5. It provides biographical information about Daniel and his companions. They meet the qualifications Nebuchadnezzar established for persons to be trained for civil service.

6. The chapter accepts selected changes in lifestyle as right and necessary in order to live and serve in another culture.

7. It introduces the theme, developed in the rest of the stories, that allegiance to God takes precedence over all other commitments. Changes in lifestyle dare not frustrate or jeopardize that primary allegiance.

8. Daniel 1 anticipates conflicts to follow. When aliens outdo natives in tasks for which the latter feel especially competent, hostility erupts. The king observes that the captives are ten times more competent than the magicians and enchanters in Babylon. That judgment will be tested!

9. It notes the lengthy span of time in which Daniel serves in Babylon, making the point that Daniel, a representative of the people of God, continues in positions of power and responsibility until the end of the exile.

OUTLINE

Historical Introduction, 1:1-2

1:1	The National Crisis
1:2	How the Sacred Vessels Arrived in Babylon

Nebuchadnezzar's Plan for the Captives, 1:3-5

1:3-4	Qualifications and Education
1:5	The Food and Drink

Ashpenaz's Selection, 1:6-7

Daniel's Decision and Proposal, 1:8-16

1:8	Rejecting the King's Food
1:9-14	The Test
1:15-16	Results of the Test

Negotiating the Training, 1:17-20

Historical Note, 1:21

EXPLANATORY NOTES

Historical Introduction 1:1-2

Accounts of Nebuchadnezzar's 598-597 B.C. siege of Jerusalem and earlier raids on it are found in 2 Kings 24:1-17 and 2 Chronicles

36:5-10. This was followed by the first major deportation of Jews. Then in 587-586 B.C. Nebuchadnezzar razed Jerusalem and took into exile those not killed (2 Kings 25; 2 Chron. 36:17-21). This was the second major deportation. *[Chronology, p. 283.]* Jeremiah referred to Nebuchadnezzar as God's servant to bring punishment to Jerusalem and Judah for refusing to obey God's word. Jeremiah also predicted that the land would be a waste and that the people would serve the king of Babylon seventy years (Jer. 25:1-14). *[Nebuchadnezzar, p. 293.]*

Jehoiakim ascended the throne of Judah in 609 B.C., after Josiah was mortally injured at Megiddo while meeting (or opposing?) the armies of Egypt under Neco (2 Kings 23:29). *[Kings of Judah, p. 288.]* In 605 B.C., the Babylonians met the Egyptians and Assyrian remnants at Carchemish. Carchemish was a city that commanded a ford of the Euphrates River. It represented Egypt's far-flung advance into Asia. There *Nebuchadnezzar* (a Jewish form of *Nebuchadrezzar*, Jer. 21:2), the crown prince of Babylon, defeated Neco, king of Egypt (Jer. 46:2; 2 Kings 24:1, 7). But then he had to rush home to be crowned king because of the death of his father, Nabopolassar. Since Judah had been a vassal state of Egypt, Nebuchadnezzar's victory at Carchemish soon brought Judah and Jerusalem under Babylon, likely by the end of 604 B.C. *[Babylon/Chaldea, p. 281.]*

If Nebuchadnezzar besieged Jerusalem in the third year of Jehoiakim (Dan. 1:1), that would have been 606 B.C. Yet Nebuchadnezzar did not become king until 605 B.C., the fourth year of Jehoiakim (Jer. 25:1). The Egyptian and early Palestinian systems count beginning months of a reign prior to New Year's Day as one year—making Nebuchadnezzar's first year the same as Jehoiakim's fourth year (Jer. 25:1). The Babylonian and the later Palestinian reckonings begin the tally for each king from the first full regnal year beginning at New Year, *after* a part year of accession. This pattern might have produced a count of the third year of Jehoiakim's reign if Nebuchadnezzar besieged Jerusalem as soon as he became king (Dan. 1:1). But it took Nebuchadnezzar several years to subdue the cities of Syria-Palestine. More plausibly, *the third year of the reign of King Johoiakim* means the "three years" of Jehoiakim serving Babylon, paying taxes 603-601 B.C., before he rebelled (2 Kings 24:1). By 601 B.C., Nebuchadnezzar had Syria-Palestine secured enough to attack Egypt, but was beaten back. This encouraged Jehoiakim to renounce allegiance to Babylonia and throw in his lot with Egypt. Yet such dating is a moot point. The writer's concern is not to harmonize dates but to root the story in world history.

The story of Jehoiakim is also difficult to sort out. Second Chronicles 36:6 tells of Nebuchadnezzar binding Jehoiakim to take him to Babylon, but then he likely died a natural death (ABD, 3:655) and "slept with his ancestors" (598 B.C.; 2 Kings 24:6). At the end of Jehoiakim's reign, Nebuchadnezzar carried "some" vessels of the house of the Lord to Babylon (2 Chron. 36:7). After his son Jehoiachin reigned three months, he, other deportees, and "the precious vessels" were brought to Babylon (36:10; 2 Kings 24; 597 B.C.). Eleven years later, at the end of Zedekiah's reign, Nebuchadnezzar burned the house of the Lord and every great house, took "all the vessels . . . and the treasures" of temple, king, and officials, along with other captives, but left some poor people to till the land (2 Chron. 36:18, 20; 2 Kings 25; 587-586 B.C.). There is agreement that the vessels and treasures of the temple and the king's palace were carried to Babylon, likely in several stages.

Thus also there were several deportations. *[Chronology, p. 283.]* Daniel and his friends were likely taken captive by Nebuchadnezzar in one of the earliest raids, perhaps in late 604 B.C., when Judah came under Babylon (cf. note on Dan. 2:1). If not then or in 601 B.C., when Nebuchadnezzar came through Palestine to attack Egypt, then more plausibly with the major deportation of 597 B.C., dated by Babylonian records (2 Kings 24:14-16).

1:1 The National Crisis

The crisis in Judah and Jerusalem was of God's doing. While 2 Kings 24:12 notes that Jehoiachin the king of Judah *gave himself up* to the king of Babylon, the writer of Daniel (like Jeremiah) sees the hand of God at work (Jer. 25:9). The book of Daniel begins by acknowledging the sovereignty of God. God is the one who *gave* (RSV; Hebrew: *natan*) the king of Judah into the hand of Nebuchadnezzar (1:2). That God is in control of history and human events is an underlying theme of the entire book. In this opening chapter, God is at work not only in national crisis but also in the personal lives of Daniel and his associates. God *gave* (*natan*) *Daniel favor* (1:9) and God *gave* (*natan*) the youths *knowledge and skill in every aspect of literature and wisdom* (1:17). The beginning of the book enables the reader to see that behind the events is the hand of a giving God. *The Lord let* Nebuchadnezzar have success in his attack on Jerusalem. He *allowed* Daniel success in negotiating a test. He *gave* the youths success in their training.

1:2 How the Sacred Vessels Arrived in Babylon

That the sacred vessels from the temple in Jerusalem arrived in Babylon is important background for the story of Belshazzar in chapter 5. When Nebuchadnezzar took captives from conquered countries, he also took their wealth and national treasures. The writer of Daniel sympathized with his Jewish kinspeople. There is sadness that the vessels (1) were taken to the land of *Shinar*, and (2) were placed in the treasury of Nebuchadnezzar's gods (and/or in his palace: 2 Chron. 36:7).

Shinar was the ancient name for Babylonia and the plain of the Tigris-Euphrates basin. The word *Shinar* came to be associated with false religion (Gen. 11:1-9; cf. Isa. 11:11; Zech. 5:11). In Shinar, the people of earth assembled to build a tower with its top in heaven. The tower, they thought, would enable them both to come to God and to deal with God through the work of their hands. It was a human effort to secure unity, fame, and security. God confused their speech and scattered them (Gen. 11:1-9).

The intimate relationship between Creator and creatures has always been based on grace and faith, not on human effort. In biblical narratives, acts of God's grace have often followed human failure. Mercy was shown to Cain by a mark, so he would not be killed (Gen. 4:15). In the case of Noah, the rainbow was a merciful sign that God would never destroy all flesh in a flood (9:8-17). However, following the tower of Babel, the great story of God's mercy begins. God called Abraham and promised to make of him a people to bless all humanity (12:1-3). In view of God's call of Abraham and his acts on behalf of Abraham's descendants, it seems hard to believe that vessels from the temple of the God of Abraham would be taken back to Shinar. Can it be that the events from Abraham to this moment are of no meaning or consequence?

The writer's sadness is compounded by the fact the vessels are placed in the treasury of Nebuchadnezzar's gods. In that day it was thought that the gods of a victorious or conquering nation had in effect conquered the gods of the defeated nation (cf. 2 Kings 18:33-35). Thus, to place the sacred vessels from the temple in Jerusalem in a Babylonian holy place seems to say that the God of Israel is impotent. He has met his match. The gods of Nebuchadnezzar have triumphed! However, the sovereignty of Israel's God is not demonstrated by what happens to sacred vessels. Instead, as the book of Daniel makes clear, it is shown by what happens in the larger history.

Nebuchadnezzar's Plan for the Captives 1:3-5

The new king of Babylon has decided to make good use of his newly imported captives. The writer relates Nebuchadnezzar's conversation with Ashpenaz, his *palace master* (Heb.: *rab saris;* NIV: *chief of his court officials*). This Hebrew term serves as a proper noun in 2 Kings 18:17 and Jeremiah 39:3, 13. Ashpenaz is a confidant of the king. As such, he would not necessarily be castrated (cf. RSV: *chief eunuch*).

1:3-4 Qualifications and Education

Nebuchadnezzar is concerned that the brightest and best be trained as civil servants. Ashpenaz is to follow certain qualifications in his selection of young men to serve the king. Nebuchadnezzar directs him to choose only those from high social level, with good physical condition, high intellectual capacity, and administrative skills.

As to social level, the youths are to be from Israelite upper classes, from the royal family and/or families of nobility. Such youths know how to act among those in high places. They will not be overawed by pomp and splendor. The word translated *nobility* is found only here and in Esther 1:3; 6:9. Since this word is from the Persian period (539-323 B.C.), its use suggests that the materials were put in writing at a later date.

As to physical condition, the youths are to be without blemish: those with physical handicaps are eliminated. They are to be handsome: only those with pleasing facial features and bodies reflecting physical perfection will be chosen.

As to intellectual capacity, the youths are to be *versed in every branch of wisdom*. Some terms (such as *akmah*, wisdom) in the list of qualifications also appear (as *akam,* wise) in the story of Joseph, another Israelite who moved in foreign court circles (Gen. 41:33, 39). Writers of the OT saw the knowledge of God as the beginning of wisdom (Prov. 1:7). Even if Nebuchadnezzar does not have this insight, he nevertheless is seeking youths skilled in living, with common sense. This includes ethical and moral behavior. *Endowed with knowledge* suggests that the youths have received a good education in their homeland and thus are well informed. *Insight* or *understanding learning* (RSV) underscores an ability to learn, quick learners.

As to administrative ability, the youths are to demonstrate competence in accepting, planning, and carrying out responsibilities.

To Nebuchadnezzar's mind, as comprehensive as these qualifications are, they are not enough. These qualifications are to be a foundation for learning what is really important to him, *the literature and language of the Chaldeans.*

In the book of Daniel, the term *Chaldean* is used in two ways. It may refer to a group of people, defined geographically as those who have settled in southern Babylon near the Persian Gulf from 1100 B.C. onward. Nebuchadnezzar himself is a Chaldean. In Daniel 5:30 and 9:1, Chaldean refers to this ethnic group. Nebuchadnezzar is likely proud of his cultural heritage, the books and tongue of his people. Yet this is hardly the meaning here. *[Babylon/Chaldea, p. 281.]*

Chaldean may also be used in a derived sense to refer to a group of people, defined vocationally, as persons well-known for their work in astrology, dream interpretation, fortune-telling, and magic. The king wants the deportees to become familiar with this large and important body of knowledge and become part of that group. Here *Chaldeans* is used for this professional class (cf. 2:2-5, 10; 4:7; 5:7, 11). The youths selected by Ashpenaz will study the omens, incantations, hymns, prayers, rituals, myths and legends, formulas, and mathematics of the Chaldeans, the experts in astrology and magic.

As the story unfolds, Nebuchadnezzar himself makes use of such expertise. Ezekiel agrees: "For the king of Babylon stands at the parting of the way, at the fork in the two roads, to use divination; he shakes the arrows, he consults the teraphim, he inspects the liver" (21:21; teraphim are little images or figurines of gods in human form used as good-luck charms and as a source of messages from the gods: cf. Gen. 31:19, 30; Judg. 18:14-20).

The course of study will be neither a quick overview nor a cram course. Nebuchadnezzar intends that the students will be with these Chaldean masters for a period of three years. Upon graduation, the youths are to enter the king's service.

1:5 The Food and Drink

Nebuchadnezzar plans to provide well for those in training. They will not only be exposed to the best teachers in the land but will also live like the king. During the entire period of study, they will eat and drink a daily allowance of his food and wine, *royal rations*, like Jehoiachin and his sons in exile (2 Kings 25:30; Jer. 52:34).

Ashpenaz's Selection 1:6-7

It is not said how many persons Ashpenaz selects for Nebuchadnezzar's training program. The book of Daniel introduces only four of them: Daniel, Hananiah, Mishael, and Azariah. All are from the tribe of Judah.

These four youths, removed from their families, their homeland, and Jerusalem, the center of worship of their God, now embark on a three-year study of practices considered an abomination in Israel. After all, Moses taught Israel at all costs to avoid divination, soothsaying, augury, sorcery, and to have nothing to do with charms, mediums, or wizards (Deut. 18:9-14).

In order to complete the break with their past, to show that they are under new authority (cf. Gen. 2:20), and perhaps also for the sake of convenience (cf. 41:45), Asphenaz changes the names of the youths. He takes away their names that refer to the God of the Israelites (with *el* or *yah*) and instead gives names which refer to Babylonian deities:

> Dani*el* (God has judged) becomes *Belteshazzar* (Bel guard his life).
> Hanan*iah* (Yahweh has been gracious) becomes *Shadrach* (Saduraku: I am fearful of god).
> Misha*el* (who is what God is) becomes *Meshach* (Mesaku: I am of little account).
> Azar*iah* (Yahweh has helped) receives an Aramaic name *Abednego* (a play on the name of a god, Nabu: servant of the shining one).

Daniel and his friends are devout and committed Israelites. Certainly, they experience great uneasiness when names referring to their God are removed and replaced by names referring to foreign deities, such as Bel.

Daniel's Decision and Proposal 1:8-16

1:8 Rejecting the King's Food

The story, which till now has moved in fast-paced style, slows dramatically. From the mention of international politics and palace regulation, the story has come to something of a stop on the question of a proposed menu. More significantly, the subject of the action words shifts from that of the government to the resolute action of a captive. Now the story becomes shaped by the captive's decision.

One wonders what leads Daniel and his friends to reject the king's food and drink. Why this, especially in the light of all they have accepted upon coming to Babylon? They do not reject Ashpenaz's appointment to receive an *education* in an area totally taboo to the

Jews, the literature and practices of the Chaldeans. They do not reject their new *other names*, even when references to their God are replaced by references to Babylonian deities. They do not reject civil service *in the king's court* under Nebuchadnezzar, the king who has destroyed Jerusalem and the temple, taken their people captive, and about whom their prophets have many harsh things to say. Indeed, the four young men exhibit a surprising openness to study another culture and to become acquainted with an entirely different thought world, such as divination.

Since they accept all these changes, it seems strange for them to reject the king's food and wine. Daniel and his companions reject the king's food because they do not want to break Jewish dietary laws. Varieties of fish and meat will likely be included that are forbidden and unclean (Lev. 3:17; 11:1-47). The eating or noneating of foods is a mark of religious identity, as still true in parts of the Orient. Then, too, the food might be prepared in unsatisfactory ways; for example, blood might not be completely drained from the meat (Gen. 9:4; Lev. 17:10-14). To *defile* oneself with food or its preparation is not a minor matter (cf. Ezek. 4:14-15). Such taboos go back to the oldest periods of Israelite history.

Though wine is not prohibited by Mosaic Law, it might have been previously offered to a pagan deity, and likewise the meat might have been so offered. In the Israelite setting, only priests (and their families, presumably) were allowed to eat a portion of a sacrifice (Exod. 29:24; Lev. 2:2-3; 1 Sam. 2:13-17). In idol worship, the evidence from the NT period might give some inkling of practices in the times of the book of Daniel; it indicates that people in worship or social gatherings and not just priests eat of meat sacrificed to idols (Acts 15:29; 1 Cor. 8, 10; Rom. 14). In Bel and the Dragon, priests sneak the meat from the idol at night (Dan. 14:1-22, in the Apocrypha). *[Supplements, p. 297.]*

If an early date is assigned to this part of Daniel, then one can note that Akkadian rituals allow pieces of meat from slaughtered sheep offered before the god Bel (identified with Marduk) to be distributed to artisans constructing new images. Perhaps some of the wine offered for libations is saved for the artisans. There were also "sacrifices of the king." The king gives orders to priests, and priests supervise rituals involving the king (ANET: 331-345). With the king and idol worship so interlocked, it is possible though not certain that the *royal rations and the wine* have been offered to idols and then are used by these royal servants (Dan. 1:16).

If a late date is given for the final form of Daniel (165 B.C.), then it fits that the book includes something about keeping dietary laws, in accord with postexilic attention to the law of Moses (Neh. 8–9). During the reign of Antiochus IV Epiphanes, such rules were an urgent matter of faithfulness for Israelites. Some conscientiously "chose to die rather than to be defiled by food," such as to eat the flesh of swine sacrificed to idols (1 Macc. 1:43-49, 62-63; 2 Macc. 6–7).

The rejection of the king's food, however, may also come from what is symbolized in eating the king's food. In the ancient Near East, food was more than a means to sustain life. In OT days, a covenant was often sealed with a meal. The food eaten by both parties made them, symbolically, members of the same clan. When Joshua and his men ate a meal with the Gibeonites, they created a bond that could not be broken, even when they learned they were tricked (Josh. 9:3-27). Mephibosheth ate at David's table like one of his sons (2 Sam. 9:7, 10, 11). On the other hand, to refuse to eat was a symbol of ruptured relationship. Jonathan "rose from the table in fierce anger and ate no food" when he learned of Saul's attempt to put David to death (1 Sam. 20:20-34). Food as a bond of fellowship goes with the Hebrew word *covenant*, which some say is derived from the root "to eat" (TDOT, 2:253-255: the more plausible root meaning is "clasp," "fetter," "binding settlement"). Eating and drinking together is often part of celebrating a covenant (Exod. 24:11; Luke 22:14-20).

Hence, for Daniel to eat the king's food is to accept his protection and in turn to give him total allegiance (Ps. 23:5). It implies a covenant of unreserved loyalty and obedience. Daniel and his companions will serve Nebuchadnezzar but not give him absolute loyalty. This can be given only to their God! Daniel and his companions will accept much of Babylonian culture and participate in Babylonian life (cf. Jer. 29:1-9), but they will reject giving Nebuchadnezzar the allegiance symbolized in eating his food and drinking his wine. To accept *royal rations* would compromise their faith in a way the other practices do not. For them, faithfulness means insisting on primary allegiance to their God. They draw the line at some point. They avoid being fully assimilated and resist total conformity. In a sense, they are citizens of two worlds. They accept involvement in the Babylonian world, but they will not surrender loyalty to their God, which includes keeping God's covenant and any dietary rules in force. Therefore, Daniel requests that Ashpenaz allow the four to eat other food.

1:9-14 The Test

In highly patriotic circles, those who refuse to wrap themselves in the flag get in trouble, and those who give such persons comfort and aid may also be in danger. Ashpenaz knows the implications of Daniel's request. He well knows that both his position and his life will be in jeopardy if his plea is granted, and especially if evidences of poor health in Daniel and his companions are traced back to his co-operation with them. Enabling them to carry out the unpatriotic act of rejecting the king's food and drink would be a serious offense.

At this point (1:9), the writer notes again God's sovereignty. God *gave* (*natan*) to Ashpenaz feelings of favor and compassion for Daniel and his friends. Perhaps this situation provides an illustration of 1 Corinthians 10:13. They have committed themselves to faithfulness in the face of temptation to idolatry, and God provides a way of escape. Consequently, Ashpenaz decides not to make Daniel's refusal an issue with the king.

Furthermore, the *guard* that Ashpenaz appoints to supervise Daniel and his friends seems open to negotiation. He complies with Daniel's proposal. Daniel and his friends will eat vegetables and drink water for ten days. The ten-day test period will make clear whether the health of the men would be hindered by this change of diet.

Perhaps the guard exchanges his own meals for the king's delicacies. If so, he may think he is benefiting from the exchange, and this guarantees secrecy. An agreement is struck. The diet of Daniel and his companions will be changed, with the guard given the assurance of final say in judging results. Then the test is begun.

1:15-16 Results of the Test

At the end of the ten-day test period, the guard sees that Daniel and his companions look healthier and better nourished than the other youths who continue to eat the king's choice foods. These four young Israelites have taken the risk of following the dictates of their faith. There are no adverse physical results. Consequently, the guard agrees to a permanent diet change. Daniel and his companions keep eating vegetables as a daily expression of their faithfulness and total allegiance to God. The motif of this story is to demonstrate that God honors faithful servants (1 Sam. 2:30) rather than that a vegetarian diet is sure to bring better health (Gen. 9:3). Note that Daniel and his friends are *fatter* than those who eat the *royal rations!*

Negotiating the Training 1:17-20

The writer has already noted two ways God exercises his power. God *gave* (*natan*) Jehoiakim, king of Judah (1:2, RSV), into Nebuchadnezzar's hands (military power). God *gave* (*natan*) Daniel favor (1:9, RSV) in the eyes of Nebuchadnezzar's chief officer (political power). Now a third is noted: God *gave* the four *knowledge and skill in every aspect of literature and wisdom* (the power of human intellect) (1:17). The writer adds that Daniel has *insight into all visions and dreams*, the mark of a prophet (Num. 12:6; Matt. 24:15). This is especially important in the light of later events (chaps. 2, 4–5).

The four young men are studying in a Babylonian culture. People tend to think their own culture is superior to others. It is probable that while the four learn the literature and ways of the Chaldeans, their teachers ridicule Jewish values. The Babylonians believe that they are invincible in military power. In scientific achievements they also deem themselves superior. *[Babylon/Chaldea, p. 281.]* God *gave* the four Hebrew youths the ability to learn all of this. Yet in the midst of the Babylonian environment, they are able to keep their faith. The daily diet of vegetables as a symbol of faithfulness likely helps them receive God's gift of learning and also keep their faith alive.

The three years of study pass quickly. When the course is completed, King Nebuchadnezzar commands that Ashpenaz bring the students to him for an interview. He is interested in the success of the study program to develop competent civil servants from among the captives.

The entire student body is brought to the king. Nebuchadnezzar interviews them one by one. Four of the group he finds to be outstanding in their grasp of Chaldean letters and wisdom. These four are identified: Daniel, Hananiah, Mishael, and Azariah. There is irony in the fact that their new Babylonian names are not used at this point. This may be the storyteller's way of attributing the competence of the four to the God to whom their Hebrew names bore witness.

After identifying the superior abilities of the four, Nebuchadnezzar gives them positions of special responsibility: *they were stationed in the king's court* (1:19). In addition he continues his interview to check the breadth and depth of their comprehension of Babylonian wisdom and understanding. Then Nebuchadnezzar comes to a startling conclusion. These four are *ten times* more competent than all the magicians and enchanters in the kingdom! (1:20).

With this bit of information, the writer sets the stage for conflicts to come. What happens when aliens excel nationals in areas in which the latter feel especially competent? Aliens praised by the king are not thereby endeared to the natives. The Babylonian professionals will soon test the king's evaluation. The young men for whom soothsaying and magic have been strange and taboo, now are more competent than those who grew up in the system. The king's view that they are ten times better than all in the kingdom, their teachers included, will not go unchallenged.

Historical Note 1:21

This introductory chapter closes with a note concerning the duration of Daniel's civil service. He serves from about 604 or 597 B.C., near the beginning of Nebuchadnezzar's reign, through the first year of King Cyrus, 538 B.C., who allows the Jews to return from exile (2 Chron. 36:22-23). *[Cyrus, p. 284.]*

Perhaps in the inclusion of this historical note there is some irony. Though the chapter begins with the dramatic rise of Nebuchadnezzar to great power and with the humiliation of the Israelite people, nevertheless, it is Daniel, the representative of God's people, who continues in Babylon in positions of power and responsibility long after Nebuchadnezzar is gone and his kingdom broken. Daniel serves until the fortunes of God's people are reversed and they are free to return home. The experience of Daniel extends from the start of the exile in Babylon to its finish.

A beginning of the difficulties of the exile is indicated in the chronological note at the outset: *In the third year of the reign of King Jehoiakim of Judah* (1:1). That beginning is superintended by an almighty God. But there is also to be an end to the exile, as mentioned in the chronological note at the close of chapter 1. Daniel continues *until the first year of King Cyrus.* The day of deliverance, like the day of wrath, is divinely superintended (Goldingay: 28). The bringing of the sacred vessels to Babylon provided background for the events of Daniel 5. So also this historical note echoes the consideration in Daniel 9 of Jeremiah's prophecy that the rule of the Babylonian king would continue for seventy years (Jer. 25:11-12).

The stories of Daniel have as their background the utter defeat of God's people; the devastation of God's holy city, Jerusalem; and the destruction of the temple, God's house, though the Most High cannot be contained therein (2 Chron. 6:18-21). How can faith in a "defeated" God continue? Indeed, if faith does survive, what form will it take? How shall it be expressed? In many respects the book of Daniel provides answers to such questions. The work of God is now seen in global proportions, reaching to all peoples and nations and languages, and extending across time.

THE TEXT IN BIBLICAL CONTEXT

Daniel, Joseph, and Esther

The story of Daniel shares many similarities with those of Joseph (Gen. 37–50) and of Esther (1–10). Like the stories of Daniel, the stories of Joseph and Esther are well planned and well arranged. The Daniel, Joseph, and Esther stories tell of righteous persons faced with great difficulties. In part, their difficulties arise because of pressures to assimilate within a foreign society, to adopt alien values, and to become acculturated. But more, the stories tell about their God. The stories are intended to call hearers to follow their examples of faithfulness, and to rely on the power and support of God.

Daniel, Joseph, and Esther are pictured as the best of Hebrew young people. They display right conduct in every situation. Daniel and Joseph are handsome (Gen. 39:6; Dan. 1:4). Esther is pleasing and attractive (Esther 2:2, 15-17). Daniel and Joseph are outstanding administrators. Joseph is the only one able to administer the huge food and relief program and is second only to Pharaoh (Gen. 41:38-44). Likewise, Daniel rises to places of high responsibility, next to the king (Dan. 2:47-49). Esther is an astute royal politician (5:1—8:8).

Daniel and Joseph are tempted. Joseph faces and overcomes the temptation of Potiphar's wife (Gen. 39:7-23). Daniel refuses the king's food (Dan. 1:8). In the face of temptations, both Joseph and Daniel set faithfulness above personal desires and aspirations. When confronted by the wiles of Potiphar's wife, Joseph says, "How then could I do this great wickedness, and sin against God?" (Gen. 39:9). In the face of the decree to prohibit prayer to anyone but King Darius, Daniel goes to his house, gets down on his knees three times a day *to pray to his God and praise him, just as he had done previously* (Dan. 6:6-10). Such loyalty to God and victory over temptations to unfaithfulness provide models for others to emulate.

Daniel and Joseph are dreamers. Joseph has two dreams related to his future (Gen. 37:5-10). The course of Joseph's story is set by the dreams of sheaves and of the sun, moon, and eleven stars. Daniel also has dreams. His related more to events in the future of the Jewish people (Dan. 7–12). In the stories of Joseph and Daniel, God gives the dreams primarily to further his purposes.

But more significantly, both are interpreters of dreams. Joseph interprets the dreams of Pharaoh's butler and baker (Gen. 40:5-23), while Daniel interprets the dreams of Nebuchadnezzar (Dan. 2, 4). Both Joseph and Daniel give full credit to God for their abilities. Joseph says, "Do not interpretations belong to God?" (Gen. 40:8). Daniel proclaims to Nebuchadnezzar, *There is a God in heaven who reveals mysteries* (Dan. 2:28). Even Nebuchadnezzar acknowledges Daniel's ability to interpret his dream: *You are able, however, for you are endowed with a spirit of the holy gods* (4:18).

The stories of Daniel, Joseph, and Esther illustrate that God overrules all things for his glory and the carrying out of his purposes. But that did not save them from many personal struggles. Joseph's brothers act in ignorance when they sell him into Egypt, yet they are actually helping to bring about God's purpose "to preserve a numerous people" (Gen. 50:20). In a somewhat similar fashion, Daniel's interaction with oriental despots leads to awareness that *the Most High is sovereign over the kingdom of mortals* (Dan. 4:17, 25, 32; 5:21). In the story of Esther are Mordecai's famous words, "Perhaps you have come to royal dignity for just such a time as this" (Esther 4:14).

The faithful work of Joseph, Daniel, and Esther have long-range implications, showing that God's redemptive purposes extend far into the future, beyond their lifetimes. Joseph believes there is much more to come. God's preserving numerous people can not end with "a coffin in Egypt" (Gen. 50:26). The faith of Joseph regarding the future is noted in the roll call of the faithful (Heb. 11:22). Similarly, Daniel looks to the future when God's kingdom will fill the whole earth (Dan. 2:35, 44) and be in the hands of the people of the Most High (7:27). The acts of Esther lead to the feast of Purim, which for every generation recalls God's deliverance (Esther 9:26-28).

Daniel, Joseph, and Esther make the point that God is with his people, guiding and preserving them wherever they are. All three are in foreign lands: Daniel in Babylon, Joseph in Egypt, and Esther in Persia. This foreshadows the NT emphasis, that with God there is no one holy land: "The earth is the Lord's" (Ps. 24:1; cf. Acts 7:47-50). At the ascension of Jesus, all authority in heaven and earth is given to him. He charges his followers to make disciples of all nations (Matt. 28:18-19).

The success of Daniel, Joseph, and Esther lies in the way they fear and obey God. God's plans for them and his people are carried out in spite of the plans of oppressive regimes to thwart them. They believe in God and trust God.

Perhaps faithful teaching in their parental homes leads to the deep faith that enables them to overcome great obstacles (Friedman: 295). They also acknowledge God's directing hand in their careers. Their stories underscore the biblical insight that God uses faithful persons, regardless of gender, to accomplish his purposes.

THE TEXT IN THE LIFE OF THE CHURCH

The Alternative Community

In today's world, the church is to be an alternative community. This has always been God's intention for his people. When Moses led the Israelites from Egypt, it was the intention of God to create a new community, quite different from that in Egypt. The new community was to have a new sense of justice, new laws, new organization, new government, and new norms of right and wrong. Paul claims that "our ancestors were all under the cloud, and all passed through the sea, and all were baptized into Moses in the cloud and in the sea, and all ate the same spiritual food, and all drank the same spiritual drink" (1 Cor. 10:1-4). The new community was called into being by divine action, and the nature of its life and action came by revelation.

To form such an alternative community is difficult because in it God's will and rule operate, in contrast to the social order where God's authority is not accepted. Paul describes the resistance to God's intention. Some became idolaters, others indulged in immorality, some put the Lord to test, others complained (1 Cor. 10:6-10).

The characteristics of this alternative community are derived from interaction with God. The Lord God reigns, not Pharaoh, nor even another Israelite. The community is to demonstrate justice, righteousness, and compassion (Isa. 5:7). Soon, however, Israel had rich and powerful kings like Pharaoh and the nations around them. Instead of compassion, the cries of the poor went unheard. Instead of allowing God to speak, to lead, and to discipline, God became a chore boy, domesticated, and confined to the temple and its ritual. The people rebelliously went their own way. To be sure, the prophets tried to recover God's original intent. Amos cried out against oppression and conspicuous consumption. Isaiah focused on God's faithfulness as he ridiculed the gods of Babylon, carried on the backs of weary beasts, unable to save themselves or those who worship them (46:1-4).

In the stories of Daniel and his companions and in Daniel's visions, the shape of God's alternative community begins to reemerge.

This instructs the church today. With Jerusalem and temple in ruins, from a human point of view, God is no longer tied to rituals and calendar. He is free to act, as he said to Moses earlier, "I will be gracious to whom I will be gracious, and I will show mercy on whom I will show mercy" (Exod. 33:19). In the stories of Daniel, God's relationship to his people again seems to be direct and personal. The Most High gives, reveals, answers prayers, and delivers. God is working in the lives of ruthless tyrants as well as faithful Jews to accomplish his purposes.

This alternative community is an intentional one. The faithful have to make costly decisions, not to take part in the strange religions or to be absorbed into the dominant culture. One can learn from how Daniel and his companions live as an alternative community. They are not "prophetic" in the sense of scolding or reprimanding their neighbors. Nor do they withdraw, condemning society as corrupt. Instead, they take advantage of much that Babylon has to offer in education and in civil service. Daniel and his companions are given new names. They accept education in disciplines and practices taboo in the society from which they come. What then makes them an alternative community?

First and foremost, they are committed to God, whom they understand to be the living God. They allow no allegiance to supersede allegiance to God. They clearly see that faithfulness takes precedence over the demands of kings or laws of the state (3:18; 6:10). From this commitment, at risk of death, springs a variety of behaviors that set them apart. There is moral integrity (6:22). Their service is not tainted by the pursuit of personal wealth (5:17). There is concern for the relief of the oppressed (4:27). They recognize that the present state of affairs is not the full and final ordering. They are persons of hope, confident that God does and will act. They have a vision of God's rule and ultimate purposes (2:44; 7:27; 12:2-3). Their lives are infused with prayer (2:17-24; 6:10; 9:3-19) and meditation on Scripture (9:1-2).

Second, they follow the instruction of Jeremiah's letter to the exiles. They are to "seek the welfare of the city where I have sent you into exile, and pray to the Lord on its behalf, for in its welfare you will find your welfare" (Jer. 29:7). The church as God's alternative community does not live to itself. It seeks the good of the broader society. It functions as salt and light (Matt. 5:13-16). If the broader society fails, the welfare of the faithful is also in peril.

Daniel and his companions do not lose identification with their historic faith tradition. However, they break out of its static dimensions and recover its original intentions. With this faith they confront and interface with the culture in which they find themselves. The knowledge that their God is in ultimate control of history allows them to confront the culture in which they live in new and dynamic ways. They are not concerned to reconstruct the past but rather to discern how God's future and his kingdom impinge on the present.

When pressures to conform are severe (chap. 3), when decisions, decrees, and dilemmas challenge their faithfulness, they resolve to obey God and rely on him, regardless of personal cost or outcome (3:17-18). Although they hold positions of civic responsibility, they do not dominate others, control thought, or exalt themselves. They are able to distinguish between human values and those revealed by their God. They put no limits on what God can do or will do. In many respects, they model the alternative community envisioned in Peter's letter to the church:

> But even if you suffer for doing what is right, you are blessed. Do not fear what they fear, and do not be intimidated, but in your hearts sanctify Christ as Lord. Always be ready to make your defense to any one who demands from you an accounting for the hope that is in you; yet do it with gentleness and reverence. Keep your conscience clear, so that, when you are maligned, those who abuse you for your good conduct in Christ may be put to shame. (1 Pet. 3:14-16)

The absolute and exclusive loyalty of God's alternative community, along with its concern for every aspect of the believer's life, gives the Christian church a decisive edge over its religious competitors. The church receives this sense of community from Judaism and yet develops further the kind of openness to interested outsiders suggested in Daniel (for example, 6:25-27). All are freely welcomed into the alternative community of the church.

Part 2

A Tract to the Nations

Daniel 2:1—7:28 (2:4b—7:28 in Aramaic)

OVERVIEW

International Language and Concerns

These chapters form an unusual tract to the nations. Daniel 2:4b to 7:28 is in Aramaic, the language of world commerce, like Koine Greek during the time of Jesus and Paul, or like English today. Aramaic texts have been found as far east as Afghanistan and as far west as Turkey. Aramaic materials from the Persian era have been found in Egypt.

Prophets of the OT have the view that God is concerned for the whole world (as in Isa. 42:4; 45:22). This belief forms the background of much of the OT. Abraham, when called, is told that through him all the families of earth would be blessed (Gen. 12:3). God's intention from the beginning has been to make his grace available to all humanity. Yet in Israel, as often happens in the church, there was a tendency to become narrow in identifying whom God loves and cares for. Isaiah believed that God loved the whole world, but his love had to center in and move from Jerusalem and the "holy land." Isaiah spoke of kings of earth bringing tributes to Jerusalem. Whatever God would do for the world, Isaiah thought, would be done through Jerusalem, the holy city (Isa. 2:1-4; 60:1-14).

Embedded in Daniel's tract to the nations, written in the language of commerce, is another view. Jerusalem is in ruins, the temple sacked, and the Israelite people in captivity. Now we learn that God reveals himself to *all peoples, nations, and languages* (4:1) through the mighty rulers of the times in contact with faithful Israelites like Daniel. The question of whether such a "tract" as a government document was actually forwarded to peoples everywhere must be left open. As the story is told, one would expect that peoples within the realm were properly informed of the king's decrees.

Some have suggested that the notion of such a tract is a literary device similar to the oracles by the prophets against the nations (as in Jer. 46-51; Amos 1-2). By means of these literary devices, the Hebrews would be assured of God's strong hand in bringing rulers to acknowledge God or to ensure God's judgment upon enemy nations. Such a tract would affirm the faith of the Hebrew people in God's power and salvation for them. Still, as presented in the story, the religious reversal by these high officials is dramatic, and the impact of their turnabout is decidedly missionary. Others across the empire if not the world could, when encouraged by an official decree, acknowledge the God of Israel as alone the sovereign God.

Patterns and Themes

This tract to the nations is carefully organized. In chapters 2–7 are six stories. The first story (2:1-49) parallels the sixth (7:1-28). The first deals with a dream of Nebuchadnezzar's, and the last reports a dream of Daniel's. In both there is a succession of four kingdoms represented by the parts of the statue in Nebuchadnezzar's dream and the four beasts of Daniel's vision. Both stories culminate with the inbreak of the kingdom of God, represented by the stone in the first and by the everlasting kingdom given to *the holy ones of the Most High* in the last. While all nations are to bow to the image in the first story, all nations will serve the living God in the last.

The second (3:1-30) and the fifth stories (6:1-28) also have parallel themes dealing with commitment to the living God. Both involve royal edicts that Daniel and his companions disobey. To their opponents, their actions are treasonous. To Daniel and the three associates, the edicts call them to deny basic faith commitments. In the second story (Dan. 3), the issue is whether something can be *added* to commitment to God. Can the worship of God also include the worship of the state? Shadrach, Meshach, and Abednego refuse to *fall down* before the statue that Nebuchadnezzar *set up*. In the fifth story (Dan. 6), the issue is whether the state can *take away* an important aspect of the worship of God. Daniel refuses to turn aside. He continues *to pray to his God and praise him.* In both stories, the issue seems to us to be a religious offense rather than a political one. But in those days (and often now!), religion and politics were interlocked, as shown by kings performing religious rituals before going into battle.

In both accounts, the Israelites were found guilty. They made their religious confession, were vindicated, and then promoted.

The third (4:1-37) and fourth (5:1-30) stories deal with two rulers confronted by the necessity to acknowledge *that the Most High has sovereignty over the kingdom of mortals and gives it to whom he will* (4:32; cf. 5:21). Nebuchadnezzar comes to his senses and praises and honors the Most High. Belshazzar, however, refuses to learn from the experience of Nebuchadnezzar. He lifts himself up against the Lord of heaven and uses the sacred vessels from the Jerusalem temple in a drunken orgy (5:22-23). Nebuchadnezzar's kingdom is restored; Belshazzar is slain.

In these six stories, the truth about God is proclaimed to the whole world by mighty world leaders, not Hebrew prophets. The text is in Aramaic rather than Hebrew, and thus it is ready to communicate to a wide audience. Also, the truth about God, who he is, and what he does, goes to the whole world from *Babylon*, not Jerusalem.

In these stories also are allusions and symbols that would have been familiar to readers in the ancient Near East and would have helped them grasp the message of the tract. The readers were at home with the use of dreams and visions as ways to articulate the involvement of gods in the affairs of humans.

The four kingdoms schema (chaps. 2 and 7) which divided history into a set number of periods was characteristic of Babylonian and Persian thought as well as apocalyptic literature. The *great mountain* that *filled the whole earth* (2:35) might have reminded the readers of Mount Zaphon, the sacred mountain of the Syrian storm-god, Baal-Hadad (lord-thunderer/smasher). They would understand the great tree of chapter 4 to be a sacred place for the gods to interact with humans.

Some of the imagery of chapter 7 would not have been foreign to Near Eastern readers. The Canaanite supreme god was called "Father of years." The one who comes with the clouds of heaven would have been identified as belonging to the divine council, since the Canaanite Baal was called "Rider of the clouds." Readers would have taken the rule of *one like a son of man* (7:13, RSV) to parallel that of Baal, who, according to their myths, secured kingship following victory over Yam, the god of the sea. Yet such imagery was used in the different pattern of the Israelite faith, based on the covenant relationship between Yahweh and his people.

Replete with religious symbols familiar in the Near East, the tract appears to make use of literary allusions to help convey to all peoples, nations, and languages the truth about the God of the Hebrews. The writer develops a powerful witness by bringing together what these rulers said to all peoples, nations, and languages about Daniel's God. Thus there is the dream of the great image with head of gold, breast and arms of silver, belly and thigh of bronze, legs of iron, and toes of iron and terra-cotta, *potter's clay* (2:41). When this image is destroyed by the great stone, which in turn fills the whole earth, it provides the context for Nebuchadnezzar's message: *Truly your God is God of gods and Lord of kings and a revealer of mysteries* (2:47).

The story of Shadrach, Meshach, and Abednego's deliverance from the *furnace of blazing fire* concludes with a message to *any people, nation, or language: . . . There is no other god who is able to deliver in this way* (3:29).

When Nebuchadnezzar loses his sanity, then comes to his senses and recognizes that the Most High rules, he shares his learning with all humanity (4:1): *Now, I, Nebuchadnezzar, praise and extol and honor the King of heaven,*

for all his works are truth
and his ways are justice;
and he is able to bring low
those who walk in pride (4:37).

The story of Belshazzar is one of stark fear in the midst of an orgy of feasting, drunkenness, and reveling. When the sacred vessels from the temple in Jerusalem are brought to his party, strange writing appears on the wall. Belshazzar's arrogance and blasphemous ways end in defeat and death. This story concludes with no words of explanation nor of warning. The events themselves provide the sobering message (chap. 5).

After placing Daniel into the *den of lions,* King Darius spends an anxious night. In the morning he finds Daniel safe and sound. Then Darius writes *to all peoples and nations of every language throughout the whole world: . . . "I make a decree, that in all my royal dominion people should tremble and fear before the God of Daniel:*

For he is the living God,
enduring forever.
His kingdom shall never be destroyed,
and his dominion has no end.
He delivers and rescues,
he works signs and wonders
in heaven and on earth" (6:25-27).

Finally, in chapter 7, Daniel has a vision of four dreadful beasts, which in many respects parallel the kingdoms in the image of chapter 2. The fourth beast is particularly dreadful. It is brought under control through the power of *the Ancient One.* The tract to the nations concludes with this message:

The kingship and dominion and the greatness of the
kingdoms under the whole heaven
shall be given to the people of the holy ones of the Most High;
their kingdom shall be an everlasting kingdom,
and all dominions shall serve and obey them (7:27).

The faithfulness of Daniel and his associates leads to proclamations to all peoples and nations and languages that this world belongs to the God of Israel, that he is in ultimate control of the universe, that he is sovereign over history (4:17), that he raises up kings and brings them down, and that behind and above international events, the living God is at work. Danna N. Fewell's comment is apt: "The central political issue in Daniel is that of sovereignty" (12). She develops the "issue" in nontraditional ways by noting the competitors to sovereignty. One of the two themes which crescendos repeatedly in the stories is "the recognition of the god of the Judean exiles as the sovereign of sovereigns" (Fewell: 132). Nebuchadnezzar can *set up* his weird image. He can force his subjects to *fall down*. But his power is insignificant when compared to the rule and might of the Lord God Almighty, who not only controls earthly kingdoms but also is establishing his own everlasting kingdom, which is given to his saints.

The tract to the nations tells stories of faithful witnesses. These persons are ready to maintain their faith without regard to personal cost. They are willing to serve the politicians of their time, but they do not allow these politicians to use them to enhance arrogant political power. There is a fine line between ministering to the high and mighty and being used by them in the service of strange gods and evil aims. Through the unwaveringly faithful life and witness of Daniel and his associates, the great men of their time come to profound insights concerning the God of Israel. These insights form the core of the tract's message to the nations.

God is in ultimate control! There is no god who is able to deliver in this way! In essence, these are words of grace and salvation, words needing to be heard by the Jews and by us. The ancient stories are also words of warning not to become fully absorbed into the culture of the powers under which they lived. This was a real temptation. When Cyrus issued the decree permitting the Jews to return to the

A TRACT TO THE NATIONS

Daniel 2–7

Chapter	**2**	**3**	**4**	**5**	**6**	**7**
	A	**B**	**C**	**C**	**B**	**A**
Theme	Kingdoms/Kingdom Four parts of statue	Test of Faithfulness (tempted to *add*—worship of statue)	Rule of God (acceptance: restoration)	Rule of God (rejection: death)	Test of Faithfulness (tempted to *omit*—prayer to God)	Kingdoms/Kingdom Four Beasts
Messenger	Nebuchadnezzar	Nebuchadnezzar	Nebuchadnezzar	Belshazzar	Darius	Heavenly Messenger
Message	*God is God of gods, Lord of kings, revealer of mysteries.* (2:47)	*There is no other god who is able to deliver in this way.* (3:29)	*Extol and honor the King of heaven, for all his works are truth, and his ways are justice; and he is able to bring low those who walk in pride.* (4:37)	*Belshazzar…was killed.* (5:30)	*He is the living God….His kingdom shall never be destroyed…. He delivers and rescues, he works signs and wonders in heaven and on earth.* (6:26-27)	*The holy ones of the Most High shall receive the kingdom and possess the kingdom forever—forever and ever.* (7:18) *Kingship…shall be given to the people of the holy ones,… an everlasting kingdom.* (7:27)

land of their ancestors and to rebuild the temple, many preferred to remain in Babylon (Ezra 1:1-5). They together with Israelites scattered elsewhere became known as the Diaspora. For others who, living under alien powers, prayed for the welfare of Jerusalem, Daniel gives words of comfort and hope. Again, in times of oppression and persecution, they are words of assurance to the faithful, affirming that their God will vindicate their faith either in life or after death in the resurrection.

The tract to the nations broadens the reader's spiritual horizons, making clear who the true God is and what he does. The tract demonstrates that the Most High God is concerned for all peoples and nations and languages. Each chapter in this tract to the nations sends a message to the world about this *God of gods* and *Lord of kings,* as charted on the preceding page.

Daniel 2:1-49

God the Revealer: Nebuchadnezzar's Dream

PREVIEW

If the time reference in 1:1 is not a slip, Daniel, Hananiah, Mishael, and Azariah have scarcely begun their training in the *literature and language of the Chaldeans* when Nebuchadnezzar has disturbing dreams.

As is his practice, Nebuchadnezzar calls in *the magicians, the enchanters, the sorcerers, and the Chaldeans* to interpret the dreams. Apparently Nebuchadnezzar has some misgiving about the authenticity and reliability of the claims of his wise men. For them to tell both the dream and the interpretation, he thinks, would certainly give credibility to their interpretation. In the heated exchange between the king and the wise men, the latter make a significant admission, *The thing that the king is asking is too difficult, and no one can reveal it to the king except the gods, whose dwelling is not with mortals* (2:11). This sets the stage for what follows. There *is* such a God, and he does indeed dwell with mortals. This one is the God of heaven, the God of Daniel and of his fathers. Most striking of all, this God is one who reveals secrets. His wisdom is made available.

In violent rage, the king commands the death of all wise men in Babylon, including Daniel and his companions, who in this crisis turn to the God of heaven in prayer. Their new education is of no avail. But God responds. Daniel's prayer-hymn of praise follows. This is the first of three occasions in which Daniel is presented as a person of prayer. Here he prays in a small group of believers. In chapter 6 he engages in personal private prayer in defiance of the king's decree. In chapter 9 he is moved to intercessory prayer on behalf of his people.

Before Daniel makes known to Nebuchadnezzar the dream and its interpretation, he gives full credit to his God as a revealer of mysteries. In so doing he shows the limitations of Babylonian wise men and yet avoids any self-aggrandizement. Daniel also demonstrates characteristics of the nonresistant personality. Without equivocation he says to Nebuchadnezzar, who has destroyed his homeland, his temple, and taken his people captive, *You are the head of gold* (2:38).

The chapter ends with two important themes that will be developed in the rest of the book: (1) The dream points to the rule of God in his eternal, universal kingdom. (2) Nebuchadnezzar learns something important about Daniel's God: *Your God is God of gods and Lord of kings and a revealer of mysteries* (2:47).

OUTLINE

A Case of Royal Insomnia, 2:1-13

2:1-2	Nebuchadnezzar's Dream
2:3-11	Nebuchadnezzar and the Chaldeans
2:12-13	Nebuchadnezzar's Decree

Daniel's Intervention, 2:14-28

2:14-23	Daniel Receives the Interpretation
2:24-28	Daniel Meets Nebuchadnezzar

The Dream and Its Interpretation, 2:29-45

2:29-30	Giving God the Credit
2:31-35	Reporting the Dream
2:36-45a	Interpreting the Dream
The Meaning of the Statue	2:36-43
The Meaning of the Stone	2:44-45a
2:45b	Asserting Reliability

Nebuchadnezzar's Proclamation, 2:46-49

EXPLANATORY NOTES

A Case of Royal Insomnia 2:1-13

The first story in the Aramaic section of Daniel begins with a third time reference (2:1; cf. 1:1, 21). Nebuchadnezzar has a bad dream in *the second year* of his reign, early 603 B.C. But in the story line, Daniel and his friends have completed their three-year training period (1:5, 18) and are now counted among *the wise men*, eligible to be executed (2:12-14). Perhaps *second year* is a dating slip. Possibly an earlier form of the story centered on Nabonidus rather than Nebuchadnezzar (Hartman, 1978:143). In this book, Nebuchadnezzar becomes a figure epitomizing and representing the line of Neo-Babylonian kings (cf. notes on 4:28-33). The Aramaic usage begins with the speech to the king by the diviners in verse 4a. While there are other sections of Aramaic in the OT (Ezra 4:8—6:18; 7:12-26; and Jer. 10:11), the Daniel section (2:4b—7:28) is the longest.

2:1-2 Nebuchadnezzar's Dream

The young king, Nebuchadnezzar, has been very active. He needed to consolidate power in order to rule effectively. The empire inherited from his father was a fairly new one. Consequently, there were minor revolts on the frontiers to the north and west, and especially in Palestine. Nebuchadnezzar defeated the Egyptians at Carchemish in 605 B.C. Even so, it was not clear what Egypt would do next. Perhaps Nebuchadnezzar's sense of insecurity contributes to his bad dreams. For Babylonians, bad dreams are considered bad omens. Thus Nebuchadnezzar's bad dream leaves him in a state of deep anxiety. In his anxiety he cannot sleep. He fears that the dream has something to do with his kingdom. *[Nebuchadnezzar, p. 293.]*

Nebuchadnezzar reasons that help in determining the meaning of his dream should be available from *the magicians, the enchanters, the sorcerers, and the Chaldeans* (here *Chaldeans* means a caste of wise men; cf. note on 1:4). From a Jewish storyteller's point of view, this is a strange crowd. There must be a smile on the storyteller's face as he repeats again and again this catalog of important people who advise the king (cf. 2:27). Had not Joseph proved superior to the magicians and wise men of Egypt? (Gen. 41). The prophet Isaiah ridiculed sorcerers for their arrogance, for their inability either to do good or to ward off evil, and for their failures to predict the future (Isa. 47:9-15). In Babylon, and wherever faithful Jews encountered other religions, they refused to accept or to make use of the occult.

2:3-11 Nebuchadnezzar and the Chaldeans

Nebuchadnezzar tells the assembled experts that he has had a dream and complains that he will have no peace of mind until its meaning is clear. The Chaldeans ask Nebuchadnezzar to tell the dream, and they promise then to give the interpretation. The Chaldeans have many books with dreams classified by subject matter. They can glean the meaning from these with certainty and authority. The large number of texts on divination found in Asshurbanipal's library in Nineveh, dated a century earlier than Daniel, indicates the popularity of this subject (ANET: 450-452).

Then Nebuchadnezzar makes an impossible demand. Refusing to tell his dream, he demands that the Chaldeans tell him both the dream *and* its interpretation. Like a typical oriental despot, Nebuchadnezzar promises dire consequences if they fail, and great rewards if they succeed. Can Nebuchadnezzar not remember his dream? There is also a Babylonian saying that if a person can not remember a dream, that person's god is angry with him.

In the face of Nebuchadnezzar's awesome threats, the Chaldeans respond a second time: *Let the king first tell his servants the dream, then we can give its interpretation* (2:7). As polytheists, they say that only *the gods* could reveal such a difficult thing (2:11). In the Bible, the dreams of Pharaoh are noted (Gen. 41), and outside the Bible mention is made of the dreams of the Assyrian kings Sennacherib and Esarhaddon. Dream manuals, known to us through archaeology, list many precedents. Thus the experts are acquainted with a large number of "case histories" and supposedly are able to work from the data of a given dream to its interpretation. But here they are without data! The bankruptcy of such activity is frequently the subject in Isaiah 40–48 (as in 41:21-24).

Since the Chaldeans are unable to tell both his dream and its interpretation, Nebuchadnezzar in anger accuses them of stalling for time. He charges them with lying to buy time *until things take a turn* (2:9), perhaps until the crisis the dream foretold is past. In his conversation with the Chaldeans, there is a hint that Nebuchadnezzar does indeed remember his dream. His demand that they tell both the dream and its interpretation is his way of testing the genuineness of the Chaldean's claims.

2:12-13 Nebuchadnezzar's Decree

Nebuchadnezzar's anger comes to a breaking point. He cuts off further conversation with the Chaldeans. The king issues a decree to kill *all the wise men of Babylon.* The storyteller notes that Daniel and his companions are to be included in the slaughter.

Daniel's Intervention 2:14-28

There are two accounts as to how Daniel comes before Nebuchadnezzar (2:14-16; 2:24-28). In both accounts one of Nebuchadnezzar's officials is introduced: *Arioch, the king's chief executioner.* In both accounts Arioch is given the unpleasant task of slaughtering the wise men of Babylon (2:14, 24). In the first account (2:14), Arioch apparently comes to Daniel. In the second account (2:24), Daniel goes to Arioch.

From the first account, one gathers that Daniel is acquainted with the king. After inquiring of Arioch as to the reason for the king's severe decree, Daniel *went in* to Nebuchadnezzar to request time so he might give the king the *interpretation* (2:16).

In the second account, after Daniel has received a vision revealing the mystery, he pleads with Arioch not to destroy the wise men (2:24). Then Daniel asks Arioch to make an appointment with Nebuchadnezzar so that Daniel can interpret the dream. A measure of Daniel's faith is also seen here in that Daniel commits himself to interpret the dream to Nebuchadnezzar before God has revealed the dream to him. Arioch hastily tells Nebuchadnezzar about the captive from Judah who is able to interpret dreams and soon introduces Daniel to the king (2:24). At this point, Daniel's Babylonian name is used: *Belteshazzar* (2:26). Instead of Daniel's offer to interpret the king's dream as in the first account (2:16), the king asks Daniel if he is indeed *able* to tell the dream and to make the interpretation (2:26).

The significance of the two accounts should not be overlooked. The first account tells how Daniel and his companions pray for the revelation of the dream and its interpretation. The second account enables Daniel to tell Nebuchadnezzar that no wise man, enchanter, magician, or astrologist could ever fulfill Nebuchadnezzar's demand. Only the *God in heaven* (2:28), Daniel's God, can do this! From the point of view of literary artistry, the two accounts reinforce each other. When heard by an audience in an oral retelling, the two accounts accent the surprising developments.

2:14-23 Daniel Receives the Interpretation

Daniel receives the revelation of the dream and its interpretation within a community of faith. Daniel and his friends are receiving a non-Hebrew education; however, their faith in the God of the Hebrews never wavers. Their refusal of the king's food and wine provides a daily reminder of their primary allegiance. Here their Hebrew names are used. The God to whom their names points, reveals the mystery as they are together.

After Daniel's talk with Arioch, Daniel returns to his companions. Daniel is not a solitary, lonely hero. Together Daniel and his friends *seek mercy from the God of heaven*. They have a prayer fellowship. They pray for a revelation so that neither they nor the wise men will be killed. In Babylon, far from the holy city, far from the temple, and immersed daily in the idolatrous lore of the Chaldeans, the young men serve Nebuchadnezzar. But more than this, they serve the *God of heaven*. This Aramaic title for God appears only in this chapter (2:18-19, 37, 44). It parallels *the Most High God* in chapters 3 to 7, *King of heaven* (4:37), and *Lord of heaven* (5:23). The title *God of heaven* appears elsewhere in the Hebrew form, but in postexilic materials (Ezra 1:2; 6:10; 7:12, 21; Neh. 1:5; 2:4), possibly as a way of counteracting the astral worship of peoples like the Babylonians (as in Isa. 40–55). The title stresses that God is the Creator also of planets and stars.

In the midst of a praying, believing fellowship, God gives a vision in the night. The *mystery* of the dream and its meaning is revealed. The word translated "mystery" (*raz*) appears in the Bible only in Daniel (2:18-19, 27-30, 47; 4:9). It is a word of Persian origin meaning a "secret" or "enigma" that can only be understood through divine revelation because it deals with God's purposes in history. Thus it is akin to the meaning of the Greek word, *mustērion* (mystery), as used by Paul in Romans 16:25.

The revelation results in a hymn of praise (2:20-23). The *name of God* is *blessed*. To bless is to empower; when used toward God, it means to give thanks, honor, and appreciation to the one named. In the blessing, the nature and works of God are expressed. Daniel's language is familiar from the Psalms (as in 72:18-19) and seems to be shaped in imitation of a thanksgiving psalm, giving thanks to God and incorporating a personal experience (as in Pss. 30, 107).

The God of heaven has *wisdom and power* (2:20) which in comparison makes the wisdom of the Chaldeans and the strength of

Nebuchadnezzar pale into insignificance. Here a double reason for blessing God is given.

The God of heaven *changes times and seasons, deposes kings and sets up kings* (2:21). This is a statement of faith. The God of Israel is in final control of history. The word *times* has the sense of duration, while *seasons* suggests the appropriate moment for something to happen (1 Thess. 5:1). God has power over kings (Ps. 75:7). Kings come and go. Kingdoms rise and fall. Behind current events, God works out his purposes. The kings on whom the stories of Daniel focus, as well as the readers of Daniel, will be made well aware of this fact.

The God of heaven *gives wisdom* and *knowledge* to those who have *understanding*. These terms, at home in wisdom literature, are especially apt, given the Chaldeans' claim to wisdom. God is the source of wisdom and knowledge, and he distributes them as he wills. This agrees with the psalmist: "The fear of the Lord is the beginning of wisdom; all those who practice it have a good understanding" (Ps. 111:10). Daniel and his friends fear the Lord. In an unusual way, God honors their commitment by revealing both the dream and its interpretation.

The eternal God also *reveals deep and hidden things*. When God reveals Nebuchadnezzar's dream and its meaning, Daniel and his friends come to realize that to their God, the past and future are the same; darkness is no barrier to him, and *light dwells with him*. In many OT passages, God is described as surrounded by light, "like a devouring fire" (Exod. 24:17) or by "rays" flashing "from his hand" (Hab. 3:4). Isaiah sees God's brightness: "The Lord will be your everlasting light" (Isa. 60:19-20). The NT expresses these ideas more clearly. Paul writes, "The king of Kings and Lord of lords . . . dwells in unapproachable light" (1 Tim. 6:15-16). While James mentions the "Father of lights" (James 1:17), John is more explicit: "God is light and in him there is no darkness at all" (1 John 1:5). This light is a sign that God is good, right, and holy, and has wisdom to share.

The thanksgiving concludes with a personal note of thanks and praise to the *God of my ancestors* (2:23). Daniel acknowledges God as the source of his wisdom and strength, the one who has answered their prayer. Daniel does not overlook the importance of a community of faith both in petition and in receiving God's answer. God *revealed to me what we asked of you, for you have revealed to us what the king ordered*. This last line of the blessing clearly states the reason why he blesses the God of heaven (2:23).

2:24-28 Daniel Meets Nebuchadnezzar

A second account of Daniel's intervention provides an important conversation between Daniel and Nebuchadnezzar before Daniel reveals the dream (2:26-28). In the conversation, Nebuchadnezzar asks Daniel, *Are you able*? (2:26). Daniel seizes the opportunity to point Nebuchadnezzar to the source of his ability, not within himself: *There is a God in heaven, who reveals mysteries* (2:28).

Step by step, the first four chapters of Daniel confront Nebuchadnezzar with the God of Israel in whom true power and ability resides. Nebuchadnezzar, along with kings and politicians before him and since, overrate their own power. Eventually, Nebuchadnezzar will come to see that power is not in his hands nor in his kingdom but in the God of Israel, the God he thought he had defeated when he took the sacred vessels from Jerusalem and led Israelites and their king captive. Nebuchadnezzar is in the process of learning that the God of the Hebrews is sovereign over both heaven and earth.

Are you able? (*kahel*, also in 4:18 [4:15 in Aramaic]; cf. 5:8, 15). This is a persistent issue in the book. Daniel is able because there is a God who is able! Nebuchadnezzar admits that Daniel is *able* because *a spirit of the holy gods* is in him (4:18). Daniel's God is *able* (*yakil*, 3:17; cf. 4:37 [4:34 in Aramaic]; 6:20 [6:21 in Aramaic]) to save from *the furnace of blazing fire* (3:17). Both Nebuchadnezzar and Darius will discover that their power is limited, that there is a God who is able (Dan. 3, 6). God's power is not limited, though evil powers may lead to a delay in his final triumph.

Before telling the dream and its interpretation, Daniel provides Nebuchadnezzar background for understanding what he will hear. The dream, Daniel says, relates to the future, *at the end of days* (2:28), the days between Nebuchadnezzar's present reign and an undefined point of time in the future.

Note the significant change in how God reveals himself. Here God reveals himself to a foreign ruler assisted by a Jewish wise person, and through the ruler to the whole world. Earlier in Israel's history, God revealed his intentions largely through the patriarchs and the prophets of Israel. In this story, God works through the subconscious mind of a Babylonian king, Nebuchadnezzar, and also through his servant Daniel. God will enable Daniel to tell and interpret the dream which he has given Nebuchadnezzar as he lay upon his bed. The ultimate meaning of this dream embraces the whole world!

The Dream and Its Interpretation 2:29-45

2:29-30 Giving God the Credit

Before Daniel tells Nebuchadnezzar his dream, he repeats two important ideas: (1) that God, who reveals mysteries, has made known to Nebuchadnezzar what will come to pass; and (2) that he (Daniel) can make no special claims for himself to be able to reveal either the dream or its interpretation. So that Nebuchadnezzar will be certain of the truth of Daniel's interpretation, Daniel first tells the dream. The protracted conversation between Daniel and Nebuchadnezzar reflects skillful storytelling. The conversation not only keeps central issues in view but also increases suspense as hearers wonder how much longer they must wait to hear the dream.

2:31-35 Reporting the Dream

Nebuchadnezzar's dream focuses on a huge, frightening, extraordinarily brilliant statue of a man. It is constructed from a strange mixture of materials, ranging from most costly gold to clay of little worth. The head is gold, the breast and arms are silver, the belly and thighs are bronze, the legs are iron, and the feet are made of iron and of fired *potter's clay*, terra-cotta (2:41). Gold and silver are precious metals. Bronze and iron are strong and hard. Clay represents brittleness and weakness, with no strength or power; used for the base, it jeopardizes the stability of the whole statue.

The statue is a picture of glory, with a head of gold. It depicts strength, but with little stability, having feet that could scarcely cohere, let alone bear the load. The statue is costly, stupid, fragile, and ready to topple! Here is a graphic description of human empires with marks of power and glory while at the same time continually confronted by internal crises, corruption, and disunity (cf. Gen. 11:1-9).

Suddenly, a stone not quarried by humans comes flying through the air. It crashes into the feet of the statue and pulverizes them. As the statue falls, all of its parts are simultaneously ground into pieces so fine that the wind blows away all traces of them. The stone, however, remains. It grows and fills the whole earth.

2:36-45a Interpreting the Dream

Having told the dream, Daniel explains its meaning. Apparently, Daniel's description of the dream squares with Nebuchadnezzar's memory. The king makes no comment. His wonder, however, increases as Daniel interprets the details.

The Meaning of the Statue 2:36-43

The interpretation is likely difficult for Daniel to report, given the experiences of Daniel and his companion. Nebuchadnezzar has brought them to Babylon as captives. He has changed their names and placed them in a reeducation program. Nebuchadnezzar has plundered Jerusalem and dislocated and made refugees of many Israelites. Yet, to this Nebuchadnezzar, Daniel says, *You are the head of gold* (2:38). How difficult to identify the number-one enemy of Daniel's people as the head of gold! But when Daniel names Nebuchadnezzar as the head of gold, he makes another important point—Nebuchadnezzar's glory and power are not the result of his ability! That Nebuchadnezzar is *king of kings* has resulted from the action of Israel's God: *the God of heaven has given the kingdom, the power, and the might and the glory* (2:37). God is the one who has extended Nebuchadnezzar's rule to include not only land areas but also all creatures—humans, beasts, and birds (2:38).

The God of Israel gives in the sense of disposing as well as granting. The Hebrew word (*natan*) translated *has given* includes in addition the sense of "appoint." In chapter 1, God *gave* Jehoiakim into the hand of Nebuchadnezzar (1:2, RSV). Then God *gave* Daniel favor in the eyes of Asphenaz (1:9, RSV). Next God *gave* Daniel and his companions the ability to learn and gave Daniel insight into visions and dreams (1:17). Now Nebuchadnezzar learns—and he will learn this more fully in chapter 4—that his power and prestige are gifts from God. In the NT, God's actions are often couched in terms of "giving." One chapter provides three examples: "God . . . *gave* his only Son" (John 3:16). "No one can receive anything except what *has been given* from heaven" (3:27). "The Father loves the Son, and *has given* all things into his hand" (3:35, RSV).

Through Daniel's interpretation, one learns that the statue of four metals represents four ages, each with a dominant world power. Scholars have wondered about the origins of such schemes. In the Jewish Sibylline Oracles (book 4; cf. 3), some parts of which date to the second century B.C., appears a ten-period scheme. But it was more common for Asiatics to outline history into four ages, as do Persian Zoroastrian texts of the sixth century B.C. Even earlier, Hesiod in the eighth century B.C. identifies four world ages with gold, silver, bronze, and iron. Perhaps Daniel reflects a scheme such as that. His pattern does not seem to be influenced by later Persian material (Lucas: 202; cf. Hartman, 1978:31-33). Tobit 14:4-14 implies a sequence of Assyria, Babylonia, and Media, and predicts the return from exile, which fits the coming Persian rule. Daniel apparently drops Assyria from the beginning and adds Greece to the end of such a series: Babylonia, Media, Persia, Greece (cf. notes on 7:4-8).

The God of Israel has made Nebuchadnezzar the head of gold. This is reflected in the message of the prophet Jeremiah. When Jeremiah encourages Zedekiah not to rebel against Nebuchadnezzar, Jeremiah quotes God as saying,

> It is I who by my great power and my outstretched arm have made the earth, with the people and animals that are on the earth, and I give it to whomever I please. Now I have given all these lands into the hand of King Nebuchadnezzar of Babylon, my servant, and I have given him even the wild animals of the field to serve him. (Jer. 27:5-6; cf. 28:14)

What kingdoms are symbolized by the statue? It is important to note that only one kingdom is identified: the Neo-Babylonian empire. Nebuchadnezzar is the head of gold. A second kingdom will be inferior to Nebuchadnezzar's. A third kingdom shall rule over all the earth. The fourth kingdom will be strong, belligerent, but unstable like iron mixed with terra-cotta (cf. Sirach 13:2). The significant revelation of the dream, however, is that God will act to *set up a kingdom that shall never be destroyed* (Dan. 2:44). It should be noted also that the stone *cut from the mountain not by human hands* hits the statue and simultaneously breaks in pieces the iron, the clay, the bronze, the silver, and the gold, so that the wind blows everything away: *not a trace of them could be found* (2:35).

A common literary device in Hebrew literature is the grouping of four items in which three form a unit with the fourth providing special importance, standing, or rank. There are many examples of this three-plus-one scheme (Talmon: 347). Daniel has three companions, Hananiah, Mishael, and Azariah. Daniel, however, is the outstanding one of the four. The three are appointed over the affairs of the province of Babylon, while Daniel remains in the king's court (2:49). In a similar way, Job had three "comforters" plus Elihu. David, the youngest son of Jesse, outranked his three older brothers (1 Sam. 17:13-14). Solomon was the outstanding son of David, outshining Ammon, Absolam, Adonijah.

Such groupings also appear in wisdom material, as in Proverbs 30:15-31:

Three things are never satisfied;
  four never say, "Enough." (30:15)
Three things are too wonderful for me;
  four I do not understand. (30:18)
Under three things the earth trembles;
  under four it cannot bear up. (30:21)
Three things are stately in their tread;
  four are stately in their gait. (30:29)

Amos couches his oracles against foreign nations in this form (1:3—2:8). "For three transgressions of Damascus, and for four, I will not revoke the punishment" (1:3). Then follow similar statements against Gaza (1:6), Tyre (1:9), Edom (1:11), the Ammonities (1:13), Moab (2:1), and finally against Judah (2:4) and Israel (2:6).

These literary forms do not require precise, literal interpretations. Often the focus is on the observation, action, event, or person involved in the fourth. In Daniel 7, the action in heaven follows consideration of the fourth beast. In chapter 8, four kingdoms will arise and from them will come a king who will be broken, not by human hands (8:25; cf. 2:34-35). The same idea appears in 11:2-4. Three kings will arise in Persia. In the time of the fourth, a mighty *warrior king shall arise*.

How then shall the kingdoms represented by the statue be interpreted? Focus should not be on naming the kingdoms. Instead, the focus should be on the action of God, who after a completed period of time will send the stone.

For some interpreters, the statue represents the reign of kings from Nebuchadnezzar to Nabonidus/Belshazzar and symbolizes the fall of Nebuchadnezzar's dynasty at the hands of Cyrus, paralleling the period of seventy years (Daniel 9). *[Nabonidus, p. 291.]* It is of interest that, counting Nebuchadnezzar, there were four Babylonian kings prior to the end of the empire. Were the statue to represent these four, the *stone* might then be Cyrus. But such an interpretation is problematic in the light of Daniel 8:20. Another suggestion has been that the statue represents the four kings mentioned in the book itself: Nebuchadnezzar, Belshazzar, Darius the Mede (5:31), and Cyrus the Persian (6:28). One of the several problems with this interpretation is the identity of Darius the Mede. *[Cyrus, the Persian/Darius the Mede, p. 284.]*

If the statue represents successive empires, which empires might they be? The movement from gold to silver, to bronze, to iron mixed with clay does indeed suggest decreasing value. But how are successive empires inferior to each other? Are they inferior because of less-capable leaders? less geographical area? population decrease? weakness militarily? economic decline? Is older thought to be better? In Daniel's fourth kingdom, inferiority is seen in divisions and instability (2:42-43).

The fourth kingdom is particularly unstable, as symbolized by an attempt to weld together iron and clay. The toes stand for kings and kingdoms that are *partly strong and partly weak* (2:42). The mixture of iron and clay is compared to weak marriages: *They will mix with one another in marriage, but they will not hold together* (2:43). This likely refers to marriages between royal families as attempts to unite kingdoms. Note that the final vision (Dan. 10–12) refers to intermarriage between the Ptolemies of Egypt and the Seleucids of Syria, two streams of successors to the generals of Alexander the Great (11:6, 17). But these marriages fail to cement relationships.

Daniel 2 has contributed a term to our dictionaries, "feet of clay." Though these kings brandish *iron* in frequent warfare, they have "feet of *clay*," flaws not apparent to the casual observer. "Defenses of clay" are worthless before God and his majesty (Job 13:11-12; cf. Isa. 41:25; Ps. 2:9; Rev. 2:27).

Chapter 2 does not name the three empires after Babylon. It is most plausible to identify the four as (1) Babylonian, (2) Median, (3) Persian, and (4) Greek, all to be destroyed by the coming universal kingdom of God (Hartman, 1978:29-42; ABD, 2:30). An ancient tradition, likely originating in Persia, named four world kingdoms, Assyria, Media, Persia, and Greece/Macedonia, succeeded by "the yoke of slavery for the Italians" (Sibylline Oracles, 4:49-104). Daniel substitutes Babylon for Assyria, since Babylon destroyed Jerusalem. In 612 B.C. Media helped Babylon conquer Assyria and in 550 B.C. became a distinct part of the Medo-Persian empire (Dan. 5:31—6:28; Esther 1:3).

Less likely would be (1) Babylonian, (2) Medo-Persian, (3) Greek, and (4) Roman empires (Baldwin: 65-68). If so, one might find clues within the book of Daniel to identify the second kingdom as the Medo-Persian empire (550-330). In a later vision, the ram with two horns (8:20) represents the Medes and the Persians. The third kingdom then would be the Greek empire established by Alexander the Great in 336 B.C., the male goat of 8:21. Daniel 2 does not name the fourth kingdom, which might be Rome. However, the fourth kingdom here is probably the same as the fourth beast in Daniel 7, the Greeks, who were eventually drawn into Rome's sphere of influence—the Seleucids by 190-188 B.C. (11:18), and the Ptolemies by 168-167 B.C. (11:30).

In the days of the Roman empire, God sent his Son Jesus and as the NT bears witness, inaugurated the kingdom of God. The earliest Christian writers tended to interpret the fourth kingdom as Rome and the stone as Jesus the Messiah (Irenaeus, *Against Heresies* 26.1). Though Nebuchadnezzar's dream predicts a succession of empires, yet when the stone hits the image, there is a simultaneous rather than a sequential disintegration. All the empires are turned to powder at once. This suggests that the rule of God is at work in the disintegration and fall of all empires regardless of the date in which the collapse occurs.

The Meaning of the Stone 2:44-45a

The stone represents the kingdom of God or the rule of God. The stone is not cut from a quarry by human hands. This indicates divine origin. It is not the product of human effort. Further, the stone coming from a source outside of human endeavors causes arrogant human structures to topple. When human empires are crushed and evil institutions are swept away, the stone remains.

In the days of those kings (2:44), God himself will come and will establish *a kingdom that shall never be destroyed, nor shall this kingdom be left to another people* (2:44)—which means that it *shall* be left to God's people. As in 7:27, the people of God receive an *everlasting kingdom, and all dominions shall serve and obey them* (see notes on 7:27 and TBC [Text in the Life of the Church] for Daniel 7). This happens when God delivers his people and they share the knowledge and worship of God with other peoples, as the book of Daniel sets out to do in the tract to the nations (cf. Isa. 61:6). In so doing, they receive God's kingdom. The stone that becomes a mountain (2:35, 44-45) shows the overwhelming worth and power of God's universal reign and calls all nations to the true worship of God. "In days to come the mountain of the Lord's house shall be established as the highest of the mountains, and shall be raised above the hills; and all the nations shall stream to it" (Isa. 2:2-4; Mic. 4:1-4).

Thus God's kingdom will have a sovereignty in the midst of kingdoms that rise and fall. The stone comes to earth from outside and symbolizes the kingdom of God. It will be indestructible. It will fill the whole earth. It will become the final reality! The kingdom of God becomes an important theme for Jesus and the early church (Luke 4:43; 9:2; 12:31-32; 13:29; 17:20-21; Acts 1:3; 8:12; 14:22; 20:25; 28:31).

2:45b Asserting Reliability

Daniel concludes his interpretation of the dream by saying that the great God, the God of Israel, has revealed to Nebuchadnezzar his plan for the future. It is ironical that in Babylon, the world center of dream interpretation, only Daniel, God's man, is able to tell both Nebuchadnezzar's dream and its interpretation. Because the God of Israel initiated the dream, recounting the dream and giving its interpretation are possible through God's faithful servant. Then Daniel reminds Nebuchadnezzar that since God acts in giving the dream and in giving interpretation, what he reports is fully reliable *and its interpretation trustworthy.*

Nebuchadnezzar's Proclamation 2:46-49

By the time Daniel finishes speaking, Nebuchadnezzar is overwhelmed. Daniel has revealed the dream—something Nebuchadnezzar and the Chaldeans have admitted can be done only through divine intervention (2:11). In addition, Daniel's interpretation makes sense to Nebuchadnezzar. Further, the dream strokes Nebuchadnezzar's ego. Nebuchadnezzar sees history unfolding before him. Though he does not grasp the significance of the stone, he does see his own place in history. It is secure. In the days to come, no human empire will be greater than his, for he is the head of gold!

Faced with the miracle of a dream revealed and with an exceptionally favorable interpretation, Nebuchadnezzar begins to worship Daniel. He falls on his face before Daniel and commands that symbols of worship, *offering and incense*, be brought. We assume that Daniel refused to receive such worship (cf. Paul and Barnabas at Lystra (Acts 14:11-18; Gal. 4:14).

The conclusion of this story is important. Nebuchadnezzar tells what he learned about Daniel's God, the God of Israel. Daniel's God, Nebuchadnezzar said, is not a mere tribal deity. He is the *God of gods*. Furthermore, since the dream depicts the rise and fall of kingdoms, Nebuchadnezzar learns that the God of Israel is sovereign over history. He is the one who moves kings at his will. In addition, as Daniel both tells and interprets Nebuchadnezzar's dream, Nebuchadnezzar learns that Daniel's God, not the Babylonian wise men, is a *revealer of mysteries*. Goldingay (57) says, "The key assertion of the book is not that there is a God in heaven: everyone believed as much. It is that, contrary to the despairing assumption of the sages (v. 11), this God reveals secrets."

Each story in the Aramaic section of Daniel ends with a revelatory statement about God that is announced to the whole world. The only exception is the story of Belshazzar (chap. 5); but even then, the death of the prince speaks eloquently of God's ability to act. Each story provides a setting to proclaim a truth about Daniel's God. Here Nebuchadnezzar, the king of Babylon, proclaims to the whole world who the God of Israel is:

1. *God of gods:* there are "no other gods before" him (cf. Exod. 20:3).
2. *Lord of kings:* he is sovereign over empires, rulers, and history.
3. *A revealer of mysteries:* he knows what is in darkness, and light dwells with him.

With the proclamation containing these exalted titles (cf. Rev. 17:14), the story quickly ends. Daniel receives high honors and gifts. He is made ruler over the province of Babylon, and head of the wise men (even before graduation from the three-year course of 1:5?). Then Daniel requests the elevation of Shadrach, Meshach, and Abednego. (In this request, their Babylonian names are used.) His request is granted. They are given positions in rural areas, while Daniel stays in the capital. The elevation of Daniel's three friends sets the stage for the test to follow (chap. 3).

THE TEXT IN BIBLICAL CONTEXT

The Stone

After Jesus' triumphal entry into Jerusalem at the beginning of Passion Week, he taught in the temple and was preaching. The leaders of the Jews confronted him, "Tell us, by what authority are you doing these things? Who is it who gave you this authority?" (Luke 20:2). Following this, Jesus tells a parable of a vineyard owner who leased his vineyard to tenants. When the time came to collect the rent, he sent a servant to collect it. But the tenants beat him and sent him away empty-handed. The landlord sent another servant, who also was beaten, insulted, and sent away empty-handed. Then the owner sent his "beloved son," thinking the tenants would respect him. Instead, when the son arrived, the tenants killed him, intending to take over the vineyard. Then Jesus said that the owner would destroy the tenants and give his vineyard to others.

To support the action of the vineyard owner, Jesus quotes several OT passages dealing with *the stone* (Luke 20:17-18).

"The stone that the builders rejected has become the cornerstone" comes from Psalm 118:22, perhaps from the time of Nehemiah when the wall of Jerusalem was rebuilt. It may refer to chosen Israel, despised by surrounding nations, but reestablished by God after the exile. What is sung about Zion finds its fulfillment in Messiah, who represents and leads faithful Israel.

"Everyone who falls on that stone will be broken to pieces" is pieced together from Isaiah 8:14-15, where the Lord of hosts becomes "a stone one strikes against, . . . a rock one stumbles over; . . . many among them shall stumble; they shall fall and be broken; they shall be snared and taken." The next part, "and it will crush anyone on whom it falls," is taken from Daniel: *As you looked on, a stone was cut out not by human hands, and it struck the statue. . . . Then the iron, the clay, the bronze, the silver, and the gold, were broken all in pieces and became like the chaff. . . . But the stone . . . became a great mountain and filled the whole earth* (Dan. 2:34-35).

In Daniel this statement is further interpreted: *The God of heaven will set up a kingdom that shall never be destroyed. . . . It shall crush all these kingdoms and bring them to an end, and it shall stand forever* (2:44-45).

In later Judaism, many of these OT verses on the stone were associated with the coming Messiah. This is paralleled by the interpretation that developed in the church (J. Jeremias in TDNT, 4:271-280). Jesus saw himself as the stone, and so did the leaders of the early church. In a sermon in Acts, Peter and John count Jesus as the stone the builders rejected (4:11). In Romans 9:33, Paul sees Jesus as the stone. There Paul cites Isaiah 28:16. The first letter of Peter develops the stone theme by inviting readers to "come to him [Christ], a living stone, though rejected by mortals yet chosen and precious in God's sight." That invitation is followed by quotations from Isaiah 28:16; Psalm 118:22; and Isaiah 8:14 (1 Pet. 2:4-8).

Living on this side of Christ's first coming, we agree with the early church that the stone is Jesus Christ and his kingdom. Since Jesus' day, the kingdom is in the process of growing to fill the whole earth. The stone that did not measure up to the builders' expectations, also turns out to be the cornerstone or the keystone, the stone that bears the weight or makes the arch possible.

To fall on the stone is to be broken. That is to say, when one comes to the recognition of need and inadequacy in brokenness, openness, and humility, one receives God's grace. On the other hand, pride, willfulness, and going in one's own way, rejecting God's grace and love, leads to destruction. When confronted by Jesus and the kingdom, persons must enter as a child. To reject him and his kingdom is to stand under judgment, for "it will crush anyone on whom it falls" (Luke 20:18).

THE TEXT IN THE LIFE OF THE CHURCH

Preaching the Kingdom

The kingdom of God is a central theme in the book of Daniel. The tract to the nations begins and ends with the kingdom: *The God of heaven will set up a kingdom* (2:44). *The kingship . . . shall be given to the people of the holy ones of the Most High; their kingdom shall be an everlasting kingdom* (7:27). Refrains describe the kingdom as *everlasting* and enduring *from generation to generation* (4:3, 34).

The kingdom is rooted in God's action in delivering the people of Israel from Egypt in order to be their king. Obedience springs from allegiance to him. The kingdom does not exist for the benefit of a special people. Rather, God's intention was that through his people, the kingdom would extend to all the nations. It is remarkable that in a desperate time, when Jerusalem was in ruins and the Israelites were in exile (sixth century B.C.), or when the Syrian king had desecrated the Jerusalem temple and was tearing up the books of the Mosaic Law (second century B.C.; 1 Macc. 1), the concept of kingdom emerges with new vigor and clarity in the book of Daniel.

Jesus began his ministry with the words, "I must proclaim the good news of the kingdom of God; . . . for I was sent for this purpose" (Luke 4:43). Jesus instructed his disciples and then "sent them out to proclaim the kingdom of God and to heal" (Luke 9:2). The kingdom always has a missionary dimension. Jesus' message was for the whole world. Yet he seemed especially concerned to bring into being an alternative community, a little flock who would enter the narrow gate and take the way that is hard (Matt. 7:13-14). By this Jesus referred to grace and the obedience that springs from grace. He called for love, for self-giving service, for justice, and for change in attitude between the rich and poor, between the sexes, and between Jews and Gentiles. The present experience of the kingdom is to be a foretaste of what will be when the kingdom of God comes in its fullness.

Not only does the kingdom of God have a present and future reality, but it also has spiritual and social dimensions. Jesus was concerned for individual change and for the formation of a group of committed disciples that would confront and penetrate society. Jesus' teachings, as found in the Sermon on the Mount, are to be experienced now. To follow Jesus means that believers commit themselves to obey his teachings about lifestyle, about peace and nonresistance, and about concern for the poor and oppressed. His followers live lives of service and self-giving love, relying upon and empowered by God's grace. It is in the church, the community of faithful disciples, that spiritual and social dimensions of kingdom living take shape. The actions of the community may be quite out of step with the values and practices of the larger surrounding society. Yet there is the profound awareness that society can be confronted and changed by the church, the alternative community of committed disciples in which God rules.

In Matthew 16, Jesus speaks of both church and kingdom: "I will build my church," and "I will give you the keys of the kingdom" (Matt. 16:18-19; cf. 18:18). The church and the kingdom are not separated, but they are not identical. The church is the body of Christ, the temple of the Spirit. As such, the church is interwoven with the kingdom. The church proclaims the good news of the kingdom and serves the kingdom. One may think of the church as exhibit A of the kingdom. Churches are colonies of the kingdom, local manifestations of the kingdom. The work of the church is kingdom work. The church is central in God's plan for advancing his kingdom until it comes in its fullness (Eph. 1:18-23; 3:9-13).

Daniel and his companions received visions of the kingdom of God, of its power, and of its universal and eternal dimensions. "God's Word pulverizes" all human empires vying with God. His rule does this "successively throughout history and climactically at the End" (Aukerman: 103-104). As a community of the faithful who refused to compromise their faith, Daniel and his friends live obediently, regardless of the cost. Thus Daniel and his companions provide an example of how the kingdom, the rule of God, is realized and experienced. This was happening in those days, is happening now in the church, and will be happening until the Lord returns. Then "the kingdom of the world has become the kingdom of our Lord and of his Messiah, and he will reign forever and ever" (Rev. 11:15).

Daniel 3:1-30

God the Deliverer: Escape from the Fiery Furnace

PREVIEW

The stories in the Aramaic section of Daniel are ancient. Whether they were put into writing at an early or late date is a continuing debate. *[Daniel: Date and Authorship, p. 285.]* In either case, the stories were transmitted orally over many years. The story of Shadrach, Meshach, and Abednego is a storyteller's story, easily told, easily remembered. It is filled with repetitions and contrasts. There is interplay between the sublime and the ridiculous. One sees opportunities to be serious—an arrogant king is humbled, while faithful persons are exalted. There are also opportunities to poke fun!

A central theme of the story about the golden image is *worship* (3:5-6, 10-12, 14-15, 18, 28). There is the interplay between *set up* (3:1-3, 5, 7, 12, 14, 18) and *fall down* (3:5-7, 10-11, 15). The story has universal dimensions, with meaning for *all peoples, nations, and languages* (3:4, 7, 29).

The many repetitions delight the storyteller. Much like the story of Daniel in the lions' den (chap. 6), the narrative is carried forward by a constant use of the simple conjunction, *so/then* (NRSV/RSV; Aramaic: *be'dayin*) (3:3, 13, 19, 21, 24, 26, 30). A storyteller would enjoy repeating the list of "great ones" that fell down before the ridiculous statue (3:2-3, 27) and the list of musical instruments (3:5, 7, 10, 15). The names of the three young men also have a cadence. Note that the storyteller seldom uses pronouns to refer to the three; time and again the names *Shadrach, Meshach, and Abednego* are repeated (3:12-14, 16, 19, 20, 22-23, 26, 28-30). Finally, the *furnace of blazing fire* struck terror but was unable to harm the three (3:6, 11, 15, 17, 20-21, 23, 26). Repetition, as Robert Alter has noted, is a trademark of Hebrew storytelling (88-113).

The story seems to have two climaxes. The story could conclude with Shadrach, Meshach, and Abednego's testimony of faith (3:17-18). God is able to deliver, they say, but even if he does not, they will continue their refusal to worship the king's image! The second climax is in Nebuchadnezzar's decree to *any people, nation, or language* that the God of Shadrach, Meshach, and Abednego *is able to deliver* (3:29).

OUTLINE

A Statue to Worship, 3:1-7

3:1	Nebuchadnezzar's Image
3:2-3	Politicians and People Come to the Dedication
3:4-7	The Decree

Shadrach, Meshach, and Abednego Accused, 3:8-15

3:8-12	The Chaldean's Malicious Report
3:13-15	The Enraged Tyrant

Shadrach, Meshach, and Abednego Refuse to Bow, 3:16-18

Shadrach, Meshach, and Abednego Condemned to Burn, 3:19-23

3:19-20	The Frustrated Tyrant
3:21-23	Into the Furnace of Blazing Fire
	Apocryphal Supplements

Shadrach, Meshach, and Abednego Delivered, 3:24-27

3:24-25	The Astonished Tyrant
3:26-27	Unbowed and Unburned

Nebuchadnezzar's Royal Decree, 3:28-30

EXPLANATORY NOTES

A Statue to Worship 3:1-7

3:1 Nebuchadnezzar's Image

Daniel has cured Nebuchadnezzar of the anxiety accompanying his bad dream (2:1-49). In the interpretation of his nightmare, Nebuchadnezzar has been confronted by the sovereignty of Israel's God, who is in ultimate control of history. The future is in God's hands.

Now that Nebuchadnezzar has been freed from the bad dream, he has to get on with being king. Nebuchadnezzar is well aware of the fragile nature of his empire. Geographically, it is widespread, embracing many peoples, cultures, religions, and political subdivisions. Nebuchadnezzar has to work for a new unity.

To create as well as to symbolize that unity, Nebuchadnezzar builds a huge image or monument (3:1). The monument, in some respects, is related to the statue of Nebuchadnezzar's dream (2:1-49). The story does not tell precisely what this image resembles. Possibly it is a stylized figure of Nebuchadnezzar. Instead of only the head being made of gold, now the whole image is likely plated with gold.

It is also possible that the image is built in honor of Nabu, a Babylonian deity. Nebuchadnezzar's name incorporates the name of this deity: "Nabu, protect my son" or "Nabu, protect my boundary." Whether an image of himself or of his god, it is a monument to Nebuchadnezzar's pride. This may explain his violent rage when persons refuse to bow to it.

The dimensions of the image are hard to imagine—ninety feet high and nine feet square. In modern times, it might be compared to a tower from which to transmit radio signals. These dimensions reflect an Akkadian mathematical system based on six rather than the more familiar ten used in Egypt. Our way of measuring time can be traced to that system, with 60 seconds to the minute, 60 minutes to the hour, and twenty-four hours to the day. The measuring rod of Ezekiel 40:5 was also six long cubits in length. Perhaps the storyteller includes the dimensions of the statue to suggest that it is both absurd and unstable. A puff of wind might easily topple it!

The site of the statue is on the plain of Dura. *Dura* is an Akkadian word meaning "city wall." Apparently the statue is erected in a fortified place in the suburbs of the city of Babylon.

A question emerges. Is this narrative historically factual or is it symbolic? (see comments on 5:1-4). Those who hold this story to be a factual account point to the Babylonian practice of erecting obelisks or statues. The statue of the Babylonian god Marduk, though no remains of it have been found in excavations, had an important place in Babylonian celebrations, as we know from their literature. The collosus at Rhodes, though in a different geographical region, was higher than Nebuchadnezzer's by ten cubits. A reference to a slave being thrown into the fiery furnace comes from the time of the "Old" Babylonian empire (1750 B.C.). The practice was not unknown, as shown in relevant data summarized by Baldwin (100). Norman Porteous (55) proposes that Daniel 3 be understood as a martyr story, similar to those related in 2 Maccabees 7. Because of the miraculous deliverance in the story, some see this narrative as "storicized history," which could then be cataloged with the story of Jonah. A further option is to think of it as a commentary on a text (such as Isa. 43:1-3; Ps. 66:10-12) made vivid in story (Goldingay: 68).

Moderns may be too obsessed with such questions of historicity. Biblical writers can convey truth in literary forms other than "historical" accounts. Still, given the emphasis on history in the OT, an emphasis remarkable for its dominance when compared to other ancient Near Eastern writings, many readers are predisposed to regard this narrative as reporting an incident in the court life of the Hebrew heroes.

The statue is created to strengthen the empire by serving as a symbol of unity. To it, all citizens, from the top to the bottom of society, are to bow in worship. The image symbolically combines both the power of the state and the power of religion (cf. 1 Macc. 1:41-64).

3:2-3 Politicians and People Come to the Dedication

When the gleaming statue is completed, Nebuchadnezzar invites all Babylonian officialdom to the dedication of the image he has *set up*. The *satraps*, heads of the provinces, are in charge of the main divisions of the empire. The *prefects* are likely military men responsible to the satraps. The *governors* are heads of territorial divisions, such as Judea or Samaria. The *counselors* are judges and justices. The *treasurers* are responsible for public moneys, and the *magistrates* are likely local law enforcers.

The frequent repetition of these categories of politicians has a satirical ring. These are the "great ones" who come to the dedication, but they have no minds of their own. They simply bow and scrape whenever the despot snaps his fingers.

The officials gather on the plain of Dura. They stand in awe before the image Nebuchadnezzar *set up*. The crowds stand expectantly, waiting for the dedication to proceed.

3:4-7 The Decree

A herald appears with the king's decree. The real meaning of the statue now becomes clear. It is a symbol of utter devotion and allegiance to Nebuchadnezzar. To worship the statue is a form of emperor worship (cf. Rev. 13). The instructions are clear. When the music plays, all officials and all citizens, *all the peoples, nations, and languages* (3:4, 7), are to *fall down* to worship the image Nebuchadnezzar has *set up*. The dedication is to be a festive event, exalting the head of the state. When all bow in worship, there will be a new, common unity in the realm.

The list of instruments in the orchestra, in good storyteller fashion, is repeated time and again. The instruments are wood—horn and pipe; stringed—lyre, trigon, and harp; and percussion—drum. In the Aramaic list of instruments are three Greek loan words: *qayteros* (Greek: *kithara*), *pesanterin* (Greek: *psaltērion*), and *sumponeyah* (Greek: *sumphō*nia). The first was a type of *lyre,* the second a *harp* of sorts, the third possibly a *drum* (NRSV) or *bagpipe* (RSV). The third word can have the sense of all the instruments "sounding together," as in a symphony; but if it referred to a specific musical instrument, it was likely a percussion one. For some commentators, the appearance of these Greek loan words suggests a late date for writing the book of Daniel. Others note that in Assyrian times prior to Nebuchadnezzar's rule, Greek musicians and instruments are mentioned in inscriptions. *[Daniel: Date and Authorship, p. 285.]*

Shadrach, Meshach, and Abednego Accused 3:8-15

3:8-12 The Chaldeans' Malicious Report

Apparently, Shadrach, Meshach, and Abednego either have not come to the plain of Dura when all the officials assembled, or when the music plays, they do not bow down. Perhaps they simply stay away so that they will not openly defy Nebuchadnezzar.

If they are at the dedication, they stand while the rest bow down. They are not directly asked to deny their God. All they have to do is to make a quick bow to Nebuchadnezzar's statue. However, to bow or even to nod in the direction of Nebuchadnezzar's statue is to acknowledge Nebuchadnezzar's claim to absolute allegiance. To bow to the statue has the same meaning as eating the king's rich food (1:8-21).

In a world of many gods and allegiances, it is hard to see why anyone would choose to have only one God. Why not bow or nod in this direction and that? The scandal of monotheism is that it narrows choices, as the apostles say of Jesus, "There is salvation in no one else, for there is no other name under heaven given among mortals by which we must be saved" (Acts 4:12). The presumed glory of polytheism is its wide range of choices.

Nebuchadnezzar's threat is clear: bow or burn! Nor is Nebuchadnezzar's command an empty threat. Two prophets, Ahab and Zedekiah, were burned by this ruler (Jer. 29:21-23). The threat of "bow or burn" is a logical position for the totalitarian mind—one empire, one king, one worship! Anything placed above the state is unpatriotic and considered treason. The tyrants acknowledge no authority beyond their own. This is why discipleship can be costly.

That Shadrach, Meshach, and Abednego refuse to bow apparently goes unnoticed, except by certain Chaldeans. At last they find an opportunity to bring down these recent immigrants from their lofty positions. They resent the skill of these Jews in their own Chaldean lore. These rivals covet the promotions of these Jews to high office. Jealous and malicious, they report Shadrach, Meshach, and Abednego's behavior to the king. The Chaldeans hope to recover lost favor with the king and at the same time unseat these immigrants from their powerful positions.

When they go to Nebuchadnezzar, they repeat his decree, emphasizing especially the punishment for those who refuse to bow (3:11). Then they report the action of the three. Their report is not false. It is simply malicious. They depict as disloyal and unworthy the men Nebuchadnezzar has elevated to positions of trust. Their charges are threefold: (1) they pay no attention to Nebuchadnezzar, (2) they reject Nebuchadnezzar's gods, and (3) they refuse to worship his golden image.

3:13-15 The Enraged Tyrant

On hearing of Shadrach, Meshach, and Abednego's refusal to worship his statue, Nebuchadnezzar goes into a fit of uncontrolled rage, like a typical tyrant accountable to no one. Not only is his authority insulted, but also he feels that his beneficence to these foreigners has been betrayed. In the midst of his rage, it is to his credit that he tries to be just. Nebuchadnezzar does not condemn these men on the basis of hearsay. He provides another occasion to bow and thus gives the three an opportunity to refute the accusations.

Shadrach, Meshach, and Abednego are called into the presence of the king. *Is it true . . . that you do not serve my gods and you do not worship the golden statue that I have set up?* he asks. Nebuchadnezzar proposes a second chance for them to worship when the music sounds forth. He renews his threat of the fiery furnace, should they refuse. Finally he concludes his remarks by ridiculing the God of the Hebrews as weak and impotent: *And who is the god that will deliver you out of my hands?* That kind of a question has been asked by skeptics before (3:14-15; cf. 2 Kings 18:33-35; 19:10-13).

The answer to this question, Nebuchadnezzar thinks, is certainly not the God of Israel! That God was defeated when Nebuchadnezzar sacked Jerusalem, robbed the temple, and took kings and citizens captive. Though earlier the king has acknowledged Daniel's God as *God of gods and Lord of kings* (2:47), this acknowledgment was given in connection with revealing mysteries. Perhaps he has forgotten. But there is much more Nebuchadnezzar has to learn. Apparently, Nebuchadnezzar has not yet made a connection between his words and his own self-perception. He sees no limits to his own authority. No human power equals his. Through his military victories, all divinities have been routed. Like Rabshakeh's question to Hezekiah (Isa. 36:18-20), Nebuchadnezzar attributes all power to himself. In the Song of Moses, God says, "See now that I, even I, am he; there is no god beside me. I kill and I make alive; I wound and I heal; and no one can deliver from my hand" (Deut. 32:39). In his arrogant rage, Nebuchadnezzar has usurped the power that God reserves for himself (cf. Dan. 5:19).

Shadrach, Meshach, and Abednego Refuse to Bow 3:16-18

At last Shadrach, Meshach, and Abednego are given an opportunity to speak. They address the king, but they use no titles of honor. In this, they are a bit discourteous. The omission suggests that Nebuchadnezzar is simply a human like the rest. They do not answer Nebuchadnezzar's question directly, for there is little they can say. Instead, they cast themselves upon the mercy of the God whom Nebuchadnezzar has defied.

The answer to the question, *Who is the God who will deliver you?* is *our God!* The faith of the three is of the deepest order. They are convinced that their God has both the authority and the power to deliver. Yet they recognize that what will happen is his to decide. They allow God to do with them as he chooses. In effect, they say, "God does not have to do what we know he can do. If our God performs a miracle of deliverance from the fiery furnace, well and good! If not, we will continue to serve him."

The word translated *serve* (Aramaic: *pela*, in 3:12, 14, 17-18, 28) appears frequently in Daniel 3. The original meaning of the root carries the notion of "doing homage" or "giving honor." The Chaldeans report that Shadrach, Meshach, and Abednego refuse to *serve* the gods of the Babylonians (3:12). Nebuchadnezzar cannot believe they will refuse to *serve* his gods (3:17). In verse 17, the response of the three is clear: *Our God whom we serve is able to deliver us*. In verse 18, their response is more radical: Even if God does not deliver, they will not under any conditions *serve* Nebuchadnezzar's god (cf. Job 13:15, NRSV note, "Though he kill me, yet I will trust in him"). Worshiping that statue would be idolatry, co-opted to serve the state in a civil religion. In no way will they let their service be compromised or divided. The issue is not whether God is capable of delivering. That is never in question in the book of Daniel. The issue is faithfulness, whether believers will reject idolatry and refuse to divide their loyalties even when their lives are at stake.

The three Israelites believe God can perform miracles. They also believe God is free not to perform miracles. They know that God hears the prayers of his children and that he knows their needs. Yet he reserves the right to respond in his own way. The NT supplies an example. When Herod imprisoned James, James was beheaded. When Herod imprisoned Peter, Peter was miraculously rescued (Acts 12).

The three standing before Nebuchadnezzar are committed to serving God. In their answer, they say nothing about being vindicated, nor is there any mention of resurrection. They serve God not because he is powerful or works miracles, but because he is the living God! Consequently, they tell Nebuchadnezzar that they will not serve other gods nor worship the image he set up. Their calm faith only increases Nebuchadnezzar's fury.

Shadrach, Meshach, and Abednego Condemned to Burn 3:19-23

3:19-20 The Frustrated Tyrant

At first when the Chaldeans came to Nebuchadnezzar with their malicious report, he was angered by Shadrach, Meshach, and Abednego's insubordination. At the outset, he wanted to avoid violent confrontation. Now their rejection of Nebuchadnezzar as benefactor, their rejection of his offer of a second chance, their rejection of his gods and his statue, and their continuing stubborn faith in God—all this is more than he can take.

Like frustrated politicians before and after, he goes to irrational extremes. An ordinary furnace fire to burn the three is not enough. The furnace has to be heated *seven times* hotter than ever! Like frustrated modern military strategists, it is not enough to have bombs that will destroy the whole earth one time. Instead, there have to be enough bombs to destroy it, not dozens of times, nor hundreds of times, but a thousand times over! Ordinary soldiers can not be used to throw these three helpless men into the furnace. The mightiest soldiers are called for this task.

3:21-23 Into the Furnace of Blazing Fire

Instead of the usual stripping of prisoners naked before throwing them into the furnace, the three are prepared for burning with their clothing on—their hats, coats, and stockings are securely fastened. Not a trace will be left of the insubordinate three—everything will be burned! For the storyteller, there is humor in this ridiculous scene of preparing the men for the fire by making sure their clothing and hats are securely fastened.

There is also irony. The king's men make the furnace hotter than ever. Then the mightiest of the king's men throw Shadrach, Meshach, and Abednego into the furnace. But the king's men themselves become the victims. They die as they carry out the frustrated politician's irrational command.

Apocryphal Supplements

A lengthy addition appears at this point in Greek versions of Daniel: The Prayer of Azariah and the Song of the Three Jews (NRSV Apocrypha). A fragment containing Daniel 3:23-24 has been found at Qumran, but without this addition, even though many think it was first composed in Hebrew or Aramaic. It consists of three parts:

The prayer: Prayer 1-22; Dan. 3:24-45, LXX (Septuagint, Greek version).
A narrative: Prayer 23-27; Dan. 3:46-51, LXX.
The hymn: Prayer 28-68; Dan. 3:52-90, LXX.

The prayer is one of repentance and supplication. At first glance it seems out of place since the three men are already in the furnace because of their faithfulness to God. Yet in the spirit of Daniel himself (Dan. 9:3-20), they are praying in behalf of themselves *and* their people: *We have sinned. . . . We, O Lord, have become fewer than any other nation* (Prayer 6, 14). The prayer is a cry for deliverance suitable to precede the report of the miracle: *Deliver us, . . . bring glory to your name, O Lord. . . . Let them know that you alone are the Lord God, glorious over the whole world* (20-22).

The narrative reports the miracle: an angel keeps the furnace cool for the martyrs (23-27).

The hymn gives thanksgiving for deliverance (29-34, 66) and a litany calling on all creation to praise God (35-68), in the mood of Psalm 148. Like Psalm 136, the hymn has an antiphonal form for public worship, typically with one line exhorting, *Bless the Lord . . . ,* and the next line repeating, *Sing praise to him, and highly exalt him forever*. The prayer and the hymn add significant dimensions to the story. The prayer reflects the piety of the youths, while the narrative and the hymn provide a contrast between Nebuchadnezzar's limited power and the awesome power and majesty of God. *[Supplements to Daniel, p. 297, has the full text.]*

Shadrach, Meshach, and Abednego Delivered 3:24-27

3:24-25 The Astonished Tyrant

Stunned by the death of his mighty soldiers, Nebuchadnezzar peers into the furnace to be sure the three are receiving their deserved punishment.

Astonished Nebuchadnezzar sees the three men standing, walking about, no longer bound hand and foot. Furthermore, there is a fourth person with them. The king who earlier blasphemously bragged of his power (3:15) is now the first to announce the extraordinary preservation of the three by their God, who *is able to deliver* (3:17, 25, 28-29).

Terrified Nebuchadnezzar asks the officials, *Was it not three men that we threw bound into the fire?* To this they agreed. How is it then, that *I see four men unbound, walking in the middle of the fire, and they are not hurt?* He adds, *The fourth has the appearance of a god.*

Many English translations say the fourth *is like the Son of God* (KJV) or *a son of the gods* (RSV; Aramaic). However, it is likely more appropriate to identify that figure as a celestial being rather than as a preincarnate manifestation of Jesus Christ. When Nebuchadnezzar is more calm, he calls the fourth an *angel* sent by God to deliver his servants (3:28). Perhaps this is a celestial figure identified as a *holy watcher* (see notes on 4:9-26), or even God himself, who promises his presence when his people go through fire (Isa. 43:2).

3:26-27 Unbowed and Unburned

Nebuchadnezzar goes to the door of the *furnace of blazing fire* and calls to the three, *Servants of the Most High God, come out! Come here!*

Once again Nebuchadnezzar is faced by the kingdom of God. In his dream (2:1-49), a stone pulverized the great statue and then filled the whole earth. Now Nebuchadnezzar's gleaming statue of gold is designed to unify his kingdom and to serve as a monument to his power and pride, but it pales in significance. In the furnace beside the statue, the Most High God is at work delivering his own.

The tyrant is defeated on the ground of his own choosing. What God is able to deliver? The answer is found on Nebuchadnezzar's lips. It is *the Most High God* (3:26). In Daniel, this title first appears here and is used by non-Jews (4:2, 17, 34) as well as Jews (4:24-25, 32; 5:18, 21; 7:18-27). The name was used by Melchizedek (Gen. 14:18-20), Balaam (Num. 24:16), and Isaiah (Isa. 14:14). The Most High is the one who controls history (Deut. 32:8). The title is for a God of universal reign. For the pagan, it means the highest among many gods. For the Jew, it is the God of Israel.

When the three come out of the furnace, they are examined by the officials. The fire has had no power over their bodies, their hair, or their clothing! There is not even the odor of fire. Only Nebuchadnezzar's ropes are burned and gone. Thus the story of Shadrach, Meshach, and Abednego turns the promise of Isaiah 43:2 into an easily grasped human experience. The three were not alone, not even in flames. Their experience illustrates the promise of safekeeping (Ps. 34:7; 91:11).

Nebuchadnezzar's Royal Decree 3:28-30

The king is faced on one hand by the unyielding faith of Shadrach, Meshach, and Abednego in their God; and on the other by the shattering confrontation with the God who delivers. So Nebuchadnezzar praises God and prepares a message for the whole world. The blessing and decree of Nebuchadnezzar provide a fitting denouement to the story. In praising the God of Shadrach, Meshach, and Abednego, Nebuchadnezzar recalls their faith (3:17), their refusal to obey his command (3:18), and their readiness to die (3:23).

As a result of their faith and God's action, Nebuchadnezzar calls on those who had earlier worshiped the golden image (3:5-7, 10-12, 14-15) to be careful now not to blaspheme the God of Shadrach, Meshach, and Abednego—or the king will enact dire penalties (3:28-29). Instead of criticizing the three Israelites for refusing to serve his gods (3:12, 14), Nebuchadnezzar commends Shadrach, Meshach, and Abednego for serving their God (3:28). He changes the command for *peoples, nations, and languages* (3:4, 7) to *fall down* before the golden image. Now they are ordered to speak respectfully about the God of Israel (3:29). Finally, the question about the ability of God to deliver (3:15, 17) is answered, not by Shadrach, Meshach, and Abednego, but by Nebuchadnezzar himself in the words of his decree: *There is no other god who is able to deliver in this way* (3:29). His announcement is an offer of grace. He introduces the Redeemer God to the world.

The story quickly concludes with Shadrach, Meshach, and Abednego receiving further promotions in the province. This dashes the hopes of *certain Chaldeans* that the three would be discredited, found disloyal, and removed from public service.

THE TEXT IN BIBLICAL CONTEXT

The Furnace of Blazing Fire

When the story of Shadrach, Meshach, and Abednego was told, Jewish hearers may have seen a deeper meaning in the *furnace of blazing fire.* The Egyptian captivity was likened to an "iron furnace" or "iron-smelter" (RSV or NRSV: Deut. 4:20; 1 Kings 8:51; Jer. 11:4). The exilic experience in Babylon was referred to as the "furnace of adversity" (Isa. 48:10).

No doubt the story of the three young men in the fiery furnace was understood by the hearers as their story in the furnace of Babylonian captivity. And later, the story of the three young men was seen as the story of the faithful in the fiery furnace of persecution under Antiochus IV Epiphanes in the second century B.C.

Symbolically, "furnace," "crucible," and "refining" had the sense of "prove," "test," or "try." The story of Shadrach, Meshach, and Abednego provided a call to faithfulness as God refined his people. "The crucible is for silver, and the furnace is for gold, but the Lord tests the hearts" (Prov. 17:3; cf. Ps. 66:10-12; Mal. 3:2-3).

This theme also appears in the NT:

> In this you rejoice, even if now for a little while you have had to suffer various trials, so that the genuineness of your faith—being more precious than gold that, though perishable, is tested by fire—may be found to result in praise and glory and honor when Jesus Christ is revealed. (1 Pet. 1:6-7)

THE TEXT IN THE LIFE OF THE CHURCH

God and Country

The story of Shadrach, Meshach, and Abednego and the fiery furnace is the second in the cycle of six stories in the Aramaic section of Daniel. In many respects this story parallels the fifth story (chap. 6) of Daniel in the lions' den. Both stories deal with servants of God living in alien territory yet attempting to keep the faith. How do persons serve and worship God when on every side the world, and especially the state, attempts to shape and control religion for its purposes?

The stories in Daniel 3 and 6 were of great worth to early Anabaptists facing persecution and death for their faith (see Braght, index under *Daniel*). Jan Woutersz van Cuyck was burned for his faith at Dordrecht in 1572. Although suffering much torture while in prison, he had managed to write a series of letters to his relatives and fellow believers. In one he says, "Rather go with Daniel in the lions' den, than that I should kneel down before wood, stone, gold, silver, bread, wine, or oil. Rather go with the young men in the fiery furnace, than worship the image, which was set up" (Braght: 918, 897-926).

In these two stories, the demands of the state comes in two forms. In the case of Shadrach, Meshach, and Abednego, the demand is to *add* the worship of the state to their faith. The temptation has always been present to try to make God and country equally important, but in practice that always results in country being regarded as the highest authority. Today this takes the form of civil religion, or religious nationalism in which the nation is the object of glorification and adoration, in which national values are religionized, national heroes are divinized, and the actions of the nation are equated with God's redemptive work. Civil religion takes its form around three interlaced ideas: (1) God has chosen and blessed one's country with greatness in order to make it an instrument to accomplish his purpose; (2) patriotism and love of one's country are equated with or are inseparable from one's religion; and (3) in times of crisis, especially war, soldiers die for both God and country.

To make God and country equally important, makes it possible for an individual to follow the demands of the state even when those demands contradict the will and way of God. Shadrach, Meshach, and Abednego saw with great clarity that their worship of God and allegiance to God stood alone. They could not add the worship of Nebuchadnezzar's statue to their faith. Then and today such refusal is seen not only as unpatriotic but also as subversive. Theirs is a risky and despised stance, held at high personal cost.

Are Christians to be, first of all, citizens of the country in which they live, or followers of Jesus? This question is critical, especially in issues related to use of national resources for the military, and when one's country becomes involved in war.

It is estimated that all the nations of the world spend one trillion dollars annually on military preparedness. It is further estimated that if 25 percent of this annual expenditure were used to improve living conditions for the world's inhabitants over a period of ten years, food, clothing, shelter, health care, education, employment, and a healthful environment could be provided for all humanity.

The unwillingness of Shadrach, Meshach, Abednego, and Daniel to allow the state to add something to or take something from their faith speaks to the church today. The temptation to silence religion is great when society is caught up in parades, fireworks, flags, and lauding of military heroes during times of war. In such activity, war is presented as an angel of light, leading to liberty and freedom, to heroism and greatness. But in reality, war is and has always been waste, terror, destruction, famine, starvation, dislocation, brutality, dismemberment, torture, untruth, and death. The God of Shadrach, Meshach, and Abednego has now revealed himself in Jesus Christ and calls his people to offer him primary allegiance. This is gathered up in the life, teaching, death, and resurrection of Jesus. Jesus taught his followers to seek first God's kingdom (Matt. 6:33). Faithful believers do not set aside or silence his teaching to love enemies (Luke 6:27, 35-36).

Later, in the story of Daniel in the lions' den, the demand of the state comes in a different form. Daniel is asked to *delete* an aspect of his faith. He is not to pray to God for thirty days (chap. 6).

The Universal Gospel

The significant insight from the book of Daniel—that God's purposes embrace the whole world—is needed in the church today. The tension between a narrowly conceived gospel and a universal gospel troubled the early church, and this tension continues to the present.

In Acts, Luke tells how hard it was for believers to understand that at Pentecost, God was creating a new people who would embrace all peoples and nations and languages. That Pentecost was a new Exodus seemed clear. When the people left Egypt, there was a wind that opened the Red Sea (Exod. 14:21). At Pentecost there was the sound of a mighty, rushing wind (Acts 2:2). In the Exodus a pillar of fire led the people (Exod. 13:21). At Pentecost flames of fire came upon this new people (Acts 2:3). But what agony early Christian leaders experienced as they came to see that the gospel was universal, that it was for all humanity! How hard it was to act upon that insight!

Some in the early church tried to keep the gospel for their own group. There was tremendous strain as the gospel went from Jews to include Gentiles (Acts 10). Paul saw clearly that there would be one new community, embracing both Jew and Gentile (Eph. 2). In Romans 11:12, 25-26, Paul foresaw the "full inclusion" of the Gentiles and the salvation of "all Israel," so that together they are the culmination of God's action in creating a new people. This new people, as many interpreters observe, Paul called the Israel of God (Gal. 6:16).

Before his ascension, Jesus' words to his followers are certainly radical: "All authority in heaven and on earth has been given to me. Go therefore and make disciples of *all nations*, baptizing them . . . , and teaching them to obey everything that I have commanded you" (Matt. 28:18-20). In this declaration, Jesus removed once and for all the concept of a holy land or place, or a privileged people. From the standpoint of the gospel, the whole world is holy land, and all peoples are objects of God's love (John 3:16).

In this day of denominations in the Christian church, believers often seem to feel that their own group has a special, exclusive place in God's love. Each denomination (or even an independent congregation) builds its own little empire. Each tends to act unilaterally without regard to what other Christians are doing. Working with other Christians is often resisted because of commitments to ideas or practices that are not near to being life-or-death issues. For this, the book of Daniel provides important correctives with its view of a powerful God, who is able and in ultimate control, whose gracious, redemptive works are for all humanity.

Daniel 4:1-37

The God Who Humbles the Proud: Nebuchadnezzar Admits the Rule of God

PREVIEW

This section of the Aramaic tract is in the form of a letter, an international communiqué, written by Nebuchadnezzar. It is addressed to the whole world, *to all peoples, nations, and languages that live throughout the earth*.

In the letter, Nebuchadnezzar describes a personal experience. His letter follows a common form, with 4:1-4 providing a typical introduction, 4:5-33 making up the body of the letter, and 4:34-37 forming the conclusion. The letter is written in the first person, except for verses 19-33, which are in third person: verses 19-27 appear to be from Nebuchadnezzar, while verses 28-33 are from someone acquainted with the reason for and the progress of Nebuchadnezzar's illness. Such an arrangement allows for shifts in point of view and also for the literary technique of repetition.

The main point of Nebuchadnezzar's letter is to tell the world that the God of Israel is the Most High God and that he is the sovereign ruler of history. Thus the letter begins with that strong statement:

His kingdom is an everlasting kingdom,
and his sovereignty is from generation to generation. (4:3)

The letter ends in *inclusio* fashion, with similar phrases or clauses repeated to enclose the unit:

> *His sovereignty is an everlasting sovereignty,*
> *and his kingdom endures from generation to generation.* (4:34)

In addition to Nebuchadnezzar's confession, a similar declaration appears on the lips of three different characters: *the watchers* (4:17), Daniel (4:25), and the *voice . . . from heaven* (4:32): God is *sovereign* and gives human leadership *to whom he will*. The strong motif of human or especially royal pride is secondary to the primary emphasis on divine sovereignty, as shown in the reason for the decree:

> *that all who live may know*
> *that the Most High is sovereign over the kingdom of mortals;*
> *he gives it to whom he will.* (4:17)

In chapter 4 as in chapters 2 and 3, Nebuchadnezzar is the central character. But in terms of story plot, Daniel has greater prominence in the first dream (chap. 2) than in the second (chap. 4). The focal point of the chapter appears at verse 26: *Your kingdom shall be reestablished for you from the time that you learn that Heaven is sovereign.*

Four characters appear in the letter:

1. King Nebuchadnezzar, the proud builder of city and empire.
2. Daniel, the man of God with a pastor's heart.
3. The celestial being behind the voice from heaven.
4. The Most High God, who is sovereign over mortals and humbles those who walk in pride.

Literary features such as repetition and key terms are notable. In the report of the dream, Nebuchadnezzar gives a description of the tree, repeated by Daniel (4:10-12, 20-21). The sketch of Nebuchadnezzar's animal behavior occurs in the dream (4:15-16) and is repeated by the *voice from heaven* (4:32) and again by the narrator (4:33). An interesting exercise is to catalog other repetitions and explore their significance. Two sets of key words occur in the chapter. *Most High* occurs in this chapter more often than in any other chapter (4:2, 17, 24-25, 32, 34). The Aramaic *'ar'a'*, sometimes translated *earth* and sometimes *ground*, appears frequently (4:1, 10-11, 20, 22; for Aramaic versification, deduct 3 verses—3:31; 4:7-8; etc.), as does *šemaya'*, the word for *heaven* (4:11-12, 15, 20-23, 25-26, 31, 33-35,

37). These features reinforce the chapter's theme on divine sovereignty.

OUTLINE

Introduction to the Letter, 4:1-3

The Body of the Letter, 4:4-33

4:4-8	Nebuchadnezzar's Dream
4:9-18	Daniel Hears the Dream
4:19	Daniel's Anxiety
4:20-26	The Interpretation of the Dream
4:27	Daniel's Pastoral Heart
4:28-33	The Proud Humbled

The Conclusion of the Letter, 4:34-37

4:34-36	Nebuchadnezzar's Praise and Restoration
4:37	Nebuchadnezzar's Testimony

EXPLANATORY NOTES

Introduction to the Letter 4:1-3

According to the story, Nebuchadnezzar writes this letter late in his career. His empire is apparently well solidified and his massive building programs in the city of Babylon completed. Babylon has become one of the wonders of the world. The letter to the nations reflects the apex of Nebuchadnezzar's reign.

The letter follows the ancient style of letter writing. It begins by naming the sender—*King Nebuchadnezzar. [Nebuchadnezzar, p. 293.]* Then those addressed are named, *all peoples, nations, and languages*. Next comes the greeting: *May you have abundant prosperity!* The greeting is followed by a brief statement of the purpose of the letter: *The signs and wonders that the Most High God has worked for me* (*performed for me*) *I am pleased* (*it is my pleasure*) *to recount* (*to tell you about, to make known*). The introduction concludes with a poem of praise to the Most High God. Parallels to this style of introduction are found in 2 Corinthians 1:1-4 and Ephesians 1:1-4.

Signs and wonders are referred to in 4:2-3 and in 6:27. God performs signs and wonders to reveal his presence and to further his work. They accompanied the exodus of Israel from Egypt (Acts 7:36) and occurred among the exiles in Babylon. Later, signs and wonders characterized and attested the ministry of Jesus of Nazareth (2:22). They were evident at Pentecost (2:43) and filled the hectic early days of the church (5:12; 6:8; 14:3; 15:12).

Nebuchadnezzar's praise to the Most High God was similar to Psalm 145:10-13:

> All thy works shall give thanks to thee, O Lord,
> and all your saints shall bless you!
> They shall speak of the glory of your kingdom,
> and tell of your power,
> to make known to all people your mighty deeds,
> and the glorious splendor of your kingdom.
> Your kingdom is an everlasting kingdom,
> and your dominion endures throughout all generations.

These similarities have given rise to questions. Was Nebuchadnezzar familiar with Hebrew poetry? Or was this letter written by a Jew and then attributed to Nebuchadnezzar? An answer to such questions is hard to come by. Still, it is interesting to speculate that perhaps Nebuchadnezzar had become acquainted with Hebrew Scripture such as the Psalms.

The Body of the Letter 4:4-33

4:4-8 Nebuchadnezzar's Dream

According to verse 4, the strains and stresses of the early years of the empire are past. The empire is secure, and a great culture is developing. An effective government is in place, conducted by the capable civil servants he has trained. The glory of the city of Babylon is beyond comparison. It captures the imagination of the world. Now Nebuchadnezzar says, *I . . . was living at ease in my home and prospering in my palace*. Nebuchadnezzar has succeeded in his desire to become a brilliant, competent, enlightened, and benevolent empire builder.

But one night, as in the earliest days of his reign, Nebuchadnezzar has a bad dream. After the dream, he lies in his bed terrified and afraid. God again uses a dream, and again God will use his servant Daniel.

As in the past, Nebuchadnezzar calls *the magicians, the enchanters, the Chaldeans, and the diviners* (4:7; cf. 2:2). But as before, they are ineffective, unable to interpret the dream. *At last Daniel came in*

(4:8). Although this is a letter, the report within it reads like a drama. Other dramatic features include: the *voice from heaven* (4:32), Nebuchadnezzar's boast following the ominous dream interpretation (4:30), and the unusual twist of a royal figure resorting to animal behavior (4:33). In this "drama" one can find plot, characterization, point of view, and "tone."

Nebuchadnezzar recalls Daniel's name change (1:7). Though Daniel's new name, Belteshazzar, points to Nebuchadnezzar's god Bel (a title for the Babylonian god Marduk), nevertheless Nebuchadnezzar makes the comment that *a spirit of the holy gods* continues to be in Daniel, a polytheistic comment that occurs three times (4:8-9, 18). Pharaoh makes a similar statement about Joseph (Gen. 41:38; see the next TBC [Text in Biblical Context]). With the memory of Daniel's earlier success in dream interpretation (2:11, 28, 47), Nebuchadnezzar shares his dream with Daniel.

4:9-18 Daniel Hears the Dream

Nebuchadnezzar addresses Daniel using his Babylonian name, *Belteshazzar*, and his official title, *chief of the magicians* (4:8; cf. 2:48). Even with these Babylonian trappings, Nebuchadnezzar recognizes and admits that *a spirit of the holy gods* is in Daniel. Then Nebuchadnezzar tells his dream to Daniel, with the confidence that since a divine spirit is with him, *no mystery is too difficult* for him.

The details of Nebuchadnezzar's dream extend from verse 10 to 17. The focal point of the dream is a great tree. In Palestine, because of desert, and in Babylonia, because of watery lowlands, much of the land is unfavorable to growing trees. As a result, trees came to be considered as sacred, and groves were thought to be the dwelling places of deity. Trees figured in ancient Near East mythology. "A lofty, preeminent, verdant, protective, fruitful, long-lived tree is a common symbol for the living, transcendent, life-giving, sustaining Cosmos or Reality or Deity itself" (Goldingay: 87; cf. Rev. 22:2). Sometimes world history would be symbolized as a tree. A tree might be thought to link heaven and earth or provide divine knowledge (Gen. 2:17; 3:1-7).

Among the Hebrews, specific trees were respected, such as Deborah's palm, under which the prophetess judged Israel (Judg. 4:5). However, Israelite religious leaders protested the groves on Canaanite hills in which strange religious rites and abominations were practiced (2 Kings 16:2-4; Jer. 2:20). Isaiah condemned the worship of trees and gardens (1:29-31). The veneration of trees may have been in the background of Nebuchadnezzar's dream. In his dream, the tree served as a stage set for action between God and humanity, in this case between God and Nebuchadnezzar.

Trees also could symbolize kingdoms and reigns (Judg. 8:8-15). Ezekiel compared Egypt to a cedar surpassing the trees "in the garden of God," rivaling God himself (Ezek. 31:2-14). Jesus used a tree as a sign for the kingdom of God (Matt. 13:31-32 || Luke 13:19).

In Nebuchadnezzar's dream, the tree is in the midst of the land, thus in the center of world activity. The tree has great height and reaches heaven, as though providing a gateway to the gods (cf. Gen. 11:4). It is visible to the whole earth, strong and large, indestructible. Its fruit feeds the nations, and its leaves provide shade for animals and humans. Birds dwell in its branches. The tree represents a mighty empire, with its ruler providing food, shelter, and protection for all creatures. With a tree like this, is God needed?

Then a *holy watcher* (messenger) comes *down from heaven* (4:13). The Aramaic word translated *watcher* (4:13, 17, 23) is found only here in the OT. The name reflects an ancient belief that celestial beings stay awake and do not sleep (cf. Ps. 121:3-4; Rev. 4:8). The term *watchers* also appears in pseudepigraphical writings for angels (as in 1 En. 12:2-4; Jub. 4:15) or generally for fallen angels (cf. Gen. 6:1-4; Job 4:18). The notion of a heavenly watcher has links to the practice of earthly kings assigning watchmen to feed information from the realm to the king (cf. Isa. 62:6). The king may also dispatch watchmen on errands. The *watchers* are celestial beings, *holy ones,* angels, part of the heavenly decision-making group, with power to announce and execute God's *sentence* (Dan. 4:14, 17; cf. 7:22; angels in spiritual warfare: 10:20-21; 12:1; TLC on Dan. 10-12; Job 1:12; 2:6-8). The word *watcher* is on the lips of Nebuchadnezzar as he reports his dream, so perhaps the term has origins in Iran (for other pseudepigraphical references, see IDB, 4:805-806).

In Daniel's interpretation, the decree of the watchers becomes a decision of *the holy ones* (4:17). Elsewhere in the OT, the term *holy ones* refers to angels of God or "heavenly beings," who attend the heavenly court over which the Lord God presides (Dan. 7:9 [*thrones*], 18, 22, 27; 8:13; Zech. 14:5; Job 1:6-12; 5:1; 15:15; Deut. 33:2-3; called "gods" in Exod. 15:11; Ps. 82:1; or "sons of God" in Gen. 6:1-4; Job 1:6, RSV). It is therefore safe to interpret *watcher* as a synonym for angel. In the Bible, angels are the messengers of God, involved in carrying out God's activity on earth. Thus angels are involved in the life of Jesus and in the beginnings of the church as recorded in Acts.

The *holy watcher* of this dream commands that the tree be *cut down* and that it be stripped of leaves, fruit, and branches so that all that found sustenance and shelter in the tree would *flee* away. Remaining will be only the *roots* and *stump* of the tree, bound with a collar of iron and bronze. Standing in a meadow, the stump will be exposed to the weather. Though not stated explicitly, the watcher shifts his focus from the empire to its head, a mighty individual, whose mind will be altered from that of a man to that of an animal. This condition will last for *seven times* (4:16). Though *time* may refer to an indefinite period (2:8), it is usually interpreted as a year (as in 7:25). Thus the judgment would be for seven years.

For Hebrew readers, such a picture of a tree, representing a king, recalls Ezekiel's parable about the large cedar tree (representing a dynasty) and the Judean king which flourished as a vine but was then uprooted (Ezek. 17:2-10). The principle of God raising up and cutting down is underscored (Ezek. 17:23-24; cf. 19:10-14). The motif of God humiliating arrogant rulers, felling a tree, is developed at length in Ezekiel 31. Ancient mythology made use of the tree motif to speak about royal power. Nebuchadnezzar's dream, however, includes the felling of the tree—a motif not included in mythology, but known from the Hebrew prophets.

The watcher who makes the announcement is identified with a group of heavenly beings able to make such plans and to carry them out, in accord with the *sentence* of *the Most High*. The purpose of their plans is to bring the living (humanity) to realize *that the Most High is sovereign over the kingdom of mortals; he gives it to whom he will and sets over it the lowliest of human beings* (4:17).

Frightened by this nightmare (4:5), Nebuchadnezzar begs Daniel for an interpretation. As in the past, the Babylonian wise men are of no help. Because *a spirit of the holy gods* (NRSV note: *a holy, divine spirit*) was in Daniel, Nebuchadnezzar believes Daniel is *able* to make the interpretation (4:18).

4:19 Daniel's Anxiety

At this point, the letter reports Nebuchadnezzar's conversation with Daniel in the third person, even though Nebuchadnezzar, still of sound mind, is able to report Daniel's interpretation himself. At verse 28 the description of Nebuchadnezzar's insanity begins. This report is by a narrator, neither Daniel nor Nebuchadnezzar. In this way the letter gains objectivity, perhaps even credibility.

When Daniel hears the dream (4:19), he is perplexed, then upset. He knows the mighty tree symbolizes Nebuchadnezzar. Over the years, Daniel has come to appreciate or at least respect Nebuchadnezzar, even though the king has destroyed his homeland and taken him captive. Daniel sees himself serving the king because God has appointed him to do so. Thus Daniel is in a unique position to communicate to the king about the God of Israel. But this is difficult because Nebuchadnezzar refuses to be accountable to anyone or to acknowledge subordination to any god or other human being.

Daniel knows the dream predicts ill for Nebuchadnezzar, so he hesitates to speak, but Nebuchadnezzar urges him on. Daniel reveals no feelings of hostility and does not say, "At last, Nebuchadnezzar will get what he deserves!" Instead, Daniel says, "*May the dream . . . and its interpretation [be] for your enemies!*

4:20-26 The Interpretation of the Dream

Daniel begins by interpreting the glory of the tree, which is like the head of gold in the earlier dream (2:38). *It is you, O king! You have grown great and strong. Your greatness has increased and reaches to heaven, and your sovereignty to the ends of the earth* (4:22). But as the tree in the dream was *cut down,* so Nebuchadnezzar will be cut down. The *decree* in verse 17 is declared by the watchers, based on the *sentence* given by God in the heavenly council; thus it is the decree of *the Most High* (4:24). Nebuchadnezzar will be stricken with a form of madness. He will be driven from human society and live out-of-doors with the animals and like the beasts of the field for *seven times* (years), until he comes to know *that the Most High has sovereignty over the kingdom of mortals, and gives it to whom he will* (4:25). The stump of the tree remains, and this means that the judgment will not be fatal (cf. Isa. 6:13; 10:5—11:10). The kingdom will be *reestablished for* Nebuchadnezzar when he comes to *learn that Heaven is sovereign* (4:26).

Heaven is a synonym for God. The Gospel of Matthew frequently uses the term "kingdom of heaven" to refer to the kingdom of God. In Jesus' story, the prodigal son says, "Father, I have sinned against heaven and before you" (Luke 15:18). In other words, the lost son sinned against God. If Nebuchadnezzar is to retain his throne, it is critical for him to acknowledge that God Almighty rules over him.

4:27 Daniel's Pastoral Heart

At this point Daniel goes beyond dream interpretation. He offers counsel. As Nathan the prophet confronted King David (2 Sam. 12:1-15), and as Elijah confronted King Ahab (1 Kings 21:17-24), so Daniel confronts Nebuchadnezzar. Daniel counsels Nebuchadnezzar to change his ways, to repent. Daniel specifically mentions injustice and oppression (4:27). Likely Daniel is scandalized by the way Nebuchadnezzar has used slave labor to build his great city with its gardens, avenues, temples, and palaces. *[Babylon, p. 281.]* It takes great courage for Daniel to put his finger on Nebuchadnezzar's shortcomings. But Daniel cares. He believes that if Nebuchadnezzar changes his ways, *practicing righteousness*, and *showing mercy to the oppressed* (RSV), God in mercy will turn aside judgment and allow Nebuchadnezzar to continue his rule. In giving this counsel, Daniel echoes the words of Jeremiah in his roll call of kings (Jer. 21:11—23:6), especially in his reprimand of Jehoiakim for not practicing justice and righteousness (22:15-17).

With a pastor's heart, Daniel calls Nebuchadnezzar's attention to his sinful ways and counsels him to repent. The verb (*peruq*), translated *break off* (RSV; NRSV note), *atone for* (NRSV), "expiate," can also mean "untie." Daniel's counsel is for Nebuchadnezzar to separate himself from his sinful ways: *Let charitable deeds replace your sins* (REB). The action Daniel calls for springs from a right relation with God. Thus Daniel's counsel goes beyond legal justice to a life of good works that reflects the character of God.

4:28-33 The Proud Humbled

What was predicted in Nebuchadnezzar's dream comes to pass. After Nebuchadnezzar's conversation with Daniel, God gives him a twelve-month grace period (4:29). But Nebuchadnezzar does not change his ways.

Nebuchadnezzar knows what has been threatened. He also knows how to avoid it. Nevertheless, one day Nebuchadnezzar is strolling on the roof of the royal palace, savoring his reputation as a builder, confirmed by inscriptions. As he looks over the great city of Babylon, he is filled with pride because he built this glorious city by his *mighty power* as a royal residence *for my glorious majesty*. Yet the city was not constructed by Nebuchadnezzar himself but by the sweat of slaves, by oppression, injustice, and exploitation of the poor. Later Cyrus the Persian compliments himself on abolishing the forced labor used by the Neo-Babylonian kings and bringing relief to the dilapidated housing of citizens (ANET: 316).

The wonders of the city of Babylon and the arrogance of kings like Nebuchadnezzar are behind the biblical use of the name "Babylon" to symbolize the arrogant, unstable achievements of humanity. Such achievements are the antithesis of the heavenly Jerusalem, the city of God. This tradition is especially evident in the book of Revelation (14:8; 16:19; 17:5, 18; 18:2, 10, 21).

Nebuchadnezzar has been unmoved by Daniel's plea. He is thinking only of himself, of his kingship, and of his city as a dwelling place for *my glorious majesty.* As Nebuchadnezzar speaks his proud words, God acts. *A voice* comes *from heaven* indicating that what was predicted will now come to pass. The *voice from heaven* features in this drama, not only as a "character" but as underscoring that there are realities beyond Nebuchadnezzar's knowledge or control. That which addresses Nebuchadnezzar from the "outside" is another pointer to divine sovereignty. Later the rabbis called such a mysterious voice from heaven *bat qol,* the resonance or echo of the voice (of God), especially valued because they claimed the Holy Spirit departed from Israel after Malachi and the last (OT) prophets died. Parallels are reported in the NT (Mark 1:11; John 12:28; Acts 9:4; 10:13) and in late Judaism.

Two things will occur, the voice announces. First, the kingdom will be taken from Nebuchadnezzar's hands. Second, he will be reduced to a tragic human figure separated from society and living like an ox for *seven times* (years), until he learns that *the Most High has sovereignty over the kingdom of mortals and gives it to whom he will* (4:32). Like persons before and since, Nebuchadnezzar is so wrapped up in his achievements that he gives little attention to God's warnings. He well illustrates the saying of Paul, "If you think you are standing, watch out that you do not fall" (1 Cor. 10:12).

Immediately a delusion comes upon Nebuchadnezzar. Some say his mental illness is similar to *lycanthropy,* a medical term based on the Greek words *lukos* (wolf) and *anthrōpos* (man). With this ailment, a person has a delusion of being a wolf. Another term is *insania zoanthropia,* because he acts like an animal. His bizarre behavior is intolerable to others, so he is driven from the beautiful city to the fields. There he eats grass like an ox, his body dampened by dew, his hair growing long, and the nails of his fingers and toes curling like claws. Nebuchadnezzar's animal-like behavior is a condition known even to modern psychiatrists. Baldwin (109) cites a psychiatrist treating two clients who thought they were becoming animals. Such symptoms have been thought to signal the onset of insanity.

A narrator might amplify the life of such a disoriented individual in great detail, but such is clearly not the interest of this story. By means of the several speeches, including Nebuchadnezzar's opening and closing parts of the letter, it is the sovereignty of God that holds center stage. God takes no pleasure in reducing his "servant" (Jer. 27:6), created in his image, to such a state. Yet God desires humility. He humbles those who will not humble themselves. In the words of James, "God opposes the proud, but gives grace to the humble" (James 4:6).

Some scholars believe that it is difficult to fit a period of seven years' sickness into what is known of Nebuchadnezzar's reign. Many hold that this illness attributed to Nebuchadnezzar was actually that of Nabonidus, his successor, who ruled from 556-539 B.C. *[Nabonidus, p. 291.]* According to The Prayer of Nabonidus, surviving from Qumran, Nabonidus wrote, "With a bad inflammation I was smitten for seven years and from men I was put away." During that time, Nabonidus took up residence in Tema, an oasis town in Arabia, while Belshazzar conducted the affairs of government in his stead (7:1; 8:1; 5:1). If this experience was transferred to Nebuchadnezzar, it is understandable since Nebuchadnezzar represents the line of Neo-Babylonian kings (punishing Israel in exile) and Nabonidus extends his reign.

Support for Nebuchadnezzar experiencing mental disorder may come from a fragmentary cuneiform text, which appears to note the king's temporary departure from Babylon. Since our secular sources of Babylonian history are far from complete, it is hardly likely that one will find external confirmation of this story as actual history. Interest in its historicity is not unimportant, yet the text is clearly written to drive home a theological point. God's absolute sovereignty, even over powerful kings, is a message forwarded by Nebuchadnezzar worldwide. Yet one should not forget the impact of such a message on the Hebrews themselves. For Jews, captive in Babylon or living in other situations of oppression, the message about the unquestionable divine jurisdiction and dominion over people in power would come as a "balm in Gilead."

The Conclusion of the Letter 4:34-37

4:34-36 Nebuchadnezzar's Praise and Restoration

At this point Nebuchadnezzar resumes his first-person account. At the end of his period of dwelling with animals, Nebuchadnezzar lifts his eyes to heaven. Earlier he has lifted up his eyes and been fascinated with Babylon and his own achievement. To lift his eyes to *heaven* means that he is ready to acknowledge the sovereignty of God. In this exercise of faith, his reason returns. There is a connection between one's sanity and one's faith and self-appraisal. Nebuchadnezzar has gone from the most powerful of men to the most pathetic. In his sojourn in the fields, he learns how frail he is. He also comes to realize that the kingdom of the Most High transcends his own.

With reason restored, Nebuchadnezzar blesses, praises, and honors the Most High God and his everlasting kingdom. As Nebuchadnezzar begins his letter with poetry extolling the power and eternal nature of God's kingdom, so he concludes his letter with poetry, extolling the virtues of the king who *lives forever* (4:34; cf. 12:7) and rules eternally both heaven and earth with self-determination and integrity. In this, he reflects Psalm 115:3; Isaiah 14:27; 40:17.

Nebuchadnezzar learns that an individual is genuinely human only when genuinely humble before God. This is at the heart of the prayer Jesus taught his disciples to pray, "Your kingdom come. Your will be done, on earth as it is in heaven" (Matt. 6:10).

4:37 Nebuchadnezzar's Testimony

Nebuchadnezzar concludes his letter with a personal testimony. He reports the return of his rule and glory. The support and confidence of counselors and noblemen are restored. When his place on the throne is reestablished, he is greater than before (4:36). But his sense of personal glory seems now to be tempered by faith as he praises, extols, and honors *the King of heaven* (4:37).

Now I Nebuchadnezzar,
praise and extol and honor the King of heaven,
for all his works are truth,
and his ways are justice;
and he is able to bring low
those who walk in pride. (4:37)

With this testimony, Nebuchadnezzar concludes his address to all the peoples of the world (4:1). He shares what he has learned about the God of Israel. Nebuchadnezzar's testimony is, in part, that *anyone* can and should acknowledge the sovereignty of Israel's God. Nebuchadnezzar represents the submission of human power to divine authority, and wise rulers will follow his example. Thus Judaism is pictured as open to others, a characteristic belief in the postexilic period (cf. Isa. 19:19-25; 45:14, 24; Zech. 2:11; 8:20-23; Tob. 14:6-7). All who confess in this way are welcome. *Even* Nebuchadnezzar! Testimonials of thanksgiving for healing are found in the Psalms (as in Ps. 30). The notion of God effecting change in humans through painful experiences (also in connection with dreams) is explained in Job 33.

From the beginning of his reign to its end, Nebuchadnezzar is confronted by the kingdom of God. In his first dream, he sees a stone which comes to earth (Dan. 2). The stone represents the rule of God not only in heaven but also on earth (cf. Matt. 6:10). The kingdom of God topples the kingdoms of men and fills the whole earth. The kingdom of God demands justice. It calls humans to live in accord with the ways of God or be humbled.

Opinions differ on whether Nebuchadnezzar became a believer. Some say no: there is no supporting historical evidence, no indication of repentance, and Nebuchadnezzar writes, *And still more greatness was added to me* (4:36). Yet there is a possibility that Nebuchadnezzar, God's "servant" (Jer. 27:6), became a "God-fearer" like Cornelius (Acts 10:2). This book tells of God's dealing with Nebuchadnezzar and Daniel's ministry to him. We hear Nebuchadnezzar's testimonies about the God of Israel—that he is God of gods, Lord of kings, a revealer of mysteries (2:47), able to deliver (3:29), right and just, and able to bring low the proud (4:37).

THE TEXT IN BIBLICAL CONTEXT

Warnings Against Pride

Synonyms for pride are arrogance, conceit, or vanity. The Hebrew language has at least six roots containing the concept of pride. They share the sense of to "lift up" and "be high." In the OT, pride is seen as a basis for sin. Isaiah 2:6-22 reflects this view. In many respects the story of Nebuchadnezzar's humiliation (Dan. 4) illustrates the words of Isaiah, "The pride of everyone shall be brought low; and the Lord alone will be exalted in that day" (Isa. 2:17). In Proverbs and Psalms, the proud are condemned and the humble are commended (Ps. 18:27; 101:5-6; Prov. 15:25). God alone is to be glorified and lifted up. The only proper boast is in the righteous deeds of Israel's God (Ps. 20:7; 34:2).

More specifically, the Bible, apart from Nebuchadnezzar, addresses the issue of the arrogance of royalty. Ezekiel has Judean kings but also Egyptian pharaohs in view when, using tree symbolism, he protests arrogance and self-exaltation (Ezek. 17:2-10; 19:10-14; 31). Ezekiel uses another metaphor about a prince presenting himself as god, the king of Tyre, compared to the first human being in paradise (Ezek. 26–28). The prophet foretells the doom of Tyre and critiques the arrogance of tyrants and others in political office. Isaiah looks at the Babylonian monarch and describes his pomp "brought down to Sheol" (Isa. 14:3-22; cf. Jer. 50:31-32). God opposes proud governments and their leaders. Jesus also condemns pride (Mark 7:21-23). He invites persons to follow himself, one "gentle and humble in heart" (Matt. 11:28). Jesus prophesies, "All who exalt themselves will be humbled, and all who humble themselves will be exalted" (Matt. 23:12).

The Need for Empowerment

Pharaoh recognizes God's presence in Joseph when he says, "Can we find anyone else like this—one in whom is the spirit of God?" (Gen. 41:38). Isaiah identifies the source of his message: "The Lord God has sent me and his spirit" (Isa. 48:16). The prophet's mission came through the Spirit: "The Spirit of the Lord God is upon me, because the Lord has appointed me" (Isa. 61:1). Jesus uses these same words at the beginning of his ministry (Luke 4:18-19).

As the Spirit is with Joseph in Egypt, so the Spirit is with Daniel in Babylonia. Yet Daniel does not make this claim for himself. It is observed in some sense by Nebuchadnezzar (4:9, 18) and the queen mother (5:11) and reported by Belsnazzar in his interview with Daniel (5:14): *The spirit of the holy gods is in you*, or as an RSV note offers, *The Spirit of the holy God.* In these verses the Aramaic word for *God* is plural (*elahin*), as in Hebrew (*elohim*, Gen. 1:1). Thus one wonders whether it is a plural of majesty (little evidence for this rhetorical device in the OT; Roop: 31); an inclusion of other celestial beings such as angels or *watchers* in the heavenly court, with God as the sovereign (more likely for Israelite speakers; cf. Gen. 1:26; Job 1:6; Dan. 4:17); or probably here on the lips of non-Israelites reflecting polytheism, *gods*. In any case, the wisdom and understanding with which Daniel interprets dreams has their source from beyond himself, from *a holy, divine spirit* (NRSV note). Those who with Daniel believe in God Most High can make a stronger claim for him: God's Spirit was working in Daniel.

Ezekiel's ministry also came through the work of the Spirit (Ezek. 3:12, 14; 11:1). He looked forward to the day when the Spirit would work in God's people in a new way: "And I will give them one heart, and put a new spirit within them; I will remove the heart of stone from their flesh and give them a heart of flesh, so that they may follow my statutes and keep my ordinances and obey them. Then they shall be my people, and I will be their God" (Ezek. 11:19-20; cf. 36:25-28).

Ezekiel also saw the path to receiving the Spirit: "Repent and turn from all your transgressions; otherwise iniquity will be your ruin. Cast away from you all the transgressions that you have committed against me, and get yourselves a new heart and a new spirit! Why will you die, O house of Israel? For I have no pleasure in the death of anyone, says the Lord God. Turn, then, and live" (Ezek. 18:30-32).

In the NT, God's Spirit was active in creating his people anew. When Mary received the news that she would bear a son, the angel Gabriel calms her fears and explains, "The Holy Spirit will come upon you, and the power of the Most High will overshadow you" (Luke 1:30-35). Jesus uses the similar words at his ascension when he promises his followers, "You will receive power when the Holy Spirit has come upon you; and you will be my witnesses in Jerusalem, in all Judea and Samaria, and to the ends of the earth" (Acts 1:8).

On the day of Pentecost, Peter quotes the prophet Joel as part of his explanation of that event. Joel looked forward to the renewal of Israel as the people of covenant, to their repentance, and restoration. This hope Peter links with the coming of the Spirit: "Then afterward I will pour out my spirit on all flesh" (Joel 2:28-29). At Pentecost, the coming of the Spirit is accompanied by the sound of a mighty wind, the tongues of fire, and believers speaking in languages of various peoples. Peter proclaims, "This is what was spoken through the prophet Joel." However, he concludes the quotation from Joel by discerning new significance in the prophecy: "Everyone who calls on the name of the Lord shall be saved." Peter applies these words to Jesus of Nazareth the crucified, resurrected Lord (Acts 2:16-24, 36).

The Holy Spirit was poured out after the resurrection and ascension of Jesus. Peter declares that Jesus, after he ascended, was "exalted at the right hand of God," a place of rule and authority (Acts 2:33). In another sermon, Peter says that heaven must receive Jesus "until the time of universal restoration that God announced long ago through his holy prophets" (Acts 3:21). In other words, Jesus will continue at God's right hand until he returns. Meanwhile, the Holy Spirit whom Jesus sent is the link between the ascended Lord and *all* those who follow him through repentance and faith (Acts 2:38), not just prophets or leaders in faith such as Joseph or Daniel.

The gift of the Spirit is available to all humanity, as Peter says at Pentecost, "to all who are far away," all who believe (Acts 2:39). The Holy Spirit empowers the church in its mission to the whole world. The Holy Spirit is the possession of the new community as a whole. Likewise, the church is a Spirit-possessed body, the temple of the Holy Spirit, and so are individual believers (1 Cor. 3:16-17; 6:19). While the NT designation is "Holy Spirit," that term is found only three times in the OT (Ps. 51:11; Isa. 63:10-11), which usually says "Spirit of God" or "Spirit of the Lord." Uninfluenced by the NT language, one would more likely conclude from the OT that an appropriate title would be the "Empowering Spirit." The energizing and enabling dimension of the Spirit's activity is highlighted in several passages (Gen. 1:2; Exod. 35:31; Judg. 11:19; Ezek. 37:1-14; Mic. 3:8). Thus the Spirit is contrasted with human weakness.

Daniel's experience reflects the enabling activity of the Spirit. In the life of Daniel, the presence of the Spirit of God was seen in his wisdom, his understanding, and his ability to interpret God's interventions in dreams and mysterious writings on the wall. The presence of the Spirit in believers is evidenced in many ways. Paul writes to Timothy, "God did not give us a spirit of cowardice, but rather a spirit of power and of love and of self-discipline" (2 Tim. 1:7). The presence of the Spirit is shown by the fruit of the Spirit, "love, joy, peace, patience, kindness, generosity, faithfulness, gentleness, and self-control" (Gal. 5:22-23). The presence of the Spirit is also evidenced in gifts for service:

> To each is given the manifestation of the Spirit for the common good. To one is given through the Spirit the utterance of wisdom, and to another the utterance of knowledge according to the same Spirit, to another faith by the same Spirit, to another gifts of healing by the one Spirit, to another the working of miracles, to another prophecy, to another the discernment of spirits, to another various kinds of tongues, to another the interpretation of tongues. All these are activated by one and the same Spirit, who allots to each one individually just as the Spirit chooses. (1 Cor. 12:7-11)

THE TEXT IN THE LIFE OF THE CHURCH

Dealing with Pride

From its earliest days, the church vigorously opposed pride. Paul warns against spiritual pride (1 Cor. 4:6-7). James writes, "God opposes the proud, but gives grace to the humble" (4:6; Prov. 3:34); "Humble yourselves before the Lord, and he will exalt you" (James 4:10). Peter advises, "Clothe yourselves with humility in your dealings with one another" (1 Pet. 5:5). He clinches his argument with the same quotation from Proverbs used by James. Then Peter adds, "Humble yourselves therefore under the mighty hand of God, so that he may exalt you in due time" (1 Pet. 5:5-6). In the NT the only appropriate pride is in God as revealed in the work and sufficiency of Jesus Christ (1 Cor. 1:28-31; Gal. 6:14; Phil. 3:3-9).

From the days of the church fathers onward, pride has been on the list of seven deadly sins. Among the sixteenth-century Anabaptists, yieldedness to God (*Gelassenheit*) and following Christ in discipleship (*Nachfolge*) were self-denying concepts that epitomized humility in their life together and in relation to outsiders. As taught and exemplified by Jesus, this means self-denial and readiness to suffer as needed in "striving first for the kingdom of God and his righteousness" (Matt. 5:10; 6:33; 16:24-26). This is not masochism because it is for a high purpose and each is still to maintain self-respect from being made in the image of God, loved by God, indwelt by the Holy Spirit, and gifted by God (Gen. 1:27; John 3:16; 1 Cor. 6:19; 12:7).

For most of the nineteenth century, humility was a dominant theme among North American Mennonites, heirs of the Anabaptists. Mennonites stand somewhat aloof in times of war when confronted by slogans of patriotism, and in times of revivalism when faced with testimonies of personal religious experience. They believe that new birth from above is essential (John 3:3). The reality of new birth, however, is not found in slogans and testimonies so much as in the *results* of the new birth—how life is lived. In the list of indicators, humility is a leading one. In addition to condemnation of personal pride, nineteenth-century Mennonites were aware that the whole community was to reflect humility. In matters of lifestyle, the church identified standards of economy and simplicity among members which were in contrast to the ostentatious and conspicuous displays of the society in which they lived. They were to show corporate humility by being submissive and yielded to one another, outdoing "one another in showing honor" (Rom. 12:10).

In the twentieth century, many Christians are forgetting about meekness and humility and instead emphasizing assertiveness and even aggressiveness. Humility, however, is still characteristic of peaceful followers of Jesus. It stands in contrast to the pursuit of social status and power through methods of domination and violence. It avoids the public parading of attainments.

The words of Nebuchadnezzar have a continued compelling force: God *is able to bring low those who walk in pride* (Dan. 4:37). This applies to personal pride and to corporate pride, whether of family, clan, ethnic group, church, or empire.

Daniel 5:1-30

The God to Be Honored: Belshazzar's Feast

PREVIEW

Belshazzar's feast, one of royal revelry, is the setting for another of Daniel's feats in problem solving. The story is one of high drama, with a king in consternation, mysterious writing on the wall (divine graffiti?), an ominous forecast, and the unexpected tragic death of a reigning monarch. The narrative is dominated by speeches, notably Daniel's speech accusing the king of failure to learn from history.

The story of the feast is closely tied to the events recorded in Nebuchadnezzar's letter (4:1-37). Belshazzar's tragic end is explained by his failure to learn from the experience of Nebuchadnezzar along with his sacrilegious use of vessels from the Jerusalem temple.

The structure of the story is simple and easily followed. The palace provides the setting for the action: (1) Belshazzar conducts a state banquet, possibly in his own honor or to divert attention from an impending invasion. (2) During the course of the banquet, Belshazzar calls for the gold and silver vessels taken by Nebuchadnezzar from the temple in Jerusalem to be used by the guests as they praise their idols. (3) When the sacrilegious activity is in full swing, there is a divine intervention. In chapter 4, God's action takes the form of a dream. Here it takes the form of fingers writing mysterious words on the plaster of the great banqueting hall. (4) Belshazzar, filled with fear, calls "the enchanters, the Chaldeans, and the diviners" for an explanation. As in times past, they are helpless (2:10-11; 4:7). The first part of the story ends with Belshazzar pale, weak, shaking, and afraid.

The story is basically carried along by a series of speeches: The queen (5:10-12), Belshazzar (5:13-16), and Daniel (5:17-28). In his speech, Daniel accomplishes four things:

1. He rejects Belshazzar's offer of rewards (5:17).
2. He recalls the experience of Nebuchadnezzar, who was given kingship by the Most High God with universal and unchallenged rule, but who in his arrogance came to learn that the Most High God has sovereignty over the kingdom of mortals (5:18-21).
3. He confronts Belshazzar with his sacrilegious behavior, which dishonors God (5:22-23).
4. Finally, he interprets the handwriting on the wall (5:24-28).

The story ends quickly with Daniel's elevation to high office (5:30) and with Belshazzar's death *that very night*, when Darius the Mede conquers Babylon (5:30). The truth of Daniel's interpretation is confirmed.

The day Nebuchadnezzar turned his eyes to heaven, his reason was returned and his reign restored (4:36). In turn, he shared with *all peoples, nations, and languages* what he learned about the King of heaven. Belshazzar knows all this but persists in ways that dishonor God. In the conclusion of this story, there is no message about God. It is not necessary to tack on a moral since the story speaks eloquently to the Jewish community, calling for faithfulness and hope even when the sacred is profaned. God posts words of judgment and in his own way brings down the oppressor.

If, as has been suggested, the book was composed by Israel's "wise," whether in Palestine or in the Diaspora, a story such as that of Belshazzar's downfall would in a compelling way communicate encouragement to the Jewish faithful. *[Daniel: Date and Authorship, p. 285.]* At the same time, the story contributes to the message of the tract to the nations. The silence following Belshazzar's defeat and death echoes the words of Nebuchadnezzar: *He is able to bring low those who walk in pride* (4:37).

OUTLINE

Belshazzar's Banquet, 5:1-9

5:1-4	Eating, Drinking, and Gross Irreverence
5:5-9	Mysterious Writing, Failure, and Fear

The Queen's Counsel, 5:10-12

Belshazzar Seeks Daniel's Help, 5:13-16

Daniel's Sobering Response, 5:17-28

5:17	Daniel Rejects Rewards
5:18-21	Daniel Recalls Nebuchadnezzar's Glory
5:22-23	Daniel Indicts Belshazzar
5:24-28	Daniel Interprets the Writing

The Interpretation Confirmed, 5:29-31

5:29	Daniel Rewarded and Elevated
5:30	Belshazzar Slain
5:31	Darius the Mede Receives the Kingdom

EXPLANATORY NOTES

Belshazzar's Banquet 5:1-9

5:1-4 Eating, Drinking, and Gross Irreverence

Belshazzar, whose name means, "May Bel protect the king," is introduced to the reader on the last day of his life. Belshazzar is the son of Nabonidus and serving as regent or viceroy during his father's absences for much of his reign. *[Nabonidus, p. 291.]* The text refers to *Nebuchadnezzar* as Belshazzar's *father* (5:2), and one may wonder if the writer is thinking of biological parentage (5:11, 13, 18, 22). Yet *father* here must mean dynastic predecessor since Nabonidus was not part of Nebuchadnezzar's family but had seized the throne through a coup. Between Nebuchadnezzar and Nabonidus were three other kings. The word *father* is used in senses other than biological (2 Kings 2:12, Elisha calls Elijah "father"). Some have suggested that through a marriage by Nabonidus with Nebuchadnezzar's daughter, Nebuchadnezzar is indeed Belshazzar's father (grandfather) in a literal sense. Anyhow, Belshazzar is in command when Babylon surrenders to Cyrus (539 B.C.) and apparently there meets his death. *[Cyrus the Persian/Darius the Mede, p. 284.]*

The question about whether the account in this chapter is historically factual perhaps cannot be answered satisfactorily. That the story has a relationship to history is certain. But what is the relationship? One might want to entertain the possibility, as suggested by Millard Lind in private correspondence, that these stories relate to history in ways that a political cartoon relates to an event. The political cartoon speaks to specific situations, oftentimes in a way that cannot be understood by those who do not know the history. Not infrequently the cartoonist exaggerates features of the history. The cartoonist does not intend to set forth history as would a historian. But the cartoonist, to be credible, cannot be unfaithful to history. Establishing the "historicity" of the account is certainly not unimportant. But the biblical text nurtures, instructs, and corrects hearers and listeners in the faith. In one's eagerness to document details, one can easily miss the overriding message of this incident: to unmask sacrilege and political arrogance and show divine punishment on those responsible.

Things are not going well in Babylon. The morale of the people is low in the face of threatened Medo-Persian invasion. Belshazzar's banquet is a diversionary tactic. In feasting, the threat of invasion can be momentarily forgotten and the ominous sense of doom can be dulled. In celebration or in despair, people often turn to alcohol. A spirit of "eat, drink, and be merry, for tomorrow we die" seems to overtake the vast assembly (cf. Isa. 22:13; Eccles. 9:7-12; Luke 12:19-20).

Belshazzar takes the initiative, staging a banquet (cf. Esther 1:3-4; 5:1-2) and leading the thousand guests in drinking wine. *Under the influence of the wine*, he gives a strange order, that the sacred *vessels* taken by Nebuchadnezzar from *the temple in Jerusalem* be brought so that *the king and his lords, his wives, and his concubines might drink from them* (5:2). The fate of the sacred vessels was in discussion in Jeremiah's day. Certain prophets announced that vessels already taken from the Jerusalem temple by Nebuchadnezzar (2 Kings 24:13; 25:13-17; 2 Chron. 36:7, 10, 18-19) would soon be returned (Jer. 27:16; 28:3). Jeremiah, while conceding the desirability of such a turn of events (28:6), said those prophets were lying. He announced in no uncertain terms, even by specifying the items, that cherished utensils and worship symbols still left in Jerusalem would be carried off to Babylon (27:19-22). Jeremiah was right. And now Belshazzar exercises what he thinks is a conqueror's prerogative.

When the Jews were permitted to return home after 538 B.C., Cyrus gave these vessels to them to take back to Jerusalem. In Ezra there is an inventory of the vessels: thirty gold basins, a thousand silver basins, twenty-nine knives, thirty gold bowls, 410 silver bowls, and a thousand other vessels; altogether, 5,400 gold and silver vessels (Ezra 1:9-11). This report makes it clear that there are more than enough vessels with which to serve all of Belshazzar's banqueters.

Belshazzar's sacrilege is twofold. First, non-Jews are drinking wine from the sacred vessels in an orgy. Second, they use the vessels as they praise *the gods of gold and silver, bronze, iron, wood, and stone* (5:4). Later, when Daniel chides Belshazzar for this behavior, he adds that their gods *do not see or hear or know* (5:23). The sacrilegious actions of Belshazzar set the stage for a confrontation between the Most High God and the gods of the Babylonians, which recalls that of Elijah and the prophets of Baal (1 Kings 18:20-40).

The Jewish prophets were quick to ridicule the impotent gods of their neighbors. Isaiah especially contrasts the gods of Babylon, Bel and Nebo, with the God of Israel. Bel and Nebo are carried by cattle. When placed on the ground, they are unable to move. If people cry to them, they cannot answer. They cannot save from trouble. In contrast, the living God carries his people, hears their cries, and saves them (Isa. 46:1-13).

There is irony in this confrontation. The official Babylonian Chronicle reports that Nabonidus has assembled the nation's gods in the city of Babylon for their protection (ANET: 306, 315). Thus many gods are present to be praised at this great banquet. Certainly with so many gods in one place, the city will be secure! they think. Certainly Belshazzar, whose name affirms Bel's keeping power, will enjoy long life. But it was not to be!

5:5-9 Mysterious Writing, Failure, and Fear

Suddenly, as in 4:31, the living God intervenes. *The fingers of a human hand appeared and began writing on the plaster of the wall of the royal palace, next to the lampstand. The king was watching the hand as it wrote.* The reader is not told at once what was written. In good storytelling fashion, suspense is built. Finally, at the end of Daniel's sobering conversation with Belshazzar, the words and their interpretation are given (5:24-28).

Likely the king's table is near the throne room on the south side of the great hall. The lampstand may be lighting the throne room. In the light of the lamp, the king sees the hand writing on the plastered wall near the throne and turns pale as his mind races. He trembles and is near collapse, the picture of one gripped by great terror.

As in moments of crisis in earlier stories (2:2; 4:7), Belshazzar calls *the enchanters, the Chaldeans, and the diviners* to explain what is going on (5:7). To encourage their best work, Belshazzar promises rewards that in his eyes are of great significance. A *purple* coat denotes royalty. (Mordecai received a mantle of purple from the Persian king Ahasuerus: Esther 8:15.) The *chain of gold* or golden neck ornament indicates high social status. The rank of *third in the kingdom* reflects accurately the situation; Belshazzar is next to Nabonidus, the recognized-though-absent ruler. Whoever interprets the mysterious writing will be next to Belshazzar, thus third in the line of authority.

As usual, the wise men are helpless; they cannot read or interpret the writing of the hand sent from God (5:8, 24). In terror, Belshazzar sinks into a deep state of shock. No one can explain to him what he has seen!

The Queen's Counsel 5:10-12

The queen, hearing of Belshazzar's strange behavior from some of the banqueters, rushes to his side, apparently without following the protocol of invitation (Esther 5:2). It is generally agreed that she is the queen-mother rather than a wife of Belshazzar. Some, however, believe the queen is the mother of Nabonidus, and thus Belshazzar's grandmother. She talks to him about *your father* Nebuchadnezzar (5:11). Since Belshazzar's father is Nabonidus, *your father* makes sense in that Belshazzar is a member in the line of Babylonian kings, the most impressive of which was Nebuchadnezzar (see notes on 5:2, above). The queen seems to be an older person since she has a clear memory of events in the distant past. Nebuchadnezzar is long gone, having died some twenty-three years earlier.

Immediately she comforts Belshazzar and suggests that Daniel be brought. By now Daniel is approximately seventy-five years of age. With Belshazzar's rise to power and Nabonidus being absent, Daniel apparently has been put on the shelf as a political adviser and is all but forgotten. The queen recalls, first of all, what Nebuchadnezzar learned about Daniel, that in him is *a spirit of the holy gods* (4:9, 18). She also remembers that Nebuchadnezzar made Daniel *chief of the magicians, enchanters, Chaldeans, and diviners* (5:11; 2:48). Her speech, citing Daniel's qualifications, will be echoed by Belshazzar (5:14).

Linked to the presence of God in Daniel's life are three characteristics: *enlightenment, understanding, and wisdom* (5:11). Contributing to his appointment as chief of the wise men are his *excellent spirit, knowledge, and understanding to interpret dreams, explain riddles, and solve problems* (5:12). Finally, the queen notes that Nebuchadnezzar (through the palace master) changed Daniel's name to Belteshazzar (1:7). The queen assures Belshazzar that if he calls Daniel, Daniel will indeed interpret the writing on the wall. *[Riddles, p. 294.]*

Belshazzar Seeks Daniel's Help 5:13-16

The shaken ruler is ready to follow the queen's suggestion. Belshazzar's drunken arrogance is gone. Nor does he exercise royal prerogatives to demand Daniel's service. Instead, he approaches Daniel quite chastened, appealing for help to overcome his terror and frustration. Belshazzar attempts to establish rapport with Daniel by citing his background, spirit, and abilities. In describing Daniel as one of *the exiles of Judah,* the king goes beyond the information supplied by the queen. The effect of this note is to highlight the oddity of the scene. A God-fearing Israelite will appear in the presence of a pagan emperor to give witness to Israel's God! Such an identification reminds readers of these strange historical events in which a victim of a king's power becomes the problem-solver for his captor! (cf. Gen. 41; 2 Kings 5).

Through identifying Daniel's person and accomplishments in a complimentary way, the king attempts to secure Daniel's help. The king's repetition of Daniel's qualifications, given earlier by the queen, is a characteristic Hebrew storytelling technique (5:11-12, 14). It also serves to spotlight Daniel in the story, even before he comes forward with the interpretation of the writing. By the speeches, attention is focused both on Daniel's gifts (5:10-12, 13-16) and on Belshazzar's monstrously evil deeds (5:17-28).

Next Belshazzar tells Daniel about his disappointment and frustration with the wise men because they are unable to interpret the inscription (5:15). Then, without a direct request or command, he invites Daniel's help. Finally, Belshazzar promises Daniel generous rewards if he gives a plausible explanation (5:16). The rewards are the same as those offered to the wise men (5:7). Belshazzar seems to think that anything can be secured if the price is right!

Daniel's Sobering Response 5:17-28

5:17 Daniel Rejects the Rewards

Though not stated in the text, Daniel likely rejects Belshazzar's gifts for several reasons. First, he does not want to be under obligation to Belshazzar. Second, he does not want the interpretation to appear connected with personal profit. Third, Daniel uses God's gifts for God's glory rather than for personal advantage. Daniel tells Belshazzar to keep his gifts *and give your rewards to someone else!* (cf. Acts 8:20).

5:18-24 Daniel Recalls Nebuchadnezzar's Glory

In order for the God-sent handwriting (5:24) to make sense, Daniel has to provide a context for his interpretation. The context contains two parts: a historical background and Belshazzar's arrogant behavior.

In the historical background, Daniel reviews the experience of king Nebuchadnezzar, briefly rehearsing material found in chapter 4 and noting God's action. God *gave* Nebuchadnezzar *kingship, greatness, glory, and majesty* (5:18). He also *gave* him a universal domain (5:19). But as a typical despot, Nebuchadnezzar did what he pleased, when he pleased, and to whom he pleased without accountability. He walked in pride and tried to act as a god. But, as Daniel points out, the God who gave him dominion was also able to bring him low (4:37). Daniel recalls the steps of Nebuchadnezzar's humiliation: (1) deposed from the throne, (2) glory taken away, (3) driven from society, (4) lost his mind, (5) lived and ate outdoors like the animals.

Nebuchadnezzar's fortunes were reversed when he came to know that *the Most High God has sovereignty over the kingdom of mortals, and sets over it whomever he will* (5:21; cf. 4:17, 25, 32). Thus Daniel reviews Nebuchadnezzar's humiliation and restoration, and identifies Nebuchadnezzar as *your father*, your predecessor (5:18; see on 5:2, above). This confrontation leaves Belshazzar without excuse. He might have learned from his "father," but like others before him, he has failed to do so (cf. Isaac repeating his father's techniques of deception [Gen. 12:10-20; 20:1-18; 26:6-11] and Jehoiakim's failure to learn from Josiah [Jer. 22:13-17, esp. verse 15]).

5:22-23 Daniel Indicts Belshazzar

Daniel indicts Belshazzar for prideful behavior on three counts: First, Belshazzar has not learned from Nebuchadnezzar's humiliation; instead, he has elevated himself. Second, he has defied the Lord of heaven when he and his fellow banqueters defiled the sacred vessels from the Jerusalem temple, using them to drink wine and to praise the idols of silver, gold, bronze, iron, wood, and stone. Third, Belshazzar has refused to honor the God *in whose power is your very breath, and to whom belong all your ways* (5:23). The speech is primarily an indictment (5:18-23), and the announcement of judgment is brief (5:24-28). This format corresponds to prophetic judgment speeches, customarily in two parts: accusation and announcement (cf. Amos 4:1-3; Mic. 2:1-5; Jer. 7:13-15). The accusation provides a reason for the judgment.

Daniel, not afraid to face Belshazzar, becomes a model. Instead of allowing himself to be used by this politician, he abruptly confronts the king with his understanding of the will and way of God. As Daniel earlier confronted Nebuchadnezzar (4:27), so now he exposes Belshazzar's pride, desecration of the temple vessels, and idolatrous worship. Though Nebuchadnezzar had taken the vessels from Jerusalem, in the course of time he had come to honor and respect the God to whom the vessels point. Belshazzar knows of this, yet brazenly defies the Lord of heaven as he and his lords in drunken revelry use them to worship powerless, senseless idols. Daniel highlights the evils of using religious vessels for banquet revelry, and of praising *the gods of silver and gold, of bronze, iron, wood, and stone.* Both these actions are also described by the narrator (5:2-4). Daniel's longer comment on Nebuchadnezzar (5:18-21) echoes the queen-mother's reference to that king (5:11). Repetition is a technique which both focuses and reinforces the emphasis.

There is a real sting in Daniel's confrontation. In effect, Daniel says to Belshazzar, "You have not learned a thing!" Nebuchadnezzar learned that his arrogance as head of a mighty empire and his pride as builder of a great city were fleeting and bordered on insanity. This learning, however, was short-lived. Belshazzar demonstrates anew the pride and arrogance associated with political power in a mighty empire. As God intervened in the life of Nebuchadnezzar, so God will intervene again to demonstrate his power in contrast to the powerlessness of the politicians and their gods.

Daniel reminds Belshazzar that his life and destiny are in the hands of God. He makes it clear that Belshazzar is not simply an automaton; he is responsible for his actions. Belshazzar's arrogant behavior will lead to his downfall: *You have not humbled your heart, even though you knew all this! You have exalted yourself against the Lord of heaven! You have been drinking wine from the vessels of his temple. You have praised the gods of silver and gold; you have not honored God* (5:22-23, abridged). Politicians, though challenged time and again about their arrogant ways, never seem to learn. In the tradition of earlier prophets, Daniel brings a powerful, needed witness. That witness is one of addressing and unmasking government.

God judges arrogance. The speech by Daniel serves as a critique of any government which may function in a way unmindful of God's controlling sovereignty. In the words of Millard Lind, "Imperial political arrogance is political insanity" (private correspondence).

The queen-mother has to remind Belshazzar of Daniel and his gifts. Daniel has to remind Belshazzar of Nebuchadnezzar's experiences in learning about the sovereignty of the Most High God. These reminders warn us and illustrate that faithfulness and spiritual insights can quickly be lost from one generation to the next!

5:24-28 Daniel Interprets the Writing

The storyteller has been building suspense by describing the terrified king's physical condition, the intervention and counsel of the queen-mother, Belshazzar's repetition of her account of Daniel and his gifts, and his indirect request for the interpretation. Further suspenseful delay is added by Daniel's long response to Belshazzar, refusing rewards, retelling Nebuchadnezzar's story, and enumerating Belshazzar's sins. Up to this point, each segment of the story contributes to the whole, but the question filling Belshazzar with terror goes unanswered. Now the mystery will be revealed.

First, Daniel tells Belshazzar that the *hand was sent* from the *presence* of the Lord of heaven (5:24). This God is living and able to act. His works are in stark contrast to the gods of silver, gold, bronze, iron, wood, and stone that are carried into the city to provide protection. In the great hall, the idols sit where they have been placed. They can not see, hear, nor respond.

Then Daniel reads the mysterious words written on the wall:

> *MENE, MENE, TEKEL, and PARSIN.* (5:25)

What has God decreed in these words? Many theories have been offered to explain their meaning. But the meaning does not reside simply in the words themselves. Rather, the meaning is found in secondary meanings from plays on the words.

Many commentators believe the words refer to weights and to coinage. For perspective, note that a talent is about what a man is expected to carry, a little over seventy-five pounds. The Aramaic word *mene* means a *mena* or *mina*, likely about twenty ounces, eventually also the name of a coin. *Tekel* is an Aramaic form of *shekel*, less than half an ounce, eventually also the name of a coin of low value. *Parsin* is plural, for "men dividing" (a mina), so it likely means two half-minas. In North American coinage, it might read, "Half dollar, half dollar, cent, two bits (a quarter)." Hence, this may refer to the line of kings after Nebuchadnezzar: Evil-merodach and Neriglissar are each worth a mina, Labashi-Marduk is worth only a shekel, and Belshazzar and his father, Nabonidus, are worth half a mina each (NOAB: 1136, OT).

The words naming the weights and coins may also be read as verbs with similar sounds. Such plays on words are also found in prophetic writings, as in *šaqed/šoqed* (Jer. 1:11-12, "almond tree/ watching") and in *qayiṣ/qeṣ* (Amos 8:1-2, "summer fruit/end"). In the form of a pun, *mene* brings to mind a verb meaning *numbered* (cf. the English noun *pound* with the verb *pound;* Goldengay: 116). *Tekel* suggests a verb meaning *weighed. Parsin* relates to a verb meaning *divided.* In his interpretation, Daniel uses the perfect-tense forms of the verbs, thus giving the sense that God's actions are already completed.

Based on the verb *numbered,* Daniel reiterates the common theme of God's ultimate control of history: God raises up, God puts down. In God's time clock, the days of Belshazzar's kingdom are *numbered*, and God has *brought it to an end*. Based on the verb *weighed,* Daniel indicates that God has been evaluating Belshazzar's performance and has found it lightweight. Based on the verb *divided,* Daniel announces that Belshazzar's kingdom is ending by division between the Medes and Persians. In a further pun, *parsin* may also refer to Persia.

The Interpretation Confirmed 5:29-31

5:29 Daniel Rewarded and Elevated

Apparently Daniel's interpretation makes sense to Belshazzar. Even though the interpretation offers him no hope, he proceeds to give Daniel the promised rewards. In light of his earlier protest (5:17), it is surprising that Daniel accepts them without any recorded protest.

5:30 Belshazzar Slain

Nebuchadnezzar repented of his pride and was restored (4:1-37). Belshazzar, however, does not repent. He gives no evidence of personal introspection nor of a desire to change his ways. When he meets Daniel, he simply parrots the queen's statements about him.

He reveals no appreciation for Nebuchadnezzar's experience and does not defend himself in the face of Daniel's indictments. Nor does the imminent judgment revealed in the mysterious words lead him to ask for mercy or for a time of grace. Belshazzar shakes in terror when the hand appears. But having heard the dreadful implications that the words imply for him personally, Belshazzar simply continues as before. He seems to believe in the protection of Bel and the efficacy of his gods of silver, gold, bronze, iron, wood, and stone.

That very night, Belshazzar is slain. There is no verbal message to the nations. The event itself speaks loudly and clearly enough. Although not specifically noted, it is generally assumed that Belshazzar's death comes with the capture of Babylon by the Medo-Persians. With the death of the monarch, the Neo-Babylonian empire comes to an end. The fall of Babylon has been foretold by the prophets (Isa. 13:17-19; 21:1-10; Jer. 51:24-58). In Isaiah 21:9, the watcher announces, "Fallen, fallen is Babylon; and all the images of her gods lie shattered on the ground."

According to the Cyrus Cylinder, "Without any battle [Marduk] enabled [Cyrus] to enter his city Babylon, sparing Babylon any calamity. He delivered into his hands Nabonidus, the king who did not worship him [Marduk]" (ANET: 315-316). Nabonidus was the premier figure in the Nabonidus-Belshazzar coregency. There are other records, and the Babylonian Chronicle offers a more detailed and somewhat varied account. Nabonidus was arrested when he returned to Babylon after it welcomed the Medo-Persian army under Gubaru/ Ugbaru (Greek: Gobyras), governor of Gutium, in Media. The gods were soon returned to their sacred cities (ANET: 306; cf. Goldingay: 107). Some reports say that the invaders diverted the Euphrates River so they could enter the city through the riverbed.

5:31 Darius the Mede Receives the Kingdom

It is unfortunate that a chapter break occurs at this point in the English Bible. The historical note of verse 31 concerning receiving the kingdom and the ruler's age should be tied to the king's first administrative acts (6:1), as in the Hebrew Bible. This Darius the Mede is most plausibly Gubaru (Gobyras), who was about sixty-two years of age when he led the Medo-Persian army into Babylon. Under Cyrus, he was vice-regent for Babylon and Mesopotamia until he died eight months later. Some think Darius the Mede is a throne name for Cyrus, whose grandfather was a Mede, according to legend. In any case, having a Mede rule Babylon at this point fits prophecy that Media would conquer Babylon (as in Isa. 13:17-19) and the ancient idea that there would be a succession of four world empires, Assyria or Babylon, Media, Persia, and Greece. *[Cyrus, p. 284.]*

THE TEXT IN BIBLICAL CONTEXT

The Hand of God

Whenever the story of Belshazzar's feast is told, hearers are fascinated by *the fingers of a human hand* that appear and begin *writing on the plaster of the wall of the royal palace* (5:5). When Daniel interprets the meaning of the words, he tells Belshazzar, *The God in whose power is your very breath, and to whom belong all your ways, you have not honored. So from his presence the hand was sent* (5:23-24).

In the book of Daniel are frequent references to the hand of God. Thus Nebuchadnezzar blesses the Most High: *He does what he wills with the host of heaven and the inhabitants of the earth. There is no one who can stay his hand* (4:35). The evil king of 8:25 is *to be broken, and not by human hands,* implying that the hand of God will be at work. In his intercessory prayer, Daniel attributes the deliverance of Israel from Egypt to God's *mighty hand* (9:15; cf. Deut. 4:34; 5:15; 7:19). The God who delivered his people from the grip of the Egyptian Pharaoh, continues to confront arrogant governments and their rulers on behalf of the faithful.

The "hand of God" is a symbol of God's power. The Hebrew idiom of "hand" representing "power" is frequent in the book of Exodus, though not always clear from the English translation (3:20; 13:3, 9, 14; 14:31; 18:10). God uses his power to deliver his people, to protect them, and to judge evildoers. Isaiah expresses this thought in the beautiful words:

> Do not fear, for I am with you,
> do not be afraid, for I am your God;
> I will strengthen you, I will help you,
> I will uphold you with my victorious right hand. (Isa. 41:10)

Jesus expresses a similar thought concerning care for his followers, "What my Father has given me is greater than all else, and no one can snatch it out of the Father's hand" (John 10:29).

The most frequent NT reference is to God's "right hand." This was considered the place of great power and glory. Most of these texts are in connection with the ascension and exaltation of Jesus and reflect Psalm 110:1:

> The Lord says to my lord:
> "Sit at my right hand,
> until I make your enemies your footstool."

Jesus ascended to a position of power and glory. At Pentecost, Peter says, "This Jesus God raised up, and of that all of us are witnesses. Being therefore exalted at the right hand of God, . . . he has poured out this that you both see and hear" (Acts 2:32-33).

At his martyrdom, Stephen sees the glory of God, and Jesus standing at the right hand of God (Acts 7:55-56). Paul instructs believers to "seek the things that are above, where Christ is, seated at the right hand of God" (Col. 3:1). In the book of Hebrews, the preacher says of Jesus Christ, "When he had made purification for sins, he sat down at the right hand of the Majesty on high" (Heb. 1:3). This preacher outlines the work of the risen, ascended Christ as a high priest: "We have such a high priest, one who is seated at the right hand of the throne of the Majesty in the heaven" (8:1). "When Christ had offered for all time a single sacrifice for our sins, 'he sat down at the right hand of God' " (10:12).

The hand of God appears and writes a message of judgment for Belshazzar to see. Even with the message interpreted by one indwelt by "a spirit of the holy gods" (5:11, 14), Belshazzar makes no effort to change or to seek mercy of the God in whose hand was his breath. That night he meets death.

Since there are no words of admonition to those who hear this story, perhaps the apostle Peter's message summarizes what needs to be heard by *all peoples, nations, and languages:*

> All of you must clothe yourselves with humility
> in your dealings with one another, for
> "God opposes the proud,
> but gives grace to the humble."
> Humble yourselves therefore under the mighty hand of God,
> so that he may exalt you in due time. (1 Pet. 5:5-6)

THE TEXT IN THE LIFE OF THE CHURCH

Teaching from Generation to Generation

The story of Daniel and Belshazzar illustrates how spiritual insights can be forgotten. Nebuchadnezzar's learnings about the Most High God seemed to be quickly lost, even though clearly recorded in his letter *to all peoples, nations, and languages that live throughout the earth* (4:1; cf. 4:2-3, 34-37) and presumably in the king's annals (cf. Esther 6:1). Belshazzar seems unaware of the implications of Nebuchadnezzar's learning: "The Most High God has sovereignty over the kingdom of mortals, and sets over it whomever he will" (5:21). Consequently, Belshazzar does not walk humbly nor honor God. Instead, he exalts himself and profanes the sacred vessels taken from the temple of the Lord of heaven. When the handwriting appears on the wall, the terrified young regent is at his wits' end.

The queen-mother is the one who remembers Daniel and comes to the banquet hall to tell Belshazzar about him. This Daniel, the queen adds, was made chief of the wise men by Nebuchadnezzar because he *is endowed with a spirit of the holy gods*. Daniel then reminds Belshazzar of Nebuchadnezzar's painful experience and its meaning.

Teaching the decrees and commandments of God has always been taken seriously by the people of God (Deut. 6:1-3). In the OT, teaching was largely oriented around the home. The central issues of faith were to be taught diligently to children. Parents were to talk of them when in the house, traveling, going to bed, and arising (Deut. 6:4-9). The central religious festival, Passover, though observed in the Jerusalem temple, was also a home observance. Undoubtedly, the faithfulness of Daniel and his companions in Babylon had its roots in their home life before being taken captive.

Teaching in the church has continuity with that in Israel. As in Israel, parents are to rear their children in "the discipline and instruction of the Lord" (Eph. 6:4). But the church encompasses considerable differences and is not an ethnic group. Entrance and participation in the church do not hinge on blood or background. Birth usually assures entrance into a biological family. New birth from above, however, signifies entrance into a new family, the family of God, through repentance and faith in Jesus Christ. While Paul clearly stresses responsibility for one's biological family (1 Tim. 5:8), the new family of God is to take first place (Mark 3:32-35; Luke 14:26). Baptism symbolizes entrance into this new family, and communion celebrates the new covenant based on Christ which binds the family together.

The Gospels were written *for* congregations, and most of the NT letters were addressed *to* congregations. This suggests that Christian teaching takes the route from congregation to parents and children. Strong teaching in the congregation makes for strong families, and not the other way around, as commonly stated.

The congregation is essential for maintaining the faith *from generation to generation* (Dan. 4:3, 34). The congregation reviews the mighty acts of God when it meets to worship (1 Tim. 2:3-7). Congregations are to deal openly with moral issues and agonize about apostasy and backsliding (1 Tim. 1:6; 3:6; 4:3; 6:9; 2 Tim. 2:17-18; 4:3-4, 10). The most effective type of Christian education for children and youth is in observing believers who model discipleship and in observing the congregation. Members participate in discussions, testimonies, preaching, prayers, screening of volunteers, scrutiny of leaders, ministering to suffering, dealing with love of money, facing persecution, and exposing all that is false.

These activities not only teach but also evangelize, as persons long to be part of a group that cares, helps, and has purpose. The practical demonstration of what life can be like when persons live together in the love of Christ, is a city set on a hill that cannot be hidden (Matt. 5:14). Such a community of believers is a springboard for God's action in the whole world. God is doing his work for the church and through the church (Eph. 1:19-23; 2:9-10).

Indirectly, the story of Belshazzar provides a significant warning to the church. If the church fails to teach the knowledge of God, his works and ways, it may quickly be forgotten, and at great peril. If that occurs, the church will be unable to confront society and its power structures with a prophetic witness or to endure the opposition which such witness arouses.

Daniel 6:1-28

The Living God: Rescue from the Lions' Den

PREVIEW

The story of Daniel in the lions' den is a classic account of court intrigue. It compares readily with the account of Shadrach, Meshach, and Abednego in the fiery furnace (chap. 3). Both are martyr stories in that Daniel and his three friends are ready to die rather than to deny their faith. In their faithfulness to God, Daniel and his companions are determined to follow their understanding of God's way whatever the cost. They "obey God rather any than human authority" (Acts 5:29).

Though there are similarities between the stories in chapters 3 and 6, there are also many differences. In both accounts there is conspiracy. In the case of Shadrach, Meshach, and Abednego, the conspirators are fellow experts in the letters and language of the Chaldeans. They are jealous because the three are more able than they (1:7, 20). In chapter 6 the conspirators are Daniel's fellow politicians, jealous of his political competence and success.

In both cases the conspirators focus opposition at the point of faith. The Chaldeans say to Nebuchadnezzar, *These pay no heed to you, O King. They do not serve your gods and they do not worship the golden statue that you have set up* (3:12). The politicians say, *We shall not find any ground for complaint against this Daniel unless we find it in connection with the law of his God* (6:5).

In both cases the conspirators focus on commands that the faithful cannot obey, even though there is a death penalty for disobedience. For Shadrach, Meshach, and Abednego, the test involves a public demonstration of opposition to an idolatrous worship of the state. For Daniel, the test involves a personal expression of faithfulness, that of prayer.

This story of Daniel is set in the beginning of a new empire. Darius had received the kingdom (5:31). His first act is to establish a network of administrators, of which Daniel is one of the top three. As in chapter 3, the story is carried along with a large use of the same conjunction, *then* (RSV; Aramaic, *be'dayin;* or without the prefix, *'edayin*). English versions resort to other conjunctions to break the monotony. The use of this conjunction fifteen times means that the story comes through the narrator and not so much through the speeches of two or three characters, as in chapter 5. This account is action-packed, as shown below. (In the Aramaic of Dan. 6, verse numbers are one higher because 5:31 is taken as 6:1. RSV is used for these examples.)

6:3 *Then this Daniel became distinguished*
6:4 *Then the presidents and the satraps sought*
6:5 *Then these men said*
6:6 *Then these presidents and satraps came by agreement*
6:11 *Then these men came by agreement*
6:12 *Then they came near and said before the king*
6:13 *Then they answered before the king*
6:14 *Then the king . . . was much distressed*
6:15 *Then these men came by agreement*
6:16 *Then the king commanded, and Daniel was brought*
6:18 *Then the king went to his palace*
6:19 *Then, at break of day, the king arose*
6:21 *Then Daniel said to the king*
6:23 *Then the king was exceedingly glad*
6:25 *Then King Darius wrote*

Upon closer examination the story also has a carefully planned structure:

The story begins and ends with Daniel prospering (6:3, 28).
The story proceeds with Darius enacting a decree that *cannot be revoked* (6:6-10).
The story climaxes with Darius enacting a new decree that supersedes the first (6:25-27).

In this story are two major contrasts: First, between two laws, *the law of God* (6:5), and *the law of the Medes and the Persians* (6:8, 12, 15). Second, between two deliverers, King Darius (6:14) and God (6:20, 27). The story assures the faithful that the law of the Medes and the Persians can be broken, and that God, not any earthly king, is able to deliver.

At the heart of the story are conversations between Darius and Daniel. In the first conversation, the distressed king wants to see Daniel delivered (6:16-18). Yet he carries out the sentence and goes to his palace to await Daniel's death. His last words to Daniel show some hope: *May your God whom you faithfully serve, deliver you* (6:16). Darius uses Daniel's Hebrew name, perhaps reflecting his sympathy for conquered people and their religion. The name Belteshazzar, given by Nebuchadnezzar, no longer appears. In the second conversation early the next morning, the king finds Daniel safe and hears his explanation, *My God sent his angel . . .* (6:19-23).

Throughout the story, Daniel stands in sharp contrast to the conspirators. They are jealous. Early on, they seek ways to discredit him. They scheme and manipulate the king. Their duplicity is apparent in proposing a decree that will enhance the king's power while destroying Daniel. They care little for truth, for the welfare of the empire, for the king, or for Medo-Persian law. Their consuming passion is to dispose of Daniel. On the other hand, Daniel has a wholesome spirit. He is an excellent administrator, careful with the smallest details (6:3-4). He is blameless before God and has not done the king any harm (6:22).

Like other stories in Daniel, the king is not presented in a positive light. Nebuchadnezzar is seen as capricious and unpredictable, ranting and raving, one who is proud and has to be humbled. Darius is presented as one who also has aspirations for greatness, even divinity (6:7). But Darius is also presented as dim-witted, easily manipulated by flattery, and unable to see the long-range implications of his actions. At best, the greatest of rulers are still human, falling far short of the attributes of divinity. Stories with such insights enabled these displaced Israelites to keep perspective on their condition. They saw that kings were not as powerful or as enduring or as insightful as they appeared. God could use them, humble them, or bypass them to accomplish his purposes.

OUTLINE

Darius Organizes His Kingdom, 6:1-5
- 6:1-3 Daniel's New Position
- 6:4-5 Daniel's Vulnerability

Collusion to Remove Daniel, 6:6-9
- 6:6-7 The Appeal to Darius's Vanity
- 6:8-9 Darius's Prayer Law

Daniel Prays to His God, 6:10

Daniel Disgraced, 6:11-18
- 6:11-14 Daniel Charged Before the King
- 6:15-18 Daniel Thrown to the Lions

Daniel Delivered, 6:19-24
- 6:19-22 Conversation at Dawn
- 6:23 Released from the Pit
- 6:24 Fate of Conspirators

The New Decree, 6:25-27

Daniel's Renewed Success, 6:28

EXPLANATORY NOTES

Darius Organizes His Kingdom 6:1-5

6:1-3 Daniel's New Position

The identity of *Darius* is one of the problems of the book. How is he to be fitted into Persian chronology? A possible answer is that Darius is another name, possibly a throne name, for Cyrus. More plausibly, Darius is Gubaru (Gobyras), who ruled over Mesopotamia as vice-regent under Cyrus. Records show that Gubaru was appointing governors until his death eight months later (ANET: 306). *[Cyrus, p. 284.]* Some have questioned the number of satraps (governors), each ruling a satrapy or a province. Some fifty years later, under Xerxes (486-465 B.C.), the number of provinces was reported to be 127 (Esther 1:1; cf. 8:9). According to the Greek historian Herodotus and tomb inscriptions, nearer to the time of our story, the number of satrapies ranged between 20 and 29, and they were subdivided into provinces. That such numbers fluctuated under different administrations is not particularly surprising. The biblical comment reflects in general what is known from other sources about the organization of the Persian empire (see notes on historical factuality at 5:1-4).

Darius enjoys the fruits of successful conquest. In order to maintain his continued domination, he has to put administrative structures in place and appoint his own people to places of responsibility. His plan is to appoint a ruling triumvirate of officials called *presidents* (6:2). Forty lesser officials, *satraps* (6:1), are made responsible to each of the three presidents.

Darius appoints Daniel as one of three presidents (6:2). Perhaps Daniel's reputation and abilities have been called to the king's attention. Since Daniel is a Jewish exile and not a Babylonian, Darius may feel reasonably sure of his loyalty.

The Persian empire extends from Egypt in the west to the Indus River in the east (or "from India to Ethiopia," Esther 8:9). To provide organization for *the whole kingdom* is a major task (Dan. 6:3). The work of the presidents and satraps is to see to it that the king will *suffer no loss* (6:2). The king does not want to lose territory through uprisings nor lose tax money through graft. Through good administration, the empire can be held together, and the king will not be overburdened.

Daniel has distinguished himself in two ways: in his personality—*an excellent spirit was in him*; and in his administration—*he was faithful, and no negligence or corruption could be found in him* (6:4). The excellent spirit is attributed to the evident presence of God in his life. He is able not only to grasp the "big picture" but also to see the significance of small details. Thus there are no instances of maladministration either through mismanagement or neglect. Because of Daniel's competence, Darius decides to appoint Daniel as his right-hand man, to govern *the whole kingdom* (6:3).

6:4-5 Daniel's Vulnerability

How the other presidents and satraps get word of Daniel's impending appointment is not told. The information leak precipitates a concerted effort to thwart Daniel's impending appointment. What they really want, however, is a way to get rid of Daniel completely.

As the presidents and satraps watch Daniel's life, they note the intensity of his devotion to the God of Israel. Daniel has been faithfully worshiping God in the days of the Babylonian empire and continues to do the same now, thus disregarding the gods of the conquerors. If

Daniel would only be vaguely "religious," there would be little ground for criticism. Daniel's devotion to God makes it clear that he has an allegiance higher than to the king or to the empire which he serves. The rivals recognize that if Daniel were to be removed, it would have to be in connection with his faith—*the law of his God* (6:5).

Collusion to Remove Daniel 6:6-9

An important feature of Persian rule is *the law of the Medes and the Persians, which cannot be revoked* (6:8). Though both Nebuchadnezzar and Darius are undisputed rulers, the Medes and Persians pride themselves in being a people of law. Nebuchadnezzar does as he wishes. Consequently, *all people, nations and languages trembled and feared before him* because *he killed those he wanted to kill, kept alive those he wanted to keep alive, honored those he wanted to honor, and degraded those he wanted to degrade* (5:19). Darius, however, is bound by *law . . . which cannot be revoked* (6:8), so much so that he labors until sundown, trying *to rescue* Daniel (6:14). *Law* is so important that Darius finds himself helpless to disregard it. The Aramaic word for *law* in this chapter, *dat* (8:9, 13, 15), was found in 1973 in an Aramaic inscription. The Persian governor of the province of Lycia (in the region of modern Turkey) gave approval for the establishment of a new cult. The provisions of his decree (Aramaic: *dat*) were for all time.

The story does not reveal what transpires between the conspirators' discovery of Daniel's vulnerability in connection with his faith and their appearing before Darius with a proposal. Undoubtedly, they see the potential conflict between the *law of his God* and *the law of the Medes and the Persians, which cannot be revoked*. They want to trap Daniel in that collision or intersection in such a way that he will be forced either to deny his God or to lose his life, because both God's law and the king's law require absolute obedience.

Daniel's prayer life provides their clue. Their scheme is to have a law enacted which carries the death penalty for anyone who prays to any man or god other than the king for thirty days. On the surface, this law is a simple way for citizens to express loyalty to king and empire. Since the law of the Medes and Persians can not be revoked, it will be impossible to do anything about the mischief the law will create in Daniel's life. His death will be certain! When the presidents and satraps come to the king, there is no hint of their ultimate purpose.

6:6-7 The Appeal to Darius's Vanity

The presidents and satraps have *conspired*, and as *conspirators* they come before the king (6:6, 11, 15). The Aramaic *hargišu* has been translated in many ways: KJV—*assembled* or (margin) *came tumultuously;* RSV—*came by agreement;* JB—*went in a body;* NRSV—*conspired and came.* In Psalm 2:1-2 and 64:2 (Heb. 64:3), the Hebrew word from the same root (*rgš*) is used with "take counsel" (*yasad*) or with "(secret) consultation" (the related noun *sod*) to suggest "secret plots" or "secret counsel" (KJV) and "scheming." It is better to use this meaning rather than "tumult" or "rage." A good choice is *conspirators;* they come conspiring.

The conspirators are persistent (6:6, 11, 15). Their proposal receives ready acceptance by the king. First, it implies loyalty to him and to his empire along with great respect. Second, he sees the proposal as a high honor. Third, the proposal pampers his vanity as he ponders, "What power they see in me!" Fourth, it attributes divinity to the king, a notion not foreign to kings before or after. And fifth, it is presented as their unanimous proposal. The conspirators, in order to impress the king with the importance of their proposal, propose a heavy penalty for noncompliance: death in the lions' den.

One notes a significant change in the form of capital punishment. Babylonians use a *furnace of blazing fire*, but the Persians use lions. This reflects the influence of Zoroastrianism on Persia. Zoroastrianism took its name from Zoroaster, who lived around 628-551 B.C. in northwest Iran. Its main body of scripture is known as the Avesta; its leading god was Ahuramazda (Ahura means "lord," and Mazda means "wise.") In this religion, fire was considered sacred and could not be used for purposes such as capital punishment.

6:8-9 Darius's Prayer Law

The speed with which Darius enacts into law the proposal of the presidents and satraps makes him appear dim-witted. Lulled by the flattery of the presidents and satraps, he thinks only of his greatness, his power, and his chance to grasp divinity (cf. Phil. 2:6). He does not take time to consider the implications of the act for the empire or the welfare of his subjects. A good law may not need change. A bad law, however, without possibility of change, can have devastating effects. Darius is unable to foresee the consequences of his decree. This certainly calls into question the role of divinity claimed by the decree. The king drafts the law and issues it over his name. He prohibits prayer to anyone but himself for thirty days. This is not a major matter to him! No one has to deny his god nor change his ways: simply pray to no one but the king for a brief period. But little things, so-called, can be really big.

Daniel Prays to His God 6:10

After the decree is signed, Daniel makes no change in his prayer practices, as the conspirators expected. The narrator records Daniel's practice in matter-of-fact fashion. Such an approach suggests that Daniel does not hesitate nor even debate within himself. Following the days of the exile and with the rise of the synagogue, personal prayers became important. Increasingly, the mark of a pious Jew was to be a person of prayer. Daniel is well aware that integrity, wise decision making, and the ability to get things done are tied to prayer. In the face of governmental prohibition and with death as the penalty, Daniel keeps on praying in his home. In this he is a forerunner of Peter and the apostles, who "obey God rather than any human authority" (Acts 5:27-32).

Daniel follows Jeremiah's letter of counsel to the exiles:

> I know the plans I have for you, says the Lord,
> plans for your welfare and not for harm,
> to give you a future with hope.
> Then when you call upon me and come and pray to me,
> I will hear you.
> When you search for me,
> you will find me;
> if you seek me with all your heart,
> I will let you find me, says the Lord. (Jer. 29:11-14)

In Daniel's house there is an *upper* room, a place for undistracted prayer. Elijah had an upper room (1 Kings 17:19), as did Elisha (2 Kings 4:10, "roof chamber" constructed on a flat roof). In the early church the disciples devoted themselves to prayer in an upper room (Acts 1:13). On a rooftop Peter received the vision to take the gospel to Gentiles (Acts 10:9).

The room had windows *open toward Jerusalem*. Facing toward Jerusalem to pray likely began in Babylon, when Jerusalem and the temple were in ruins. This may have resulted from remembering Solomon's dedicatory prayer,

> If . . . they pray to thee toward this city that you have chosen and the house that I have built for your name, then hear from heaven their prayer and their plea, and maintain their cause. (2 Chron. 6:34-35)

The windows are open. Daniel makes no attempt to hide his prayer. He is easily observed. Before the open window, Daniel gets *down on his knees*. There is some evidence of Israelites customarily standing for public prayer and kneeling for private prayer (cf. Neh. 8:5-6; Luke 22:41; but see 2 Chron. 6:13; Ps. 95:6). Kneeling also implies intensity, humility, and submission. Daniel prays *three times a day*, at dawn, midday, and evening (Dan. 6:10). This is in harmony with Psalm 55:16-17:

> But I call upon God
> and the Lord will save me.
> Evening and morning and at noon
> I will utter my complaint and moan,
> and he will hear my voice.

In his times of prayer (6:10-11), Daniel also gives *praise* (NRSV) and *thanks* (RSV) to God, *seeking mercy* (NRSV), making *petition and supplication before his God* (RSV). Daniel's prayers are well-rounded. They include thanksgiving for what God has done, is doing, and will do in his life. They also include intercession for the state in which he lives and serves (cf. Jer. 29:7), for fellow Israelites (cf. Dan. 9:4-19), and for himself especially in this time of crisis. In the midst of his heavy responsibilities as a president, he takes time to pray. Daniel keeps on praying as he has in the past. He does not close the windows nor pull down the shades to pray in secret. Through prayer Daniel declares his allegiance to and confidence in his God, denying the ultimacy of Darius and his "irrevocable" laws. Daniel is ready to die for his faith.

Daniel Disgraced 6:11-18

6:11-14 Daniel Charged Before the King

After the decree is signed, the conspirators began surveillance of Daniel's home. Much to their satisfaction, they find Daniel praying to his God (6:11). Today Daniel's action would be called civil disobedience.

Immediately, the conspirators go to the king. They report Daniel's violation of the decree. So that the king rather than the conspirators will bear the responsibility for what will follow, they ask, *Did **you** not* *sign an interdict?* The king, unaware of the startling news to come, readily admits his decree: *The thing stands fast, according to the law of the Medes and the Persians, which cannot be revoked* (6:12). Both the conspirators' question and the king's assertion reinforce earlier statements in the story (6:7-8). The assertion about the unchangeability of the Medo-Persian law occurs for a third time in verse 15. By means of such repetition, the storyteller accomplishes two things. First, the text exposes the fragility of so-called unchangeable government law, since it is contradicted by Darius's later decree (6:26-27). Government, for all its iron-clad laws, is not nearly as permanent as it pretends to be. Second, in ironical fashion the story points forward to the climactic and supposedly irrevocable (!) decree that in all of Darius's dominion, *people should tremble and fear before the God of Daniel* (6:26).

Then they break the news. The conspirators have feelings of scorn, disrespect, and hatred for Daniel. Their identification of Daniel as *one of the exiles from Judah* seems to reflect also an anti-Jewish feeling. Their report climaxes with Daniel's treasonous activities: he disregards both the king and his decree; he prays to his God three times a day. The conspirators suggest that as an alien, Daniel can no longer be trusted. They further imply that Daniel's prayer to an alien God is a political act of rebellion against the king himself.

The story does not tell why the king is *distressed* with the conspirators' report. Is he distressed because the presidents and satraps are able to precipitate Daniel's downfall? Because Daniel ignores his decree? Is he distressed with himself for having been maneuvered into a position he did not foresee and from which he cannot easily extricate himself or Daniel? Is he distressed with his law? Is he *determined to save Daniel* and *rescue him* because he values Daniel as a leader or as a personal friend? Whatever the reason, the king now sees clearly that his law is a bad one. If the law is allowed to stand, a highly competent administrator will be lost unfairly. If the law is ignored, the sacred principle of unchangeableness of Medo-Persian law will be lost, opening the way for serious deterioration of law and order. Perhaps the king is distressed by all of the above. *The Jerusalem Bible* says, "He racked his brains until sunset to find some way out" (6:14). Daniel is trapped, and so is the king.

6:15-18 Daniel Thrown to the Lions

Darius is under the pressure of personal distress. But as the day passes, pressure comes from another source. When the conspirators see that the king is taking no action to enforce the death penalty, they come to the king. For the third time a reference is made to their collusion (6:6, 11, 15). Again the conspirators do not reveal their real purpose—to get rid of Daniel! Instead, they come as great patriots, loyal to the king, committed to Medo-Persian law and order. They speak glowingly of the unchangeabless of properly enacted laws of the Medes and Persians. Patriotism is often the refuge of scoundrels. It is frequently used also to divert attention from unaddressed domestic problems or from international misadventures.

The king summons Daniel to appear for sentencing. There is a marked contrast between Darius's behavior and that of Nebuchadnezzar in the case of Shadrach, Meshach, and Abednego. In both instances, questions of authority and divinity are at stake. Nebuchadnezzar was in furious rage (3:13) and blasphemously questioned, *Who is the god that will deliver you out of my hands?* (3:15). Darius, however, is saddened and distressed. He says to Daniel, *May your God, whom you faithfully serve, deliver you!* (3:16). It is not clear whether this is an expression of hope or an attempt to give Daniel final words of encouragement. Is it a prayer to Daniel's God for deliverance? If so, it is similar to the "wish prayers" of the apostle Paul (1 Thess. 3:11-13; 5:23-24; 2 Thess. 2:16-17; 3:5, 16). Or is it a statement of faith that Daniel's God will deliver?

As the story is told, the prayerlike statement by the king anticipates the climax of the chapter where the king makes a confession about the God who delivers, and where he orders all to worship this God (6:26-27). Whatever the king's intent, with these words Daniel is thrown to the lions. A stone is placed upon the opening of the den. In the material used to seal the opening, they place the mark of the king's signet ring and those of his lords, *so that nothing might be changed concerning Daniel* (6:17). The unchangeable law of the Medes and Persians has intersected with the law of Daniel's eternal God. Will God act or will the law of the Medes and Persians prevail?

Fearful for Daniel's life, angry with himself for what he has done, and frustrated with a law that can not be changed, the king goes *to his palace*. That night is different from those that have gone before, with *fasting* instead of food. He cannot relax. *No diversions* are *brought to him, and sleep fled from him* (6:18, RSV). Translators do not agree on what is not brought to him: the Aramaic word *daawan* is rendered variously as *diversions* (RSV), *food* (NRSV), *eating and . . . entertainment* (NIV) such as *musical instruments* (Davidson: 149); cf. 1 Sam. 16:23), *concubines* (JB), or *woman* (REB).

Daniel Delivered 6:19-24

6:19-22 Conversation at Dawn

The sleepless night goes slowly. As soon as it is light, the king hurries to the lions' den to see if his prayers for Daniel are answered and his hopes for Daniel's deliverance are realized. Out of great anguish of spirit, the king cries out as he nears the den, *O Daniel, servant of the living God, has your God whom you faithfully serve been able to deliver you from the lions?* (6:20). This question is remarkable in what it implies. It reflects a night of deep thought and new insight. Darius begins to understand the relationship between Daniel and his God. Daniel is a servant. God's will, rather than personal desires and aspirations, guide Daniel's life.

Just as important, Darius has come to see that Daniel's God is different from gods of metal, wood, and stone with which he is familiar. Daniel's God is *the living God*. Such a title for God suggests, says one scholar, "not merely that God is alive rather than dead, but that he is active and powerful, awesome and almighty, involved in bringing judgment and blessing" (Goldingay: 133). Darius also recognizes Daniel's unwavering commitment to serve his God regardless of the cost. The king tests his new insights with his question: *Has your God . . . been able to deliver you from the lions?*

When Darius hears Daniel's voice, his new insights are confirmed. Daniel's reply to the king is courteous: *O king, live forever!* (6:21). This is the only instance in the book of Daniel in which an exile addresses a king in this way. But there is more than courtesy in Daniel's reply. The king has called Daniel's God *the living God*. In Daniel's reply, he affirms Darius's kingship by wishing him long life. Thus Daniel indirectly calls attention to the limited power and brief life of earthly kings when compared to the King of heaven, the living God. Daniel's reference to God sending *his angel* to *shut the lions' mouths* (6:22) is in line with the notion that angels are in the service of Almighty God (Heb. 1:14), and that one of their functions is to afford protection (Matt. 26:53). Daniel's reply is a commentary on Psalm 91:9-13:

> Because you have made the Lord your refuge,
> the Most High your dwelling place,
> no evil shall befall you,
> no scourge come near your tent.
> For he will command his angels concerning you
> to guard you in all your ways.

Daniel's answer stresses two points: first, his innocence (a legal term) before God; and second, that he has done the king *no wrong* (6:22). Daniel has disobeyed the law of the Medes and Persians. However, when the laws of the empire conflict with the law of God, the faithful will break the law of the empire with a clear conscience. Consequently, Daniel sees himself as *blameless* before God and King Darius. In 6:23, the narrator adds that God intervened because Daniel *trusted in his God.*

In his response, Daniel also opens for examination the plot of the conspirators. They were hoping to force Daniel to deny his God or to appear disloyal to the king. By putting loyalty to God first, Daniel remains innocent before God, kept from doing harm to the king or to the empire. Even though Daniel is a key character in the story, he is silent throughout the entire story except for his answer to the king. That answer pinpoints the subject of God's deliverance, a key feature of God's action as presented in OT story (Exod. 6:6) and poetry (Ps. 30:1-3). It is the subject of the king's later decree (Dan. 6:26-27), and the note of God's deliverance is sounded again in 12:1-3. Is this single speech by Daniel intended by the narrator to hint at the significance of the story?

6:23 Released from the Pit

Greatly relieved, the king orders Daniel's release. As in the case of Shadrach, Meshach, and Abednego (*not even the smell of fire came from them*, 3:27), so with Daniel: *No kind of harm was found on him*. The storyteller and not Daniel nor the king gives the reason: *because he had trusted in his God*. According to the NT, it is through faith that the men and women of God "shut the mouths of lions" and "quenched raging fire" (Heb. 11:33-34). God's intervention and spectacular deliverance from death points forward within the book to the resurrection motif (12:1-3; cf. Heb. 11:19, 35).

6:24 Fate of Conspirators

Upon Daniel's release, the king orders the conspirators, their children, and their wives to be cast into the den of lions. The lions' mouths are no longer shut. Before reaching the bottom of the pit, their bodies are broken. Though jarring to Christian sensibilities, this feature of retribution and of family solidarity in guilt and punishment is in harmony with Mosaic Law (see TBC, below). The entire story stands as an elaborate illustration of Psalm 57:4, 6: "I lie down among lions that greedily devour human prey. . . . They dug a pit in my path, but they have fallen into it themselves." Porteous (87) comments somewhat mischievously that these verses "might almost have suggested the story of chapter 6 to an inventive story-teller!"

The New Decree 6:25-27

Upon Daniel's deliverance and the demise of the conspirators, Darius takes action. He not only revokes the old prayer law; he also replaces it with a new decree. Through a letter he publicizes this action among *all peoples and nations of every language throughout the whole world*. After the usual salutation, he reviews the new decree. It states that the God of the Israelites is not simply to be tolerated: instead, all citizens are to *tremble and fear before the God of Daniel* (6:26). The theme of non-Israelites acknowledging Israel's God is a major message of the tract to the nations (Dan. 2–7). Yet the theme occurs elsewhere in the OT tradition (as in Exod. 18:11; Ezek. 36:20-21, 36).

Then Darius enumerates the reasons for his new decree:

1. The God of Daniel is the *living God*.
2. *His kingdom* and *dominion* have *no end*.
3. *He delivers and rescues*.
4. He *works signs and wonders in heaven and on earth*.

Darius comes to realize all this through Daniel's deliverance *from the power of the lions*.

Daniel's miraculous escape from the lions also demonstrates the impotence of Darius's pagan deities. Like Nebuchadnezzar, Darius comes to see that human claims to power and permanence stumble and fall before God's sovereignty and power, before his eternal law, and before his abiding presence. Darius's new decree, however, is as misdirected as the old one, since people cannot be compelled by law to turn to God or to worship him.

In this story, as in earlier stories, humans who claim greatness, power, and authority are confronted by the God to whom the faithful bear witness. As a result of this witness, powerful leaders come face-to-face with the power of Daniel's God. The confrontation leads the pagan kings, in turn, to call all the peoples of earth to *tremble and fear* before the living God. The whole world must hear about the living God. The tract to the nations brings truths about this God effectively to *all peoples, nations, and languages* (4:1; cf. 3:29; 6:25).

In the blessing Daniel gives to the God of heaven (2:20-23), in the testimonies of Nebuchadnezzar (2:47; 3:29; 4:3, 34, 35, 37), and in the letter of Darius—the rule of God, his power, his eternal nature, his universal concern, and his ability to act on behalf of his people are not only clearly set forth, but also are dramatically illustrated! The book of Daniel speaks to a faltering, discouraged people, helping them renew their strength and giving them hope. Throughout the tract to the nations is this double-pronged message. At one level it speaks to God's people; in a second and more striking way, it speaks to the nations about Daniel's God.

The living God's *dominion has no end* (6:26). This is the only eschatological note in the story, but a necessary one. The trials of the moment must be seen in the light of God's ultimate triumph.

Daniel's Renewed Success 6:28

The story begins with Daniel's successful service as one of three presidents. Daniel is at the point of receiving another promotion from Darius the king. Instead of promotion, Daniel is framed and disgraced. The story ends with Daniel's recovery of his place of responsibility. Daniel continues to serve under Darius the Mede and Cyrus the Persian *[Cyrus, p. 284]*. This concluding paragraph makes the point that it is possible for persons of faith both to survive and to overcome. Like the leader in Psalm 2, Daniel is conspired against and disgraced. But the living God is at work. The conspirators are broken; the target of their evil plot is restored. The psalm concludes

> Now therefore, O kings, be wise;
>   be warned, O rulers of earth.
> Serve the Lord with fear. . . .
> Happy are all who take refuge in him. (Ps. 2:10-11)

If Daniel went to Babylon with the first group of captives in 597 B.C. (or 604 B.C.?), he now is an old man, since Darius and Cyrus come to power over Babylon in 539 B.C. The visions in the chapters that follow take place earlier. The vision in chapter 7 is dated in the first year of Belshazzar (around 554 B.C.? 549 B.C.? 545 B.C.? It is unclear when he began as co-regent with his father). The vision of chapter 8 comes in Belshazzar's third year.

THE TEXT IN BIBLICAL CONTEXT

Retribution

One of the Ten Commandments prohibits giving malicious witness, which would include the entrapment planned by the conspirators against Daniel (Exod. 20:16; cf. 23:1; Lev. 19:16). The Mosaic *lex talionis* (law of retaliation) stipulates "life for life, eye for eye, tooth for tooth" (Deut. 19:21).

> If a malicious witness comes forward to accuse someone of wrongdoing, then both parties to the dispute shall appear before the Lord, before the priests and judges who are in office in those days. . . . If the witness is a false witness, . . . then you shall do to the false witness just as the false witness had meant to do to the other. (Deut. 19:16-19)

The fate of the conspirators and their wives and children is in harmony with OT understandings of family solidarity in guilt and punishment. That families should perish with offenders was in those times an accepted practice. This is illustrated in OT stories about Korah (Num. 16), Achan (Josh. 7), Saul's house (2 Sam. 21:1-9), and Haman (Esther 9:13, 25). Guilt was thought to affect a whole social group, especially the family. In Achan's case, other family members were accessories, surely knowing and then not reporting that Achan hid the forbidden booty under their tent floor. The fate of the conspirators against Daniel is an example of this ancient viewpoint of solidarity in guilt, that families should suffer with offenders.

Yet Amaziah, in connection with the death of his father (2 Kings 14:1-6), followed another Mosaic rule modifying this ancient belief of corporate guilt:

> Parents shall not be put to death for their children, nor shall children be put to death for their parents; only for their own crimes may persons be put to death. (Deut. 24:16; cf. Jer. 31:29-30; Ezek. 18)

The punishment on the conspirators also corresponds with the prophecy of Isaiah that as Israel is delivered, the oppressor will be destroyed in God's judgment:

> Yes, all who are incensed against you
>   shall be ashamed and disgraced;
> those who strive against you
>   shall be as nothing and shall perish. (Isa. 41:11)

Various proverbs also speak to the fate of such conspirators in God's righteous dealings:

> Whoever digs a pit will fall into it,
> and a stone will come back on the one who starts it rolling. (Prov. 26:27)
> Those who mislead the upright into evil ways
> will fall into pits of their own making. (Prov. 28:10)
> A false witness will not go unpunished,
> and a liar will not escape. (Prov. 19:5)
> Their mischief returns upon their own heads,
> and on their own heads their violence descends. (Ps. 7:14-16)

Jesus teaches his followers a higher way than seeking "eye for an eye" retribution. "Do not resist an evildoer. . . . Love your enemies and pray for those who persecute you" (Matt. 5:38-48). Paul also warns believers against taking vengeance into their own hands. "Leave room for the wrath of God. . . . If your enemies are hungry, feed them. . . . Do not be overcome by evil, but overcome evil with good" (Rom. 12:19-21; cf. Deut. 32:35; Prov. 25:21-22). Paul does recognize that the governing authority acts as "the servant of God to execute wrath on the wrongdoer" (Rom. 13:4). In Daniel 6:24 the governing authority, King Darius, gives the *command* that the conspirators are to suffer the same penalty they have devised for Daniel. Yet it is good to note that the story does not have Daniel clamoring for that sentence against his enemies.

Daniel and Jesus

In the detailed account of events leading to Daniel being cast into the den of lions, some interpreters have seen parallels between Daniel and Jesus. Both were victims of conspiracy and innocent of wrongdoing. Both prayed before arrests and faced rulers who sought ways to release them (but who in the end honored their laws). Both were "entombed" with a stone that was sealed. In both cases, God intervened and vindicated those who trusted in him. Daniel trusted in his God (6:23). Jesus trusted his Father (1 Pet. 2:21-24).

As interesting as such parallels might be, the analogy falls far short. Jesus died and was raised. In Daniel's case, he reported that an angel shut the lions' mouths. In Jesus' life, death, resurrection, and ascension is the watershed of history. Through Jesus, God brings victory over Satan, sin, and death. Rather than to become overly enamored with Daniel as a prototype of Jesus Christ, it is better to focus primarily on Daniel's faithful obedience. Daniel in many ways illustrates the discipleship to which Jesus called others: "Follow me" (John 1:43; 12:26; 21:19, 22).

The Living God

In the stories of Daniel, various names appear for *the God of Daniel* (6:26), *of Shadrach, Meshach, and Abednego* (3:29), and of the loyal Israelites (11:32). God is the *God of heaven* (2:18-19, 37, 44), *God of gods and Lord of kings* (2:47). God is *the Most High God* (3:26; 4:2; 5:18, 21) but most often simply *the Most High* (4:17, 24-25, 32, 34; 7:18, 22, 25, 27). God is *King of heaven* (4:37) and *the Ancient One* (7:13). In the story of Daniel's deliverance from the lions' den, the most significant of the names appears: *the living God* (6:26).

The living God is a most important name in both OT and NT. The "living God" is the one who spoke on the mountain in the midst of fire when the law was given (Deut. 5:26). The "living God" demonstrated his presence by driving out the tribes before Israel after they crossed the Jordan (Josh. 3:10). When Israel was confronted by Goliath, David asked, "Who is this uncircumcised Philistine that he should defy the armies of the living God?" (1 Sam. 17:26).

According to the prophet Jeremiah (10:10),

> The Lord is the true God;
> he is the living God and the everlasting King.

This name appears in Jeremiah's poem mocking false gods and idols. The poem describes the work of making and decorating idols. In contrast to the living God, idols are like "scarecrows in a cucumber field" (10:5). They cannot move or walk. They cannot speak. They cannot do evil or good. The teaching attributed to them is "stupid and foolish" (10:8). Isaiah, too, ridicules the worship of idols. He contrasts the creator God (Isa. 42:5) who carries his people, with Babylonian gods that are heavy loads on weary beasts and cannot save themselves or those who worship them (Isa. 46:1-8).

The name *living God* implies much more than simply "God is alive, not dead." The living God acts, is conscious and aware of what is going on, and is powerful (Dan. 5:23). This God controls the affairs of humans and nations, raises up, and puts down. This God judges and blesses. When humans are arrogant, the living God is able to humble them. If humans overestimate their power and defy his rule, God is able to intervene and to humble them. When humans are overwhelmed and in dire need, God is a refuge and strength. Darius learns and proclaims that, in contrast to his gods, *the living God* rules forever. This God rescues and saves, performing signs and wonders.

In the NT, the name "living God," fills a prominent place. In his great confession, Simon Peter replies, "You are the Messiah, the Son of the living God" (Matt. 16:16).

At Lystra, Paul and Barnabas are thought to be the gods Hermes and Zeus. In great consternation Paul cries out,

> Why are you doing this? We are mortals just like you, and we bring you good news, that you should turn from these worthless things to the living God, who made the heaven and the earth and the sea and all that is in them. (Acts 14:15)

The church is "the temple of the living God" (2 Cor. 6:16). "The church of the living God" is "the pillar and bulwark of truth" (1 Tim. 3:15). The church is composed of both Jews and Gentiles, who together are called "children of the living God" (Rom. 9:26).

The living God is "the savior of all people" (1 Tim. 4:10). The blood of Christ will "purify our conscience from dead works to worship the living God" (Heb. 9:14).

The believers at Thessalonica "turned to God from idols, to serve the living and true God" (1 Thess. 1:9). Believers are to take care lest they "have an evil, unbelieving heart that turns away from the living God" (Heb. 3:12), since "it is a fearful thing to fall into the hands of the living God" (10:31). The believer's pilgrimage is to the city of the living God (12:22). On the way, "the seal of the living God" gives protection to "the servants of our God" (Rev. 7:2-3).

Darius writes to *all peoples and nations of every language* that the God of Daniel is *the living God, enduring forever. His kingdom shall never be destroyed, and his dominion has no end.* The *God of Daniel* is the central figure of history. The past, the present, and the future are in his hands (Dan. 6:25-27).

The poems of the book of Daniel, whether expressed by Daniel (2:20-23) or by kings (4:3, 34-35, 37; 6:26-27), emphasize the greatness of God. There is no emperor so great that he is not under the control of the living God. To be deported to a strange land raised questions in the minds of Israelite exiles about the power of *their God* (11:32). In their testing, they needed reassurance. Darius's letter announces the climactic revelation about the God of Israel: This God is the living God! Because this God is living, he can reveal mysteries, humble arrogant rulers, and deliver the faithful. The Most High God is the living God.

THE TEXT IN THE LIFE OF THE CHURCH

Martyr Stories

The story of Daniel in the lions' den and the story of Shadrach, Meshach, and Abednego (chap. 3) are like martyr stories. Believers are ready to die rather than to deny their faith. Faithful persons are confronted by demands of the state which if obeyed, would compromise their worship of God. In the case of Shadrach, Meshach, and Abednego, the king demands that they worship the statue. In the case of Daniel, the king requires him to cease praying to his God for thirty days. Shadrach, Meshach, and Abednego are thrown into a *furnace of blazing fire;* Daniel is thrown into a den of lions.

The focus of these stories is not on miraculous deliverance. Instead, the focus is on the readiness of persons to accept whatever is threatened while they refuse to deny any part of their faith. When deliverance takes place, the focus is not on God's intervention; instead, the focus is upon what is learned about God.

Too often these stories have been mishandled, especially with children. After the story of Daniel in the lions' den is told, the storyteller will say, "Now boys and girls, if you pray like Daniel, then God will also keep you safe!" The ability of God to deliver is not in question. Shadrach, Meshach, and Abednego as well as Daniel know that God is always able (3:17; 6:20). The three young men, however, express the appropriate stance: If God delivers, well and good! If he does not deliver, well and good! Whatever happens, we will be faithful (3:17-18).

In telling these stories today, the church must exercise caution lest the relationship with God is reduced to a triumphal, commercial transaction: if you do this, then God will do that! This is especially true in matters related to health, where some say, "If you have faith, then healing will occur." When God intervenes, it is to accomplish his purposes, not ours. God says to Moses, "I will be gracious to whom I will be gracious, and will show mercy on whom I will show mercy" (Exod. 33:19). Concerning this, the apostle Paul comments, "So it depends not on man's will or exertion, but on God who shows mercy" (Rom. 9:16).

In the early days of the church, "Herod laid violent hands upon some who belonged to the church. He had James, the brother of

John, killed with the sword" (Acts 12:1-2). When Herod saw that this pleased the Jews, he arrested and imprisoned Peter. But God intervened. Like Daniel, Peter says, "The Lord has sent his angel and rescued me from the hands of Herod" (12:11). Both James and Peter were persons of faith; yet one died, the other lived. The author of Hebrews writes of those who "by faith" "escaped the edge of the sword" or "were killed with the sword" (Heb. 11:34, 37).

Martyr stories have always been a source of strength for the persecuted. Graphic details of the martyrs of a Jewish mother's seven sons are provided in the 2 Maccabees. The mother cheers on her sons to remain resolute as one by one they face death by torture (2 Macc. 7). Martyr stories have been important in the wider history of the Christian church and also among the Anabaptists of the sixteenth century. The Anabaptists saw themselves, like Daniel, caught in the conflict between two kingdoms, the kingdom of God and the kingdom of Satan. They also saw this as a bloody battle. The death of saints was seen as a victory, and as a testimony against the persecutors. They looked forward to the day when the situation would be reversed, when persecutors would be judged and the anticipated victory of Jesus Christ would be full and complete (Braght).

At the heart of the Anabaptists' willingness to die for their faith was the cross. Anabaptists believed that they must accept the cup which Jesus drank and be baptized with the baptism with which he was baptized (Mark 10:38-39). For them, that baptism often meant death. They knew that Paul alluded to baptism as dying (Rom. 6:3-5). Conrad Grebel wrote to Thomas Müntzer, September 5, 1524, "True believing Christians are sheep among wolves, sheep for the slaughter. They must be baptized in anguish and tribulation, persecution, suffering, and death, tried in fire, and must reach the fatherland of eternal rest not by slaying the physical but the spiritual. They use neither worldly sword nor war" (*Sources:* 290).

The outstanding writing by Menno Simons on this subject is in "The Cross of the Saints," 1554. The tract contains six sections:

1. Who the Persecutors Are
2. Why They Persecute the Saints
3. Biblical Examples (OT, NT, with Daniel, and the three in the furnace)
4. Excuses of the Persecutors
5. The Blessings of Cross-bearing
6. Promises for Those Bearing the Cross (Menno Simons: 579-622)

The theme of martyrdom is found in numerous Anabaptist hymns. A good example is that of Jorg Wagner (1527) found in the *Ausbund* (1564), "He who would follow Christ."

> Christ's servants follow him to death,
> And give their body life and breath
> On cross and rack and pyre.
> As gold is tried and purified
> They stand the test of fire. (*The Mennonite Hymnal:* 344)

Thieleman Jansz van Braght has made an outstanding collection of martyr stories, first published in 1660 in Dutch with a long title and now known as *Martyrs Mirror*. In the preface of this book the author identifies three characteristics of true Christians. They are (1) "baptist minded," (2) defenseless or nonresistant, and (3) ready to take torture and death for the sake of Jesus. The author compiled stories of martyrs from the time of Jesus through the Middle Ages. Then he recorded martyr stories of Anabaptist men and women from 1524 to 1660. The stories of Daniel 3 and 6 are often mentioned as inspiration for the Anabaptist martyrs (Braght: 1-1157; see index).

The Anabaptists believed that martyrdom was the lot of God's people from the beginning of time. God's people suffered from the time of Abel. For them, the cross was the event at the center of all history and a principle guiding the way God's people should act.

Suffering was seen apocalyptically. It was part of that great drama, the conflict between God and Satan. The forces of Satan—the dragon, the beast, the false prophets—are let loose against the defenseless flock of the faithful. In the midst of suffering and death, believers looked forward to God's final acts in history when God would set things right. The persecutors will be judged as "every eye will see him, even those who pierced him; and on his account all the tribes of earth will wail. So it is to be. Amen" (Rev. 1:7).

The concept of martyrdom is at the root of nonresistance. The concept of believers baptism carries the idea of following the Lord even in death. Those who accept baptism are to expect death. First John 5:8 has often served as a baptismal text. There are three witnesses—the Spirit, the water, and the blood. In this text, those sixteenth-century Christians observed that the one being baptized had received the new life in the Spirit. The water called attention to forgiveness, washing away of sin, and a new way of life. The blood referred to faithfulness to Christ "even unto death" (Matt. 26:38; Rev. 2:10), since baptism involved the cross.

Baptism implied readiness to suffer. This is what the Swiss Brethren meant in the term *Gelassenheit*, which they understood as yieldedness to God, readiness to follow Jesus as a lamb among wolves (Luke 10:3), willingness to love enemies and pray for persecutors (Matt. 5:44-48). Thus readiness to be a martyr and practicing nonresistance were two sides of the same coin for them. They were ready to suffer; they rejected vengeance and the use of the sword.

For troubled people, the biblical and Christian martyr stories have always been a source of strength. The real-life example of believers ready to die rather than to compromise faith is stronger than a proposition, whether as an admonition or the declaration of a principle. With such living and dying models, more youth and adults can "dare to be a Daniel" and stand firm in "the faith that was once for all entrusted to the saints" (Jude 3).

Daniel 7:1-28

The Rule of God, His Angels, and His People: Daniel's Dream

PREVIEW

Without question, chapter seven is the high point in the book of Daniel. It is pivotal in that it completes the Aramaic tract to the nations (2:4b—7:28) and at the same time with its vision (or dream), sets the stage for the visions that follow. The stories in chapters 1-6 relate to Daniel and his friends. The visions beginning with chapter 7 are reported to have come to Daniel in his old age.

The tract to the nations speaks to *all* (or *any*) peoples, nations, and languages (3:29; 4:1; 6:25; 7:14). It presents truths about the God of Israel announced by the great leaders of the times, growing out of their experience with this God: The God of Israel is *God of gods and Lord of kings and a revealer of mysteries* (2:47). No other god *is able to deliver in this way* (3:29). *All his works are truth, and his ways are justice; and he is able to bring low those who walk in pride* (4:37). *He is the living God. . . . He delivers and rescues, he works signs in heaven and on earth* (6:26-27).

In many respects, the tract to the nations is an offer of grace. The testimonies are invitations to all peoples, nations, and languages to know and to honor this God.

The tract tells the peoples of the world who God is and what he does. At the same time, it speaks to his saints, encouraging them and giving them hope in times of exile and great persecution.

Chapter 7 is also a fitting introduction to the visions and themes found in chapters 8–12. In each of the visions, a heavenly messenger provides understanding. In chapter 7, this figure is an attendant standing in the heavenly court (7:16). In the two succeeding visions, the archangel Gabriel provides understanding (8:16; 9:22). In the final vision, a celestial being (Gabriel) comes to make Daniel understand (10:10-14).

Each of the visions tells of the coming of a dreadful king who will oppress the people of God (7:24-25; 8:23-24; 9:27; 11:29-45). This is the meaning or the truth concerning the fourth beast (7:19). The activity of this evil king is developed in each of the visions. Each vision indicates that God's people will be severely oppressed for a limited time (7:25; 8:14; 9:27; 12:7). Each of the visions predicts the end of this arrogant king (7:11; 8:25; 9:27; 11:45). In the visions that follow chapter 7, God's offer of grace to the world is rejected by the kings of the world. However, in the midst of tempestuous international affairs, there are the faithful, the people of God, the people of grace, who live lives of holiness and peace, led by *the wise* (11:33).

Following the introductory note (7:1), the dream or vision begins. The interpretation is part of and within the total dream. The dream moves back and forth between earth and heaven, between the horrible and the sublime, between violence and serenity, and between human chaos and divine order.

The vision begins with four vicious beasts rising out of the sea (7:2-8). After the wild antics of the fourth beast are reported, the scene suddenly shifts to heaven, to the throne room of *the Ancient of Days* or *the Ancient One*, where beauty, peace, and order prevail, and where judgment is about to commence (7:9-10, RSV, NRSV).

Just as suddenly, the scene shifts back to earth. Divine decrees are swiftly executed. The fourth beast is slain. The power to rule is stripped away from the other three, though their lives are spared for an indefinite period (7:11-12).

With the execution of the heavenly sentences on the earthly kings, the dream returns again to the heavenly court. A mysterious figure, *one like a son of man, like a human being*, appears before *the Ancient of Days, the Ancient One* (7:13, RSV, NRSV). He is given a glorious, universal rule in an eternal, invincible kingdom.

Within the dream, Daniel asks a heavenly attendant for an interpretation (7:15-16). Daniel is given a general explanation: *As for these four great beasts, four kings shall arise out of the earth. But the holy ones of the Most High shall receive the kingdom and possess the kingdom forever—forever and ever* (7:17-18).

Not satisfied with this brief statement, Daniel requests and receives further information about the fourth beast (7:19-23). The beast is soon destroyed, and in turn *the kingship and dominion and the greatness of the kingdoms under the whole heaven shall be given to the people of the holy ones of the Most High; their kingdom shall be an everlasting kingdom, and all dominions shall serve and obey them* (7:24-27). The chapter ends with a postscript indicating the completion of the dream and Daniel's response (7:28).

In the story of Nebuchadnezzar's humiliation, the theme, *the Most High is sovereign over the kingdom of mortals*, appears three times (4:17, 25, 32). In a similar way, chapter 7 repeats the theme, *the holy ones of the Most High shall receive the kingdom* (7:18, 22, 27).

Too often interpreters have unduly concentrated on the meaning of the fourth beast and its actions. However, the focus of the heavenly attendant's interpretation is upon *the Ancient One*, upon the *one like a son of man (human being)*, and upon the universal rule and kingdom given to this figure (7:14), to *the holy ones of the Most High* (7:18, 21), and eventually also to *the people of the holy ones of the Most High* (7:27). God rules. Tyrants are destroyed. The chaos that results from the kingdoms of this world exercising their power is not the last word. The court of heaven sits in judgment on the beasts of history. They are destroyed, while the faithful saints receive the rule and dominion that only the Most High can give.

No greater message of hope could be given to a people in exile, to a people enduring bitter persecution, or to the faithful today living in the midst of violence, bloodshed, and corruption!

OUTLINE

Introduction, 7:1

Description of Daniel's Dream, 7:2-14

7:2-8	Four Great Beasts (on Earth)
7:9-10	The Ancient One (in the Heavenly Court)
7:11-12	The Beasts Judged (on Earth)
7:13-14	One Like a Son of Man (in the Heavenly Court)

The Interpretation of the Dream, 7:15-27

7:15-16	Daniel's Condition and Request
7:17-18	A General Interpretation
7:19-22	Daniel Asks About the Fourth Beast
7:23-27	A Detailed Interpretation

Postscript, 7:28

The structure of chapter 7 follows a fourfold organizational pattern: First, an introduction (7:1). Second, the dream (7:2-14). Third, the interpretation (7:15-27). Fourth, a postscript (7:28). Each of these sections in turn has four parts, leading to an alternate outline:

1. The Introduction:
    - 1.1 The date (7:1)
    - 1.2 The reception of a vision (7:1)
    - 1.3 Place of reception (7:1)
    - 1.4 Decision to write the vision (7:1)
2. The Dream
    - 2.1 On earth (7:2-8)
    - 2.2 In the heavenly court (7:9-10)
    - 2.3 On earth (7:11-12)
    - 2.4 In the heavenly court (7:13-14)
3. The Interpretation
    - 3.1 Daniel's request (7:15-16)
    - 3.2 Heavenly attendant's response (7:17-18)
    - 3.3 Daniel's request (7:19-22)
    - 3.4 Heavenly attendant's response (7:23-27)
4. A Postscript
    - 4.1 Notice of completion (7:28)
    - 4.2 Daniel's thoughts (7:28)
    - 4.3 His physical condition (7:28)
    - 4.4 His use of material (7:28)

In addition there are: four winds (7:2); four beasts, which are four kings (7:3, 17) or four kingdoms (7:23); four wings (7:6); and four heads (7:6). A group of four is a common literary device in Hebrew literature (see notes on 2:36-43).

EXPLANATORY NOTES

Introduction 7:1

Daniel's dream occurs in the first year of King Belshazzar. This would place it chronologically between the stories found in chapter 4 and chapter 5. *King Belshazzar of Babylon* died in 539 B.C. He had been placed in the position of responsibility by Nabonidus in his third year, around 554 B.C. (ANET: 313). *[Nabonidus, p. 291].* Daniel has this dream, therefore, about fifteen years before the Persian invasion in 539 B.C. During the days of Belshazzar, Daniel is put on the shelf, so to speak, as a civil servant. During these days of less activity, Daniel receives a disturbing vision. The dream is so vivid, so disturbing, and with its God-given interpretation so far-reaching in scope and importance that Daniel *wrote down the dream* (7:1). This is said only for this vision in the book of Daniel. It is written so that every detail of the dream with its interpretation, which was also part of the dream, will not be lost. What follows is what Daniel *saw* (7:2). This is a recurring theme: *I saw* (7:2, 7, 13), *I watched/looked* (7:4, 6, 9, 11, 13, 21).

Description of Daniel's Dream 7:2-14

7:2-8 Four Great Beasts (on Earth)

As Daniel sleeps one night, he dreams that he is taken to the shore of a great sea—possibly he stands on a cliff overlooking the Mediterranean Sea, a familiar scene from his boyhood. The mention of night gives a sense of mystery and fear.

As he looks out over the sea, the *four winds of heaven* are *stirring up the great sea*. The four winds of heaven appear three times in Daniel (7:2; 8:8; 11:4; cf. Rev. 7:1). Here the winds relate with the four beasts (kings; 7:2, 17), later with the *male goat* (another king; 8:8), and with a powerful *warrior king* (11:3-4). The four winds of heaven often refer to the four points of the compass: north, south, east, and west. The meaning may be deeper than this. Since the four winds of heaven appear in connection with earthly kings, the term also suggests divine action. Since *the Most High has sovereignty over the kingdom of mortals, and gives it to whom he will* (4:25), *the four winds of heaven* are a sign of his universal rule over the whole earth.

The four winds of heaven are *stirring up the great sea*. The picture is that of a whirlwind churning the waters. The sea symbolizes that which is limitless, restless, dangerous, and uncontrollable. In this dream, the sea represents humanity, those on the earth (7:17). Isaiah likens the commotion of the nations to the roaring of mighty waters (Isa. 17:12-13; cf. 57:20-21), as did Jeremiah, who compares cruel and merciless invaders to the roaring of the sea (Jer. 6:23).

As the winds of heaven churn the waters, *four great beasts* come *up out of the sea*, "manifestations of primeval chaos" (ABD, 2:32). It is not unusual for animals and birds to symbolize nations (as in Ezek.

17:3-10; 19:2). The tribes of Israel are symbolized by animals—Judah as a lion, Issachar a donkey, Naphtali a deer, Benjamin a wolf (Gen. 49; cf. the former Soviet Union symbolized by a bear, the USA by an eagle). For Israelites, the sea is the home of monsters of chaos: Rahab, the dragon, and Leviathan (Isa. 27:1; 51:9; Ps. 74:13-14; 89:9-10; cf. Rev. 13:1). These beasts are awesome and terrible. Later the interpreter says the four beasts that emerge from the sea are *four kings* that will *arise out of the earth* (7:17). Thus in a general way, the four beasts parallel the four kingdoms of Nebuchadnezzar's dream (2:1-49; see notes on 2:36-43).

The motif of four kingdoms is certainly at home in the book of Daniel. That animals symbolize kingdoms is a notion also found in 1 Enoch 85–90. But it remains debatable how the two books are related. Likely 1 Enoch is dependent on Daniel. Some have wanted to compare the descriptions of the animals to Babylonian engravings of animals, but the two have only minimal features in common.

The **first beast** is *like a lion* with *eagles' wings.* The lion is the king of beasts, and the eagle the king of birds. The lion symbolizes majesty, the eagle power. The combination of the lion and eagle indicate that this king has great dominion and strength. The prophet Ezekiel likens Babylon to an eagle (Ezek. 17:3-14).

As Daniel looks, *its wings were plucked off* and *it was lifted up from the ground and made to stand on two feet like a human being; and a human mind was given to it* (7:4). It is generally agreed that the first beast refers to Nebuchadnezzar and the Neo-Babylonian empire. His kingdom was stripped from him (4:32) until he lifted his eyes to heaven. Then he resumed his posture as a human and his mind and kingdom were restored (4:36). As Nebuchadnezzar was the *head of gold* (2:38), so in Daniel's dream, the first beast also stands for Nebuchadnezzar.

The **second beast** is *like a bear. It was raised up on one side, had three tusks in its mouth among its teeth and it was told, "Arise, devour many bodies"* (7:5). The Daniel 7:16 interpreter of the dream does not indicate which kings are symbolized by the beasts. How much time and energy of God's people would have been conserved had the heavenly interpreter told Daniel, "This beast represents that king." Perhaps in the wisdom of God the kings are not named so that Daniel's dream can be applied and reapplied across the centuries. On and on, the winds of heaven stir up the events of history. Kings and kingdoms rise; in their arrogance, power, and pride, they challenge even heaven, only to be brought down in humiliation and defeat.

Meanwhile, God accomplishes his purposes through his *holy ones* (angels) and his *people* (7:18, 27; cf. 8:13, 24).

The kings of chapter 7 may represent the same kingdoms alluded to in chapter 2. As in chapter 2, it is not clear whether these kingdoms rise sequentially or simultaneously. As the stone reduced all kingdoms to powder at the same time (2:35), so judgment on the four beasts occurs simultaneously (7:11-12). When attempting to identify historically which beast represents which kingdom, there is wisdom in being tentative rather than dogmatic.

Tentatively, the second beast, the bear, represents the Medes, who were prophesied to destroy Babylon (Jer. 51:11; Isa. 13:17-19; 21:2). By extension, one might count it as standing for the Medo-Persian empire. Cyrus himself was the grandson of a Mede (according to legend) and so would be part Persian and part Mede. He began his reign over the Persians around 559 B.C. as a vassal of the last king of the Medes, his maternal grandfather. He rebelled and in 550 B.C. conquered Media. Then in 539 B.C., Babylon fell before his army led by Gubaru the Mede (Darius?) and became part of the Medo-Persian empire (5:31; 6:8). *[Cyrus, p. 284.]* The three ribs or tusks may refer symbolically to the Babylonians, the Medes, and the Persians; or to individual kings. The bear is raised up on one side; perhaps this means that, after the Medes were conquered by the Persians under Cyrus, they played a less-significant role than the Persians in the Medo-Persian empire. Eventually there is a tendency to drop the reference to the Medes and refer to the Persian empire. The command *Arise, devour many bodies!* points to the expansion of the Medo-Persian empire, which eventually included territories now found in Egypt, Israel, Jordan, Syria, Turkey, Russia, Iraq, Pakistan, and Afghanistan.

The **third beast** is *like a leopard* with *four wings of a bird on its back and four heads; and dominion was given to it* (7:6). Note the dominance of *four*. Four winds, four beasts, and now four wings and four heads. The most plausible interpretation is to see in the four wings and four heads, an empire extending in all directions, the Persian empire. Dominion is *given to it;* this underscores a theme of the chapter, that God is over the human rulers (7:17, 25, 32). Some interpret the leopard as a sign for the Persian empire under four kings: Cyrus (Ezra 1:1), Ahasuerus (Ezra 4:6, Xerxes I), Artaxerxes (Ezra 4:7), and Darius the Persian (Neh. 12:22), all part of a Persian ruling house called the Achaemenids. These rulers extended the Persian empire from Egypt and Turkey on the west to the Indus Valley on the east; they were historically important for over two centuries, from 559 B.C., when Cyrus assumed power, until Alexander the Great overthrew Darius III in 330 B.C.

A common interpretation is to identify the leopard with the amazing career of Alexander the Great—but the Greeks seem to fit better for the fourth beast. *[Alexander the Great, p. 276.]* In 336 B.C. the youthful king invaded Asia Minor to liberate the Greeks residing there. He met and defeated Darius at Issus in 333 B.C. and then advanced rapidly to the east. He took Tyre, Sidon, Gaza, and Damascus. Alexander died at a young age in Babylon in 323 B.C. His empire was divided among four of his generals. Of particular significance to the book of Daniel are successors to two of these generals: the Ptolemies ruled Egypt and until 200 B.C. controlled Palestine; the Seleucids reigned over the territory from Syria to the east and dominated Palestine from soon after 200 B.C. until the Jews gained political independence in 142 B.C. The leopard, therefore, might suggest Alexander the Great establishing his empire with lightning speed, symbolized by the *four wings.* Following Alexander's untimely death, his empire was divided among four leaders, Cassander, Lysimachus, Seleucus, and Ptolemy, perhaps the *four heads.*

The dragon-like **fourth beast** is described in great detail. Daniel mentions again that it is night (7:2, 7). Darkness underscores the terror and foreboding aroused by the appearance of the fourth beast. Its description is threefold: *terrifying and dreadful and exceedingly strong* (7:7). There is no creature in the animal world to which the beast can be likened. No known animal is as vicious, destructive, or ruthless as this one. This beast engages in no constructive enterprise of any kind. All its activities are carried out by its military—the great iron teeth which chew up and destroy everything in its path. Whatever it does not chew up and spit out in little pieces, it pushes over and stomps with its feet for the sheer joy of destruction.

This fourth beast is *different from all the beasts that preceded it* (7:7) and likely stands for the Greeks and especially the Seleucids. Whereas the actions of kings symbolized by the lion, the bear, and the leopard may not be defensible, yet their behavior can be understood and explained. Not so with the fourth beast. Its evil is so widespread and its depravity so pervasive that there is nothing with which to compare it. An ordinary beast has two horns; this one has *ten horns*. In other words, its ability to attack, to gore, to kill, and destroy is five times greater than anything known previously.

In the midst of these ten horns (evil multiplied), an eleventh one sprouts up. This small horn grows and replaces three of the horns that are *plucked up by the roots* (7:8), leaving eight horns. The emerging horn becomes the symbol of evil, like the "eighth" horn of Revelation 17:11. In apocalyptic literature, numbers have significance. *[Apocalyptic Literature, p. 280.]* Seven is fullness or perfection. Since six is one less than seven, it suggests deficit or failure to attain completeness. Six then is seen as evil. Thus 666 is evil compounded (Rev. 13:18, likely referring to Nero). In the same way, eight is one more than perfection (seven plus one). It means superabundance, of good or of evil. In Revelation 21:8, those with eight types of evil behavior are placed in the lake of fire. Thus eight horns befit this horrible, evil beast of Daniel 7. This latest horn has *eyes* like humans and a *mouth speaking arrogantly*. With its eyes it probes every nook and cranny, like the secret police of totalitarian regimes. It brags, boasts, lies, and threatens with an arrogance that defies description, and it is the model for the beast found in Revelation 13:1-10.

This dragon-like beast is not clearly identified. Some believe it represents an evil political regime or figure of Daniel's day. The most plausible interpretation is that it represents the Greeks, and the ten horns are for ten rulers succeeding Alexander the Great, especially the line of the Seleucids, with the dominant horn speaking for the great oppressor of the Jews, Antiochus IV Epiphanes. Thus the vision of four beasts reflects a widespread belief that the Near East had been governed by four kingdoms: Babylonia (replacing Assyria), Media, Persia, and Greece (ABD, 2:30).

Other interpreters believe the fourth beast represents the Roman empire or a figure who will emerge in the end times, the antichrist. *[Antichrist, p. 277.]* Some think it is a sign of especially demonic political leaders who emerge in history. They are ruthless and attain great power, often over vast domains, destroying not only enemies but also their own people and structures of society. Then they are brought low. Recent examples might include Hitler, Idi Amin, or Saddam Hussein (see notes on 7:11-12).

There are vigorous supporters for each of these views. No position is without questionable details. The identification of the fourth beast often reflects an attempt to establish a system of thought or to support the bias of an interpreter. The text itself simply does not say which king was symbolized by the fourth beast. If the leopard means Alexander the Great's empire, and if the fourth beast represents another empire following Alexander's or the Greeks, and if there were ten kings before the exceedingly evil king emerged, then a lengthy period of time is intended either from Daniel's time or from that of Alexander the Great.

Most plausibly, the dream points to Alexander and the Greeks as the fourth beast and to Antiochus IV Epiphanes (175-164 B.C.) as the horn *speaking arrogantly*. Antiochus conquered Egypt, then under three rulers, and so plucked up *three of the earlier horns* (7:8). He rose to power through murder and violence and led the first organized massacre of Jews in history (although Esther 3 and 9 report one attempted). Thus he fits the picture of a king wearing out *the holy ones* (angels) and prevailing over them and the righteous people they represent (7:21, 25, 27). The goal of Antiochus was to unite the world with a common language (Greek), a common king (himself), and a common religion.

Accounts of Antiochus's dreadful actions are found in 1 and 2 Maccabees. His forces killed those who possessed "the book of the covenant" or kept the Mosaic Law (1 Macc. 1:57). They sacrificed pigs on the altar of the temple (1 Macc. 1:47, 54; cf. Dan. 9:27) and converted it for the worship of Zeus (2 Macc. 6:2). His agents hung circumcised babies from the necks of their mothers and paraded them around the city before hurling them to death from the wall (1 Macc. 1:60-61; 2 Macc. 6:10). Antiochus IV Epiphanes could well be the *mouth speaking arrogantly*. (See notes on 7:23-27.) *[Antiochus Epiphanes, p. 279.]*

While the fourth beast is mouthing *great things* (RSV), the scene shifts abruptly from earth to heaven, to the heavenly court. As always, the focus is not on the raging kings in the sea of humanity; instead, the focus is on the King of heaven and what he is doing.

7:9-10 The Ancient One (in the Heavenly Court)

The sea of humanity is ravaged by beastly rulers who maintain their position through destruction and military might. The real hope for humanity is elsewhere, in the heavenly throne room with *the Ancient of Days* (RSV) or *the Ancient One* (NRSV), and one *like a son of man* (RSV), *like a human being* (7:13). The sights and sounds of verses 2-8 contrast strikingly with those in 9-10. One moves from a night of horror, violence, and commotion on earth to brilliant heavenly light with beauty, peace, and order.

In the dream, Daniel looks into heaven itself. As he watches, *thrones were set in place* for the assembly of the heavenly court (cf. Job 1:6). Daniel's attention is caught by an elderly figure, *the Ancient One* or *the Ancient of Days* (NRSV, RSV; 7:13, 22). For this term, capitalization indicates deity in the KJV, RSV, and NRSV, but some modern translations differ; JB translates it as *one of great age.* We can assume that this is God himself. The sacred name, Yahweh (LORD), or the name Adonai (Lord) is not used here as in Daniel's prayer in chapter 9. The elderly one *took his throne* as a judge (7:9; cf. 1 Kings 22:19-22; Isa. 6:1-9), surrounded by others of his heavenly court on *thrones* of judgment. In the OT, the others who share in this decision making and judging are *holy ones*, angels (see notes on 4:9-18 and below). In the NT, believers share this role now in the church and later on a wider basis in the fulfillment of God's kingdom (cf. Matt. 18:18; 19:28; Luke 22:30; 1 Cor. 4:8; 6:3; Rev. 20:4).

Some have noted similarities between *the Ancient One* in Daniel and a Canaanite myth about El of the Ugaritic pantheon. In the late 1920s, archaeologists discovered literature from the fourteenth century B.C. at Ugarit in ancient Phoenicia. In stories about deities found on these tablets, several portray an old deity, El, "father of years." This chief god El, gray-haired and gray-bearded, is greatly venerated. Baal, "rider of the cloud," is his son. In the story, Yamm, "sea," tries to unseat Baal, in defiance not unlike that of the beasts in Daniel's vision. Baal, however, slays Yamm the aggressor and, as one destined for kingship, has a temple-palace built for himself by El's permission. Here Baal takes his seat as king of the earth. Yet there are significant differences: in Daniel 7, the signs of chaos are from human kings, not other gods; and resolution is provided through a court scene rather than a battle (7:9, 22, 26; ABD, 2:32).

This story in turn has links with a Babylonian myth *Enuma Elish*, which also tells of the rebellion of some monsters arising from the ancient ocean, of the destruction of a giant monster figure whose body is split to form heaven and earth, and of the destroyer being given a royal position governing heaven and earth. The motifs of rebellion and of a fatherlike deity found in Daniel are not strange in the context of the ancient Near Eastern world. To seek to establish direct links between these myths and Daniel raises problems, but it is possible that such myths may have provided background for the vision.

The description of *the Ancient One* in Daniel is highly symbolic. To take one's seat means that judgment is to begin. *His clothing was white as snow* and *the hair of his head like pure wool*, suggesting heavenly purity and majesty. In the transfiguration, Jesus' garments "became dazzling white" (Mark 9:2-8). The angel at the tomb on the resurrection morning had "raiment white as snow" (Matt. 28:3).

Fire accompanies the presence of God: *his throne was fiery flames, its wheels were burning fire* (7:9). God met Moses at a blazing bush (Exod. 3:2). When the law was given at Mount Sinai, the Lord "descended upon it in fire" (19:16-25). In both OT and NT, "God is a devouring/consuming fire" (Deut. 4:24; Heb. 12:29). Since fire is used to purify metals (Mal. 3:2-3), the fiery flames suggest judgment. God acts to cleanse, to purify. The first step is judgment. Judgment upon the four beasts is to begin. The throne on which the Ancient One sits is modeled after a chariot, as in Ezekiel 1. This should comfort the Israelite exiles. God is ready to oversee and judge the whole earth, into which Jews are scattered. From this throne *a stream of fire issued*. It is this fire that burns the fourth beast (7:11).

Daniel observes that the throne room is a place of great activity with *a thousand thousands* serving him and with *ten thousand times ten thousand* standing ready to follow his command—the angelic *host of heaven* (8:10). In Hebrew poetry, ten thousand often appears as a parallel to thousand. Thus, the idea is not that exactly one hundred million are attending him. Rather, the thought is simply of a large number. This parallelism is found in Psalm 91:7: "A thousand may fall at your side, ten thousand at your right hand" (also, Deut. 32:30 [RSV]; 1 Sam. 18:7; Mic. 6:7).

According to the Bible, heaven keeps records, and *books* becomes a lively metaphor for that. *The court sat in judgment, and the books were opened* (7:10c). The nature of these books differs from reference to reference. One set of records contains information concerning the destiny of persons as decreed from the beginning of time: the book of life (Ps. 139:16; Rev. 13:8; 17:8). This is similar to the register of members of the theocratic community (Exod. 32:32-33; Ps. 69:28; Isa. 4:3; Dan. 12:1; Mal. 3:16). Another set contains legal records of the deeds of persons both good and bad, obedient and disobedient (Neh. 5:19 taken with 13:14; Isa. 65:6; Ps. 51:1; 109:14). There are three references to these books in Daniel (7:10; 10:21; 12:1). The book of truth (10:21) seems to refer to what is decreed by God, while 7:10 can refer both to what is decreed and to records of deeds, and 12:1 is a register of the righteous. The faithful ones gain hope and strength from their trust that heaven keeps accurate books, with no auditor needed. For the unfaithful, these books provide adequate grounds for God's actions in judgment.

The books are opened, showing that the judge has read all relevant material concerning the case before rendering his decision. These books likely contain briefs needed for the trial. The verdicts are recorded elsewhere, as *judgment* is *given* (7:22; cf. the Lord's indictment of Israel, Hos. 4–5).

The vision does not go into detail. The trial begins, but then the vision returns to earth. The action that follows indicates that a verdict has been reached and that sentences are imposed. In the next scene, the sentences are carried out. The divine judgment is further explained (7:22, 26).

7:11-12 The Beast Judged (on Earth)

Daniel's attention to the action in the heavenly court is diverted by the loud arrogant words of the latest horn of the fourth beast. Perhaps these are words of self-defense addressed to the judge. Considering the beast's power and position, he feels no need for an attorney.

As Daniel looks, *the beast was put to death, and its body destroyed and given over to be burned with fire.* Apparently, the sentence of the heavenly court is death for the fourth beast. There is no mention of human instrumentality in carrying out the sentence. Elsewhere in the book, angels are involved in executing God's sentences and in spiritual warfare (4:14, 17; 6:22; 7:21-22; 10:20-21; 12:1). God acts quickly; a consuming fire streams from his presence (7:10). The writer of Hebrews says, "He makes his angels [messengers] winds, and his servants flames of fire" (1:7 [from Ps. 104:4]). Those who "willfully persist in sin" have to face "a fearful prospect of judgment, and a fury of fire that will consume the adversaries" (Heb. 10:27). The beast's body is to be burned, a sign of extreme wickedness and final humiliation (Lev. 20:14; 21:9; Josh. 7:25).

A sentence is also carried out on the other three beasts. *Their dominion* is *taken away* (7:12). God gives dominion, and he takes it away. In chapter 2, the entire statue is destroyed; so here, the dominion of all four beasts is taken away—simultaneously in the dream, which encapsulates God's judgments in history. As pinnacles of power pass from one empire to the next, the peoples of nations remain. *Their lives were prolonged for a season and a time:* the peoples continue on indefinitely so that God can accomplish his purposes through them as he wills. If these beasts represent the Babylonian, Medo-Persian, and Greek empires, God allows their peoples to survive but without exercising dominion, as Isaiah foresees:

> I will soon lift up my hand to the nations,
> and raise my signal to the peoples;
> and they shall bring your sons in their bosom,
> and your daughters shall be carried on their shoulders.
> Kings shall be your foster fathers,

> and their queens your nursing mothers.
> With their faces to the ground they shall bow down to you,
> and lick the dust of your feet.
> Then you will know that I am the Lord;
> those who wait for me shall not be put to shame. (Isa. 49:22-23)

This oracle is realized in Daniel 7:26-27: *the greatness of the kingdoms under the whole heaven shall be given to the people of the holy ones [angels] of the Most High*.

The fourth beast with its horn speaking arrogantly has been variously identified as Antiochus IV Epiphanes, Rome, and in later times as Islam, the pope, communism, capitalism, the European Economic Community, and/or the antichrist. Since these beasts are not specifically identified, the vision can be applied and reapplied across the centuries as situations of great evil arise, flourish, and then are doomed. This pattern confronts the people of God from time to time and place to place. Daniel's vision affirms the rule of God in the midst of inhuman oppression. It is continually a source of confidence and hope.

7:13-14 One Like a Son of Man (in the Heavenly Court)

With judgment on the beasts carried out, the scene again changes abruptly, returning to the heavenly court. The scene is introduced with the line *I watched in the night visions*. This expression appears three times: first at the beginning of the vision (7:2), second when the horrible fourth beast emerges (7:7), and third with the coming of one *like a son of man* (7:13, RSV; NRSV: *human being*), the most important scene. Only poetry can convey the sublime nature of this scene.

Again there is great contrast. The beasts represent human empires in rebellion against God. Now appears one like a human being who comes *with the clouds of heaven*, suitable for a ruling figure. In the Exodus, the "glory of the Lord appeared in the cloud" (Exod. 16:10). At the giving of the law, God says to Moses, "I am going to come to you in a dense cloud" (Exod. 19:9). In the NT, when Jesus is transfigured, "A cloud came and overshadowed them; and they were terrified as they entered the cloud. Then from the cloud came a voice that said, 'This is my Son, my Chosen; listen to him!' " (Luke 9:34-35). At the ascension, Jesus "was lifted up, and a cloud took him out of their sight" (Acts 1:9). Clouds are associated with the coming of "the Son of Man" or Jesus Christ (Matt. 24:30; Mark 14:62; Acts 1:11; 1 Thess. 4:16-17; Rev. 1:7; see TBC, below).

There came one like a son of man (RSV), one in human likeness, *one like a human being* (NRSV) in appearance. This figure is *like* a human, in contrast to the kings (7:17), who are humans but appear beastly and demonic in their actions (7:3-8, 19-21), as the interpreter makes clear. Yet Nebuchadnezzar did regain some human dignity and mind (see notes on 7:4; 4:36). The one who comes in the clouds in human appearance, though traditionally identified as the Messiah in later interpretations, is likely (for the writer and the first readers) the archangel *Michael,* the patron angel of the Israelites (cf. 10:13, 21; 12:1). In Revelation 14:14, "one like the Son of Man," "seated on a cloud," is an angel, as in Daniel 7 (ABD, 2:32, 35). Similarly, Gabriel appears in human form but with angelic splendor (Dan. 8:15-16; 9:21; 10:5-6), and in Ezekiel, God appears as a man (1:26).

This scene takes place *after* the verdicts are reached and the sentences carried out on the four beasts. The Ancient One is on the throne. Then one like a son of man (human being) is *presented before him* for the purpose of receiving kingship. This one is given sovereignty like God's, *an everlasting dominion* (7:14; cf. 4:3). Here is assurance that history is more than the distressing, terrifying rule of beasts. The pretense of the beasts to wield absolute authority is cut short by heaven. Broken and silenced are the arrogance, greed, destruction, and loud mouth of the little horn. Now to one like a human figure, heaven grants true heavenly authority to be exercised on earth, ruling God's world as God would have it ruled. *All peoples, nations, and languages should serve him:* sovereignty belongs not to earthly kingdoms but to heaven.

This is the seventh appearance of the term *all peoples, nations, and languages* (3:4, 7, 29; 4:1; 5:19; 6:25; 7:14). All peoples, nations, and languages tremble before Nebuchadnezzar (5:19), but Nebuchadnezzar learns that the Most High God alone has lasting sovereignty (4:1-3). Darius also learns that the God of Daniel alone has everlasting sovereignty (6:26). Now all peoples, nations, and languages learn that this sovereignty is given to this humanlike figure, who will exercise sovereignty over all empires to follow.

Hence, although the one like a son of man is never called a king or Messiah in Daniel, he is given royal powers and prerogatives, and all nations will serve him (7:14). The bearer of that sovereignty is the enthroned heavenly patron of the people of God, who are suffering at the hands of kings rebelling against heaven (ABD, 6:138). The message is that the righteous will be delivered, and all nations will serve them, too (7:27). The sovereignty given this figure is **universal:**

all peoples, nations, and languages should serve him; **eternal:** *shall not pass away*; and **all powerful:** *shall never be destroyed* (7:14). Understandably, later Jewish and Christian interpreters of Daniel recognized messianic qualities in this figure coming with the clouds of heaven (see TBC, below).

The Interpretation of the Dream 7:15-27

The dream and its interpretation go together to make up the total dramatic vision. The vision embraces scenes on earth, scenes in heaven, Daniel's feelings, conversations with a heavenly attendant, and the dream's interpretation.

7:15-16 Daniel's Condition and Request

When Nebuchadnezzar awakens from his dream, his spirit is troubled, and he wants to know its meaning (2:1, 3). As Daniel's dream progresses he, too, is troubled and alarmed. In his dream Daniel sees heavenly beings, so he *approached one of the attendants* to find out *the truth*, the meaning of the dream. The heavenly attendant is not identified but might be the archangel Gabriel, who elsewhere provides understanding and can have *the appearance of a man* (8:15-16; 9:21). Thus *Gabriel, whom I had seen before in a vision* (9:21) might refer to this vision as well as the one of chapter 8. The heavenly attendant gives a brief answer to Daniel's request.

7:18-19 A General Interpretation

The heavenly attendant's answer falls into two parts. The vision moves back and forth between the beasts on earth and the heavenly court. The brief interpretation refers first to the beasts and then to the action in the heavenly court.

The interpretation of the four beasts is brief: *As for these four great beasts, four kings shall arise out of the earth* (7:17). The interpretation of the action in the heavenly court, however, takes a strange twist. In the heavenly court, dominion, glory, and kingdom are given to one like a son of man so that all peoples, nations, and languages should serve him. In the interpretation, however, *the holy ones of the Most High shall receive the kingdom, and possess the kingdom forever—forever and ever* (7:18; cf. 7:21, 27).

The coming kingdom takes away the kingship and power grasped by the beasts in their attempts to rule the world. There is only one kingship, and that is in the control of heaven. That kingship is given to a humanlike figure that came with the clouds. In the interpretation, the recipients of the kingdom are plural: *the holy ones* (Aramaic: *qadišin*, in 7:18, 22, 25, 27; cf. Hebrew: *qedošim*) *of the Most High* receive and possess the kingdom.

Elsewhere in the book of Daniel, *holy ones/watchers* refers to heavenly beings, angels (see notes on 4:9-18; 8:13; chapters 10–12; TLC on Dan. 8; cf. Deut. 33:2-3; Ps. 89:6-8; Zech. 14:5). The task of the holy ones is to convey divine messages, accompany the Lord, act at his direction, and protect Israel. When the writer refers to *people of the holy ones* (7:27; 8:24) or *holy people* (12:7), the word *people* (*'am*) is added to a form of the word *holy*. In the KJV and RSV, the term *the holy ones* is rendered as *the saints* in chapter 7. Early in Israel's history, the concept of a holy people was applied to the Israelites. The Lord says, "If you obey my voice and keep my covenant, you shall be my treasured possession out of all the peoples. Indeed, the whole earth is mine, but you shall be for me a priestly kingdom and a holy nation" (Exod. 19:5-6; cf. Dan. 12:7).

Likely *the holy ones* here are angels, led by Michael. These angels *receive the kingdom* and *possess the kingdom* through the gift of God, in behalf of and with *the people of the holy ones.* In receiving the kingdom there is no note of militarism nor of rule through human military might. The war with the arrogant horn is successful when the Ancient One gives judgment for them (7:21; 11:20-21; 12:1). The people of the holy ones are nonresistant and are *given* the kingdom (7:27). This is in contrast to some Hasideans (*hasidim* or holy ones) of 1 Maccabees 2:42-48 who become warriors; they offer themselves willingly for the law but organize an army to rescue the law out of the hands of the Gentiles and kings.

7:19-22 Daniel Asks About the Fourth Beast

In Daniel's dream, evil kingdoms are represented by beasts. The kingdom of the holy ones is represented by a humanlike figure. Like many today, Daniel is fascinated by the fourth beast. He wants to know about it, who it is and what it means. In his eagerness to have the truth *concerning the fourth beast*, he fails to focus on the Ancient One and the one like a son of man (human being). He requests additional information and repeats much of the material recorded in verses 7-14, yet also adding details and actions not noted earlier.

As Daniel rehearses what he has seen, he adds to the description of the fourth beast *claws of bronze* (7:19). He also offers the observation that one horn seems greater than the others (7:20), an expression that has led some interpreters to believe that the eleven horns represent eleven contemporary states rather than a series of Hellenistic rulers beginning with Alexander the Great. That Antiochus IV Epiphanes was indeed the eleventh king in a sequence of rulers after Alexander the Great is difficult to establish historically. Many believe, however, that this personification of evil refers to Antiochus.

As Daniel continues his question, he gives much new information:

1. The horn *made war with the holy ones* (cf. Rev. 13:7).
2. The horn *was prevailing over them.*
3. This continued *until* the *Ancient One came; then judgment was given for the saints of the Most High.*
4. *The time came when the holy ones gained possession of the kingdom.*

Earlier the picture of the fourth beast is that of biting, breaking, and stomping. Now the object of the beast's fury becomes clear: *the holy ones of the Most High* (7:21; cf. 8:10, *the host of heaven*). The beast challenges heaven and its decrees in a conflict that is parallel with the way the beast makes war on earth. Thus the scene matches reports in 1 Maccabees of how Antiochus tried to deprive faithful Jews of their language, their sacred books, and their temple. For a period of time, Antiochus may prevail and *destroy . . . the people* (Dan. 8:24), but God will intervene.

The Ancient One sits in the heavenly court, as a judge, and the books are opened. Only now is it learned that when the judge rules against the beast, he rules for *the holy ones* (7:22) and *the people* they protect (7:27). With the sentence upon the four beasts carried out, *the holy ones gained possession of the kingdom*. In verse 14, *one like a son of man (human being)* is given the kingdom; now Daniel makes it clear that the righteous receive *kingship and dominion* (7:27). In the vision, the Ancient One is putting down arrogance, but there is no explanation for giving the kingdom *to the people of the holy ones of the Most High.* In 9:18 we hear Daniel appeal for the Lord to show his *great mercies* to his people.

Unlike the beasts grasping for absolute power, dominion, and kingdom, the *one like a son of man* serves under God. He receives the kingdom and in turn shares it with *the people of the holy ones* (7:27). The fact that the beast prevails over *the holy ones* (7:21) and *the saints of the Most High* (7:27, RSV) leads to his fall. However, the righteous people are given victory even in earthly defeat! To them, the "poor in spirit," the "meek," those who refuse to fight, is the kingdom given (Matt. 5:3-12, 44). This scene anticipates Paul's observation:

> You have come to fullness in him, who is the head of every ruler and authority. . . . He disarmed the rulers and authorities and made a public example of them, triumphing over them in it [the cross]. (Col. 2:10, 15)

7:23-27 A Detailed Interpretation

The heavenly attendant, in response to Daniel's request, provides little additional information about the fourth beast and repeats some of the earlier information. The focus is on the eleventh horn of the fourth beast. Its origin is traced back to a worldwide conquest different from previous conquests not in kind but in intensity and scope. This could be a reference to the far-reaching empire of Alexander, broken to pieces upon his death. From this division ten horns (7:7) or ten kings will arise (like the ten toes of 2:42). This is likely a round number. From these an eleventh shall rise. This one will be different in terms of murder and violence. He will *put down three kings* (7:20, 24; see notes on 7:8). Though other identifications are possible historically and symbolically, this king seems best identified as Antiochus IV Epiphanes. The *mouth speaking arrogantly* (7:8, 11, 20) is guilty of three crimes:

1. *He shall speak words against the Most High* (7:25). That is, he blasphemes the God of Israel (cf. notes on 8:11).

2. *He . . . shall wear out the holy ones of the Most High*. Antiochus persecuted the saints of the Most High. He plundered Jerusalem, looted the temple, took captives, placed in Jerusalem a citadel for his troops, and drove the faithful into hiding (1 Macc. 1:20-40).

3. *He . . . shall attempt to change the sacred seasons and the law*. Antiochus also interfered with Jewish religious practices, holy days, and offerings. *Changing times* reflects the Jewish thought that the unfolding of human history is in the hands of God, not humans (Dan. 2:21). By forcing his way to the throne and subjugating other nations, including Israel, Antiochus was at cross-purposes with God. Although there is no supporting evidence, Antiochus might have tried to impose a change from a 364-day solar calendar to a 360-day lunar calendar, creating havoc in setting dates for regular religious celebrations. Antiochus certainly did attack such rituals: "He directed them to follow customs strange to the land, to forbid burnt offerings and

sacrifices and drink offerings in the sanctuary, to profane sabbaths and festivals . . . so that they would forget the law and change all the ordinances" (1 Macc. 2:44-49).

The books of Maccabees describe how Antiochus attempted to stamp out the Mosaic Law. Unfortunately, in the view of the faithful, many Jews were ready and willing to adopt the Greek way of life. Many were ready to surrender Jewish religious practices for those promoted by Antiochus. "They built a gymnasium in Jerusalem, according to Gentile custom, and removed the marks of circumcision, and abandoned the holy covenant. They joined with the Gentiles and sold themselves to do evil" (1 Macc. 1:14-15). "But many in Israel stood firm and . . . chose to die rather than to . . . profane the holy covenant; and they did die" (1 Macc. 1:62-63).

The climax of Antiochus's evil was the "desolating sacrilege" (1 Macc. 1:54). *[Abomination That Desolates, p. 276.]* This is referred to four times in Daniel (8:13; 9:27; 11:31; and 12:11; cf. Mark 13:14; Matt. 24:15). Antiochus called himself "Epiphanes," which means "god manifest." He thought his facial features resembled those of the Olympian Zeus, and increasingly depicted himself with the traditional profile of Zeus on his coins and with a crown of rays, like Helios, the sun god. On the altar of the Jerusalem temple he erected an altar to Zeus, perhaps with meteorites to be worshiped (Goldstein, 1976:145-152). This emptied the temple of true worshipers, and God himself certainly departed, according to Israelite understanding (as in Ezek. 11:22-23).

According to the heavenly attendant's interpretation, the beastly king will dominate the holy ones *for a time, two times, and half a time* (7:25; cf. 8:14; 9:27; 12:7, 11, 12). In chapter 4, here in chapter 7, and in 12:7, *time* likely refers to a year. Thus one year plus two years plus one-half year equal about three and one-half years.

The word *time* (*'iddan*) may also refer to an indefinite period or season. Since seven is considered the number of perfection, to be arrested midway or cut in half indicates extreme evil. Thus three and one-half times represents a limited period of intense evil. In addition, this also reflects an idiom referring to an extended period of time suddenly cut short. Thus "a period, a double period, a quadruple period," on through to seven periods (an eternity), is suddenly cut in half. The horn that grasps and usurps dominion is cut down in God's time and in God's way. Revelation 13:5-8 draws from Daniel 7 and speaks of forty-two months or three and one-half years. In Revelation, the forty-two months also represent a period of terror and demonic evil before God's victorious intervention.

Daniel 7:1 claims that this vision came to Daniel in Babylon in the first year of Belshazzar. The events purport to be in Jerusalem many years hence. The heavenly attendant makes it clear that the beastly king's devastation will be short-lived. This was indeed the case, as history shows. The time between the desecration of the temple in (Nov.-Dec.) 167 B.C. (1 Macc. 1:54) and its rededication in (Dec.) 164 B.C. was three years and ten days. By starting the period earlier, when Apollonius captured Jerusalem for Antiochus and the Syrians committed blasphemous acts (1 Macc. 1:29-35; 2 Macc. 5:24-26), it is possible to arrive at a period of three and one-half years (Dan. 7:25). The value or necessity of such attempts, however, is debatable.

The heavenly attendant elaborates on the scene set in heaven (7:26; cf. 7:10). In the vision, the beast's destruction has already taken place. In the interpretation, the action is still to come. Though God's people are given into Antiochus's hand for a limited period by decree of the heavenly judge (7:25), his dominion is taken away and utterly destroyed.

Then comes the climax of the vision. Heaven acts on behalf of *the people of the holy ones of the Most High* (7:27). To them are given *kingship and dominion. Their kingdom shall be an everlasting kingdom, and all dominions shall serve and obey them.*

The heavenly attendant does not explain the nature of the kingdom *given* to the righteous. With the rededication of the temple and the death of Antiochus in late 164 B.C., oppressive regimes did not disappear.

There is, however, an eternal dimension to the rule of saints. This is beautifully described in Revelation 22:1-5, when God's servants worship him and the Lamb, and "they will reign for ever and ever" (see TBC, below).

Postscript 7:28

To receive a divine message is an overwhelming experience. Daniel's vision is mysterious. There is both terror and serenity, cause for despair and encouragement. Daniel's report of his reaction to the vision encourages his readers. If Daniel scarcely understands its meaning, it follows that his readers also will be perplexed and find it difficult to interpret and to identify with many facets of the vision. Yet throughout the vision, in the midst of troubled times, God is powerfully present and at work on behalf of his people. To grasp the significance of that insight is of greater value than attempting to explain each detail of the vision.

In the postscript, Daniel includes four items:

1. Daniel marks the end of the vision.
2. He describes his inner spirit as *terrified*, disturbed, perplexed.
3. He notes his physical condition—the vision has left him weak and pale.
4. He mentions his thoughts. What he has seen and heard keeps turning over in his mind again and again. He examines each detail so that nothing will be lost while he hopes that he might come to a fuller understanding of the vision.

THE TEXT IN BIBLICAL CONTEXT

Son of Man

The Hebrew phrase *ben-'adam*, literally "son of man," means human being. This term (in Hebrew and RSV) appears in Psalm 8:4 (cf. Heb. 2:6; Ps. 144:3, *ben-'enoš*); 80:17 (in Hebrew, 80:18); and 146:3—always with meanings similar to that in Ezekiel (as in 2:1), where it is used over fifty times. "Son of man" designates Ezekiel simply as a human being, a descendant of Adam, a "mortal." The phrase suggests the limited significance of the prophet in comparison to the might and majesty of God, who choses to speak to and through him.

The most important occurrence of this phrase in the OT is in the Aramaic of Daniel 7:13, *bar 'enaš*. The RSV follows the Aramaic more literally and helps the reader link it with Jesus' words:

> *With the clouds of heaven*
> *there came one like a son of man* (NRSV: *like a human being*),
> *and he came to the Ancient of Days* (NRSV: *the Ancient One*)
> *and was presented before him.*

When the vision of Daniel 7 was shared with other Israelites, it is doubtful that they thought the *one like a son of man* (RSV) or *like a human being* (NRSV) referred to the Messiah, although this is a later Jewish and Christian interpretation. The original hearers likely thought that the phrase referred to a humanlike appearance of Michael, the archangel responsible for Israel (10:21; 12:1). Michael and his accompanying *holy ones*, angels, possess the kingdom for and with their people, the righteous and faithful Israelites who dwell on earth. The nations will serve them. This is paralleled at Qumran in The War Rule (1QM), chapter 17:

> This is the day appointed by [God] for the defeat and overthrow of the Prince of the kingdom of wickedness, and He will send eternal succour to

the company of His redeemed by the might of the princely Angel of the kingdom of Michael. . . . Peace and blessing shall be with the company of God. He will raise up the kingdom of Michael in the midst of the gods, and the realm of Israel in the midst of all flesh. (Vermes: 122)

The Daniel text refers to a celestial figure. Earlier some interpreters thought that this figure was linked to mythology of an archetypal man; but that linkage, if it exists, is tenuous at best. More probably, the figure is to be understood as an angelic representative of the faithful community which is passing through suffering. Perhaps Jesus used the term "Son of Man" because it was not popularly connected with messianic thought and thus gave him a vehicle through which to reshape messianic expectations (cf. Mark 2:10; 28; 8:31, 38; 9:9, 12, 31; 10:33, 45; 13:26; 14:21, 41, 62; and parallels). If so, then Jesus exercised a unique option in the use of the expression, by which, however, his sonship to God and messiahship would be safeguarded.

Some feel that Jesus used the term "Son of Man" to emphasize his humanity and dependence upon God his Father to carry out his work. In that case, Jesus drew upon Ezekiel's use of the expression for "mortal" rather than Daniel's celestial figure. Yet that Jesus invoked this self-designation simply to signify his humanity (and nothing else) is problematic and disputed, partly because of the dominion given to the Daniel figure coming with the clouds (7:13). The latter is obviously behind Mark's references to the Son of Man coming in/with clouds "with great power and glory," with assisting "holy angels," and as an exalted ruler and judge (8:38; 13:26-27; 14:62; cf. John 5:25-29; 1 Thess. 4:16-17; Rev. 1:7, 13-17; Gardner: 149, 383).

Others have wisely concluded that in the Gospels, "Son of Man" is an honorific title by which Jesus claimed for himself the kind of heavenly given authority and ruling status granted the humanlike figure of Daniel 7:13. As Son of Man, Jesus claimed authority to forgive sins and to be lord of the Sabbath (Mark 2:10, 28). He said that the Son of Man is to suffer, give his life a ransom for many, and rise again (8:31; 10:45). This may have some connection with Daniel's vision of the suffering of *the holy ones* and their *people* (7:21, 27) and the first clear biblical reference to resurrection, which includes leading others to righteousness (12:2-3).

It is difficult to trace the line of development from *one like a son of man* in Daniel 7:13 to "the Son of Man" in the Gospels (a messianic title). To attempt this requires study of late Jewish books such as the pseudepigraphical 1 Enoch and the apocryphal 2 Esdras (4 Ezra). First Enoch is a composite work representing numerous periods and writers, likely written from the second century B.C. to the first century A.D. in Hebrew and Aramaic (Charlesworth, 1:5-8). It is much like Daniel in presenting visions and apocalyptic material. This book contains 108 chapters that treat angels and the universe, the triumph of righteousness, astronomical data, the future of Israel, rewards and punishments, and the final judgment. Several titles refer to the Messiah, such as the "Anointed One," the "Righteous One," the "Elect One," and the "Son of Man" (for the latter: 1 En. 46:2-4; 48:2; 62:7, 9, 14; 63:11; 69:26-27; 70:1; 71:1).

First Enoch depicts the one who is Messiah and Son of Man "as a pre-existent heavenly being who is resplendent and majestic, possesses all dominion, and sits on his throne of glory passing judgment upon all mortal and spiritual beings" (E. Isaac in Charlesworth, 1:9; cf. ABD, 2:35). The portrait of this deliverer is drawn from Daniel 7 and other OT texts (such as Ps. 2; Isa. 11, 42, 49, 52–53).

At least some of the book of Enoch was apparently known in the days of Jesus and the early church. Jude 14-15 refers to Enoch, and a number of NT phrases or clauses can be paralleled in Enoch, showing that such apocalyptic imagery was floating around (Charles, 2:180-181). In the Qumran scrolls, however, the "Son of Man" texts from Enoch are missing, even though most chapters from Enoch are represented. Thus the possibility must be left open that the "Son of Man" sections may be Christian additions to this Jewish book. So it is possible, but hardly certain, that Jesus took the title "Son of Man" from Enoch. Much more likely, Jesus took this title directly from Daniel (Bruce, 1969:26-30). In doing so, Jesus supported his claim to the everlasting kingdom (7:14). In the Christian era, believers understood that the vision of *one like a son of man* in Daniel 7:13 was being fulfilled best in Jesus. They counted the church as the new and restored Israel (Gal. 6:16).

In the apocryphal book of 2 Esdras, chapter 13 presents a vision of a man coming from the sea and flying with the clouds. The phrase "something like the figure of a man" (13:3) echoes Daniel 7:13. This is the Messiah, whom God calls "my Son," preexistent and hidden until the last days, when he is revealed (cf. 7:28). He will reprove and destroy evil nations and gather a peaceful multitude, the ten "lost" tribes of Israel. The core of this book is from a Jewish writer near the close of the first century A.D., later than the Gospel of Mark and after the split between synagogue and church. Christians later added chapters 1–2 and 15–16 and used the book. Somewhat similarly, the pseudepigraphical 2 Baruch of the same time period has God speak of "my Anointed One" with glorious appearance, a heavenly figure foreign to OT texts about the coming king. Yet this book "presumes the messianic identification of the central figure in Daniel 7 and his judicial functions" (ABD, 6:141; cf. "Son of Man" article, 6:137-150).

The NT presentation of Jesus of Nazareth builds on this vision in Daniel 7. In the announcement of Jesus' birth, Gabriel says to Mary, "Of his kingdom there will be no end" (Luke 1:33). Jesus begins his ministry preaching the "good news of the kingdom of God," indicating that he is "sent for this purpose" (Luke 4:43). Jesus is confessed as the one who came in human likeness (Rom. 8:3; Phil. 2:7). He ascends into heaven in a cloud (Acts 1:9), and as Son of Man will return in a cloud with power and great glory (Luke 21:27). Before his ascension, Jesus says, "All authority in heaven and on earth has been given to me" (Matt. 28:18). Jesus inaugurates the reign of God, which includes disciples of "all nations" (Matt. 28:19).

In Daniel's vision, the relation between *the Ancient of Days* (RSV) or *the Ancient One* (NRSV), and *one like a son of man* (RSV) or *like a human being* (NRSV) is similar to the NT's picture of the Father and the Son, especially in John's Gospel: "The Father had given all things into his hands" (13:3). "I do as the Father has commanded me" (14:31). "All that the Father has is mine" (16:15). "The Father himself loves you, because you have loved me and have believed that I came from the Father. I came from the Father and have come into the world; again, I am leaving the world and am going to the Father" (16:27-28). "Father, glorify me in your own presence with the glory that I had in your presence before the world existed" (17:5).

Jesus initiated the kingdom of God on earth, as anticipated in Daniel 7. This is proclaimed in the NT epistles (as in 1 Cor. 15:21-25; Col. 1:11-14; 1 Thess. 2:12; 2 Tim. 4:1; Heb. 12:22-29; 2 Pet. 1:10-11). In many respects, Daniel's vision anticipates the ascension of Jesus (cf. Heb. 1:2-3, 8; 9:24-28; 12:22-29).

In the NT (RSV), the title "Son of Man" appears 94 times. It is always used by Jesus himself, except by opposers repeating his words (John 12:34), by Stephen (Acts 7:56), by Hebrews (2:6) in a quotation of Psalm 8:4, and by John describing the glorified Christ in terminology reminiscent of Daniel 7 and 10 (Rev. 1:13; cf. Gardner: 149).

The title "Son of Man" has helped believers grasp the uniqueness of Jesus. The designation attests to Jesus' sonship to God. In the Fourth Gospel, John writes, "No one has ascended into heaven except the one who descended from heaven, the Son of Man," who is God's "only Son" (John 3:13-17). Here clearly the Son of Man is God's Son, from heaven. He is human, on earth. As John 1:14 makes clear, Jesus' coming is to reveal the grace and truth of God and to reconcile humanity to God.

The designation "Son of Man" attests to Jesus' messiahship. Jesus did accept the title "Messiah" on the lips of others (Matt. 16:16-20; Mark 14:61-62; cf. 10:47). Yet it is significant that Jesus did not use this title for himself, possibly to avoid the military and worldly political associations that accompanied many Israelites' expectation of the Messiah. Jesus found the "Son of Man" title more useful as he communicated the messiahship God intended for him. It was particularly appropriate for Jesus and the church to draw from Daniel 7:13 since the Son of Man was in direct contrast to the arrogant political and military beasts that continually ravage the sea of humanity (cf. Mark 1:13).

For Christians, the title "Son of Man" identifies Jesus with the church in a manner reminiscent of the connection between *one like a son of man* and *the people of the holy ones of the Most High* (Dan. 7:13, 27). In Matthew 16:13-20, Jesus asks his disciples, "Who do people say that the Son of Man is?" After a variety of answers, Peter says, "You are the Messiah (Christ), the Son of the living God." Upon this confession, Jesus declares, "I will build my church." As to the keys of the kingdom, however interpreted, God has given the Son of Man the authority to forgive sins on earth (Mark 2:10; Matt. 9:6). Jesus shares with his followers the privilege of declaring forgiveness to those who come in repentance and faith (Matt. 9:8; 16:19; 18:18; John 20:21-23; Gardner: 153-154).

"Son of Man" signifies Jesus' universal lordship. At Jesus' trial, the high priest asks, "Are you the Messiah (Christ), the Son of the Blessed One?" Jesus replies, "I am; and you will see the Son of Man seated at the right hand of the Power, and coming with the clouds of heaven" (Mark 14:61-62). Then before his ascension, Jesus asserts his universal lordship, "All authority in heaven and on earth has been given to me" (Matt. 28:18; cf. Acts 1:8).

The title "Son of Man" attests to Jesus' work as an advocate. In Acts, when Stephen uses the title, it has special significance. Jesus said, "Every one who acknowledges me before others, the Son of Man also will acknowledge before the angels of God; but whoever denies me before others will be denied before the angels of God" (Luke 12:8). As Stephen is being stoned, he looks to heaven and cries out, "I see the heavens opened and the Son of Man standing at the right hand of God" (Acts 7:55-56). Stephen has just acknowledged Jesus before the high priest and the council. In turn, Stephen is acknowledged by the Son of Man. The Son of Man reveals himself as Stephen's advocate at God's right hand (cf. 1 John 2:1).

The designation "Son of Man" signifies that Jesus is judge of all people. In Matthew 13:41-53, Jesus says, "The Son of man will send his angels, and they will collect out of his kingdom all causes of sin and all evildoers, and they will throw them into the furnace of fire, where there will be weeping and gnashing of teeth." Drawing from Daniel 12:3, Jesus adds, "Then the righteous will shine like the sun in the kingdom of their Father." Jesus, though Son of God, became one with all humanity and is thus qualified to be a judge. Paul in his sermon at Athens emphasizes this climactic work of Jesus Christ: "God . . . commands all people everywhere to repent, because he has fixed a day on which he will have the world judged in righteousness by a man whom he has appointed, and of this he has given assurance to all by raising him from the dead" (Acts 17:30-31; cf. Rom. 2:16; Rev. 20:11-15).

Visions of the Throne

In Daniel's dream, it seems as though he is given the privilege to look into heaven and to see the throne of God (7:1-28). As recorded in the Scriptures, several have had similar experiences.

The first such account is about Moses, along with Aaron, Nadab, Abihu, and seventy elders of Israel. "They saw the God of Israel. Under his feet there was something like a pavement of sapphire stone, like the very heaven for clearness. . . . They beheld God, and they ate and drank" (Exod. 24:9-11).

When Jehoshaphat, king of Judah, and Ahab, king of Israel, inquired of the prophet Micaiah, son of Imlah, about going to battle against the Syrians, Micaiah said, "Therefore hear the word of the Lord: I saw the Lord sitting on his throne, with all the host of heaven standing beside him to the right and to the left of him . . . " (1 Kings 22:1-40).

When the prophet Isaiah received his call to serve the Lord, he reported, "In the year that king Uzziah died, I saw the Lord sitting on a throne, high and lofty; and the hem of his robe filled the temple." Then follows a description of the seraphim and Isaiah's confession of sinfulness in the presence of the holy God. In several ways Isaiah's call (Isa. 6:1-9) parallels Daniel's experience of the voice and the touch (10:9-10).

Ezekiel also saw the throne. His description paralleled the accounts of others. He saw living creatures like Isaiah. The throne was in appearance like sapphire. On the throne "was something that seemed like a human form." The throne was like a chariot with wheels, and from the throne issued fire (Ezek. 1:5, 13, 18, 26). Daniel's vision moved back and forth between earth and the heavenly throne. Daniel also saw a fiery, chariot-like throne (7:9-10). In addition, a heavenly attendant interpreted what Daniel saw both in heaven and on earth.

In the NT, Stephen, the first known Christian martyr, was in the midst of an angry violent crowd. "He gazed into heaven and saw the glory of God and Jesus standing at the right hand of God. 'Look,' he said, 'I see the heavens opened and the Son of man standing at the right hand of God.' " Upon this testimony, the crowd "dragged him out of the city and began to stone him" (Acts 7:54-60). The apostle Paul apparently had a vision of the throne of God. He wrote that he was "caught up to the third heaven . . . into Paradise and heard things that are not to be told, that no mortal is permitted to repeat" (2 Cor. 12:1-4).

The longest and most detailed vision is that of John in the book of Revelation (4:1—5:14). He describes the throne of God, the thrones of twenty-four elders, the four living creatures, and the incessant activity around the throne. The focus is upon the one seated on the throne and upon the Lamb. As in Isaiah's vision, John affirms the holiness of God. In Revelation, two great anthems of praise are recorded, the hymn of creation (4:11) and the hymn of redemption (5:9-10). In the climax of the vision of the throne, the heavenly host praises the Lamb with a sevenfold benediction, and then the entire creation—in heaven, on earth, and under the earth—responds in affirmation.

These throne visions have a deeper purpose than merely to satisfy human curiosity. They affirm faith, give hope in the midst of difficulty, and encourage obedient service.

The focus is upon the occupied throne. God is on the heavenly throne, even when the earthly throne is vacant (as when King Uzziah died: Isa. 6:1) or when earthly thrones are occupied by tyrants. In this respect the heavenly throne differs from earthly thrones, for the One upon the throne is not a despot: *All his works are truth, and his ways are justice* (Dan. 4:37). Further, the throne visions make the point that there is reality behind and beyond earthly existence. The heavenly throne is occupied by the glory of God. In the NT, God is joined on the throne by the Son of Man (Acts 7:56), Jesus Christ (Heb. 1:3, 8), "the ruler of the kings of the earth" (Rev. 1:5; 3:21), the "Lamb that was slaughtered" (5:6, 12-13; 7:10, 17). Thus it now can be called "the throne of God and of the Lamb" (22:3).

Before the throne there is worship of God. But one learns that heaven is also concerned both for creation and for all humanity—for *all peoples, nations, and languages* (Dan. 7:14). In Daniel is a clear statement of eschatological (end-time) expectation that God's people will rule the nations. As authorized by God, his people are to reign over all *dominions* (7:27), and this kingdom shall not *be left to another people* (2:44). Thus God's people become the mediator of God's blessings to the whole world (cf. Gen. 12:3; Isa. 19:23-25; Zech. 14).

Christians believe that God's concern for all nations is picked up best in Jesus Christ and the church (Luke 10:1-16; Matt. 28:18-20; Eph. 2:11-22). Salvation through Christ is ransoming saints from "every tribe and language and people and nation" and making them "to be a kingdom and priests serving our God, and they will reign on earth" (Rev. 5:9-10). The concern is that *all . . . should serve* God (Dan. 7:14, 27).

Visions of the throne affirm that history is in God's hands, that the trials and persecutions of the saints are temporary, and that God knows and takes care of his people.

THE TEXT IN THE LIFE OF THE CHURCH

The Peaceful Kingdom

If the acts of Antiochus IV Epiphanes are a focal point for the visions of Daniel and for 1 and 2 Maccabees, then these materials reflect two distinct approaches to realizing God's rule. In Daniel, the suffering righteous ones remain faithful to God even unto death. They do not take matters into their own hands, preferring rather to wait and let the God of heaven deal with oppressors. On the other hand, the Maccabees used force. They, too, were ready to die. They remembered Hananiah, Azariah, and Mishael's deliverance from the flame, and Daniel's deliverance from the mouth of the lions (1 Macc. 2:59-60). But rather than wait for God to act, they took the route of military might to "avenge the wrong done to your people" and to "pay back the Gentiles in full" (1 Macc. 2:67-68). In Daniel's vision, kingdom and dominion are given by God (7:26). They are received by the people, not seized!

In the NT, it is clear that the kingdom presented to the Son of Man is given to the saints, followers of Jesus. Believers are receiving a kingdom that is eternal and cannot be shaken (Heb. 12:28). Kingdom citizens, saints, experience now as a foretaste what will be when the kingdom comes in its fullness, when "they will see the Son of man coming in a cloud with power and great glory" (Luke 21:27).

The kingdom given to the saints is not a worldly political one. All too often the primary tools of politics are lies and violence. Time and again the outrageous lying of governments and politicians are laid bare—hiding secret deals, distorting the truth, disclaiming knowledge of facts at hand, and manipulating people to "buy" false opinions and views. Lying by public figures and politicians is at the heart of the decay in nations today. This is like the "imperial hegemony and revolt against God" portrayed in Daniel 2 and 7 (Aukerman: 106). At the same time, politicians "lord it over others" and often act as "tyrants," as though their ultimate tool to solve domestic or international problems is violence (Mark 10:42-45). This, too, is part of the tension between the church and the state.

It is always tragic when lies, violence, manipulation, and distortion of the truth find their way into the life of the church. The intention of Jesus Christ, the head of the church, is truth: his words and ways become normative—love God, love neighbor, love self, and love the enemy (cf. Mark 12:29-31; Matt. 5:43-48).

The church is the body of Christ (Eph. 1:23). It is made up of both Jew and Gentile (Eph. 2:11-22) and is the new Israel of God (Gal. 6:16). The title "saints" or "holy ones" is applied to its members. This name indicates not only continuity with the people of God in the past, but also a manner of life. Believers are a "holy priesthood," a "holy nation, God's own people" (1 Pet. 2:5, 9). They are "rescued from the dominion of darkness and transferred . . . into the kingdom of his beloved Son" (Col. 1:13).

Jesus echoed the words of Daniel: "Do not be afraid, little flock, for it is your Father's good pleasure to give you the kingdom" (Luke 12:32). Then Jesus gave a series of admonitions about lifestyle, priorities, and readiness for the master's return. In Luke 21:8-36, Jesus also describes kingdom-style living in the midst of political turmoil which stretched from the destruction of Jerusalem to the end of the world, when the kingdom will come in its fullness (21:31).

Kingdom living is not militaristic. It is strange that religious fundamentalists (whether Hindu, Muslim, or Christian) often take to themselves worldly political rule, interpret their holy books rigidly, consider themselves alone to be right, oppress those who differ, and attempt to make everyone in their image. In so doing, they become like the beasts of Daniel! The reign of saints (Rev. 3:21; 5:9-10) is exercised in a strange way, the way of the cross, trusting in salvation through Christ. Evil is confronted and overcome by the cross (1 Pet. 2:19-25; Col. 2:13-15).

Rome through its provincial rulers and armies oppressed the faithful in the days of Jesus and the early church. The Anabaptists of the sixteenth century suffered from the swords of princes and bishops. But through the centuries, Christians have recognized that through Jesus, God initiated the ultimate downfall of worldly empires and the establishing of his rule. Jesus taught his followers to pray,

> Your kingdom come.
> Your will be done,
> on earth as it is in heaven. (Matt. 6:10)

Part 3

Reading Scriptures and Receiving Visions

Daniel 8:1—12:13 (in Hebrew)

OVERVIEW

Shift to Hebrew Language and Concerns

At this point the book of Daniel returns to the Hebrew language. Chapter 1, the introduction to the book, is in Hebrew, while the tract to the nations (2:4b—7:28) is in Aramaic. A variety of reasons have been suggested for this arrangement. Some scholars believe that the entire book was originally in Aramaic and that the first chapter and the latter part of the book were translated into Hebrew so that it would be more acceptable in the Hebrew canon. Persons familiar with these languages suggest further that the translator was an Aramaic-speaking person since the Hebrew—in word order, use of pronouns, and simplicity—is not characteristic of classical Hebrew prose.

Another reason may be related to the content. The tract to the nations is addressed in the language of commerce to a worldwide audience, *all peoples, nations, and languages*. It is about the God of the Hebrews, who he is and what he does. Hence, the book speaks to both Jews and non-Jews. As is so often the case, the words of Scripture speak to different people in different ways, according to their need. A Scripture passage can speak to one person as a word of conviction that leads to salvation. The same passage may speak to another as a word of insight leading to sanctification. Through renowned world leaders, the tract informs the world of *the living God* (6:26) and thus offers grace to the world. At the same time, to Jews in exile or in severe testing, the tract inspires hope and encourages faithfulness to their God.

In the visions to follow, the focus shifts from universal proclamation to areas of special concern to the Jewish people: Palestine *the beautiful land* (8:9; 11:16, 41); Jerusalem, God's *holy mountain* (9:16); God's *sanctuary/temple* (8:11; 9:17; 11:31), the *covenant* (9:4; 11:28-32), and the people of God, Israel (9:7, 15, 20).

The remaining five chapters (8-12) contain three visions. Each further develops themes already found in Daniel's first vision (Dan. 7). Daniel's second vision is of a ram and a male goat along with an interpretation (Dan. 8). Following meditation (on Jeremiah 25:11-12; 29:10-14) and a lengthy prayer of confession, an angel brings Daniel (in a third vision) a message concerning seventy weeks of years (Dan. 9). His fourth vision reveals times of violence and war leading to the rise and downfall of a dreadful king and to the deliverance of the faithful (Dan. 10-12).

In the four visions of chapters 7-12, a profile emerges of this dreadful king along with dreaded developments, if one assumes similar subject matter for the four visions.

1. The rise of a violent, arrogant, ruthless king, likely Antiochus IV Epiphanes (175-164 B.C.). *[Antiochus IV Epiphanes, p. 279.]*

> *Another horn appeared, a little one coming up among them, . . . [with] a mouth speaking arrogantly.* (7:8)
> *Out of one of them came another horn, a little one, which grew exceedingly great.* (8:9-11)
> *The prince who is to come.* (9:26)
> *In his place shall arise a contemptible person. . . . He shall devise plans against strongholds.* (11:21, 24)

2. This king will oppress the people of God.

> *This horn made war with the holy ones and was prevailing over them. . . . He shall . . . wear out the holy ones of the Most High.* (7:21, 25)
> *He shall destroy the powerful and the people of the holy ones.* (8:24)
> *After the sixty-two weeks, an anointed one shall be cut off.* (9:26)
> *For some days, however, they shall fall by sword and flame, and suffer captivity and plunder.* (11:33)

3. This king will oppose Jewish worship.

> *He . . . shall attempt to change the sacred seasons and the law.* (7:25)
> *[The little horn] took the regular burnt offering away from him and overthrew the place of his sanctuary. . . . It cast truth to the ground.* (8:11-12)
> *He shall make sacrifice and offering cease.* (9:27)
> *Forces sent by him shall occupy and profane the temple. . . . They shall abolish the regular burnt offering.* (11:31)

4. This king will commit an unspeakable sacrilege (foreign worship in the temple: cf. 1 Macc. 1:54; 2 Macc. 6:2-5).

For how long is this vision concerning the regular burnt offering, the transgression that makes desolate? (8:13)
In their place shall be an abomination that desolates. (9:27)
They shall . . . set up the abomination that makes desolate. (11:31)
The abomination that desolates is set up. (12:11)

5. The time of outrageous sacrilege will be cut short.

They shall be given into his power for a time, two times, and half a time. (7:25)
For two thousand three hundred evenings and mornings; then the sanctuary shall be restored to its rightful state. (8:14)
For half of the week he shall make sacrifice and offering cease. (9:27)
He shall prosper until the period of wrath is completed. (11:36)
It would be for a time, two times, and half a time. (12:7)
There shall be one thousand two hundred ninety days. (12:11)
Attain the thousand three hundred thirty-five days. (12:12)

6. God removes the king. (References to *end* refer primarily to the end of this king rather than to end-time in an eschatological sense.)

Then the court shall sit in judgment, and his dominion shall be taken away, to be consumed and totally destroyed. (7:26)
The vision is for the time of the end. . . . I will tell you what will take place later in the period of wrath; for it refers to the appointed time of the end. (8:17, 19)
He shall be broken, and not by human hands. . . . Seal up the vision, for it refers to many days from now. (8:26)
Until the decreed end is poured out upon the desolator. (9:27)
There remains an end at the time appointed. (11:27)
Until the time of the end, for there is still an interval until the time appointed. (11:35)
At the time of the end the king of the south shall attack him. (11:40)
He shall come to his end, with no one to help him. (11:45)
Keep the words secret and the book sealed until the time of the end. (12:4, 9)

7. The faithful are restored to their place in God's eternal kingdom.

The kingship and dominion and the greatness of the kingdoms under the whole heaven shall be given to the people of the holy ones of the Most High; their kingdom shall be an everlasting kingdom. (7:27; cf. 2:44)
Seventy weeks are decreed for your people and your holy city: to finish the transgression, to put an end to sin, and to atone for iniquity, to bring in everlasting righteousness, to seal both vision and prophet, and to anoint a most holy place. (9:24)
At that time your people shall be delivered. . . . Many of those who sleep in the dust of the earth shall awake, some to everlasting life. . . . Those

who are wise shall shine like the brightness of the sky, and those who lead many to righteousness, like the stars forever and ever. (12:1-3)

Visions Given and Sealed

In each of the visions, Daniel is confronted by heavenly beings. In chapter 7, his vision is interpreted by *one of the attendants* standing in the heavenly court (7:10, 16). In chapter 8, the vision of the ram and male goat is interpreted by Gabriel. In chapter 9, after Daniel's meditation and prayer, Gabriel again appears to announce the seventy weeks of years. In chapters 10–12, several heavenly beings appear: *a man clothed in linen* (10:5), *one in human form* (10:16, 18), and at the end of the vision, *two others* stood along with the one clothed in linen (12:5). The heavenly beings attest to the divine origin of the visions and also to their truth and reliability (8:26). In addition, they provide Daniel with strength and courage (10:18; 11:1).

These visions are given dates that would be late in Daniel's career. The chapter 7 vision would fit around 554 B.C., in the first year of Belshazzar (7:1; ANET: 313). The chapter 8 vision comes two years later, in the third year of Belshazzar (8:1). The chapter 9 vision is given in 539-538 B.C., the first year of the reign of Darius the Mede (likely ruling under Cyrus; 9:1). The fourth vision, Daniel 10–12, comes in the third year of Cyrus, 536 B.C. (10:1). The meaning of these visions will become clear many days (years) hence. From the vision of the ram and male goat (8:1-22), it is safe to assume that the coming of the outrageous king will be many years after Alexander the Great. In chapter 9, seven plus sixty-two weeks of years (69 x 7 = 483 years) will pass (9:25)—the time of Persian rulers and some Hellenistic dominion—before the outrageous king will appear in the seventieth week of years.

Daniel is instructed to seal up the visions until that time (8:26; 12:4, 9). If the visions came in the sixth century B.C., they were to be kept sealed until the days of the dreadful king. If they were to be opened at the apex of the career of Antiochus IV Epiphanes (175-164 B.C.), their meaning would then be clear. On the other hand, if these materials were written during the days of Jewish suffering under Antiochus and attributed to the ancient personage, Daniel, the effect is the same. *[Daniel: Date and Authorship, p. 285.]* In either case, the message to the afflicted faithful is that the court of heaven is in control. God is faithful to his people. Though the forces of evil and oppression may reach extreme levels of horror and persecution, they are of short duration. The faithful are not exempt from suffering. But the severest oppression and the most demonic regimes are broken in ways that can scarcely be anticipated or explained, at *the appointed time of the end* (8:19), when *the decreed end* (9:27) is realized.

If these visions of Daniel were written at the time of the Maccabees, they suggest an alternate way for the faithful to confront the excesses of Antiochus and the renegade Jews who adopted Hellenistic ways and religions. The Maccabees took the way of prayer and violence (1 Macc. 3:43-44). *[Maccabees, p. 290.]* The wise, represented by Daniel (and partially by 2 Macc.), embraced the way of prayer and peace, and some were martyred while waiting for God to deliver his people (cf. 1 Macc. 1:63; 2:29-38; 2 Macc. 6:11). Thus the Jewish community was split at least three ways in response to Hellenism.

The visions of Daniel stress the sovereignty of God in times of crisis along with the importance of prayer. God is the one who brings to naught the arrogance, deceit, violence, destruction, irreligion, and persecution of tyrants. God is also the one who strengthens, restores, purifies, and gives understanding to the faithful.

Daniel 8:1-27

Daniel's Vision of the Ram and the Goat

PREVIEW

The structure of Daniel's vision of the ram and the goat is similar to that of chapter 7. Both have an introduction and a postscript. The introductions provide dates for the visions. The postscripts describe the effects of the vision upon Daniel, both physically and emotionally.

The vision of the ram and male goat is in two parts, the vision itself and its interpretation, both of which make up the vision. Daniel does not receive the vision and then in a more wakeful state gain its meaning. Rather, the interpretation is part of the vision.

Visions and dreams by their nature are disjointed and symbolic. It is hard for anyone to relate a dream logically, sequentially, or coherently. This helps to explain why the interpretation has the same disjointed qualities as the vision. Not every detail of the vision proper is interpreted. At the same time, the interpretation supplies information not anticipated in the vision. Thus both parts have to be pieced together to discern the overall meaning. The very nature of a vision cautions against any attempts to make exact, literal interpretations of every detail.

A ram appears, then a male goat. There is conflict. The male goat's horn is broken, and in its place four horns emerge. Out of one of the horns comes a little horn that opposes God and violently oppresses his people. Things are so bad that even heavenly observers are concerned. They wonder, "How long can this go on?" To this question a cryptic answer is given. Daniel is perplexed by what he has seen. Then the angel Gabriel appears to help Daniel understand what he has seen and how the indignation will end (8:19; 11:36). Gabriel identifies the ram as the Persian empire and the male goat as Greece. He outlines the breakup of Alexander the Great's empire into four parts, out of which will come the king who will oppress the people of God. But this arrogant king will also be broken. Gabriel emphasizes, finally, that these events are in the future. Daniel is filled with horror and dismay by the vision. He admits that he fails to understand it.

OUTLINE

Introduction, 8:1

The Vision, 8:2-14

8:2	In Susa
8:3-4	A Charging Ram
8:5-8	A Flying Goat
8:9-12	Emergence of the Evil Little Horn
8:13-14	Concerned Holy Ones

The Vision Interpreted, 8:15-26

8:15-17a	Gabriel Appears
8:17b-22	The Time of the End
8:23-26	A Dreadful King

Postscript: Daniel's Response, 8:27

EXPLANATORY NOTES

Introduction 8:1

Daniel's vision of the four beasts (7:1-28) is said to have come in the first year of Belshazzar (7:1). The vision reported here comes in the third year. Belshazzar was in his place of responsibility about fifteen years, until 539 B.C. (5:30). Since he took office in about 554 B.C., then this vision is to be dated around 552 B.C. With the mention in this introduction (8:1) of the former vision of chapter 7, there is a hint that the two visions are related in content. For a somewhat generalized schematic diagram of that relationship, see notes just before TBC.

The Vision 8:2-14

8:2 In Susa

This vision and the one beginning in chapter 10 are the only ones given a geographical setting. Daniel is actually in the city of Babylon, but in this vision he sees himself in *Susa the capital.* The future action will be in Jerusalem. Susa was located at the foot of the Zagros mountains in the ancient *province of Elam* (in the modern province of Khuzistan in Iran), north of the Persian Gulf. Since this is a vision, it really does not matter that Susa was destroyed in 646 B.C. It survived modestly until the Persian Darius I in 521 B.C. chose to rebuild it as the main capital of the Persian empire and the royal winter residence (ABD, 6:242-245). Daniel is in Babylon, the center of political action of his world. His visionary location in the (later) Persian capital suggests that the vision's message is for a time other than the present. Antiochus the Great, the grandfather of Antiochus IV Epiphanes, was killed in Susa in 187 B.C. while looting a temple of Bel.

Furthermore, the ruins of this city, located about two hundred miles east of Babylon, are along a canal called *the river*, Chaour, or *Ulai* in Akkadian. Literarily, a vision by a river is something of a type-scene (by the Nile, Gen. 41:1; by "the river Chebar," also a canal, Ezek. 1:1). Perhaps the word *'ubal* (*river*) should be *'abul* (*gate*, as in LXX [Septuagint Greek]). Thus JB reads, *gazing at the vision I found myself at the gate of the Ulai* (8:2). Later Daniel is joined by one with a human appearance who cries *between the leaves of the Ulai gate* (8:15-16, JB note).

8:3-4 A Charging Ram

Daniel's vision is about sheep and goats with the male of each representing a leader of a political power. First a ram comes into view. From Gabriel's interpretation, the ram represents the Medo-Persian empire (8:20). One of the two horns is *higher* and *the longer one came up second;* this represents the larger influence of the Persians and the fact that the Persians overcame the Medes. The scene parallels that of the bear raised up on one side (7:5). As the bear had three ribs, so the ram charged in three directions—west, north, and south. Cyrus, whose reign over the Persians began around 559 B.C., conquered the Medes nine years later in 550 B.C., and then the Babylonians in 539 B.C. The Medo-Persian Empire embraced territories now found in Turkey, Egypt, Israel, Jordan, Syria, Russia, Iraq,

Pakistan, and Afghanistan. The latter ones, in an easterly direction, are apparently not in view in the vision.

In Ezekiel 34, the symbol of a ram is associated with leadership (shepherds) and perhaps also with nations which oppress Israel (NOAB: 1104, OT). Here the ram represents a mighty military power. *All beasts*, other nations, fall before the Medo-Persian rulers. There is no way to escape their domination and *power*. They are accountable to no one, doing as they *pleased*. Arrogant and proud, they *magnified* themselves (8:4, RSV; *became strong*, NRSV).

8:5-8 A Flying Goat

Out of the west comes a male goat. Male goats are more aggressive and usually stronger than rams. Later Gabriel also identifies this animal figure (8:21). It is the king of Greece, Alexander the Great, who races *across the face of the whole earth*, conquering much of the known world. *Without touching the ground* is a sign of the speed with which Alexander subdued kingdom after kingdom, from Greece all the way to India between 334 B.C. and his death in 323 B.C., after he met and defeated Darius at Issus in 333 B.C. *[Alexander, p. 276]*. This conflict between Alexander the Great and the Medo-Persian ruler is described in verses six and seven. Perhaps Alexander's rapid conquest is symbolized by the *four wings* of the leopard in Daniel's first vision (7:6). But it is more likely that the *terrifying and dreadful and exceedingly strong* fourth beast (7:7) is a double for this *male goat* and stands for the Greeks.

Like the ram, the goat *magnified himself exceedingly* (RSV; *grew exceedingly great*, NRSV). However *at the height of its power, the great horn was broken* (8:8). History tells us that two things stopped Alexander's dramatic conquest to the east: first, the mutiny of his troops at the Ganges River; second, his untimely death from a fever as a young man of thirty-three years (356-323 B.C.). Following his death, the empire was divided among his four generals: Cassander, Lysimachus, Seleucus, and Ptolemy. Thus the *four prominent horns toward the four winds of heaven* reflect in a general way the breakup of Alexander's empire (on *four*, see notes on 7:2). The *four heads* mean the division of his empire. *[Selucids, p. 295. Ptolemies, p. 294.]*

8:9-12 Emergence of the Evil Little Horn

Between verses nine and ten, a long period of time passes. In the earlier vision, a sequence of ten kings precedes the emergence of a little horn speaking great things (7:8). That period, it seems, spans the time between the death of Alexander the Great (323 B.C.) and the rise of Antiochus IV Epiphanes (175 B.C.). Here details of the conflicts between the Ptolemies and the Seleucids are overlooked. These will be dealt with in Daniel's final vision (chap. 11).

The *little horn* (Antiochus) comes out of the Seleucid line of kings, whose control is centered in Syria. In the middle of his career (169 B.C.), Antiochus leads military expeditions toward Egypt, the south (1 Macc. 1:16-19; 2 Macc. 5:1-10; cf. Dan. 11:15-17); toward Pakistan, the east (1 Macc. 3:27-37); and toward Palestine, the *beautiful land* (Dan. 8:9; 1 Macc. 1:20-35; 2 Macc. 5:1-26; cf. Dan. 11:41; on *beautiful*, cf. Ezek. 20:6, 15; Jer. 3:19).

As the king grows great, he attempts to invade and dominate in a new direction, *the host of heaven* (Dan. 8:10). This description of the evil king echoes Isaiah's critique of the king of Babylon (Isa. 14:13-14). The host of heaven often refers to a heavenly army. In this vision, it refers to the angels of the host who represent the Jewish people. This king throws *down to earth some of the host and some of the stars* and tramples them. The king's attacks on the angels that protect the Israelites is matched by the way he tramples the Jews on earth (8:24; 7:21). There is correspondence between celestial and earthly events. A defeat of the Jews is also a defeat of their guardian angels.

Even against the prince of the host, this horn/king *acted arrogantly* (8:11). This Prince is the God of Israel, supreme over the hosts of heaven as kings rule nations. Not satisfied with earthly conquest, Antiochus takes on God himself, the Prince of the host, ruler of the universe, the host of heaven, and all humanity. The king's challenge to God centers in attacking the worship of God by God's people in God's temple. He takes away *the regular burnt offering* of every morning and evening and overthrows *the place of his sanctuary*. The *regular burnt offering* is the daily offering prescribed in Exodus 29:38-42 and here may represent the whole elaborate ritual of sacrifice.

The records show that Antiochus took authority over the Jerusalem temple, and in doing this he usurped that which belonged to God alone. Antiochus acted *arrogantly* against God by proclaiming his own self-deification and claiming divine honors for himself as Epiphanes, "god manifest." He likely claimed to be a manifestation of the Olympian Zeus, for whom he renamed the Jerusalem temple (cf. 7:8, 11, 20; 11:36; 1 Macc. 1:10; 2 Macc. 4:7; 5:21; 6:2). His enemies, however, noted that he was a fierce tyrant and called him Epimanes, "utterly mad" (Polybius 26.1a.1). This defiant little horn belongs with those world rulers who claim to be god and marshal their forces against God, God's *host*, and God's people (Dan. 7:21; 8:24; Isa. 14:12-15; Ezek. 28; 38:14-16; Ps. 2:1-3). *[Antiochus IV Epiphanes, p. 279.]*

The temple thus was made useless to the Israelites. Instead of the people of God entering its gates, another "host" took over the holy precincts. Antiochus garrisoned troops in the vicinity of the temple. These Gentiles were free to roam not only the city of Jerusalem but also into the temple itself. They turned the temple into a shrine for Hellenistic-Canaanite worship artifacts and practices. Thus the temple was overthrown, not in the sense of destruction as in 586 B.C. or A.D. 70. Rather, it was defiled by alien worship, emptied of true worshipers, and made useless as a place to worship the God of Israel.

The horn *cast truth to the ground* (Dan. 8:12; cf. Isa. 59:14-15). By truth may be meant the Torah, the Hebrew Scriptures. Antiochus tried to strip Jewish sacred books of all authority. Torah scrolls were confiscated and destroyed by tearing them to pieces and burning them. The king condemned to death anyone found to possess the book of the covenant or to be adhering to the law (1 Macc. 1:56-57).

The horn *kept prospering* (Dan. 8:12) and *was active and successful* (JB). As the king became more radical and as his power grew, he regarded himself as divine (see above).

8:13-14 Concerned Holy Ones

Events on earth, according to the book of Daniel, are ultimately controlled by heaven. They are also observed in heaven. Two holy ones (angels; see notes on 4:13-17; 7:17-27) observe the unbridled oppression of God's people by Antiochus IV Epiphanes, and they discuss the matter. One of them asks, *For how long is this vision concerning the regular burnt offering, the transgression that makes desolate, and the giving over of the sanctuary and host to be trampled?* For people under duress, the age-old question "How long?" is understandable (as in Ps. 13:1-2; Isa. 6:11; Hab. 1:1; Rev. 6:10). Then the other replies, *For two thousand and three hundred evenings and mornings; then the sanctuary shall be restored to its rightful state.*

In the question of the holy one is the mysterious phrase *the transgression that makes desolate* (8:13). This refers to the intrusion of foreign religion into the temple. Officials authorized by Antiochus IV

Epiphanes set up an altar to Zeus in the Jerusalem temple in (Nov.-Dec.) 167 B.C. (1 Macc. 1:54; 2 Macc. 6:2-5). *[Abomination, p. 276.]* The holy one wonders, "How long will this continue, this detested thing which appalls the faithful and empties the temple of worshipers and of God himself?" (see also notes on 12:5-6).

The response is equally cryptic. Since the regular burnt offering consists of morning and evening sacrifices, the number 2,300 is to be divided by two. Thus it would be 1,150 days, not far from three and one-half years, until the temple would be restored. As in 7:25 (see notes there), the period represents a brief time of intense evil. This passage also provides background for Revelation 11:2, where the city will be trampled for forty-two months. Similarly, Jesus predicts that after the destruction of Jerusalem (A.D. 70), it will be "trampled on by the Gentiles, until the times of the Gentiles are fulfilled" (Luke 21:24). If it means 2,300 days, that is nearly seven years and could refer to the seven years of Daniel 9:27.

In Daniel's visions, periods of time tend to have symbolic significance. They should not be seen as exact in length. The rededication of the Jerusalem temple happened three years and ten days after the altar to Zeus was erected in it (1 Macc. 1:54; 4:52-53) and three and a half years after Apollonius captured Jerusalem for Antiochus (cf. Dan. 7:25; 9:27; 12:7; 12:11-12, resetting the date a bit later).

The Vision Interpreted 8:15-26

8:15-17a Gabriel Appears

As the vision continues, Daniel is perplexed. He seems fully awake, yet in the vision he is still near the Ulai canal! The focus of the vision is on Jerusalem, the faithful people, and the temple. There appears a manlike figure, "a vigorous young man." Then *by the Ulai*, or *between the leaves of the Ulai gate* (JB, note), Daniel hears a human voice. It is from a celestial being speaking human language, perhaps even the voice of God (cf. 4:31, *a voice came from heaven*). The voice says, *Gabriel, help this man understand the vision.*

Canonically, this is the first place in Scripture that an angel is mentioned by name. In the OT, only in Daniel are angels named ("Satan" likely means "an accuser" in 1 Chron. 21:1; Job 1-2; Zech. 3:1-2). The name *Gabriel* means "mighty man of God" or "God is my strength." The archangel Gabriel appears in the vision as a man, setting the stage for the next chapter calling him *the man Gabriel* (9:21). In the book of Daniel, Gabriel is primarily a revealer. In Luke,

Gabriel announces the birth of John (1:11-20) and the birth of Jesus to Mary (1:26-38). He stands in the presence of God (1:19). Thus he can say to Zechariah, "Do not be afraid; . . . your prayer has been heard" (Luke 1:13). To Mary he says, "Do not be afraid; . . . you have found favor with God" (1:30). Gabriel is both a messenger and a revealer of God's purpose.

Gabriel comes *near* to Daniel to help him understand the vision. In Hebrew thinking, when a messenger of God is present, God is also fully present (Gen. 16:7-13; Exod. 23:20). Confronted by the divine presence, Daniel is filled with fear and falls prostrate, *face to the ground.* This parallels the experience of Ezekiel (1:28). To fall on one's face is an extreme form of reverence.

8:17b-22 The Time of the End

Gabriel speaks, *Understand, O mortal, that the vision is for the time of the end.* This is the third time the root for *understand* (*bin*) in the sense of "discern" appears: Daniel seeks *to understand* (8:15); a voice instructs Gabriel to *help* Daniel *understand* (8:16); and Gabriel begins the interpretation of the vision by calling Daniel to *understand* that the vision is for the time of the end.

The question arises, End of what? Is it the end of time? Likely not. Gabriel's terminology must be seen in the context. The holy one asks, *For how long is . . . the sanctuary and host to be trampled?* (8:13). Gabriel refers to *the end* of *the period of wrath* (8:19) and concludes that *it refers to many days from now* (8:26). Perhaps the period of *wrath* refers to God's judgments upon his people because of their sins. Sometimes God uses unbelieving kings as his servants to execute that wrath (8:19; 9:16; 11:36; cf. 1 Macc. 1:64; 3:8; 2 Macc. 5:17, 20; 6:12-16; 7:38; 8:5; Jer. 25:9; 27:6; Rom. 1:18; 13:4). The *time of the end* is the end of the little horn's rebellion against God, when God intervenes in judgment against Antiochus IV Epiphanes. For Daniel, the time is far ahead. A reader in the second century wants it now!

After Gabriel's introductory remark, Daniel falls into a *trance.* This is a comalike state that accompanies the heaven-sent visionary experience. In the final vision, Daniel will experience this again (10:9-10; cf. Gen. 15:12, Abraham's deep sleep; 2 Cor. 12:2-4). Both times Gabriel touches Daniel and sets him upon his feet (cf. Ezek. 1:28—2:2). The touch is to awaken and to strengthen him.

Gabriel continues the interpretation. Much of the information has already been examined in connection with verses 3-8. Additional bits of information are supplied. Concerning the division of Alexander's empire, Gabriel observes that the succeeding kingdoms lack the strength and sovereignty of Alexander's (8:22). Gabriel sees the succession of kings between Alexander and Antiochus Epiphanes as heaping evil upon evil.

8:23-26 A Dreadful King

When the transgressions have reached their full measure, then a king will arise whose evil will outdo all that has gone before. Similarly, Paul writes that those who hindered him from proclaiming the gospel to Gentiles "have constantly been filling up the measure of their sins; but God's wrath has overtaken them at last" (1 Thess. 2:16).

Gabriel lists the characteristics of this dreadful king:

1. *A king of bold countenance* (8:23). It is reported that Antiochus IV Epiphanes thought he had the facial features of Zeus, and that in the shrine for Zeus erected in the Jerusalem temple, the image had the body of Zeus with the face of Antiochus. This was matched by his adoption of the name Epiphanes ("god manifest").

2. *One who understands riddles* (8:23, RSV). *Skilled in intrigue* (NRSV) as a rendering of the Hebrew *idot* ("riddles") is possible, but it puts a negative cast to the description. For the most part, *idah* is used in the OT simply as "riddle" or "enigmatic question" (as in 1 Kings 10:1). Solomon was able to solve difficult situations (1 Kings 3:16-28). Further characterization shows that this despot is malicious and deceptive (8:25). But the translation *one who understands riddles* is here preferred with the sense that this person is clever and even shrewd in untangling hard cases (cf. Dan. 5:12). *[Riddles, p. 294.]* Perhaps this king tried to enhance his superior ability by contact with "other powers," such as the occult.

3. *One strong in power,* causing *fearful destruction,* who *shall succeed in what he does* and *destroy the powerful and the people of the holy ones* (8:24). This is a picture of outward prosperity but at horrible cost. He destroys both property and people that stand in his way. The picture is one of ruthless tyranny not unlike that of Nebuchadnezzar's (cf. 5:19).

4. *By his cunning he shall make deceit prosper* (8:25). Antiochus was notorious for his cunning, which involved flattery, shameless insolence, plots, misrepresentation, double-crossing, surprise attacks, and ruthlessness (11:21, 23, 24, 27, 32). The books of Maccabees

record his treachery in saying one thing and doing another (1 Macc. 1:29-32), and his manipulation of the high priests (2 Macc. 4:7-29).

5. *In his own mind he shall be great* (8:25). Like the ram that *became strong* and *magnified himself* (8:4, NRSV/RSV), and like the male goat (8:8), the little horn magnifies itself (8:11). Gabriel repeats this charge of arrogance-without-accountability. Antiochus especially targeted the Jews for violence. Those to be destroyed are *many*, a term usually applied to the Jews (see notes on 12:2).

6. He *shall even rise up against the Prince of princes* (8:25). This refers to the supreme leader, God himself. Antiochus in arrogance, rebellion, and violence, deifies himself and defies the God of Israel. He expresses his contempt by desecrating the temple, by destroying the books of the Torah, by banning worship of the God of Israel, by polluting the Jerusalem temple with the worship of Zeus, and by oppressing and slaying the faithful. This rebellion climaxes his grasp for power. But his power will be no match for the greater power. Gabriel announces the end of the rebellion. The point has come for God to intervene. The major space in the interpretation has been taken with a description of the little horn that becomes great. The interpreter does not lay stress on the kings of the Medes and the Persians, but on what follows after the territorial thrust of the male goat, the Grecian empire. From the succession of rulers, the spotlight is put on one ruler specifically. *[Antiochus IV Epiphanes, p. 279.]*

Two things should be observed. First, in his own time and in his own way, God will act. How God will break Antiochus is not said. As the horn of Alexander the Great is broken (8:8), so Antiochus will be broken. Though not made explicit, the description of God's action recalls the stone in Nebuchadnezzar's dream (2:34, 45). The stone cut from a mountain *not by human hands* breaks in pieces the mighty kingdoms.

Second, *not by human hands* underscores again the nonresistant theme of Daniel. Gabriel's message suggests that the violent, militaristic resistance of the Maccabeans to Antiochus is not an appropriate expression of faithfulness. *[Maccabees, p. 290.]* *God* will act on behalf of his people.

Gabriel concludes his interpretation by affirming its reliability. The vision of the *evenings and mornings* is true (8:14). The time of the indignation will be short-lived (8:19). Here there is no interpretation, only confirmation. The angel's words are not primarily concerned with calendaring. The vision has stressed the fearsome actions of the crafty despot and that, quite apart from human hands, his power will be snapped. Daniel is to *seal up the vision*. This means that Daniel is to keep the vision a secret because it refers to the distant future. It has no relevance to the time of Daniel or his contemporaries. There is no immediate application.

Postscript: Daniel's Response 8:27

The vision of the little horn coming to power and challenging the worship of God so overwhelms Daniel that he is in bed and *sick* for several days. Later Daniel returns to work for Belshazzar's regime, thus showing that he has not left Babylon. He is in Susa only in his vision. Even with Gabriel's explanation, Daniel still does *not understand* the vision (8:15-17, 27). It is to become clear centuries later. The vision will be unsealed in the days when Antiochus comes to power, when he desecrates the temple and oppresses the saints. *[Antiochus IV Epiphanes, p. 279.]*

The vision in chapter 8 concludes the set of three visions which lean heavily on symbolism (cf. Dan. 2, 7). Subsequent visions will have angelic figures and interpretations, but they will not depend on symbols such as metals (chap. 2) or animals (chaps. 7-8). The pattern of interpretation followed in this commentary holds that these visions are, so to speak, nested inside each other with respect to interpretation. The vision of the statue spans the period from the Babylonian empire till the Greek empire, followed by the universal reign of God (chap. 2). The vision of Daniel 7, generally thought to accord with Daniel 2, begins with the Babylonian empire, pictured as a lion, but concentrates on the fourth, *terrifying and dreadful and exceedingly strong* beast, likely intended to describe Antiochus IV Epiphanes. This will so be charted, with the understanding that the arrogance of the last beast (and of the other beasts) erupts in other empires, too.

The third vision (chap. 8) describes in greater detail the first vision's kingdoms of Medo-Persia and Greece, with major attention given to the arrogant antagonist who as Antiochus Epiphanes may well be representative of tyrants everywhere, and ultimately of any antichrist figure.

The diagram gives empire identities to the metal and animal symbols. To do so is simplistic but perhaps initially helpful. The symbols point to more than a straightforward identification. The first two visions elaborate on the nature of God's intervention (chap. 2) or his adjudication in judgment (chap. 7). The third vision is silent on the manner of terminating the human kingdom except for the comment, *he shall be broken, and not by human hands* (8:25). The first two visions end with the establishment of God's kingdom; not so the third.

DIAGRAM OF THREE VISIONS

Empires	Daniel 2	Daniel 7	Daniel 8
Babylonian	head of gold	lion	———
Median	chest of silver	bear	———
Persian	thighs of bronze	leopard	ram
Greek	legs of iron and clay	dragon-like fourth beast	male goat
Rulers	toes	horns	horns
Antagonist	———	little horn (Antiochus IV Epiphanes)	little horn (Antiochus IV Epiphanes)
Divine *Agent*	the stone that becomes a mountain	one like a son of man, and holy ones	not by human hands
Outcome	earthly kingdoms pulverized; God's kingdom established	beast destroyed; dominion given to holy ones and their people	little horn broken

(A less-plausible alternative is counting the four human empires as Babylonian, Medo-Persian, Greek, Roman. Later Daniel refers to Romans as *a commander* and *Kittim* [11:18, 30]).

THE TEXT IN BIBLICAL CONTEXT

The Coming Distress

The abomination that makes desolate is referred to four times (8:13; 9:27; 11:31; and 12:11). It is the altar of Zeus erected by Antiochus IV Epiphanes in the Jerusalem temple on the altar of burnt offerings.

This sacrilege emptied the temple of true worshipers and of God himself, according to Jewish understanding. *[Abomination, p. 276.]* The phrase appears in 1 Maccabees 1:54-59, written around 100 B.C., and in the synoptic Gospels: Matthew 24:15; Mark 13:14; and Luke 21:20 (without the word "abomination"). Paul foretells the same type of desolating sacrilege in 2 Thessalonians 2:3-4, and Revelation 13:12 tells of emperor worship enforced.

In response to a disciple's observation about the temple, "What large stones and what large buildings!" Jesus replies, "Do you see these great buildings? Not one stone will be left here one stone upon another; all will be thrown down" (Mark 13:1-2).

Later Peter, James, John, and Andrew ask Jesus privately, "When will this be, and what will be the sign when all these things are about to be accomplished?" (Mark 13:1-4). In response, Jesus speaks at length about the interval between his ascension and his return and deals with three separate matters: (1) the destruction of Jerusalem, (2) the persecution of the new community by authorities within and outside of Judaism, and (3) the continuing life of the new community looking to the end of the present age. Jesus' discourse in content and style resembles the apocalyptic material of Daniel and draws heavily from it. Note also that the material in Mark 13, Matthew 24, and Luke 21 introduces the passion account, the eschatological and apocalyptic event by which all human activity is and will be weighed. The death of Jesus is the final battle in the war against sin and death. One wonders, however, why this Synoptic Apocalypse does not refer to resurrection, as in Daniel 12:2-3.

From the words of Jesus, it is difficult to tell whether he envisions the time between his ascension and return as long or short. The "last days" signify the period between his ascension and return (Acts 2:16-17; Heb. 1:2). The incarnation, the crucifixion, the resurrection, and the ascension make up the center of the great saving act of God which spans all time and eternity. The interval between the ascension and the return, when the kingdom of God comes in its fullness, is in the hand of God (Mark 13:32). If there is delay, it is planned to allow humans to come to repentance and faith (cf. 2 Pet. 3:8-9).

Signs will announce that the return of the Son of Man is near (Mark 13:5-23, 29), and yet it will be sudden and unexpected (13:33, 35). Not even the Son of God knows when (13:32). Because no one knows when the Lord will return, disciples are warned to watch, to be ready, carrying out the tasks assigned (13:33-37). The preceding signs are not given to enable observers to predict the exact time of his return. Instead, they are given so that believers—in every age and throughout the whole world—who are so easily distracted from readiness, may be called back again and again to continue to "watch" and take heed.

In both Matthew 24:15 and Mark 13:14, the reference to "the desolating sacrilege" comes in Jesus' discussion of the fall of Jerusalem. Luke is more specific: "When you see Jerusalem surrounded by armies, then know that its desolation has come near" (Luke 21:20). Matthew is more explicit in referring to this sacrilege "standing in the holy place," the temple—thus tying the remark to Daniel 8:13; 9:27; 11:31; 12:11). In the nature of prophecy, a fulfillment at a given time may not exhaust the prophecy.

Thus, the comment about *the abomination that makes desolate* (8:13) can accurately describe the action of Antiochus IV Epiphanes. That catastrophe of Gentiles desecrating the temple and instituting strange worship becomes a prototype echoed in later events and in actions by the Romans. One example is Caligula's decree in A.D. 39-40 (later rescinded) to convert Jewish places of worship into shrines for the imperial cult and erect a statue of the emperor as Zeus in the Jerusalem temple (perhaps reflected in 2 Thess. 2:4). Other examples are the destruction of the temple by Titus and the Romans in A.D. 70 (foretold in Mark 13); Hadrian's construction there of a temple honoring Jupiter around A.D. 130; and attempts to enforce emperor worship (Rev. 13:8, 12; 19:20). Similarly, the dreadful king, as the incarnation of evil, describes Antiochus IV Epiphanes, and that description fits other tyrants in human history. It may ultimately characterize a figure called antichrist. *[Antichrist, p. 277.]*

It was a common practice in the day of Jesus and in earlier centuries for conquering nations to assert their sovereignty over a defeated nation by dethroning its gods and replacing them with the gods of the conqueror (though Cyrus showed interest in restoring temples and local worship; Ezra 1). With the actions of Antiochus IV Epiphanes in mind, Jesus anticipated the result of Roman occupation and Jewish resistance. The time would come when the Roman imperial-eagle standards would be placed in the temple area. Whether in the war of A.D. 66-70 or in the revolt of A.D. 130-135, the words of Jesus in Mark 13:14-20 (and parallels) were dramatically fulfilled. Archaeological discoveries give dramatic evidence to the destruction inflicted by the Romans. The note "let the reader understand" (Matt. 24:15) reminds the new community of the horrors faced by the faithful in the days of Antiochus IV Epiphanes and warns that a similar challenge will soon confront them. Jesus drew on Daniel 12:1 to describe the coming *anguish.*

Whatever happens, Jesus' new community keeps looking to the end of the age, to the return of the Lord. Christ's description of his return is also drawn from Daniel: "Then they will see the 'Son of man coming in clouds' with great power and glory" (Mark 13:26; cf. Dan. 7:13-14).

THE TEXT IN THE LIFE OF THE CHURCH

Angels, Ministering Servants

Chapter 8 introduces the angel Gabriel, who appears again in chapter 9. Gabriel may have been the heavenly messenger who spoke to Daniel in chapter 7. The angel Michael is named in chapters 10 and 12.

In the Old Testament, angels fill a significant role. Their appearance symbolizes the glory and beneficent presence of God. The "Blessing of Moses" reports that when the law was given at Sinai, the Lord was accompanied by "myriads of holy ones" (Deut. 33:2). Stephen says his critics "received the law as ordained by angels, and yet . . . have not kept it" (Acts 7:38, 53). Paul also wrote that the law "was ordained through angels by a mediator" (Gal. 3:19; cf. Heb. 2:2). The prophet Zechariah (14:5) expected the Lord to come in victory, "and all the holy ones with him."

Angels were messengers of God, as in Daniel 7–9. They were servants of God, sent to minister to and to serve the people of God (Heb. 1:7). Angels urged Lot to leave Sodom (Gen. 19). An angel ministered to Hagar (Gen. 16). The angel of the Lord appeared to Moses in the burning bush (Exod. 3:2, 4; Acts 7:30, 35), showing that at times God himself may appear as an angel of the Lord (cf. Gen. 16:7, 13; Exod. 14:19, 24). An angel "touched" Elijah and provided food when he sat discouraged under the broom tree (1 Kings 19:4-8; cf. Dan. 8:18). An angel protected Daniel in the lions' den and his three friends in the fiery furnace (6:22; 3:28). In the literature produced in intertestamental times, as for example in 1 Enoch, much is said about angels. Names and hierarchical status are noted. One reads about good angels and bad angels and about the destiny of the latter. They may travel in disguise (Tobit 5–6).

When Jesus was born, the angel of the Lord along with a multitude of angels announced his birth to the shepherds (Luke 2:8-15). Angels ministered to Jesus in the wilderness (Matt. 4:11) and as he prayed on the night of his betrayal (Luke 22:43). Luke's story of the founding and expansion of the church as told in Acts is filled with stories of angels. An angel of the Lord opened prison doors to release the apostles (Acts 5:19), and one directed Philip down the road between Jerusalem and deserted Gaza (rebuilt elsewhere) to meet an Ethiopian official (8:26-39). Angels were active in the events leading to the conversion of Cornelius (10:3, 7, 22; 11:13). An angel of the Lord enabled Peter to escape from his prison cell (12:7-11).

The death of Herod Agrippa I was through the intervention of the angel of the Lord, according to Acts (12:22-23). This tyrant was acclaimed as "a god" and met his end "eaten by worms," on both counts much like Antiochus Epiphanes. In his death, Antiochus fulfilled his name Epiphanes, "god manifest," in a way he did not intend: "He who only a little while before had thought in his superhuman arrogance that he could command the waves of the sea, . . . was brought down to earth and carried in a litter, making the power of *God manifest* to all. And so the ungodly man's body swarmed with worms" (2 Macc. 9:8-9, italics added). Both Herod and Antiochus were broken but *not by human hands* (Dan. 8:25).

In Daniel's visions, the archangel Michael *contends* for Israel (10:21), and fiery judgment comes directly from God upon the Greeks (7:10-11; cf. Heb. 1:7). A destroying angel may be sent to carry out God's judgments (Exod. 12:23; 2 Sam. 24:16; Isa. 37:36). An angel appeared to Paul during a great storm at sea to give a message of hope and salvation (Acts 27:23-24). According to the Bible, angels are assigned to churches, nations, and individuals (Rev. 1–3; Deut. 32:8; Dan. 10:13, 20-21; 12:1; Matt. 18:10).

Are angels bringing messages, serving God, and ministering to the church today? Some people suggest that the subject of angels should be treated like Santa Claus in connection with Christmas. Others, however, theologians such as Karl Barth and evangelists such as Billy Graham, believe in the real existence of angels. In modern times, persons are so committed to scientific explanations that the work of angels may wrongly be ascribed to natural phenomena. Could it be that unexpected insights, moments of protection, or times of profound comfort might be the work of these messengers of God?

Beyond that, the church has the responsibility to perform many of the tasks assigned to angels. The same word in Hebrew (*mal'ak*) or Greek (*angelos*) can be translated *angel*, *messenger* (of God), or *agent*, depending on the context. Believers are to be messengers, angels of mercy, announcing peace and salvation, that "God reigns"

(Isa. 52:7; Rom. 10:14-17; Dan. 4:3; 6:26; 7:9). They are to bring prophetic words of warning and of impending judgment, like those brought to Lot, Nebuchadnezzar, and Belshazzar—but not to enact God's judgment; vengeance is the Lord's (Rom. 12:19; Deut. 32:35). Believers are to proclaim the good news of salvation and to call persons to repentance. They are to comfort, protect, and strengthen those in need. Perhaps they can aspire to be like Stephen; when he gave his testimony of faith in his time of crisis, all who sat in the council saw that "his face was like the face of an angel" (Acts 6:15).

Daniel 9:1-27

The Meaning of Jeremiah's Prophecy

PREVIEW

When one passage of the Bible interprets another part, we rejoice. Yet in chapter 9 Gabriel gives Daniel an interpretation of Jeremiah's prophecy concerning *seventy years* that is more puzzling than the original text (Jer. 25:12; Dan. 9:2).

Though separated in time by seven or eight years from the *third year of the reign of Belshazzar* (546 B.C.; Dan. 8:1) to *the first year of Darius* (539-538 B.C.; 9:1), chapters 8 and 9 form a unit. Both chapters have similar structures. In both, Gabriel points to the coming outrages of a dreadful king. Chapter 8 records Daniel's visionary overview of world history, followed by Gabriel's interpretation of the vision. In chapter 9, Daniel's prayer provides an overview of holy history in which Israel's unfaithfulness is contrasted with God's faithfulness. Following Daniel's prayer, the angel Gabriel appears in a vision to interpret *the word of the Lord to the prophet Jeremiah* (9:2) concerning the seventy years on which Daniel was meditating before his prayer.

The prayer of Daniel is like an insert (9:4-19). One could go immediately from verse 4b to verse 20 without destroying the sense of the chapter. The reader, however, is greatly enriched by the inclusion of Daniel's prayer. It reveals the type of supplication anticipated by

Solomon, a prayer of repentance to which God responds (1 Kings 8:46-53). It also provides insight into the prayers Daniel likely offers when three times a day he kneels at his window, *open toward Jerusalem* (6:10-11).

In Daniel's prayer, the word *LORD* is printed in NRSV eight times in small capital letters. This signifies that Daniel uses the sacred name for God, known only to the Israelites and rarely uttered. This is the only passage where the name *Yahweh* (*LORD*) appears in the book of Daniel (9:2, 4, 8, 10, 13, 14 [twice], 20). The use of this name in Daniel's prayer reflects his special relationship with the God of Israel. Similarly here, *Adonai* (*Lord*) is used eleven times as a substitute for the personal name of God, *Yahweh*, and only once elsewhere in Daniel (1:2; 9:3, 4, 7, 8, 9, 15, 16, 17, 19 [thrice]; cf. addressing the king [1:10] or an angel [10:16-19; 12:8] as *adoni, my lord*).

OUTLINE

Introduction, 9:1-2

9:1	Date
9:2	Meditation on Scripture

Daniel's Intercessory Prayer, 9:3-19

9:3-4a	Preparation for Prayer
9:4b-14	"If They . . . repent" (1 Kings 8:47-48)
9:15-19	"And Plead" (1 Kings 8:47, 49)

Heaven's Response: A Vision, 9:20-27

9:20-23	Gabriel's Arrival
9:24-27	Gabriel's Interpretation of Seventy Years

Sevenfold Chastisement	9:24
First Seven Weeks of Years	9:25a
Next Sixty-two Weeks of Years	9:25b
Final Week of Years	9:26-27

EXPLANATORY NOTES

Introduction 9:1-2

9:1 Date

In the first year of Darius refers to Darius the Mede, who was likely Gobyras/Gubaru, ruling Mesopotamia for eight months under Cyrus, or perhaps Cyrus himself (see notes on 5:30; 6:1, 28). Cyrus issued the decree for the exiles to return to Jerusalem (2 Chron. 36:23). The first year would have been 539-538 B.C. *[Cyrus, p. 284.]*

9:2 Meditation on Scripture

Daniel has been studying Jewish sacred books such as Jeremiah. This is the first time this book refers to *the books* (in other words, holy books or Scriptures). Daniel mentions specifically *the word of the Lord to the prophet Jeremiah* (9:2). Other visions come without being dependent on Daniel's action. But the vision which follows the prayer is prompted by Daniel's study of Scripture. He is likely meditating on these passages:

> This whole land shall become a ruin and a waste, and these nations shall serve the king of Babylon seventy years. Then after seventy years are completed, I will punish the king of Babylon and that nation, the land of the Chaldeans, for their iniquity says the Lord. (605 B.C.; Jer. 25:11-12)
>
> For thus says the Lord: Only when Babylon's seventy years are completed will I visit you, and I will fulfill to you my promise and bring you back to this place. For surely I know the plans I have for you, says the Lord, plans for your welfare and not for harm, to give you a future with hope. Then when you call upon me and come and pray to me, I will hear you. When you search for me, you will find me; if you seek me with all your heart, I will let you find me, says the Lord. (594 B.C.; Jer. 29:10-14a)

Daniel's study has led both to puzzlement and then to prayer. The puzzle comes from Jeremiah's prediction of seventy years (cf. Zech. 1:12). With the defeat of the Babylonians, Daniel wonders about the meaning of the seventy years of Jeremiah's prophecy. Jeremiah did not say that Israel would be in exile seventy years but that they would serve Babylon seventy years, after which God would punish the Babylonians and their land for their iniquity (Jer. 25:11-12). God would visit Israel "when Babylon's seventy years are completed" (Jer. 29:10) and when the land of Israel has "made up for" its Sabbath years not kept (2 Chron. 26:21; Lev. 25:1-7; 26:34-35; cf. 1 Macc. 6:49, 52). Now that Babylonian rule is terminated, Daniel wants to know what the implications will be for his people. Nebuchadnezzar came to power in 605 B.C., and now it is 539-538 B.C.

Approximately *seventy years* has passed, a human lifetime. It should also be observed that the number *seventy* is the result of multiplying seven times ten, which suggests "completion" to those who see meaning in numbers. Likely Jeremiah intended the seventy years to refer to a completed period rather than to precisely seventy years.

To calculate 70 precisely, one wonders what dates should be

used for the count. At the early end, Nineveh fell to the Medes and the Babylonians in 612 B.C. In Nebuchadnezzar's first year (605-604 B.C.), Jeremiah made his prophecy of "these nations" serving Nebuchadnezzar for 70 years (Jer. 25). Judah likely submitted to Babylon in late 604 B.C. In the fourth year of Zedekiah, 594 B.C., Jeremiah (29:10) again prophesied that the Israelites would serve Babylon 70 years. *[Kings of Judah, p. 288.]* The fall of Jerusalem could be calculated from 597 B.C. (first major deportation) or from 587/586 B.C. (temple destroyed and second major deportation).

At the other end, one could use 539 B.C. (fall of Babylon), 538 B.C. (Cyrus's decree for return from exile), or 520-516 B.C. (temple rebuilt). There are 70 years between the temple destroyed and the temple rebuilt, a key symbol for the nation (Zech. 1:12). *[Chronology, p. 283.]* From the 594 B.C. prophecy to 538 B.C. is 56 years. The length of the largest captivity was about 48 years, from 587/586 B.C. to 538 B.C. (2 Chron. 36:20-23, taking 70 as a round number). From the fall of Nineveh (612 B.C.) to the fall of Babylon (539 B.C.) is 73 years. From Nebuchadnezzar's defeat of Egypt (605 B.C.) to the decree for return (538 B.C.) is nearly 70 years. Since Jeremiah refers to "Babylon's seventy years" (29:10a), they are best taken as an imprecise reference to the period of Babylon's domination over surrounding nations. It is about a lifetime, such as Daniel's (Ps. 90:10; Ezra 3:12; Hag. 2:3), and certainly much longer than the false prophet Hananiah's 594 B.C. prediction of two years! (Jer. 28).

Daniel's Intercessory Prayer 9:3-19

9:3-4a Preparation for Prayer

The question of Israel's future is extremely important to Daniel. Jeremiah indicated the importance of prayer in bringing restoration. Solomon also recognized that in the event of being carried captive, the prayer of repentance and supplication would bring forgiveness and restoration (1 Kings 8:46-52). Consequently, Daniel makes vigorous preparation for prayer.

The prayer is laced with vocabulary and concepts drawn, quite likely, from other parts of Jeremiah. Daniel, to judge from the prayer, is steeped in Scripture. It would be a good exercise to examine the prayer for its linkages with Jeremiah and other Scriptures, such as Deuteronomy, with prayers such as Solomon's (1 Kings 8:23-53), or with prayers after the exile (Ezra 9:6-15; Neh. 1:5-11; 9:5-37).

Daniel reports, *I turned to the Lord God* (9:3), *turned my face to the Lord God* (RSV). This means that he faces toward Jerusalem, the city of God, in accord with Solomon's prayer that captives should "pray to you toward their land" (1 Kings 8:48; cf. Dan. 6:10). His prayer and supplication is supported with *fasting and sackcloth and ashes*. Daniel's prayer is one of penitence. Hence, it is fitting that these symbols of self-abasement precede his prayer. Neither food nor personal appearance is to interfere with his concentration on prayer.

In structure and content, the parallels between Daniel's prayer, Ezra 9:6-15, and Nehemiah 1:5-11; 9:6-37 suggest a type of penitential prayer common to the second-temple period and to the emerging synagogues.

9:4b-14 "If They . . . Repent" (1 Kings 8:47-48)

Daniel's prayer begins with his recognition of God's greatness and awesomeness (9:4). The description of God as having and bringing righteousness (*ṣedaqah*) is frequent (9:7, 14, 16, 24); it is likely an echo from Jeremiah's writings (cf. Jer. 12:1: "You will be in the right [*ṣadiq*], O Lord") as well as other Scriptures (such as Ps. 119:137). God's righteousness contrasts sharply with Daniel's people, who are not righteous (9:18). Daniel lists characteristics of God. He identifies the qualities of *mercy* (*raḥamim*, plural) and *forgiveness* (*selihot*, plural; 9:9). The note on compassion links with a section in Jeremiah's Book of Consolation (30:1—31:40). God is "deeply moved, his compassion (*raḥamim*, a word associated with "womb") is stirred. Mother-like, God's affections are aroused as the wayward son Ephraim repents (Jer. 31:20).

Early in the prayer, Daniel acknowledges that God is forgiving; at the end of the prayer, he appeals for God to exercise that forgiveness toward his people. In addition, he describes God as *keeping covenant and steadfast love* (*berit* and *ḥesed;* 9:4). Though largely petition, the prayer is rich with its ascriptions to God (cf. Neh. 1:5-6). On his knees, one may imagine, Daniel lifts his hands heavenward as he acknowledges this awesome God.

But then, so one can visualize, Daniel falls forward with his face to the ground as he catalogs Israel's sins, using a variety of terms. Repeatedly he confesses that *we have sinned* (*ḥata;* 9:5, 8, 11, 15c) and uses the related noun for *sin* (9:16, 20, 24). Some form of this root word is found more than 600 times in the OT and thus is a common way to speak of evil. It is also used of slingers hitting the target without missing (*ḥata*) the mark (Judg. 20:16). Twice Daniel confesses the evil of acting *wickedly* (*rašaʿ*; 9:5, 15c). The word signifies the opposite of doing good; in the Psalms it frequently describes wrongdoing or acting unjustly. Twice, too, the list includes the evil of rebellion (*marad*) (9:5, 9). A classic instance of defying authority is Israel's refusal to move into the land at Kadesh-barnea (Deut. 1:25-26). Twice, too, Daniel points to iniquity (*ʿawon*), essentially perversity and waywardness (9:13, 16). There are two references to Israel *turning aside* (*sur*), stepping off the correct track (9:5, 11).

Daniel continues the rehearsal of failure. Israel did not obey (*šamaʿ*, *listen to*) God and his prophets (9:6, 10, 11, 14). Such language is characteristic of Jeremiah, who used forms of the word "obey/listen" 184 times. The accusation "You have not listened" is found thirty times in Jeremiah. Beyond all these evils, there is the people's failure to understand God's *truth* or *fidelity* (9:13, RSV/NRSV). Thus Daniel catalogs evil and gathers together all sin, every kind, to its full extent. In light of Israel's sinfulness resulting in captivity, and in memory of Solomon's prayer, Daniel's prayer of confession and repentance indicates that he takes Scripture seriously. Solomon's prayer provides the outline and terminology for Daniel's intercession:

> If they sin against you, . . . and you are angry with them and give them to an enemy, so that they are carried away captive to the land of the enemy, far off or near; yet *if they* come to their senses in the land to which they have been taken captive, and *repent*, and *plead with you*, . . . saying, "We have sinned and have done wrong; we have acted wickedly"; *if they repent* . . . and pray to you toward their land, . . . then hear in heaven your dwelling place their prayer and *their plea*, . . . and forgive your people. . . . Let your eyes be open to the plea of your servant, and to the plea of your people Israel, listening to them whenever they call to you. (1 Kings 8:46-52, italics added)

Daniel highlights the sins of the leaders, *our kings*, *our princes*, . . . *our officials* (9:6, 8). Perhaps he is thinking of Jeremiah's roll call of kings, especially Jehoiakim, indicted for greed, showiness, and neglect of the poor (Jer. 22:13-17; cf. 22:11—23:6). Kings, shepherds, are seen as contributors, along with the rest of society, to the evil situation (cf. Jer. 23; Ezek. 34; Neh. 9:32-33). Daniel, himself a government official, is sensitive to the large responsibility of those who rule.

The prayer throughout emphasizes the extreme contrast between the character of God and the condition of his people. The central plea of Daniel's prayer of repentance is gathered up in the contrasts between God's *righteousness* and the people's dishonor and *open shame* (9:7-8), between God's *mercy and forgiveness* and the way the people *rebelled against* God (9:9). The basis for Daniel's prayer is his recognition of God's grace as revealed in righteousness, mercy, and forgiveness. Toward the end of his prayer, Daniel says specifically, *We do not present our supplications before you on the ground of our righteousness, but on the ground of your great mercies* (9:18).

Daniel's repentance embraces all his kinspeople, those who remain in Judea and Jerusalem, and those who have been carried far away. All are guilty of treachery, and in open shame their faces betray their guilt. They look like persons caught in immoral acts.

In his prayer Daniel turns from addressing God to addressing the people directly (9:12-14). Some see this as a "prayer sermon" in which Daniel explains why the disaster has come upon them. The fact of exile in a distant land should not have come as a surprise. Long ago *the curse and the oath* for transgressing the law were set forth in the *law of Moses*, the Pentateuch (9:11). The people of Israel are familiar with priestly teachings that promise sevenfold punishment for disobedience (repeated four times: Lev. 26:18, 21, 24, 27). They are familiar, too, with the blessings and curses of Deuteronomy 27–30.

In this prayer sermon, Daniel underscores God's autonomy. God gave repeated warnings (9:12), but there was no obedient response. Therefore, the dreadful destruction of Jerusalem and of the temple are to be seen as just acts on God's part (9:13-14). God activated all the curses that resulted in the present calamity, *as it is written* (9:13). This is a phrase important to Jewish and Christian interpretation of Scripture. Scripture must be taken seriously. Note the form of Daniel's prayer of repentance upon meditating on the word of the Lord to Jeremiah the prophet (9:2). It indicates that Daniel himself has studied Scripture and followed it carefully.

Others see Daniel's direct address to the people as a "summons to repentance." This is a standardized speech form that appears frequently in the OT (cf. 2 Kings 17:13; Jer. 3:12-13; Neh. 1:8-9). There are usually four parts:

1. An accusation: *All Israel has transgressed your law and turned aside, refusing to obey your voice.* (9:11)
2. An admonition: *We did not entreat the favor of the Lord our God.* (9:13)
3. A threat: *The Lord kept watch over this calamity.* (9:14)
4. A promise: *The Lord our God is right.* (9:14)

The suffering of exile and in the days to come *the abomination that desecrates* (9:27) are traceable to the same cause: *We have disobeyed his voice* (9:14). Later, in the days of Antiochus IV Epiphanes, the second temple stands, but it is stripped of all that contributes to the worship of the God of Israel. The sanctuary is contaminated by the presence of the altar to Zeus (2 Macc. 6:1-2). Disaster follows disobedience. Daniel prays as he does because he believes that God is faithful, merciful, and forgiving. Daniel confesses that to God belongs righteousness, because God is righteous. Daniel also believes the ancient teachings that prayers of repentance will restore relationships with God, because he is the God of steadfast love, the covenant-keeping God (9:4).

9:15-19 "And Plead" (1 Kings 8:47, 49)

What would undo the calamity? Not new forms of piety. Not more sacrifices nor armed intervention. What has been lacking and what is needed to bring about change is repentance. Daniel turns from speaking to his fellows to addressing God: *And now, O Lord our God* (9:15). Daniel returns to God's acts in the Exodus. The deliverance from Egypt was one of the great events in forming Israel's faith. References to the Exodus are made to emphasize God's grace and to encourage obedient response to this gracious act (cf. Exod. 20:2; Deut. 6:21-25). Here it provides the backdrop for confession of sin and a plea for mercy.

Daniel repentantly confesses, *We have sinned, we have done wickedly*. He pleads on the basis of God's *righteous acts* to turn his anger and wrath from *your city Jerusalem*, and from *your holy mountain,* where the temple once stood. On behalf of the people, Daniel acknowledges that what happened to Jerusalem and to the people resulted from *our sins* and *the iniquities of our ancestors* (9:16). They are under the *wrath* of God (see notes on 8:19; 11:36).

Now therefore signals the turn in the prayer to supplication (9:17). The first half of the prayer has not contained a petition; Daniel has confessed the greatness of God and the awfulness of Israel's sin (9:4-14). Only now does he make his requests. The first half of the prayer is bracketed largely by noting God's righteousness (9:7, 14); the second half, although still sounding the note of God's righteousness, leads off with God's activity in the Exodus. Daniel confesses the people's sin against the One who redeemed them from Egypt and recognizes the calamities that followed sin. He prays,

1. That God's anger and wrath would turn away from Jerusalem and the holy mountain (9:16).
2. That God would cause his face to shine upon the sanctuary which is desolate (9:17).
3. That God would respond on the basis of his great mercy (9:18).

In his supplications, Daniel like Nehemiah (1:6) uses the terminology of Solomon's prayer, "Let your eyes be open to the plea of your servant, and to the plea of your people Israel, listening to them whenever they call to you" (1 Kings 8:52).

Daniel urges several reasons why God might be moved to respond to his supplication:

1. God's people are experiencing the reproach of their neighbors (9:16).
2. God's reputation is at stake, and so it is for the sake of his name that a new *act* of deliverance is needed (9:17, 19).
3. The city of Jerusalem and its people *bear* God's name (9:18-19).
4. God's mercies are sufficiently great to meet Israel's failures (9:18).

Daniel's requests, in lawyer fashion, are well argued. His prayer is intense and passionate, but also thoughtful.

The prayer of repentance is like that prescribed by Jeremiah and also like that of Solomon's prayer. Jeremiah (3:22b-25) supplies his people with a model prayer of repentance which has points of resemblance with Daniel's prayer: acknowledgment of shame and confusion of face; a forthright statement, "we have sinned"; a recognition of evil that reaches back to previous generations; vocabulary of failure to obey; and a declaration that salvation and mercy must come from God. On the other hand, some expressions in Daniel's prayer seem to be inspired by Solomon's prayer (1 Kings 8:23-53, esp. 48-53): "Let your eyes be open, . . . listening to . . . your people, . . . brought . . . out of Egypt." Thus Daniel's prayer seems modeled after other OT prayers of repentance. His prayer, in turn, becomes a model for others.

Daniel's reference to the Exodus also suggests that the present calamity is so great that another act of salvation in the magnitude of the Exodus is necessary, a similar manifestation of God's *mighty hand* (9:15, 19). As the Lord glorified himself in rescuing his people from Egypt, so now God should act, *for your own sake, O Lord* (9:17, 19).

Daniel prays, *Let your face shine upon your desolated sanctuary* (9:17). This calls to mind part of the Aaronic benediction (Num. 6:25). In Daniel's day the temple is desolate, destroyed in 586 B.C. The temple, considered a vehicle of God's blessing, is itself in need of that blessing. Daniel prays for its restoration for the Lord's sake, so that God would not be a stranger in his own land (cf. Jer. 14:7-8). This prayer also has implications for the days of Antiochus IV Epiphanes, when the temple was desecrated and desolate.

Daniel's prayer climaxes with a series of requests in imperative form (9:19):

O Lord, hear;
O Lord, forgive;
O Lord, listen and act and do not delay.

There is hardly another prayer in the Scripture so urgent. God is called upon to relieve Daniel's people burdened by sin and afflicted by merciless oppression. God is to act without delay—for his own sake (9:17, 19), to bring salvation to the city and to his people, who *bear your name.*

To act *for your own sake* suggests that since God has punished his disobedient people, thus showing to the whole world his righteousness and justice, he should now reveal to the world his *steadfast love* (9:4), *mercy, and forgiveness* (9:9) by restoring his people. In acts of restoration, God would reveal himself more fully. For Daniel, the present crisis is a discredit to those who bear God's name. The present crisis is also a discredit to God's own name. Thus Daniel prays that God would restore his people and his city, *for your own sake* (cf. Ezek. 20:9, 14, 22; 36:20-22).

Daniel knows that God has already decreed the time and manner of his intervention in human affairs (cf. 7:22, 25-27; 8:25). Why then does he pray? His prayer suggests several reasons. Through prayer, Daniel like Moses expresses his agony and cries out to God to have mercy on his people even though they have sinned grievously (Exod. 32:31-32). God listens to such true leaders. In prayer, formal and reasoned appeals are made to God's mercy. There is a recognition of God's autonomy and of his will not to destroy that which is his own. In prayer, there is hope. God's faithfulness in the past gives confidence that he will act in the present crisis. Though the effects of calamity may never be removed, yet relationships with him can be restored, because he is a covenant-keeping God (9:4).

Heaven's Response: A Vision 9:20-27

Daniel's long prayer might have distracted the casual reader from the initial question. Yet Daniel's urgency reinforces that question: How should the seventy years of Jeremiah's prediction be interpreted? (9:2). This is a desperate rather than an academic matter. Now comes the answer.

9:20-23 Gabriel's Arrival

While Daniel is *speaking*, *praying*, *confessing*, and *presenting* his *supplication*, the angel Gabriel appears in a vision as he has in a previous vision, likely the one of chapter 8 (cf. 8:16), though some suggest the one of chapter 7 (cf. 7:16). Daniel has been praying for an indefinite period. The angel appears at *the time of the evening sacrifice* (9:21). This time reference is a reminder that faithful Jews remember the worship practices of the temple before it was destroyed. Gabriel comes *in swift flight*. This is the first text to suggest that angels have wings like other heavenly creatures such as the seraphim (Isa. 6:2) or the cherubim (Exod. 25:20). The scene corresponds to ancient Near Eastern depictions in drawings, reliefs, and statues.

Gabriel appears like a *man* (9:21) and speaks like one. Gabriel, to judge from other biblical references, is a key messenger angel (8:16-17; cf. Luke 1:19). Indeed, the Hebrew word *mal'ak* and the Greek *angelos* can be translated as "messenger" or "angel" (see TLC for Dan. 8). Jewish literature of the first two centuries B.C. and A.D. (such as 1 Enoch) lists hierarchies of angels and names many demonic figures. Gabriel addresses him: *Daniel, I have now come to give you wisdom and understanding. At the beginning of your supplications a word went out, and I have come to declare it, for you are greatly beloved. So consider the word and understand the vision* (9:22-23).

The appearance of Gabriel indicates that Daniel's prayers are heard and will be answered. The answer, however, is not directly related to the prayer. Prior to his prayer, as Daniel was meditating on Jeremiah (25:11-12; 29:10-14), he wondered about the *seventy years* and their relation to his people's present situation. When Gabriel appears, he comes to give *wisdom and understanding. Understanding* is a gift from God and requires constant diligence. It involves character and is more than IQ. *Understanding* is insight backed up by or in harmony with a moral life. Even before Daniel prays, when he was in the process of self-abasement, God had prepared *a word* for Daniel (9:23). This Gabriel will deliver.

This word mentions the restoration and rebuilding of Jerusalem as a counting point (9:25) but does not otherwise relate to the return of the people from captivity. Instead, the word gives new meaning to the original, inspired words of Jeremiah about the seventy years. This revelation is brought to Daniel because *you are greatly beloved*. Daniel is held in high esteem by God, as was another servant (cf. Isa. 42:1). Consequently, God sends the new revealing word in the form of a vision. Daniel is instructed to give serious attention to what will follow. The answer to Daniel's prayer assumes return and restoration, then gives serious understanding about further troubles to come.

9:24-27 Gabriel's Interpretation of Seventy Years

Sevenfold Chastisement 9:24

Gabriel supplies a simple solution to Daniel's problem concerning the seventy years. Jeremiah (29:10) gives the Lord's promise that "when Babylon's seventy years are completed," he would bring Israel back to Jerusalem. But those "seventy years" need to be interpreted. According to Gabriel, *seventy weeks are decreed* (Hebrew: *seventy sevens*). Since in Jeremiah the reference is to years, the more usual rendering in Daniel 9:24, *seventy weeks of years*, makes sense (RSV). Jeremiah's "seventy years" become years to the count of seventy times seven (weeks), or 490 years. The explanation for the 490 years derives from Leviticus (26:18, 21, 24, 27), which threatens a "sevenfold" punishment for disobedience and unfaithfulness. The land needed to make up its unkept sabbatical years (see notes on Dan. 9:2). The seventy years of exile and suffering which resulted from disobedience and unfaithfulness will be multiplied sevenfold, as promised in Leviticus. *[Seventy Weeks of Years, p. 295.]*

According to Gabriel, the 490 years will culminate in six blessings for Daniel's people and for the holy city. The statement that follows is not related to the whole world, as in chapter 7. Instead, the reply relates to Daniel's prayer for "your city, . . . your holy mountain, . . . and your people" (9:16). God is in ultimate control of history, both secular and sacred, but as Gabriel makes clear, God's special concern here is for Jerusalem, the temple, and faithful Jews. Three of the six blessings deal with sin: (1) *to finish the transgression*, (2) *to put an end to sin, and* (3) *to atone for iniquity*. Three deal with restoration: (1) *to bring in everlasting righteousness*, (2) *to seal both vision and prophet, and* (3) *to anoint a most holy place*.

The first three appear to be a direct response to Daniel's confession made in his prayer, *We have sinned* (9:5), and to his supplication, *O Lord, forgive!* (9:19). In this, Gabriel parallels the words of Isaiah (40:1b-2), "Jerusalem . . . has served her term." Yet this *word* from God was given *at the beginning of* Daniel's prayer (9:23). The message points to a time in the future. In quick reply to Daniel's prayer, the angel tells of already-decreed blessings. Indeed, the word that Gabriel brings does not deal with past events except that the extended period of seventy weeks of years is *to atone for the iniquity* of the Israelites. Instead, the message sheds light on what is to come. God determines the outcome of future events, in response to Israel's past unfaithfulness and Daniel's intercessory prayer. These gracious acts of God are to prepare the people for persecution and suffering that will come under the *abomination that desolates* (Dan. 9:27).

God's faithfulness has been demonstrated in delivering Shadrach, Meshach, and Abednego from Nebuchadnezzar's burning fiery furnace and Daniel from the lions' den. In the word to Gabriel, God's deliverance will bring *an end to sin, . . . atone for iniquity, . . . and bring in everlasting righteousness* (9:24). The verb "to atone" (*kipper*) has the sense of "to cover, cleanse, or cancel." It would not be far off the mark to think of forgiveness and pardon as bringing closure. From the time of Daniel to the time of the crisis under Antiochus, God has promised deliverance as persons turn in repentance to the living God (9:5) and experience him as the forgiving and righteous One.

But this does not depend *on the ground of our righteousness, but on the ground of your great mercies* (9:18). These gracious acts of God are designed to create and maintain a faithful community, *your people* (9:19), not a collection of isolated, independent individuals. In many respects, Daniel 9:24 reveals the righteous God (9:7, 14, 16) who longs to establish his righteousness among his people.

The three aspects of restoration in a measure parallel the first three notes on sin. In place of transgression, eternal righteousness is brought in. Righteousness, the character of God (9:14), will be realized. Sealing *both vision and prophet* (9:24) is paralleled in 8:26 (cf. 12:4, 9). Here *prophet* refers to Jeremiah (Dan. 9:2), not to Daniel. The sealing suggests that Jeremiah's prophecy will be obscure in the period of time just ahead. Sealing also means to confirm, to prove genuine or true. Thus the prophecy of Jeremiah will be fulfilled and confirmed as true (Deut. 18:21-22).

In the clause *to anoint a most holy place* (9:24), *place* can be translated *thing* or *one.* The combination of *anoint* and *holy one* has led some to see in this verse a prediction of Jesus of Nazareth as the Messiah. As heartening as that interpretation is, there is no compelling exegetical reason to interpret 9:24-26 as referring either to the first or to the second coming of Jesus Christ.

The anointing of a most holy place refers to the restoration of the sanctuary *to its rightful state* (8:14) after *the sanctuary and host* was given over *to be trampled* (8:13). There will be a reanointing of the altar, other sacred objects, and priests as in the beginning (Exod. 29:36; 30:26-31; 40:9-15). The reconsecrating occurred after the desecration of Antiochus IV Epiphanes (1 Macc. 4:36-59).

The promises of verse 24 recapitulate the promise in chapter 8, where Gabriel's vision looks forward from Daniel's day to the dreadful time under Antiochus. The text itself (in the interpretation given here) does not point to a messianic *holy one* (an alternate translation). Those who advocate a messianic interpretation follow two lines of thought. According to one line, the Messiah, Jesus, comes into view at the end of the sixty-ninth week, so that the final week of seven years is the time of Jesus. *[Seventy Weeks of Years, p. 295.]* This final week begins with his baptism. Three and one-half years later, his death effectively puts an end to sacrifice (Payne).

Others, dispensationalists, also fit the appearance of the Messiah at the end of the sixty-ninth week, with a following interval. They take the final week as the end time when the antichrist makes a covenant with many for one week (9:27). Such an interpretation separates the seventieth week from the sixty-ninth by a long time interval. It is out of step with the apparently continuous succession of the seventy weeks of years. Moreover, dispensationalists focus on the fortunes of the Jewish people, as indicated by the language about rebuilding Jerusalem and the use in this chapter of the covenant name of the Lord, *Yahweh*. Messianic interpretations also lean for support on the phrase *anointed one* in 9:26. Many hold that expressions such as "the Lord's anointed" or "anointed one" (*mašiaḥ)* were not in OT times a technical term for a coming Messiah. Kings were anointed (1 Sam. 10:1; Ps. 2:2) and so were priests (Lev. 4:3). The term "Messiah" for the coming deliverer is in use by the Qumran community (ca. 2nd century B.C.) and most frequently by Jesus and the NT writers. *[Antichrist, p. 277]*.

First Seven Weeks of Years 9:25a

As Gabriel moves into the essence of the vision, he again uses the word *understand.* In his greeting Gabriel has explained his purpose, *to give you wisdom and understanding* (9:22). Then he encourages Daniel to *consider the word and understand the vision* (9:23). Now Daniel is told to *know therefore and understand.* The purpose of

Gabriel's message is to enable Daniel to understand what will be ahead. Gabriel proceeds to unfold the 490 years into three segments. The first segment is seven weeks of years, 49 years. It spans *from the time that the word went out to restore and rebuild Jerusalem until the time of an anointed prince* (9:25).

A *word* went forth in 9:23 that Gabriel is *to declare* and includes all the information in 9:24-27. Another *word* appears in 9:25, limited to the first *seven weeks* of years. This word proclaims the rebuilding of Jerusalem and finally the coming of an anointed one, a *prince.* Here the Hebrew word *nagid* signifies a leader who may be a political ruler (1 Sam. 9:16); but the word is also appropriate for a chief priest (Jer. 20:1; Dan. 11:22).

Is the *anointed prince* Cyrus the Persian (Isa. 45:1)? an Israelite leader such as a high priest? the destroying figure mentioned in Dan. 9:26? or Zerubbabel or Joshua/Jeshua (520 B.C.; Ezra 3:2; Hag.; Zech. 3–4, esp. 4:14)? There is no consensus, but one of the latter is more probable since Zerubbabel (governor of Judah, of the line of David) and Joshua (high priest) are both anointed, active in rebuilding the temple, and so prominent in Ezra and Zechariah. Of the two, Joshua the priest is more likely since 11:22 similarly calls the high priest Onias III *the prince of the covenant*. The text provides no clues to specific events between the word *to rebuild Jerusalem* and *the time of an anointed prince. [Seventy Weeks of Years, p. 295].*

Next Sixty-two Weeks of Years 9:25b

Then *for sixty-two weeks it shall be built again with streets and moat, but in a troubled time*. In the next period of 434 years, Jerusalem stands rebuilt but in troubled times. The city has *streets and moat.* Here the Hebrew word *ḥaruṣ* should be translated *conduit.* Thus Jerusalem stood with its protective walls and water system. The period of 434 years was reviewed briefly in 8:5-12, 20-23. It embraced the Medo-Persian Empire, the Greek Empire, and the succession of Hellenistic kings and kingdoms.

Final Week of Years 9:26-27

At the end of the sixty-two weeks of years, the vision comes to its climax in a final week of years. The events of the final week recall the coming of the bold and arrogant king in chapter 8.

Gabriel's vision, as in chapter 8, comes to the era of Antiochus IV Epiphanes and his devastation of the people, the city, and the temple in Jerusalem. *An anointed one shall be cut off and shall have noth-*

ing almost surely refers to the pious high priest Onias III (*prince of the covenant*, 11:22), displaced by his Hellenizing brother Jason when Antiochus came to power in 175 B.C. Jason was replaced by Menelaus in 172 B.C. In 171 B.C., Menelaus had Onias killed, "put out of the way" (2 Macc. 4:34). *[Antiochus IV Epiphanes, p. 279.]* The expression *shall have nothing* is ambiguous, as shown by the versions: *no one will take his part* (REB); *unjustly* (TEV; cf. 2 Macc. 4:35, "unjust murder").

The prince who is to come is the main actor in the concluding week of years and is doubtless the *desolator* of 9:27, Antiochus IV Epiphanes. *The troops of the prince . . . shall destroy the city and the sanctuary.* Some commentators hesitate to identify the prince as Antiochus since he did not totally level the city and its sanctuary. This is true if to destroy means literally tearing it down, as occurred in Jerusalem in A.D. 70. However, there are many forms of destruction. One is to render places unusable, especially to worshipers. On the way back from a military expedition against Egypt in 169 B.C., Antiochus feared a revolt in Judah. In a rage, he took Jerusalem by storm, looted the temple, and "shed much blood." In "three days eighty thousand were destroyed, forty thousand in hand-to-hand fighting, and as many were sold into slavery as were killed" (1 Macc. 1:20-24; 2 Macc. 5:5-21).

Two years later, in 167 B.C., forces from Antiochus profaned the temple and then made it unusable by faithful Jews by installing the worship of Zeus in it (1 Macc. 1:54; 2 Macc. 6:2). The *troops of the prince* can refer to his general, Apollonius, who at that time sacked the city and built a fortified citadel near the temple (cf. 1 Macc. 1:29-40; 2 Macc. 5:24-26). He came with an army of 22,000, pretended peace, and on the Sabbath ordered his troops to parade. They killed Jews who came to watch the parade, then "rushed into the city" and "killed great numbers of people" (2 Macc. 5:24-26). "He plundered the city, burned it with fire, and tore down its houses and its surrounding walls. They took captive the women and children, and seized the livestock" (1 Macc. 1:31-32). "Residents of Jerusalem fled," replaced by "strangers," "renegades," "sinful people," meaning Jews who supported the Seleucids; along with Samaritans and Gentiles who accepted Hellenization (1 Macc. 1:34-61). Judas Maccabeus and others found refuge in the wilderness to remain undefiled and prepare for resistance (1 Macc. 1:52, 62-63; 2:27-31; 2 Macc. 5:27).

In Christian interpretation of the text, special note has been taken of such words as *anointed.* Together with other readings, some have concluded that the text refers to events in the life of Jesus or even to the end of time. Close attention to the text combined with information about events of the second century B.C., however, yields the interpretation given here. *[Seventy Weeks of years, p. 295.]*

Its (or his) end shall come with a flood, and to the end there shall be war. Desolations are decreed. Until the death of Antiochus IV Epiphanes, his reign was characterized by war and desolation. The end of every tyrant is inevitable; like the water of a mighty flood, it cannot be held back or redirected.

He shall make a strong covenant with many for one week. The story of certain Jews giving up their religion and its practices is told in the books of Maccabees: "Then the king wrote to his whole kingdom that all should be one people, and that all should give up their particular customs. All the Gentiles accepted the command of the king. Many even from Israel gladly adopted his religion; they sacrificed to idols and profaned the sabbath" (1 Macc. 1:41-43).

Three and a half years into this final week the prince makes *sacrifice and offerings cease.* "The king sent letters by messengers to Jerusalem and the cities of Judah; he directed them to follow customs strange to the land, to forbid burnt offerings and sacrifices and drink offerings in the sanctuary, to profane sabbaths and feasts, to defile the sanctuary and priests, to build altars and sacred precincts and shrines for idols, to sacrifice swine and unclean animals, and to leave their sons uncircumcised . . . so that they should forget the law and change all the ordinances" (1 Macc. 1:44-49). The officials were compelling Jews to eat swine's flesh (2 Macc. 6–7). The climactic act was to erect an altar to Zeus in the temple itself, perhaps with meteorites to be worshiped (Goldstein, 1976:145-152). Gabriel announces that in the *place* of sacrifice and offering *shall be an abomination that desolates.*

The Hebrew behind the phrase *in their place* is obscure. REB says, *in the train of these abominations*; RSV, *upon the wing of abominations.* Some have wanted to connect *wing* with the high point or pinnacle of the temple. Since this desolation happens with the altar, one could take it to refer to the horns, the top corners of the altar (Goldingay: 263). Here the term *abomination that desolates* refers to the same outrage as the *transgression that makes desolate* (8:13). *[Abomination, p. 276].*

The desolating abomination will come to its end at the time decreed by God. Such outrage is short-lived. The desolator, Antiochus, will come to his end (cf. 8:14, 25). The desolating sacrilege (167 B.C.)

continued a little over three years until the temple was cleansed, the altar rededicated, and daily sacrifices resumed (Dec. 164 B.C.; 1 Macc. 1:54; 4:52-58). Antiochus, the man who thought he could "walk on the sea," died about the same time (late 164 B.C.). Pain and worms in his bowels brought him down after an unsuccessful attempt to plunder Persian temples. In life, "Epiphanes" thought he was "god manifest"; in death, he made "the power of God manifest" (1 Macc. 6:1-16; 2 Macc. 5:21; 9:1-29; see TLC for Dan. 8). The words of Gabriel recall a prophecy of Isaiah, "Destruction is decreed, overflowing with righteousness. For the Lord, the Lord of hosts will make a full end, as decreed, in all the earth" (Isa. 10:22-23).

When Gabriel completes his speech, no further comments are made. Readers today, like Daniel, are not given help to *understand the vision* (9:23). It is filled with familiar words, yet from the vision itself, one can hardly discern precise meanings or make specific identifications. People have laid varied interpretations upon common words used as part of the visionary explanation: *prophet, holy place, to anoint a most holy place* (or *thing* or *one*), *anointed prince, squares and moat* (or *conduit*), *flood, covenant, place* (or *wing* or *train*), *abomination, desolates, decreed end*, and *desolator*. The best key comes from correlating the vision with rebuilding the temple after the exile (520 B.C.; Ezra, Zech.) and especially with events of the second century B. C. (169-164 B.C.; 1-2 Macc.).

The visions, however, speak to all generations in all parts of the world. Daniel's visions (chaps. 7-9) make several points:

1. God acts in history both "secular" and "sacred."
2. God is aware of his people.
3. God confronts and overcomes the destructive forces of oppression and violence that would destroy his people.
4. God inaugurates his kingdom, and in the present his people can experience foretastes of what will be when his kingdom triumphs.
5. Prayers of repentance and supplication are always appropriate.

THE TEXT IN BIBLICAL CONTEXT

Forgiveness and Restoration

Daniel's prayer of intercession for his people is one of the great prayers of the OT (9:4-19). Daniel loves God. He loves God's people. He acknowledges the sins of God's people and longs for their forgiveness and restoration. Like the saints of all ages, Daniel knows the God of Israel as one of steadfast love, who keeps promises and is righteous, merciful, and forgiving. This God hears and answers prayers, knows the needs of his people, and is able to act.

The prayers of the NT move in a new world of grace, as well as in a new framework—after the life, death, resurrection, and ascension of Jesus, his pouring out of the Spirit, and establishing his church.

The apostle Paul interceded for the same people in his generation: "My heart's desire and prayer to God for them is that they may be saved. I can testify that they have a zeal for God, but it is not enlightened. For, being ignorant of the righteousness that comes from God, and seeking to establish their own, they have not submitted to God's righteousness" (Rom. 10:1-4). Both Daniel and Paul recognize that restoration depends not *on the ground of our righteousness, but on the ground of your great mercies* (Dan. 9:18). Yet there are new understandings because of the coming of Jesus Christ.

According to Paul, God introduced in Jesus Christ the measure of righteousness toward which the commandments and ordinances had pointed: "For Christ is the end of the law so that there may be righteousness for everyone who believes" (Rom. 10:4). The gospel of Jesus Christ is the "power of God," and in the gospel the "righteousness of God is revealed" (Rom. 1:16). Paul defines the gospel as the "gospel of God, . . . promised beforehand through his prophets in the holy scriptures, . . . concerning his Son, . . . descended from David . . . and declared to be Son of God with power according to the Spirit of holiness by resurrection from the dead, Jesus Christ our Lord." Paul adds that through Jesus Christ, grace and apostleship are received to bring about "the obedience of faith among all the Gentiles for the sake of his name" (Rom. 1:1-5).

For Daniel, the power of God is demonstrated in his bringing *your people out of the land of Egypt with a mighty hand* (Dan. 9:15). For Paul, the counterpart to the Exodus is the power of God in the resurrection. Paul prays that persons would know

> what is the immeasurable greatness of [God's] power for us who believe, according to the working of his great power. God put this power to work in Christ when he raised him from the dead and seated him at his right hand in the heavenly places, far above all rule and authority and power and dominion, and above every name that is named, not only in this age but also in the age to come. And he has put all things under his feet and has made him the head over all things for the church, which is his body, the fullness of him who fills all in all. (Eph. 1:19-23)

This leads to another difference between Daniel and Paul. Daniel anticipates that the return of his people from Babylon and the restoration of the city of Jerusalem and its temple would demonstrate the righteousness, mercy, and power of God. Paul, however, goes far beyond this. The church, the new "Israel of God" (Gal. 6:16), is made up of both Jew and Gentile reconciled into one new community through the cross. As fellow citizens, they form a new nation, a new household, a new holy temple, a dwelling place of God in the Spirit. All of this is based on Jesus Christ (Eph. 2:19-22). Furthermore, "through the church the wisdom of God in its rich variety might now be made known to the rulers and authorities in the heavenly places. This was according to the eternal purpose that he has carried out in Christ Jesus our Lord" (Eph. 3:10-11).

Daniel prays for God's face to shine upon the Jerusalem sanctuary *for your own sake, O my God* (Dan. 9:19). That prayer is limited in scope when compared with Paul's vision. Paul is global in perspective, desiring to bring about the obedience of faith "among all the Gentiles for the sake of his name" (Rom. 1:5).

Finally, Daniel prays, *O Lord, in view of all your righteous acts, let your anger and wrath, we pray, turn away from your city Jerusalem* (Dan. 9:16). Beyond this, Daniel seems unable to go. But now, as Paul writes,

> We were by nature children of wrath, like everyone else. But God, who is rich in mercy, out of the great love with which he loved us even when we were dead through our trespasses, made us alive together with Christ—by grace you have been saved—and raised us up with him and seated us with him in the heavenly places in Christ Jesus, so that in the ages to come he might show the immeasurable riches of his grace toward us in Christ Jesus. (Eph. 2:3-7)

The variant circumstances surrounding Daniel and Paul account for some of the differences in the two prayers. Nonetheless, the two share a common orientation toward God, his grace, his forgiveness, and his willingness to bring about restoration.

Experiencing Gabriel's Promise

In Jesus, believers experience the deliverance Gabriel anticipates *to finish the transgression, to put an end to sin, and to atone for iniquity, to bring in everlasting righteousness* (9:24). Paul writes,

> You were washed, you were sanctified, you were justified in the name of the Lord Jesus Christ and in the Spirit of our God. (1 Cor. 6:11)
>
> All this is from God, who reconciled us to himself through Christ; . . . in Christ God was reconciling the world to himself, not counting their trespasses against them. . . . We entreat you on behalf of Christ, be reconciled to God. . . . For our sake he made him to be sin who knew no sin, so that in him we might become the righteousness of God. (2 Cor. 5:18-21)
>
> Apart from the law, the righteousness of God has been disclosed . . . [and is] through faith in Jesus Christ for all who believe. (Rom. 3:21-22)

Christians now enjoy in Christ that which is dimly foreseen in the word Gabriel shares with Daniel. Though *your people* and *your holy city* are in the background (9:24), the word focuses on God's action in dealing with the sin of his people and establishing righteousness.

Gabriel communicates a word to Daniel on sin, atonement, and righteousness—the essence of salvation. These are issues the prophets searched out and "into which angels long to look" (1 Pet. 1:10-12). Peter captures for the early church and for the church today the heart of Gabriel's conversation with Daniel as he speaks of deliverance and new life in a hostile world. For Peter and for the church, deliverance and new life are in Jesus Christ. Jesus was made manifest "at the end of the ages" (1 Pet. 1:20) to call into being "a holy nation, God's own people," who have "received mercy" and are given the assignment to "proclaim the mighty acts of him who called you out of darkness into his marvelous light" (1 Pet. 2:9-10).

THE TEXT IN THE LIFE OF THE CHURCH

Predictions Lead to Hope

A significant portion of chapter 9 centers on Jeremiah's prophecy concerning seventy years (Jer. 25:11-14; 29:10). On this matter, fascination with predictive aspects of prophecy reaches great heights. As Daniel meditates on Jeremiah's writing, he wonders whether it furnishes a timetable for events related to Jerusalem.

Upon his arrival, Gabriel tells Daniel that the seventy years actually represent seventy weeks of years stretching into the future and broken into segments of seven weeks, sixty-two weeks, and a final week of years. There would be oppression but also hope for the time *when the decreed end is poured out upon the desolator* (9:27).

The Bible does contain predictions, some of which are quite general. Ezekiel predicts that the sheep of Israel will be scattered, but God will gather them again under a shepherd after his own heart

(Ezek. 34:7-24). The church sees Jesus fulfilling this prediction.

Some predictions are in the form of promises. For example, God promises to write his law on human hearts (Jer. 31:31-34). This theme becomes important in the NT (Heb. 10:11-18; Rom. 2:15). Some predictions, like Gabriel's word about Jeremiah's seventy years, seem quite specific (Dan. 9:24-27). The apparent precision has led Christians to spend immense amounts of time and energy trying to connect each segment of the seventy years with an identifiable event in the past, present, or future. *[Seventy Weeks of Years, p. 295.]*

To what extent should the church, in attempting to interpret Gabriel's predictions, tie them to specific events in history or to the future? All too often, interpretations tied rigidly to future events prove to be in error.

Some parts of the OT are seen by the NT writers to be predictions fulfilled in the life of Jesus, even though this was not the original intent of the original writer. Many predictions appear in apocalyptic literature. The very nature of such writing should caution us against interpreting it as though it is a historical record. To use the Scriptures to predict the future in detail tends to miss the mark. The Bible warns against sin and is primarily a guide to salvation, to fullness of life in Christ, and to hope. Some predictions supposedly based on the Bible claim to provide early warnings about international affairs. They tend to discount international cooperation, reinforce nationalism, and raise fear and efforts to save one's own skin. If properly handled, predictions encourage hope. When the church finds itself in the midst of a world torn by oppression, strife, hatred, and violence, the predictions of the Bible point to a sovereign God who cares for his people and is working out his purposes for all.

The calendaring of Daniel 9:24-27 is not abundantly plain nor does it fit neatly into any time scheme. But it does provide hope. It assures believers that God limits evil and is able to change perverse humans and bring to naught corrupt social institutions.

In Daniel, predictions are made for times of crisis. The desecration of the temple and the cessation of temple offerings were disasters. Today, as then, the question comes, "How long?" (cf. Rev. 6:10). *Do not delay!* (Dan. 9:19).

The Bible does not supply answers to questions about current affairs even though some persons try to find them there. Rather, in times of stress, books like Daniel give hope to the church. Hope empowers the church to endure. Hope holds out the promise of renewal and restoration. Hope encourages the church to practice the way of love. Hope enables the church to focus on God's acts of transformation. Hope inspires mission, as the church under the power and authority of Jesus obeys his command to "make disciples of all nations" (Matt. 28:19).

Daniel 10:1—12:13

Daniel's Vision of the Future

PREVIEW

Chapters 10:1 to 12:13 form a unit, and its structure is complex. There is a long introduction (10:1—11:1) leading to the central message of the heavenly being (11:2—12:4). In the introduction, Daniel receives word of a coming revelation. A divine messenger appears, before whom Daniel falls prostrate. The heavenly messenger explains that his message relates to the Jewish people in the days to come (10:12-14). Daniel falls to the ground once more. A second heavenly messenger touches Daniel's lips, strengthens him, and affirms the dependability of the message.

The heavenly message, extending from 11:2 through 12:4, spans the historical period from the rise of Alexander the Great to the end of the Seleucid king, Antiochus IV Epiphanes (ruling 175-164 B.C.). Kings are not named, yet through a general knowledge of the history, one can identify kings to the south and west of Palestine and kings to the north and east. *[Seleucids, p. 295.]*

An Interpretative Angle of the Vision

The vision of chapter 11 is a sketch of world history reaching from approximately 600 B.C. to 164 B.C. If this material was written in the second century B.C., it serves as a message to the faithful, to encourage endurance during a time of the dreadful persecutions of 169-164 B.C. In the second century it was not unusual for Jewish writers to attribute their compositions to persons out of the past who were held in high respect for their courage, piety, and wisdom. They were not intending to be deceptive. They only wished to give their writings additional authority. Thus Daniel was chosen to "predict" history, to encourage Jews in the days of crisis under Antiochus IV Epiphanes.

On the other hand, if the vision was written by Daniel in the sixth century B.C., the message is the same. Kingdoms rise and fall. Political power is illusory and short-lived. God's people suffer at the hands of tyrants whose political power deludes them into thinking themselves as gods. Severe persecution, too, is short-lived. If the early date is accepted, then greater stress falls on prediction. However, the message that God is in control of history, that he is mindful of his people, and that he rewards those who remain faithful—that message is of greater significance than debates over dates. *[Daniel: Date and Authorship, p. 285.]*

Regardless of one's view concerning the time of writing, the reader today should not attempt to identify every part of the vision with events in history. To harmonize Daniel's predictions with known facts of history or to prove that a second-century B.C. writer had all facts of history accurately in hand is to miss the point. It may be interesting to make the events of Daniel 11 match history to support a theory of inspiration, or to reflect twentieth-century ideas of how history should be written. Too often such efforts lead to debates that obscure the essential meaning and purpose of Daniel.

The vision concludes with Daniel conversing with the heavenly beings (12:5-13). Daniel asks when the events will occur. An answer is given cryptically. The call to faithfulness is the central concern.

From the outset, the vision presents itself as predictive. It is for *the end of days* (10:14). The focus is on the people of God and their *beautiful land* (11:16, 41) as they are caught in conflicts between the great powers of the time. The power to the south sweeps across Palestine to confront the north. In turn the power of the north sweeps across Palestine to confront the south. Ultimately, a king arises in the north who personifies all that is evil (11:21). He is proud and arrogant. His abilities and great power are used only for evil purposes. Lies and deceit pervade all his actions. When frustrated, he vents his rage against the people of God. He desecrates the temple, persecutes the faithful, and defies the God of gods as he comes to see himself as a god above all. In the end, his military might, his great wealth, and his ruthless domination are of no avail.

Many interpreters agree that the infamous king of the north who climaxes the vision is Antiochus IV Epiphanes (ruling 175-164 B.C.). Daniel's vision unveils acts of this Antiochus, sometimes in ambiguous ways, perhaps to encourage imaginative interpretation. The books of 1 and 2 Maccabees describe these events in more detail, apparently with the writer of 1 Maccabees trying to "correct" Daniel and the writer of 2 Maccabees seeking to support Daniel (Goldstein, 1976:42-54; 1983:63-70). The history of the period is complex, full of intrigue and conflict, and there are some discrepancies in the sources. Yet it is clear that Antiochus died from a mysterious illness late in 164 B.C., soon after he heard of his general's defeat by the Maccabees in a key battle *[Antiochus IV Epiphanes, p. 279.]* Since the king in question is unnamed, there is room to regard the descriptions and destiny as appropriate to all tyrants across history who blatantly defy the almighty God, up to and even including an end-time figure often called the antichrist. *[Antichrist, p. 277.]*

OUTLINE

Introduction, 10:1—11:1

10:1	The Promise of a Vision	
10:2-3	Daniel's Preparation	
10:4—11:1	The Arrival of the Heavenly Messenger (Gabriel)	
	Time, Place, and Appearance	10:4-6
	Daniel's Reaction to the Sight and Sound	10:7-9
	The Heavenly Messenger Responds to Daniel	10:10—11:1

The Message, 11:2—12:4

11:2	Persian Kings	
11:3-4	A Warrior King	
11:5-20	Turning Tides Between South and North	
	A Powerful Prince	11:5
	An Alliance Between South and North	11:6
	North Invaded by South	11:7-8
	South Invaded by North	11:9
	North Continues Harassment of South	11:10
	Resistance of Southern King	11:11-12
	Invasion by Northern King	11:13-15
	Triumph and Fall of the North	11:16-19
	Northern King's Tribute Collector	11:20

EXPLANATORY NOTES

Introduction 10:1—11:1

10:1 The Promise of a Vision

In the third year of King Cyrus of Persia, Daniel is informed of a coming vision. Daniel's captivity spans most of the rule of Nebuchadnezzar and reaches the time of Cyrus. *[Cyrus, p. 284.]* The promise of a vision comes in Cyrus's third year, 536 B.C., about seventy years after Nebuchadnezzar became king (see notes on 1:1, 21).

So that there is no confusion, the reader is told that the Daniel who will receive this vision, is the Daniel of chapter 1, *who was named Belteshazzar* (10:1; 1:7). Thus the reader is assured of the unity of the book. Here one is led to expect themes similar to those of the earlier stories of Hebrew heroes and powerful kings, as well as interpretations of visions. The vision to come is inseparable from the rest of the book. The first verse is written in third person (10:1; cf. 7:1). It introduces the time of the vision, the one receiving the vision, the essential content of the vision, and Daniel's grasp of its meaning.

The introductory paragraph calls Daniel's experience a *vision*. It is a vision in that heavenly beings appear who bring a message. There are no strange events or awesome beasts as in other visions (Dan. 7–8). The introduction notes two things about the *word* (*message* or *oracle*): first, it is *true*, reliable; second, it concerns *great conflict*, warfare. The long introduction to the vision concludes with another remark about truth: *the book of truth* (10:21). The mention of *conflict* is good storytelling technique and heightens the interest of the reader. The *conflict* likely does not refer to Daniel's inner conflict in trying to understand the vision. Instead, it points to celestial conflict between (probably) Gabriel and the opposing prince of Persia and then the prince of Greece (10:13, 20), matched on earth by conflict between the kings of the north and south as detailed in chapter 11.

Daniel pays attention to the oracle, and *he understood the word.* This was quite different from his experience in 8:27. There he was *dismayed* and *did not understand* the vision. At the end of this vision, however, he does not fully understand and asks for further information (12:8).

10:2-3 Daniel's Preparation

With knowledge of a coming, divine revelation, Daniel prepares himself for receiving it. His preparation consists of three things: mourning, fasting, and neglecting of personal grooming. Surprisingly, perhaps even to Daniel, his preparation continues for three weeks. The explanation for the long delay will be given in verse 13, when the heavenly messenger explains that he was detained by *the prince of the kingdom of Persia* for twenty-one days. During the three weeks, however, Daniel's preparation does not go unnoticed by heaven (10:12).

The practice of *mourning* appears in other places in the OT. In two instances it was related to national or political reverses. Samuel "grieved" over the rejection of Saul as king (1 Sam. 15:35—16:1). Ezra was "mourning" over the unfaithfulness of the returned exiles (Ezra 10:6; cf. Neh. 8:9). Those who knew the ruinous state of Jerusalem "mourned" (Neh. 1:4). Since Daniel's mourning comes during the scheduled Passover and Feast of Unleavened Bread, Daniel may be mourning because it is not possible for him properly to observe them away from the temple. The later actions of Antiochus in desecrating the temple "turned into mourning" these celebrative events (1 Macc. 1:39, 45-47). Daniel senses that the coming message will contain words of trouble for his people. The rituals of fasting and neglecting of bodily grooming were thought to heighten spiritual insight and sensitivity. The thoroughness of Daniel's preparation also lends authority to the revelation, because the one receiving the revelation is personally fully prepared. Daniel's earlier search into Scripture became the prelude for a revelation (9:2). Here likewise his search after God is preparatory to a divine disclosure (10:3).

10:4—11:1 The Arrival of the Heavenly Messenger (Gabriel)

Time, Place, and Appearance 10:4-6

Daniel notes both the date and the place of the messenger's appearance. The date is *the twenty-fourth day of the first month*. The place is on *the bank of the great river* (*that is the Tigris*) that flows through Babylon. As far as we know, there is no significance to the date except that the Passover falls on the fourteenth of the first month, with the Feast of Unleavened Bread from the fifteenth to the twenty-first (Lev. 23:5-6). Thus, the days for these events pass by during Daniel's three weeks of preparation. The messenger appears to Daniel by the Tigris River, similar to the experience of Ezekiel, who was by a river when his vision came (Ezek. 1:1; cf. notes at Dan. 8:2).

Next, Daniel describes the appearance of the celestial being who appears as a *man*, in human form but with angelic splendor—likely the angel Gabriel, as in 8:16 and 9:21. In some ways this heavenly being resembles the living creatures or cherubim of Ezekiel 1:4-25 (cf. Exod. 25:10-22; 1 Kings 6:23-28; Rev. 4:7). This passage provides background for the vision of the Son of Man, the exalted Christ, in Revelation (1:12-16).

The celestial being in human form is *clothed in linen*, a priestly garment (Lev. 6:10; 16:4), with *a belt of gold from Uphaz* (10:5). This was the finest gold—24 carat (cf. Jer. 10:9). His body is like *beryl*, and his arms and legs gleam like *burnished bronze*—features noted in Ezekiel's vision (Ezek. 1:7, 16). His *face like lightning* reminds one of John's vision of the Son of Man with a face "like the sun shining with full force" (Rev. 1:16). The voice of the messenger is *like the roar of a multitude* (10:6). In John's vision, the voice is "like the sound of many waters" (1:15). One can compare this to the thunder of a great waterfall like Niagara Falls (Canada/USA) or Iguazu Falls, in the rain forest where Brazil meets Argentina, and twenty yards higher and a mile wider than Niagara. The messenger reflects the holiness and majesty of God (Dan. 7:9-10; Ezek. 1:26-28). (On angels, see notes on Dan. 4:9-18; 7:9-27; and TLC for Dan. 8.)

Daniel's Reaction to the Sight and Sound 10:7-9

Apparently, Daniel is in the company of other men when the vision comes. They do *not see the vision*, but they sense that something awesome is occurring. So *they fled and hid themselves.* Daniel's experience seems to parallel that of Saul on the Damascus Road. When the Lord Jesus appeared to Saul, those with him according to one account saw nothing but heard the voice and were speechless (Acts 9:3-8; cf. John 12:29).

The writer does not further describe the appearance of the celestial visitor but does give the reaction to this vision at length. The overpowering nature of the vision is sketched by observing its effects (cf. the effects of the devastating locust given in Joel 1:4-12).

Left alone, standing before the heavenly being, Daniel is overcome. He becomes weak, loses his color, and is deathly pale. At *the sound of [the messenger's] words,* Daniel collapses (10:9). He falls to the ground face down, in a trance. In yet another way, Daniel's experience parallels Ezekiel's (1:28) and John's (Rev. 1:17).

The Heavenly Messenger Responds to Daniel 10:10—11:1

In this prolonged introduction, a variety of themes are intertwined. All are designed to lend authority to Daniel, who passes on the message received from the celestial being. First, the authority of Daniel as a message bearer is not to be questioned, since his experience is similar to that of Ezekiel (1:1-28) and Isaiah (6:1-13), recognized prophets. As noted, Daniel's depiction of the heavenly messenger parallels the vision of Ezekiel. Daniel's experience is also like the call of Isaiah, similarly overwhelmed when he received the heavenly vision. He could not speak till his lips were touched. Isaiah also received a message of grave importance for God's people. Like him, Daniel is ready to serve.

Second, Daniel is identified by the heavenly being as one *greatly beloved* by God (10:11; cf. 9:23). Such affirmation gives credibility to Daniel's life and service.

Third, the heavenly visitor identifies himself as one among many heavenly beings who carry out God's plan for history, as inscribed in the book of truth (10:21; cf. note on 7:9-10). He calls himself a coworker with Michael, the patron angel who oversees the history of Israel (10:21; 12:1). Yet the heavenly visitor does not give his name. Since Daniel's experience with Gabriel in 8:15-19 and 9:21-23 parallels this event so closely, it makes sense to identify the heavenly messenger as Gabriel.

In the course of the interview, Daniel is touched three times (10:10, 16, 18). It is not clear whether he is touched by the heavenly being who first appears, or by other angels who join the first. In the first instance, a hand lifts Daniel from a prostrate position to his hands and knees. Then the heavenly visitor tells Daniel to listen carefully and stand on his feet. The angel indicates that Daniel's prayers during the time of preparation have been heard (10:12). His coming is in response to Daniel's prayer.

The celestial visitor shares information about events in the heavenly realm that have delayed his coming. For twenty-one days, *the prince of the kingdom of Persia opposed* him, but *Michael, one of the chief princes, came to help* in the struggle (10:13). The opposition of the nation-angel of Persia (rather than from princes of other countries) is matched by history the angel unfolds, in which the downward spiral begins with Persia (11:2). The Lord's armies, the host of heaven, are engaged in conflict, in accord with long tradition in the OT (as in Num. 10:34-36; Deut. 33:2-3; Josh. 5:14-15; Judg. 5:20; Isa. 13:4; Dan. 8:10; at Qumran in the War Rule, 1QM 12). Paul mentions the church's struggle "against the cosmic powers of this present darkness, against the spiritual forces of evil in the heavenly places" (Eph. 6:12). Other NT texts refer to such spiritual warfare (Matt. 16:18; Mark 3:24-27; Luke 10:18; John 12:31; Jude 9; Rev. 12:7-12; 19:11-21; see TLC, below).

In Jewish tradition, each nation has its patron angel (as do individuals and churches in the NT: Matt. 18:10; Acts 12:15; Rev. 1:20; cf. Gen. 48:16). According to Deuteronomy 32:8-14, the Lord of Israel, the Most High God, placed a subordinate in charge of each of the other nations. These are angels, "gods" or "sons of God," *holy ones,* divine beings who belong to the heavenly court and sit for judgment on the thrones surrounding the Ancient One (cf. Dan. 7:9; Job 1:6; Qumran version of Deut. 32:8; Wink, 1984:18-35; 1986:88-93). Alongside Yahweh, the gods of other nations are worthless, and Israel should not worship them (Deut. 32:15-21; TDOT, 1:274). In Deuteronomy, the Lord is directly guarding Israel (cf. Exod. 23:20: the angel is the Lord in person). According to later tradition, as in Daniel, the Lord has assigned a patron or guardian angel to Israel—Michael, *one of the chief princes* (10:13), *your prince* (10:21), and *the great prince, the protector of your people* (12:1).

In 1 Enoch and other pseudepigraphical books, the archangel Michael frequently appears (as in 1 En. 9:1). These works and Qumran also know Michael as the patron angel of Israel (as in T. Mos. 10:2; 1 En. 20:5; 1QM 17:6-8). He intercedes for Israel before God (T. Levi 5:5-6; cf. Tob. 12:15) and is a champion of God's people against enemies (2 En. 22:6 [J]; 1QM 9:14-15; cf. ABD, 4:811). In the NT, Jude 9 notes that the archangel Michael disputed with the devil about the body of Moses but depended on the Lord to rebuke the devil. John sees Michael and his angels defeat the great dragon called the devil and Satan (Rev. 12:7-12; cf. 1 Thess. 4:16).

The angels of the nations "represent the actual spirituality and possibilities of actual entities. The power of the angel-prince of Persia here reflects the political power of the Persian empire, before which puny Judah, its temple destroyed, its land desolate, and its people captive in Babylon, must have appeared insignificant" (Wink, 1986:89). The king of Assyria can speak contemptuously of the "gods of the nations," which he has conquered (2 Kings 18:33-35). These nation-angels have a will of their own and can resist the will of God, who limits himself and does not violate their freedom. Daniel's prayer makes an opening for God "to act in concert with human freedom," leading to war in heaven—showing that "every event on earth has its heavenly counterpart" (Wink, 1986:90-91; cf. 2 Sam. 5:24). The nation-angels represent "the invisible spirituality that animates, sustains, and guides a nation," whether for good or evil (Wink, 1986: 92-93).

Though the vision begins with a reference to Cyrus, king of Persia (10:1), real power is in the hands of heaven. Moreover, heaven is clearly in contact with earth. Michael, whose name means "Who is like God?" comes to Gabriel's aid, thus enabling him to come to Daniel with the message. The message concerns events to come that will affect the people of God *at the end of days* (10:14; 2:28). *End of days* (*'aarit hayyamim*) refers to some time in the future, as in Numbers 24:14 ("days to come"). Similarly, the phrase *time of the end* (Dan. 8:17; 11:35, 40) refers to the end of a climactic event or period of time. Neither expression necessarily refers to the ultimate eschatological end of time, yet 12:1-4 may be reaching in that direction.

Upon Gabriel's report of the conflict in heaven, Daniel falls to the ground speechless (Dan. 10:15; cf. Luke 1:20-22). Then Daniel's lips are *touched* (10:16), like Isaiah's (Isa. 6:1-8). Isaiah senses his sinfulness. Daniel senses his weakness. Upon receiving the touch of the live coal from the altar, Isaiah is ready to go to God's people. Daniel, however, is touched again (Dan. 10:18) and reminded of God's love for him. Daniel is told not to fear. With his strength returning, Daniel is ready to listen.

Before sharing the promised message, Gabriel tells of his *return to fight against the prince of Persia*, whom Michael has been holding off (10:13). After that, *the prince of Greece will come*, and he and Michael will be contending also against that nation-angel (10:20-21; cf. 12:1). Here the writer provides background for the coming vision, the fall of Persian kings and the rise of (the Greek) Alexander the Great (11:1-4) and the kings that follow him (11:4—12:1). The Jews are a small powerless group located in Palestine. Wave after wave of powerful aggressors sweep over their land from many points of the compass. One empire after another exercises dominion over God's people. Yet God is in control and responds to the prayers of the faithful, like Daniel. His people will survive. God knows what will happen, since the events are already written in the book of truth (10:21).

There is artful parallelism and repetition in this long introduction to the vision. The two sections (10:8-14 and 15-21) each make the same points shown in this chart:

Detail	***Section 10:8-14***	***Section 10:15-21***
strength sapped	10:8 (twice)	10:16-17; 18 (twice)
face to the ground	10:9	10:15
roused by a messenger	10:10	10:18
called *greatly beloved*	10:10	10:19
told *Do not fear*	10:12	10:19
why the angel came	10:12	10:20-21
prince of Persia	10:13	10:20

Such repetition emphasizes the remarkable nature of Daniel's experience and sharpens, as mentioned, the authoritative nature of what is to be revealed. The longest vision report of the book (Dan. 11) is now to be disclosed, with a most impressive staging. With this lengthy introduction, the writer alerts readers to pay special heed to the message and thus implies that receiving visions from God is no light matter. Daniel 10 provides information about

1. Daniel's preparation.
2. The appearance of the heavenly messenger.
3. The conversation between the messenger, Gabriel, and Daniel—the one greatly beloved by God.
4. Parallels between Daniel and Ezekiel in receiving visions.
5. Parallels between Daniel and Isaiah in the "touch" and "call."
6. The book of truth—happenings on earth already decreed and the outcome determined by heaven.
7. Angelic protectors of the people of God—enabling the faithful to survive, regardless of how severe the struggle on earth will be.

The heaping up of these insights not only builds suspense, it also provides a context for receiving the message. In addition to establishing authority and reliability, it also encourages hope and confidence even though the message is of wars and suffering.

The Message 11:2—12:4

The materials that follow point to selected events from the time of Daniel up to and including the reign of Antiochus IV Epiphanes. The climax of the vision is Antiochus's outrageous reign. Chapter 11 parallels much of the vision of chapter 8. Both describe the conflict between Persia and Greece (11:2-4; cf. 8:1-8) and the coming of the Greek empire (11:3-4; 8:8). Both give attention in climactic fashion to the arrogant and bold king (11:21-39; cf. 8:9-14, 23-26).

Initially the materials focus on Persian kings whose rule extended from 539 B.C. to 334-331 B.C., when defeated by Alexander the Great. Upon Alexander's death and the breakup of his empire, the focus shifts to the conflicts between two parts of the divided empire: the king of the north leads the Seleucids, who control Syria (territories north and east of Palestine); and the king of the south leads the Ptolemies, who control Egypt (south and west of Palestine). After the Persian collapse, the scope of the vision spans a period of approximately 150 years, during which time the north and the south dispute over control of Palestine.

The details of the vision (at least through 11:39) are readily correlated with the history of the period. Hence, some have considered the *vision* (10:7) not to have future reference but to be veiled history writing (Porteous). Others seek to make the case that the material is predictive prophecy (Baldwin). Still others write of quasi-predictions and note how the experiences of persecution in the second century B.C. are interpreted with the help of scriptural phrases and ideas (Goldingay). Without subtracting from the reality of predictive prophecy, the tilt of the following comments is along the line suggested by Goldingay. Daniel 11 essentially uses a heavenly angle of vision to interpret historical events from the decline of Persia to the rule of Antiochus IV Epiphanes, with predictions of his end. As a prophet (Matt. 24:15), Daniel is called to be a true link between the human and divine worlds, to receive God's commentary on the news. *[Chronology, p. 283, lists kings and verses alluding to them.]*

11:2 Persian Kings

The message begins with Gabriel saying, *Now I will announce the truth.* The messenger will share with Daniel what is written in *the book of truth* (10:21) concerning the days ahead.

The message begins with Persian kings after Cyrus: *Three more kings shall arise in Persia. The fourth shall be far richer* (11:2). This fourfold formula is found in Near Eastern and biblical literature (cf. notes on 2:36-43). It signifies a complete unit of three followed by a fourth that in some way outdistances the other three (cf. note on 2:36-43). The formula is a literary technique to move swiftly to the point of emphasis, the fourth item (cf. Prov. 30:15-31; Amos 1:3—2:8).

There actually were more than four kings in this period of two hundred years, but they are difficult to identify. Following Cyrus (Dan. 10:1), the *three* notable kings probably are Cambyses, Darius I, and Xerxes I (486-465 B.C.), who invaded Greece in 480 B.C. but suffered setbacks. After struggles, there was a peace settlement of 448, during the reign of Artaxerxes I (465-425 B.C.), but the rivalry continued, with Persians dominating Greek cities of Asia. Perhaps the *fourth* king is Darius III, the last king of Persia. The sense is that there is a series of kings of the Persian royal family, the Achaemenids. Then one arises significantly different, richer and stronger, who will *stir up all against the kingdom of Greece*. After all, the Greeks were pressured by the Persians for centuries, and under Alexander the Great in 334 B.C. they were finally ready to take charge. Darius III was the last Persian king and thus symbolizes the cumulative riches and strength of the Persian empire pitted *against . . . Greece.*

11:3-4 A Warrior King

Then a warrior king shall arise (11:3). This refers to Alexander the Great, who became king in Macedonia in 336 B.C. His father, Philip II, had through diplomacy and military skill become master of the whole Greek mainland by 338 B.C. but was assassinated before he could make war on Persia. His son Alexander was a brilliant military strategist who invaded and conquered the territories between his homeland and India in rapid fashion (cf. 8:5). Upon putting together this vast empire, the largest the world had known, Alexander caught a fever in 323 B.C. and died. His empire was *divided toward the four winds of heaven*, among four of his leading generals. *[Alexander, p. 276.]*

11:5-20 Turning Tides Between South and North

The selected conflicts that follow are between the Ptolemies, who control Egypt, in the south; and the Seleucids, who control the area to the north and east of Palestine. *[Chronology, p. 283.]* In these conflicts of the third and second century B.C., armies often marched through Judea. The Jews were pawns in these international conflicts. Yet the central concerns of the messenger are with *the beautiful land* (11:16, 41), *the temple* (11:31), *the holy covenant* (11:28, 30), and *the wise* among the people (11:33, 35; 12:3, 10). There will be great trouble, but there will be deliverance for the faithful. For this period there is no suggestion that suffering is the result of divine displeasure for current sins, but it is within the 490 years of 9:24-27, *to atone for* preexilic *iniquity* in a sevenfold fashion (see notes on 9:24-27; 11:21-45).

A Powerful Prince 11:5

The sequence of selected events begins with Ptolemy I, who ruled Egypt 323-282 B.C. That *one of his officers shall grow stronger than he* may refer to a particular event in history. Antigonus, who in the division of Alexander's empire received the area now called Turkey, attempted to maintain the unity of Alexander's empire. In 319 B.C. he seized Jerusalem and then attacked Babylon in 316 B.C. Seleucus I fled to Egypt in 315 B.C. to serve as a commander for Ptolemy I. Together they defeated Antigonus at Gaza in 312 B.C. In 301 B.C. at the battle of Ipsus, Antigonus was defeated by the other four of Alexander's generals and lost his life. Seleucus recovered his territory and gradually took over Antigonus's land—with the result that Seleucus became stronger than Ptolemy I (11:5). Egypt, however, controlled Palestine until the time of Antiochus III the Great (223-187 B.C.). See 11:16.

An Alliance Between South and North 11:6

After some years, nearly fifty years later (250 B.C.), Ptolemy II (282-246) tried to build relationships with the Seleucids through the marriage of his daughter Berenice to Antiochus II Theos (261-246 B.C.). To do this, Antiochus divorced his wife, Laodice, thus cutting off his sons, Seleucus and Antiochus, from succeeding him to the throne. The marriage, however, did not last. Two years later Antiochus II went back to Laodice. But Laodice had her revenge by arranging the death of Antiochus II, Berenice, her Egyptian attendants, and the son of Berenice and Antiochus II. Then Laodice's son, Seleucus II Callinicus (246-225), began to rule in Syria. In the same year, Berenice's father, Ptolemy II Philadelphus, died and his son

Ptolemy III Euergetes (246-222 B.C.) began to rule in Egypt.

North Invaded by South 11:7-8

Ptolemy III Euergetes was a brother to Berenice. To avenge the death of his sister, Berenice, of his nephew, and of Berenice's Egyptian attendants, Ptolemy III invaded the north, the Seleucid empire. He took Antioch, and Seleucia on the Mediterranean, and had Laodice murdered. Ptolemy III returned to Egypt with *their gods, with their idols and with their precious vessels of silver and gold* (11:8). To take a nation's gods and sacred ceremonial vessels indicates humiliating defeat, not only for the people but also for their gods (cf. 1:2; 5:2-4, 23; Jer. 52:17-23). Ptolemy III was kept from further conflict with the north because of trouble at home.

South Invaded by North 11:9

After Ptolemy III returned home, Seleucus II Callinicus, son of Laodice, continued on the northern throne. Two years later Seleucus II felt strong enough to set matters straight with Ptolemy III. In 242 B.C. he invaded Egypt, but had to return into his own land in defeat.

North Continues Harassment of South 11:10

Seleucus II was succeeded by his two sons, Seleucus III Soter (226-223 B.C.) and Antiochus III Magnus (Antiochus the Great) 223-187 B.C. Antiochus III recaptured Seleucia (219 B.C.), which had been taken by Ptolemy III.

Resistance of Southern King 11:11-12

When Ptolemy IV Philopator (222-204 B.C.) came to the Egyptian throne, he decided to halt the harassment from the north. With a large army he met Antiochus III at Raphia, an Egyptian outpost on the Palestine frontier in 217 B.C. According to ancient history (Polybius, *Hist.* 5), Ptolemy had 70,000 foot soldiers (lost 1,500), 5,000 cavalry (lost 700), and 73 elephants. Antiochus III had 62,000 foot soldiers (lost 10,000 plus 4,000 prisoners), 6,000 cavalry (lost 300), and 102 elephants. Ptolemy IV was victor (11:11) but did not take advantage of his success. He went to Jerusalem and was eager to enter the temple but reportedly was deterred by God (3 Macc. 1-2). After regaining Palestine and Phoenicia, he then was defeated at Banias and made peace. He did *not prevail* (11:12) in the sense that he did not push on to complete victory over the north.

Invasion by Northern King 11:13-15

In the next decade and a half, Antiochus III invaded what is now called Turkey and also campaigned to the east to regain the boundaries of the old Seleucid empire. Through his success, he gained the title "Magnus" or "the Great." He made an alliance with Philip V of Macedonia with the hope of invading Egypt. As 11:14 indicates, *many shall rise up against the king of the south.*

During this time Ptolemy IV died (204 B.C.) and was succeeded by an infant son, Ptolemy V Epiphanes (204-180). There was an Egyptian insurrection against the child king. In addition, Antiochus III the Great and his allies prepared for a full invasion of Palestine. He went as far as Gaza in 201 B.C. He met the Egyptian general Scopas near Paneas (later Caesarea Philippi) in 200 B.C. The Egyptians withdrew. Jerusalem changed hands three times in as many years. In 198 B.C. Antiochus met and defeated a garrison left in Jerusalem by Scopas. From this time, Judah was completely under Seleucid rule. Antiochus the Great prevailed over Egypt since there was *no strength to resist* (11:15). Apparently, within Egypt itself there was also dissension and insurrection.

While battles raged between north and south, the messenger refers briefly to the condition of the Jews in Palestine. Apparently, the Jews were in a quandary. They did not know what to do nor what direction to take as the major powers of the day *advance like a flood and pass through* their land (11:10). It is not clear what their concerns were, beyond the well-being of their homeland and maintaining their faith. Their land was a highway for warring nations. Certainly the Jews were aware of Isaiah's vision that there will be an altar to the Lord in Egypt and a highway from Egypt to Assyria, and that Egypt and Assyria will join Israel in worshiping the Lord (Isa. 19:19-25). They were also aware of the prophet's messages concerning Jerusalem as the center of God's activity affecting the whole earth (Isa. 60:9-14). Among the Jews, however, were *the lawless* (wild men) who believe that Jewish hopes as expressed in the prophet's visions would be realized if they were to take matters into their own hands on the side of the Seleucids. They joined insurrections against the regent of the child king Ptolemy V of Egypt (Josephus, *Ant.* 12.3.3-4). These violent efforts, the messenger points out, were doomed from the beginning: *They shall fail* (11:14). But later the Seleucids did prevail and take possession of Palestine (11:15, as noted above).

Triumph and Fall of the North 11:16-19

Having overcome Egypt, Antiochus the Great was now dominant. He *shall take the actions he pleases* (11:16). No one could stop him—for a while! In 198 B.C. Antiochus the Great overcame the Egyptian garrison in Jerusalem and was in firm control of Palestine, including Judea, *the beautiful land* (11:16).

Instead of moving into Egypt to destroy the Ptolemies, Antiochus the Great pursued another course. He made peace by giving his daughter Cleopatra to Ptolemy V Epiphanes in marriage in 195 B.C. (11:17). To the surprise of Antiochus, Cleopatra did not cooperate with his plan to *destroy the kingdom*, to further subjugate Egypt. Instead, she was completely loyal to her husband and to her new country. She stood solidly behind a plan to create an alliance between Egypt and the rising Roman power. Hence, the scheme of Antiochus to dominate Egypt did *not succeed* nor give him *advantage* (11:17).

Frustrated, Antiochus the Great turned his attention *to the coastlands* (11:18). He attacked Egyptian colonies in Asia Minor, settled 2,000 families from Mesopotamia in Lydia and Phrygia, then went westward to Greece. The Romans turned him back at Thermopylae in 191 B.C. In Asia Minor, the Roman *commander* Lucius Scipio defeated him at Magnesia in 190-189 B.C. and forced him permanently to the eastern side of the Taurus range of mountains, eastern Cilicia and Syria, putting *an end to his insolence* (11:18). This was the turning point in his power. Antiochus the Great became a vassal of Rome and had to send twenty hostages to Rome, including his son Antiochus IV. Warlike all the way, he was assassinated in 187 B.C. as he looted a temple of Baal in Susa to pay tribute to Rome. *He shall stumble and fall, and shall not be found* (11:19). The motif is common: at the moment of triumph, disaster may strike and all is lost (cf. his son in 11:43-45).

Northern King's Tribute Collector 11:20

Antiochus III the Great was succeeded by his son Seleucus IV Philopator (187-175 B.C.). The story of Seleucus IV is a tragic one. His main occupation was raising money to pay the tribute Rome imposed on his father. He sent his minister Heliodorus to confiscate funds in the treasury of the Jerusalem temple, but the Syrians were frightened off by an apparition sent by God, according to 2 Maccabees (3:7-39; 5:18). His rule was unpopular, and his end *not in anger or in battle* (11:20)—assassinated in 175 B.C. by Heliodorus in a coup attempt.

This lengthy rehearsal of conflicts between the kings of the south and the kings of the north sets the stage for the coming of the northern king who is the focus of the vision, Antiochus IV Epiphanes. This king devastated the Jewish people, defied their God and covenant, and defiled their temple and glorious land.

11:21-45 The Dreadful King of the North

Antiochus IV Epiphanes (175-164 B.C.) came to power upon the death of Seleucus IV Philopator (175 B.C.). Antiochus pushed Hellenization in culture and religion upon his subjects and brought terrible persecution upon the Jews. *[Antiochus IV Epiphanes, p. 279.]* The story the heavenly messenger tells about this dreadful king falls into five segments:

11:21-24	His Rise to Power
11:25-28	His First Invasion of the South
11:29-35	His Second Invasion of the South
11:36-39	His Defiance of the God of Gods
11:40-45	His Final Southern Campaign and End Predicted

His Rise to Power 11:21-24

In 190 B.C. this Antiochus (later called IV), younger son of Antiochus III the Great, was taken to Rome as a hostage. He lived there in splendor for fourteen years. Seleucus IV Philopator sent his own son, Demetrius, to Rome to replace his brother Antiochus, who did not then return to the capital city, Antioch. Instead, he stopped in Athens and soon became a public official there. Heliodorus, who had murdered Seleucus IV Philopator, attempted to take the throne. When news of his brother's death came to him, Antiochus left Athens for Antioch and thwarted Heliodorus's conspiracy.

When Heliodorus fled, Antiochus seized power and usurped the throne through *intrigue* (11:21). It is said that he posed as a guardian of the young son of the murdered Seleucus IV, functioning as a puppet king. Our text says that *in* the *place* of Seleucus IV Philopator *shall rise a contemptible person*, "a sinful root" (1 Macc. 1:10), Antiochus IV Epiphanes, *on whom royal majesty had not been con-*

firmed (11:21). Demetrius, the son of Seleucus IV, was next in line for the kingship, but he was hostage in Rome. Demetrius I Soter did eventually occupy the throne, but not until the death of Antiochus IV.

Armies shall be utterly swept away and broken before him (11:22). This points to the constant warfare of his reign. Antiochus IV deposed *the prince of the covenant*, the Jewish high priest Onias III (11:22; cf. 9:26). Onias had come to Antioch to gain the help of Seleucus IV to settle a conflict he had with Simon, an extreme Hellenizer encroaching on his jurisdiction over the city market. Simon had told the Syrian governor Apollonius of great sums of money in the temple treasury. Apollonius sent Heliodorus to confiscate those deposits, but he was deterred by popular protests and miracles, according to 2 Maccabees 3–4. Then Seleucus IV died and Jason, a brother of Onias, offered Antiochus 350 talents of silver for the office of high priest. Antiochus IV accepted the offer, kept Onias in the capital, and had Jason installed in 175 B.C. Three years later, Menelaus outbid Jason for the high priesthood. Jason was deposed, and Menelaus reigned as "a cruel tyrant" for ten years (2 Macc. 4:23-50; 13:3-8). In turn, Onias exposed Menelaus's theft of gold from the temple to pay overdue tribute to the king. Menelaus had Onias murdered (2 Macc. 4:32-34).

Behind the intrigues was the question of how Judea should be governed. Would the Torah be the law of the land? Or would Judea become a Hellenistic state, with citizenship based on accepting "the Greek way of life," "foreign ways," and "new customs contrary to the [Mosaic] law"? Antiochus called for the latter, to promote unity in his realm (1 Macc. 1:41-42). Jason purchased a permit from Antiochus to establish a gymnasium and register inhabitants of Jerusalem in an "Antioch in Jerusalem" organization. Thus they could practice and promote Greek ways, for prestige and commercial advantage (2 Macc. 4:9-22; 1 Macc. 1:11-15, 41-53). As this project developed, it was opposed by Jewish experts in the Mosaic Law—which helps to account for the king later deciding to crush this opposition by trying to eradicate observance of the Torah (1 Macc. 1:54-57; 2 Macc. 6:1-11; Dan. 11:30-32; ABD, 4:437-438). By doing business with *a small party*, Jewish aristocrats, "renegades" who favored Greek customs above the Torah and would pay for privileges, Antiochus IV was able with this *alliance* to *become strong* in control of Judea (11:23; 1 Macc. 1:11). *[Antiochus IV Epiphanes, p. 279.]*

Near the end of Jason's high priesthood, Antiochus sent Apollonius to attend the coronation of Philometor in Egypt (172 B.C.).

While there, he discovered that Philometor's advisers were hostile to Syria and laying claim to Palestine. So Antiochus and an army went up to Jerusalem to ensure its loyalty to the Syrians and were "welcomed magnificently by Jason and the city" (2 Macc. 4:21-22). No doubt the Syrians had earlier, later, and even now gained wealth in Palestine through plundering and bribes; they rewarded their supporters and made sure that Jason would send "money to the king."

As carrier of the tribute to Antioch, Jason delegated Menelaus, who double-crossed him and outbid Jason for the high priesthood. Menelaus did not regularly pay what he promised. But he did steal some gold vessels of the temple to give to the king's deputy and to sell (2 Macc. 4:23-29). Thus Antiochus took much wealth from Judea, something *his predecessors* had not done, then used the booty in senseless ways, *lavishing plunder, spoil, and wealth* on his Jewish supporters (11:24). *He shall devise plans against strongholds, but only for a time.* His oppression of the Jews would be of limited duration.

His First Invasion of the South 11:25-28

In 170 B.C. Egypt attempted to recapture Palestine. Antiochus IV defeated the Egyptian army, invaded Egypt in 169 B.C., and was able to take Ptolemy VI Philometor (181-146 B.C.) prisoner. Philometer had followed bad advice from members of the Egyptian court, *plots . . . devised against him* (11:25-26). Powerful Egyptian nobles then crowned Ptolemy VII, Philometor's brother, king in Alexandria. Next, Antiochus IV and Ptolemy VI united to depose Ptolemy VII. This seems to be the background for 11:27: *The two kings, their minds bent on evil, shall sit at one table and exchange lies, but it shall not succeed* (11:27). Each attempted to carry out his own agenda, so it came to nothing. God, however, does have a calendar. *For there remains an end at the time appointed* by God (11:27; cf. 11:24).

Meanwhile, a "false rumor" came to Jason (see notes on 11:22-23) that Antiochus had been killed in Egypt. So Jason went to Jerusalem to unseat Menelaus, who had succeeded him as high priest (2 Macc. 5:5-10; ABD, 1:270; 169 B.C.). When Antiochus heard of this, he "took it to mean that Judea was in revolt" against his own authority and not only against Menelaus, who was not keeping up regular payments to the king but was stealing temple treasure for him (2 Macc. 4:27; 5:11-21). So troubles in Judea and at home called Antiochus IV away from Egypt. Enraged, he returned with much booty and stopped in Jerusalem to *work his will* (Dan. 11:28). His troops sacked the city and "shed much blood." Menelaus even guided Antiochus into the temple so he could loot it, and his forces took any hidden treasures they found (169 B.C.; 1 Macc. 1:19-28; 2 Macc. 5:1-23).

Antiochus appointed Philip, a Phrygian, to govern Jerusalem. Philip along with Andronicus of Samaria were to incorporate Greek worship and culture among the Jews. The Jews themselves were divided. Some were determined to be faithful to the Torah, while others were ready to accept Hellenistic ways. Philip was unable to handle the Jews (2 Macc. 5:22-23).

The term *holy covenant* appears three times in the context of Gentile intrusion into the temple. It refers to the Jewish covenant people with their Torah and temple (Dan. 11:28, 30). *Holy covenant* is similar to *people of the holy ones* (7:27) and *holy people* (12:7).

Note the pessimism of the writer concerning powerful rulers, their military might, and their international alliances. Their plans shall not succeed, for the end is yet to be at *the time appointed* (11:27).

His Second Invasion of the South 11:29-35

Regardless of how mighty or self-determining rulers appear to be, nevertheless their actions are *at the time appointed* (11:29). The messenger reasserts God's ultimate control of history as prewritten in the book of truth (10:21).

A short time after Antiochus returned to his capital, he learned that Ptolemy VI Philometor and Ptolemy VII agreed to rule Egypt together. Antiochus had hoped they would be rivals, weakening each other. But Philometor in a double cross was able to outwit Antiochus the double-dealer (11:27; cf. 8:25). Then the Egyptians negotiated an alliance with Rome.

Furious, Antiochus set out for Egypt with his armies (168 B.C.). This invasion, however, would not be like the last one. This time *the ships of Kittim* (11:30), a figurative term for Roman forces under Popilius Laenas, intercepted Antiochus on his way to Alexandria and ordered him to leave Egyptian territory. *Kittim* is similar to the name of a Phoenician city on the island of Cyprus and can be applied to any westerners. The story is that Popilius drew a circle around Antiochus in the sand and demanded his decision to withdraw before stepping out of the circle. In humiliation, Antiochus agreed to return home—*he shall lose heart and withdraw* (11:30).

With his foreign and domestic programs collapsing, Antiochus was *enraged* and took harsh action *against the holy covenant* (Dan. 11:30). Jerusalem was still resisting Hellenization, so he sent Apollonius to teach it a lesson—"to kill all the grown men and to sell the women and boys as slaves." Apollonius pretended peace, then killed many people on the Sabbath day (167 B.C.; 1 Macc. 1:29-40; 2 Macc. 5:24-27). At this time, Judas Maccabeus with others escaped to find refuge in the wilderness.

Antiochus IV soon prohibited *the regular burnt offering* at the temple according to Jewish ritual and set up in the temple the *abomination that makes desolate*, the altar of the Greek god Zeus, perhaps with meteorites to be worshiped (Dan. 11:31; Goldstein, 1976:145-152). Antiochus identified the Olympian Zeus with the God of Israel and with himself (see notes on 11:36-39; cf. 2 Macc. 6:1-6; 1 Macc. 1:44-54). *[Abomination, p. 276.]* There are clues that he thought he was purifying and restoring the original Jewish religion (Goldstein, 1976:125-160). However, the Gentiles used the temple for debauchery, prostitution (as for Syrian fertility cults), and unfit sacrifices. Antiochus directed the people to make altars and shrines for idols outside the temple, to sacrifice swine there, and to eat that sacrifice (in opposition to Lev. 11:7; Deut. 12; and the reforms of 2 Kings 23. See 1 Macc. 1:47; 2 Macc. 6–7).

Antiochus outlawed observance of Sabbaths, traditional festivals, circumcision of babies, and even confessing oneself to be a Jew. He ordered Jews to partake of sacrifices in monthly celebrations of his birthday and to help in honoring Dionysius (Bacchus), the god of the grape harvest. The king issued a general decree that Jews who did not change over to Greek customs were to be killed (2 Macc. 6:7-11).

The Jewish people seemed hopelessly divided into at least three groups. Some were ready to accept the ways instituted by Antiochus, to *violate the covenant*. At the same time, many were *loyal* to the God of Israel and his ways as revealed in the Torah, and ready to *stand firm and take action* in resistance to sacrilegious Hellenization (Dan. 11:32). But among those who were committed to the Torah, there was disagreement. How should faithfulness be expressed? By violent resistance? This was the way of the Maccabees. Or would faithfulness follow the way of the escape from Egypt and the return from exile, waiting for God to deliver them? In either case, loyalty to the Torah would be difficult.

Some pious Jews believed that God forbids violent rebellion and trusted prophecies that God would protect Sabbath-observers who took refuge in the wilderness (cf. Isa. 32; 55:12-13; 56:1-2; 58:11-14; Jer. 2:2-3; 17:19-27; Zech. 4:6; Exod. 16:29). They did not defend themselves on the Sabbath and were slaughtered by the king's troops on that day of rest. So others decided to defend themselves even on the Sabbath (1 Macc. 2:29-41; 2 Macc. 6:11; Goldstein, 1976:164, 235-236). The martyrs would have to wait for vindication of their faith in the resurrection (see notes on Dan. 12:2-3 and TBC, below).

The wise (*maśkilim*) is a technical term in Daniel for a group of leaders (11:33, 35; 12:3, 10; Anderson: 139). They apparently are recognized experts in the Torah who *give understanding* and enlightenment to the people, teaching them the reasons for loyalty. But loyalty to God would bring suffering by *sword, flame, captivity, and plunder* (11:33). There was about a year of unrelieved persecutions before Mattathias and the Maccabees began an armed revolt. The military solution to faithfulness appealed to many. To save their necks, *many* Jews who earlier embraced the Hellenistic culture and religious ways, now joined the militaristic Maccabees *insincerely* (11:34). They hoped to be spared the zealous but vicious attacks of the Maccabees on their renegade fellow countrymen, the Hellenized Jews (1 Macc. 2:44-48). Though the Maccabees eventually secured Jewish independence, the Jewish state was short-lived (1–2 Macc.; 142-63 B.C.). *[Chronology, p. 283.]* The Maccabees would only provide *a little help* to those who *fall victim* (11:34). But what are their accomplishments when compared to the ultimate deliverance that will come at *the time appointed* (11:35)?

Thus the heavenly messenger does not encourage military defense or reprisals. Testing will come, but God does not permit it to go beyond its allotted measure. *The wise* realize that faithfulness and suffering even unto death may lead to the people being *refined, purified, and cleansed* (11:35; 12:10; cf. 2 Macc. 7:30-38). Even if they *fall*, their true faith cannot be crushed by any human power (11:35) and there is hope for resurrection (12:2-3).

God is in charge of history. Those caught up in armed resistance to Antiochus IV were not to be followed. Arms are ridiculed (11:34). *The wise* took their stand against Antiochus IV but not with physical force. His values, his pride, his intrigue, his prodigal use of resources for evil—all these were abhorrent to the people of God. Antiochus will be overthrown! In the meantime, *the wise* will help many to understand the ways of holiness as they look for God to bring the crises to an *end* in his own time and way (11:35; 12:3, 10). The wise will reflect Isaiah's insights that militarism is rejection of the Lord of hosts, who will protect and deliver (Isa. 31:1-8). God works through *the wise,* not the men of violence, to fulfill the vision.

The wise or the discerning likely represent a circle of influence from which the book of Daniel itself has come. They are teachers of the Torah who see current political events as superintended by God and know that there will be an *end* to the vicious attacks of arrogant despots. *The wise* trust God instead of meeting violence with violence. Their nonviolent approach is grounded in the kingly rule of a merciful God. They are discerning, encouraging others to adopt the same view, and *lead many to righteousness* (12:3). Daniel is of their number, as both the stories (Dan. 1-6) and the visions make clear (Dan. 7-12). *[Daniel: Date and Authorship, p. 285.]*

His Defiance of the God of Gods 11:36-39

The king shall act as he pleases (11:36; cf. 11:28, *work his will*). Like oriental despots before him, Antiochus IV knows no accountability beyond himself. As said earlier of Nebuchadnezzar, *he killed those he wanted to kill, kept alive those he wanted to keep alive, honored those he wanted to honor, and degraded those he wanted to degrade* (5:19). No one could challenge the authority of Antiochus IV without suffering for it. Similar words were spoken of the Persians, *the ram,* that *did as it pleased and became strong* (8:4); and of Antiochus the Great, who shall *take the actions he pleases* (11:16).

The arrogance of Antiochus was climaxed by his attempt to deify himself. *He shall exalt himself and consider himself greater than any god* (11:36). This description of Antiochus is echoed by Paul as he depicts the "lawless one," who "takes his seat in the temple of God, declaring himself to be God." But the Lord "will destroy [him] with the breath of his mouth" (2 Thess. 2:3-4, 8). Unlike the Persian kings who attributed their successes to Ahura Mazda, Antiochus attributed divinity to himself and wanted his subjects to worship him, in a sometime tradition of ruler-cult among the Greeks (cf. Alexander the Great, ABD, 1:149). He assumed the divine name, *Epiphanes,* which means "[god] manifest." The king fancied that his own face was a match for that of Zeus. On some of his coins, he is crowned with rays like the sun god; the coins increasingly represent him with traditional features of the Olympian Zeus, and carry the words *theos epiphanes* (god manifest) and *nikēphoros* (bringing victory; IDB, 1:150). It is said that the common people did not call him *Epiphanes.* Instead, as a pun, they called him *Epimanes*, "mad man."

The climax of Antiochus's self-aggrandizement as divine came at the point of speaking *horrendous things against the God of gods* (11:36). This *Lord of kings* is the God of Israel (2:47), *Prince of princes* (8:25), King of kings and Lord of lords (Deut. 10:17; 1 Tim. 6:15). For the Jews, the king's astounding actions climaxed when he had an altar to Zeus placed in the Jerusalem temple. Antiochus took his own "divinity" seriously. He believed that religion would enable him to tie his empire together (1 Macc. 1:41-42). This mere man was arrogant enough to see himself as a god above any other god, the catalyst to unite all things in himself.

The heavenly messenger indicates that Antiochus would *prosper until* the *period of wrath* (RSV: *indignation*) *is completed* (11:36). One might think of the rage of Antiochus (11:30). More likely, it means that *God's wrath* and discipline has justly fallen upon the Israelites for their sin, but that God will soon show mercy to the nation. The exile is clearly seen as God's *wrath and* punishment for Israel's sin in former generations (9:16). There are hints that the suffering under Antiochus is the result of divine displeasure, but the book of Daniel does not specify which generation's sin called forth God's *wrath* (see notes on 8:19). The seventy weeks of years (490) and the sevenfold punishment principle (Lev. 26) imply that present agonies result from the sins of generations before the exile (see notes on 9:24-27). The books of the Maccabees, however, claim that this *wrath* came because Jews were currently breaking God's law (1 Macc. 3:8; 2 Macc. 5:17, 20; 7:33-38). God is the one who has *determined* things. Being merciful, God will see that his wrath upon his people *is completed* and not overlong, and that Antiochus is stopped (11:36).

The book of Daniel emphasizes again and again that God is sovereign in both heaven and on earth. However, this does not mean that humans are simply automatons or puppets. Human actions do make a difference. Often the deeds of kings and generals delay or unwittingly contribute to the accomplishment of God's purposes. The events of history seem to have behind them the spiritual realm. This is illustrated by the role of the church in the collapse of the Soviet empire in the early 1990s. When Antiochus at the apex of earthly power confronts the power of heaven, the outcome is easily predicted.

Daniel 11:37 and 39 provide additional insights into Antiochus's arrogance in claiming divine honors for himself. As far as known gods were concerned, Antiochus elected to make the Olympian Zeus (identified with himself) the god of the Seleucid empire. This was in place of *the gods of his ancestors* and the cult of Adonis, the *one beloved by women* (Tammuz, Ezek. 8:14), the Sumero-Akkadian vegetation god. Thus *he shall pay no respect to any other god* and *shall consider himself greater than all* (11:37).

Antiochus magnified Zeus partly because Zeus was god of his soldiers who occupied garrisons in Jerusalem and other cities of Judah. Antiochus depended on these soldiers to enforce his will on the people. Thus a *foreign god* helped him *deal with the strongest fortresses.* Some *will acknowledge him:* Antiochus IV encouraged Jews who denied their faith and adopted Greek ways and worship. He would make these apostate Jews *more wealthy* (11:39). They were given silver, gold, gifts, and places of responsibility (1 Macc. 2:18). And more, Antiochus was eager to sell important posts to the highest bidder: he *shall distribute the land for a price* (11:39; cf. 2 Macc. 4:24).

This litany of the blasphemous acts of Antiochus is a continuation of the revelation of the heavenly messenger. There is nothing here or in the next section (11:40-45) that suggests a future "antichrist." This idea may be latent in the text, with Antiochus IV Epiphanes as a type figure. Although history is linear, events in one era may correspond in a cyclical fashion with events in other eras. Thus this description of the dreadful king in many ways typifies the actions of similar tyrants before and after, including the possibility of a dreadful future personality such as an "antichrist." The text itself, given the setting, is not to be interpreted as intending to describe a future antichrist or "lawless one" (2 Thess. 2:3).

His Final Southern Campaign and End Predicted 11:40-45

The *him* of 11:40 refers to Antiochus IV. The messenger angel now predicts things that are to happen *at the time of the end*—a subject that has been lurking in the background thus far (11:27, 35). This does not refer to the end-time in an absolutely final eschatological sense; instead, it refers to *the end* of the outrages perpetrated by Antiochus (cf. 8:13-14, 19; 11:27, 35, 40; 12:4, 9-13).

The information in the next paragraph does not follow the course of documented history, as do earlier sections of Daniel 11. Likely the vision is to be dated in about 165 B.C., before Antiochus died. Since these predictions were never fulfilled in detail except that Antiochus *did* come to his end, some interpreters think 11:40-45 refers to some distant point in history.

This section predicts that the Ptolemies of Egypt will provoke the dreadful king, Antiochus IV, who will wage war against them in blitzkrieg fashion with a mighty army of *chariots and horsemen, and with many ships* (11:40). In his *advance against countries* in the south, he shall *pass through like a flood*, even across *the beautiful land* (Israel). There will be many deaths, but *Edom and Moab and the main part of the Ammonites* will be spared (11:41). These are specifically mentioned since they were hostile to the Jews and supported Antiochus. Consequently, they shall *escape from his power*. Antiochus is to take total control of Egypt and also Libya and Ethiopia (11:43).

The dreadful king will experience great success. But he is to be called back by rumors of revolts in his home territory, there to meet death (like Sennacherib, Isa. 37:7). The dreadful king will hear alarming *reports from the east and the north* (11:44). He will return *with great fury* to put down revolts by bringing *destruction to many* (11:44). Here, as in 12:2-3, the term *many* refers to faithful Jews (cf. Isa. 53:11-12). Jerusalem has been a special target of his hatred.

He will come into Palestine between the Mediterranean and the *beautiful holy mountain*, Jerusalem itself. There along the coastal route, he is to set up headquarters of *palatial tents* for a major assault. But at this point the dreadful king *shall come to his end*. He dies, *with no one to help him* (11:45). This echoes the earlier statement: *He shall be broken, and not by human hands* (8:25).

However, records show that Antiochus IV died in late 164 B.C. in the east, in Persia. Pillaging a temple of Nanea (or Anahita; equated with Artemis, Aphrodite, or Diana) in Elymais (biblical Elam), he was withstood by local citizens. He escaped and fled toward Babylon. According to 1 Maccabees 6:1-17, news came to him that his armies in Judah had been routed, that the wealth of his armies had been taken by the Jews, and that the abomination he erected in the temple had been torn down. Hearing this news, Antiochus was "badly shaken, . . . took to his bed, and became sick from disappointment." He died from a mysterious illness after making Philip, one of his friends, ruler over all his kingdom. Antiochus did die shortly after the Jerusalem temple was rededicated, but there was hardly time for that news to reach him (Goldstein, 1976:307). Other accounts claim that he died in the east of consumption (Appian, *Syr.* 66) or of worms, punished by God (2 Macc. 9; Josephus, *Ant.* 12.9).

Since the descriptions of the end of Antiochus (who throughout has been identified as the "dreadful king") do not fit known historical events, what is to be done with this paragraph (Dan. 11:40-45)? Some feel such material must reflect specific, identifiable events, and so they project its fulfillment into the future when someone like Antiochus will arise at the end of time. But, as previous explanations have shown, the events of the second century B.C. are too carefully chronicled in this vision to set aside the identification with Antiochus IV even in this paragraph.

There are other ways of looking at this material. First, one may take the position that 11:40-45 is in a *vision* (10:8) written during the days of Antiochus IV, perhaps in about 165 B.C. *[Daniel: Date and Authorship, p. 285.]* The writer reflected recent history affecting Israel up to his day and had confidence that the end of the outrage and suffering was certain. Based on past performance, the writer anticipated that Antiochus would launch yet another expedition against Egypt, and with great success. But the end would come as Antiochus planned a final assault against the beautiful, holy mountain, Jerusalem.

Second, one may observe that at this point the writer adopts a totally different approach. He clothes the demise of Antiochus not in a veiled recounting of history but with scriptural allusions to show that as God acted in the past, so he would soon act to alleviate the present crisis. The *whirlwind* (11:40) calls to mind Isaiah 21:1-2, in which "whirlwinds" symbolize how the "betrayer betrays, and the destroyer destroys." To *pass through like a flood* (11:40) recalls Isaiah 8:8 about how the king of Assyria "will sweep on into Judah like a flood." At the height of his success, Antiochus will hear *reports from the east and the north, . . . and he shall go out* (11:44) recalls Sennacherib in Isaiah 37:7. As Antiochus will return *with great fury to bring ruin and complete destruction to many* faithful Jews on *the beautiful holy mountain* (11:44-45), so would the Assyrian "shake his fist at the mount of the daughter of Zion, the hill of Jerusalem" (Isa. 10:32).

That Antiochus is to die near Jerusalem recalls the words of Joel that God would judge the enemies of Israel in the valley of Jehoshaphat, the "valley of decision" (Joel 3:2, 12-15; location unspecified, but near Jerusalem; tradition points to the Kidron valley just east of the city). The death of Antiochus is so climactic for Daniel that for him to die near Jerusalem would be appropriate. It is here also that Ezekiel anticipated climactic events (Ezek. 38:14-16; 39:2-4). Insights of Scripture are brought to bear on the subject of the *end* of the wicked. The situation is not unlike Messianic prophecies, whose fulfillments are true but happen (or may still happen?) in ways different from what was expected (as with Isa. 9:1-7).

Third, since this paragraph predicts the death of a ruthless tyrant, there was wisdom in avoiding specific details concerning how his death would occur, lest there be reprisals (cf. Rev. 17–18, referring to the fall of Rome without using the name; 17:9, 18). More important is the message to be conveyed: That God has control over the most powerful and ruthless tyrants, even Antiochus IV, who arrogantly claims to be Epiphanes, god manifest! The heavenly messenger reviews the career of Antiochus with all its arrogance, violence, and blasphemy. Here is an evil regime, overextended, exploitative, and cruel; overripe for revolt, collapse, and God's judgment. For such a tyrant, the end must surely come! It will come at the apex of his power. It will come when his hatred for the people of God has reached the moment of greatest peril. The heavenly messenger makes it clear: *He shall come to his end, with no one to help him* (11:45). Exactly how and when doesn't really matter.

Fourth, the interpretation of the materials in chapter 11 cannot be exclusively historical because there have been many like Antiochus in other times and places who have come to their end in God's own time and way. Across the centuries, rulers have arisen who have persecuted the people of God. They are selfish and irrational. They turn their reign into idolatry as war and politics are interwoven with a substitute and false religion, a cult of worshiping state or ruler. And then they are judged by God and die. Thus Antiochus IV is a typical model for all arrogant rulers who in life pretend to be "god manifest" but who in death make "the power of God manifest to all" (2 Macc. 9:8).

It is overinterpreting to hold that in the end-time, a character will appear who in literal ways will do exactly what stands written about Antiochus IV. Yet it is appropriate to observe that from time to time, tyrants like Antiochus have appeared. At the end of history, there could well be a tyrant like him. How and when God will bring the present age to a conclusion is not for us to know (Mark 13:32; Acts 1:7), nor do these materials locate our present moment of history on God's time line. Daniel may be used to interpret current international convulsions or predict the end. However, a good purpose can be served thereby only if that interpretation calls us to be faithful to God, critiques arrogant human powers, and reminds us that God will judge all and bring history to its end as he chooses. Thus Daniel 11 inspires hope in the midst of adversity.

12:1-4 Deliverance of the Faithful

With the death of the tyrant, the messenger concludes his revelation with information about the people Antiochus tried to exterminate.

At that time (*'et*, 12:1) connects with 11:40 and does not begin something new. The story told in chapter 11 is held together by references to *time*, especially that time when Antiochus will meet his end. His atrocities will continue *only for a time* (11:24). The end will be *at the time appointed* (11:27). *At the time appointed he shall . . . come into the south* (11:29). The fall of Antiochus is referred to as *the time of the end* (11:35, 40). Thus this verse refers to the end of Antiochus. The word *time* (*'et*) appears in three more places in this same verse (12:1): *There shall be a time of anguish, such as never occurred . . .* (*till that time* [RSV]). *But at that time your people shall be delivered.* The repeated phrase *at that time* beats like a refrain for the death of Antiochus and the deliverance of the faithful Israelites.

Behind the overthrow of Antiochus, heaven is at work. While Antiochus is threatening God's people and destroying their worship, the people have a champion in the heavenly court: *Michael, the great prince, the protector of your people.* As noted earlier, each nation has its patron or guardian angel (cf. notes on 10:10—11:1). Michael is responsible for Israel and protects the faithful against enemies (such as Persia, Greece, and Antiochus: 10:13, 20; 12:1). He will arise and seal the doom of Antiochus.

Meanwhile, Israel will suffer *anguish* as never before experienced since nations appeared. This reflects the fact that Antiochus was the first to attempt to annihilate not only the people but also their worship. In times past they were invaded, taken captive, and harassed by neighbors. But this was the first known pogrom in their history (cf. the plans for one in Esther). There is a hint that the anguish under Antiochus would introduce more tribulations preceding the end of the age, but this is not spelled out.

The time of deliverance will come as Michael intervenes. The prophecy is that Michael will confront and overcome the patron angel of Antiochus. The reintroduction of Michael, whose name means "Who is like God?" recalls the introduction to the vision (10:13, 21). Already there, Michael, Israel's patron angel, was overcoming opposition to the Jews. This was a prelude to his decisive help now at the end. The upshot of his intervention will be eventual deliverance for God's people.

The names of the faithful and loyal are *written in the book* (12:1;

cf. notes on 7:10). This refers to the book of life (Ps. 69:28; 139:16; Luke 10:20; Rev. 20:12-14). The faithful are not to be eternal victims to Antiochus's plan *to bring ruin and complete destruction to many* (11:44). The faithful are to live! Michael will intervene on their behalf. The heavenly messenger says, *Your people shall be delivered*, not dispatched to the realm of death.

The attention of the angel now turns to those who died or will die martyr deaths during this time of anguish brought on by Antiochus. What will happen to them? Verse 2 is closely connected with what has gone before. It is frequently claimed that neither in the time of Daniel nor in the days of Antiochus was there a clearly developed doctrine of the resurrection. But L. J. Greenspoon has challenged such a conclusion (see TBC, below). Daniel 12:2 is a significant passage concerning resurrection: *Many of those who sleep in the dust of the earth shall wake, some to everlasting life, and some to shame and everlasting contempt.*

In Greenspoon's judgment, the innovative piece to resurrection teaching in Daniel is that not only are the righteous awakened but also the wicked (Greenspoon: 282). In 12:2, *many* refers to Jews (the majority in contrast to "the few") and is used in an inclusive sense: "the many who cannot be counted," "the great multitude," or even "all" (cf. Isa. 53:11-12; Mark 10:45; 14:24; 1QH 4:27; 1QS 6:1; TDNT, 6:536-545). It is possible that *many* includes Gentiles being raised, but that is probably not in the picture here; in the term *many of those*, "of those" points to a (Jewish) part of those who *sleep in the dust of the earth* (Hartman, 1978:307). Jews who die in this crisis *are* raised and receive reward or punishment. At this stage, it is unclear to what extent the resurrection hope includes Israelites from previous centuries. Earlier texts leave one with the impression that the wicked will remain in Sheol. Daniel's statement, chronologically the last in the OT on the subject, envisions a resurrection of both righteous and wicked Jews.

Belief in resurrection from the dead became quite strong at the time of the Maccabees (cf. 2 Macc. 7:9, 23). It grew out of the belief that God would vindicate and reward the faithful who were suffering and dying under the oppression of the likes of Antiochus. When oppression and wickedness reached their zenith, they counted on God to intervene. In his vindication and judgment, the righteous though dead would be raised and not lose their reward of everlasting life, and apostates would be raised for judgment and everlasting shame (for OT antecedents, see TBC, below).

The final focus of the heavenly messenger is upon a group within the faithful, *the wise. Those who are wise shall shine like the brightness of the sky; and those who lead many to righteousness, like the stars for ever and ever* (12:3). *The wise* (*maśkilim*) are teachers of the Torah who understand and are able to discern. They are faithful to the Torah when a compromise of faith is demanded by tyrants, and they *lead many to righteousness. The wise* are meek and *stand firm.* They are able to make others understand and give themselves to refine and cleanse others, even those who may come with wrong motives. Although many of the faithful will *fall victim,* yet *many* are being *cleansed.* They *understand* that heaven is working behind the earthly scenes and wait for God to deliver them (see notes on 11:33, 35; 12:10). Hellenized Jews despised the teachings and the example of these wise, some of whom lost their lives (12:2). But in the resurrection, their lots are to be reversed. The wise are to be given not only life but also are favored with high honor: *They shall shine like the brightness of the sky, . . . like the stars forever and ever* (12:3).

This scene is similar to one of Isaiah's servant songs: "See, my servant shall prosper; he shall be exalted and lifted up, and shall be very high" (Isa. 52:13). "The righteous one, my servant, shall make many righteous" (Isa. 53:11-12). Again, *many* refers to the congregation of Israel. This term, *many*, is also used in the NT, as in Mark 10:45 and Hebrews 9:28.

These final words of the heavenly messenger are intended to emphasize the glory to be conferred upon the faithful spiritual leaders of God's people. The words can be appreciated when contrasted with what is said of Antiochus. When Antiochus, described as a horn, began his treacherous rule, he magnified himself *as high as the host of heaven*, cast down *some of the stars*, and even challenged *the prince of the host* (8:10-11). Antiochus pursued power and glory, even to seeking a place among the stars. But this was beyond his grasp. His character, his methods, his cunning, his deceit, his violence, his blasphemous attacks upon God's people and their worship—all these will result in his being *broken, and not by human hands* (8:25). This is to happen when *the decreed end is poured out upon the desolator* (9:27). The arrogant man *shall come to his end, with no one to help him* (11:45). Here is a clear contrast and even irony: Antiochus, wise in intrigues, grasping for the stars, is upstaged by those truly *wise*, who do not grasp for stars but receive the gift of shining like the stars—and not just for a human lifetime, but *forever and ever.*

The faithful are to rise to everlasting life (12:2). To shine as the stars is reserved for the wise teachers, who lead many to righteousness. The parallelism of the two halves of 13:3 show that one group of leaders is under discussion. Jesus includes all the righteous in his promise: "The righteous will shine like the sun in the kingdom of their Father" (Matt. 13:43). In any case, this honor comes as a gift. It is not earned, grasped, or seized. The wise receive the honor that kings of the earth seek in wrong ways and in vain.

This climactic statement concerning the new life and glory of the community of faith takes its place alongside the other messages of hope. At the beginning of Daniel: *The God of heaven will set up a kingdom that shall never be destroyed, nor shall this kingdom be left to another people* (2:44). In the middle of the book: *The kingship and dominion and the greatness of the kingdoms under the whole heaven shall be given to the people of the holy ones of the Most High; their kingdom shall be an everlasting kingdom, and all dominions shall serve and obey them* (7:27). And now at the end of the book: *Many of those who sleep in the dust of the earth shall awake, some to everlasting life. . . . Those who are wise shall shine like the brightness of the sky, and those who lead many to righteousness, like the stars forever and ever* (12:3).

Gabriel instructs Daniel to *keep the words secret and the book sealed until the time of the end*. This marks the end of the heavenly messenger's revelation (12:4.). To seal means to keep this truth secret until the generation for whom the message is intended. When the message is made known, it will be a source of joy, uprightness, and wisdom. The vision may appear strange and puzzling to readers, but when the end arrives, they will understand.

A similar instruction was given in 8:26 (cf. Isa. 8:16). In chapter 8, the vision is to be sealed because *it refers to many days from now.* Here it is *until the time of the end.* In both, the meaning is the same. Daniel is to keep the visions secret until the time of Antiochus IV Epiphanes—ostensibly from the third year of Cyrus, 536 B.C. (10:1), until the days of the outrageous rule of Antiochus (175-164 B.C.).

During the period between Daniel and Antiochus, the word of God is sealed up. *Many shall be running back and forth, and knowledge* [RSV] *shall increase* (12:4). Some translations, including the NRSV, opt for a different meaning: *and evil shall increase.* This change, made on the basis of the Greek translation (cf. 1 Macc. 1:9, "evils"), requires amending the Hebrew *da'at* (*knowledge*) to *ra'ah* (*evil, disaster,* or *suffering*). Alternatively, some linguists think that another meaning of *da'at* was "suffering." But sense can be made from the Hebrew text as it stands, and according to the principle of retaining the more difficult reading, *knowledge* is to be preferred.

The increase of knowledge recalls the words of Amos:

> The time is surely coming, says the Lord God,
> when I will send a famine on the land;
> not a famine of bread, or a thirst for water,
> but of hearing the words of the Lord.
> They shall wander from sea to sea,
> and from north to east;
> they shall run to and fro, seeking the word of the Lord,
> but they shall not find it. (Amos 8:11-12)

Daniel 12:4 does not refer to the twentieth century with its improved transportation, its explosion of technical knowledge, and the information highway! Rather, it points to the time *prior* to Antiochus IV Epiphanes, when there would be no further word from God. Persons hurried to and fro to find such a word, but without success. However, when the vision is unsealed in the days of crisis during the rampage of Antiochus, then the famine for the word of God will cease. Then the word Daniel has sealed up will be available to all. Meanwhile, *knowledge shall increase:* God will enable persons, like Daniel, to draw meaningful observations from the flow of historical events.

Conclusion 12:5-13

12:5-6 How Long?

With the revelation of the heavenly messenger completed, the vision returns to 10:19. *Two others appeared, one standing on this bank of the stream and one on the other* (12:5). The scene is like the dialogue between the two angelic figures of 8:13, where one asks, *For how long is this vision concerning . . . the transgression that makes desolate?* Here in 12:6, one of the two angels asks the *man clothed in linen* (cf. 10:5, likely Gabriel), *How long shall it be until the end of these wonders?*

The word *wonders* (*pela'ot*) points not to human capabilities but to God's acts. Thus the question refers to the wonderful and mighty acts of God in relation to Antiochus IV Epiphanes (described in 7:25-26; 8:14, 25; 9:27; 11:36, 45). As in 8:13, the question is stated in the form of a lament, "How long?" (cf. Ps. 74:10; 79:5; 80:4; 89:46; Rev. 6:10). How long will it be until God takes decisive action on behalf of his oppressed people?

12:7 The Messenger's Response

The man in linen responds in a strange way, raising both hands *toward heaven* (12:7). To raise one's hand in this way is part of taking an oath, calling God to witness. Raising both hands symbolizes the gravity of what will be said. For a parallel, compare John's vision, Revelation 10:5-6.

Then Daniel hears *him swear by him who lives forever* (cf. 4:34) *that it would be for a time, two times, and half a time; and that when the shattering of the power of the holy people comes to an end, all these things would be accomplished* (12:7).

This response of the man in linen again repeats the set period of three and a half times (see notes on 7:25; 8:14; 9:27). *The shattering of the power of the holy people* (12:7) refers to the dreadful suffering under Antiochus described in 11:21-45. The climax of this outrage, however, will be short-lived (see note on *wrath,* 11:36). When *the decreed end is poured out upon the desolator* (9:27), at *the time appointed* (11:27, 35), *what is determined shall be done* (11:36), and *all these things would be accomplished* (12:7).

12:8 Daniel Requests Further Explanation

Daniel hears these words, but he does *not understand.* He receives his visions *in the first year of King Belshazzar* (7:1), *in the third year of the reign of King Belshazzar* (8:1), *in the first year of Darius* (9:1), and *in the third year of King Cyrus* (10:1). In those days Daniel's interests are in his people and in their return from captivity to the homeland. Yet strangely each of the visions focuses on the coming of a king in the distant future who will violate God's people and try to crush their worship of God.

Daniel is puzzled by the discontinuity between his concern for his people's return from captivity and the vision of a future tyrant. He asks, *My lord, what shall be the outcome of these things?* (12:8).

12:9-13 Final Words of the Messenger

The heavenly messenger makes it clear that the vision is for the time of Antiochus, *the time of the end* (11:35, 40; 12:4, 9). He repeats again that the contents of this vision, like those before, are to *remain secret and sealed* until that time (12:9). In John's vision, the prophecy is not to be sealed because the time is near. However, as in Daniel, the wicked continue in wickedness and the holy in holiness

(Rev. 22:10-11). The heavenly messenger has final words of encouragement: *many* [Jews] *shall be purified, cleansed, and refined* (12:10).

Daniel is to *go* his *way* and live a life of purity (12:13). These words emphasize again that the faithful do not take into their own hands the task of violently changing history, as did the Maccabees. The focus of the faithful is to be upon holiness, purity, and meekness. Their lives are in contrast to the *wicked*, who *continue to act wickedly* (12:10). The *wicked*, apostate Jews, act the way they do because they do not *understand* the ways of God. *The wise* are the ones who understand the ways of God in the time of crisis and can teach all the faithful (11:33, 35; 12:3; see notes at 11:33-35). When confronted by an Antiochus, they are ready (if necessary) to *fall by sword and flame, and suffer captivity and plunder* (11:33). Their lives are demonstrations of holiness and meekness as they wait on God. *Many* faithful Jews, who follow *the wise*, will also suffer and *be purified, cleansed, and refined* (12:10).

The man in linen finally answers the question, How long? *From the time that the regular burnt offering is taken away and the abomination that desolates is set up, there shall be one thousand two hundred and ninety days* (12:11). There is no satisfactory explanation of the difference in the count of the days: 1150 (8:14), 1290 (12:11), and 1335 (12:12). Perhaps there is hidden symbolism in the numbers. Some wonder whether, as time passed in anguish under Antiochus, new and variant calculations were recorded that set this *end* a bit later to give God time to act. Those today who set the time of the end eventually also have to adjust their calculations (cf. Mark 13:32; Acts 1:7). It does seem that 12:11 is a correction of 8:14, since the same predicted event is under discussion, the cleansing of the temple and the restoration of the regular burnt offering. Daniel 12:12 likely refers to a slightly later event, the death of Antiochus, when Michael arises on behalf of the Jews (11:45—12:1).

In the days of Antiochus IV Epiphanes, many calendars were in use. The lunar calendar had 354 1/4 days. The solar calendar had 365 1/4 days. Early Babylonians followed a lunar-solar calendar and inserted a month every two or three years. There was a Macedonian Seleucid calendar (from autumn 312 B.C.), and a Babylonian Seleucid calendar (from spring 311 B.C.; Goldstein, 1983:32). The Jews used the latter, but there was much debate and confusion. Dates for religious festivals were of great importance, and the calendar followed was critical in determining dates of significant events. When did an event occur? When did it begin? When did it end?

The time of events mentioned by the man in linen in 12:11-12 is not clear. When does counting begin? When Antiochus plundered Jerusalem and massacred Jews in 167 B.C.? Did the counting start slightly later with the cessation of the Jewish burnt offering? Or with the erecting of the abomination? When does counting cease? At the removal of the abomination? The cleansing and rededication of the temple? The death of Antiochus? The text does not say.

The messenger does say that there is a limited period of crisis during which the faithful must live carefully. The crisis will be of short duration, and it will end. Two ways of reckoning are given, perhaps to accommodate different calendars or starting or ending times. One is 1290 days, the other is 1335 days. One is a period of 3 years and 7 months, the other 3 years and 8 1/2 months. From the account given in 1 Maccabees, it was approximately 3 years from the first pagan sacrifice to the rededication of the altar in the Jerusalem temple (1 Macc. 1:59; 4:52-53; but 2 Macc. 10:3 calls it 2 years), which happened about 3 1/2 years after Antiochus captured Jerusalem (cf. Dan. 7:25; 8:14; 9:27; 12:7).

The man in linen concludes with a beatitude, *Blessed is he who waits* and endures the period of crisis. This recalls Isaiah 30:18,

> Therefore the Lord waits to be gracious to you;
> therefore he will rise up to show mercy to you.
> For the Lord is a God of justice;
> blessed are all those who wait for him.

Again Daniel is addressed: *Go your way* (12:9). In essence, Daniel is told to continue to live his life to the full. Death will come soon enough, and then comes *rest* (12:13). As one of the *wise,* after death Daniel will experience resurrection life, as envisioned in 12:2-3. He *shall rise for* his *reward* with the *holy people* (12:7) *at the end of the days* (12:13). This expression has the same meaning as *time of the end* in 12:4, in which case the *reward* appears to be more immediate. One must leave open the possibility that in this instance *end of the days* could mean end-time resurrection. In Daniel 12, *the end* seems to be a deliberately evocative term, heralding something far more significant than the mere end of the wicked Antiochus—God's ultimate victory over evil (Anderson: 145-146).

The book of Daniel ends in great tranquillity. Daniel's work is done. He is free to go on his way until the end of his earthly life. Daniel can rest in peace, because of the knowledge that he has filled the place God wanted him to fill, both in life and in death. He can rest in peace because of his confidence that God will unfold history in his time and in his way, that God will overcome evil, and that he, Daniel, will be raised for his *reward*. Daniel's life demonstrates that the faithful do not simply wait for a time when faithful living is possible. Instead, in the midst of crises, their lives demonstrate the way of life characteristic of the kingdom that *shall stand forever* (2:44).

In the second century B.C., the day came when Torah scrolls were burned, circumcised babies were tied to their mother's necks for joint slaughter, a mad man sat on the throne, and oppression, injustice, war, and human sin abounded (1 Macc. 1). Yet even then it was possible, individually and as a faithful community, for believers to grapple with issues of love, justice, and peace and to live lives that were hopeful and obedient to God. This is the central thrust of Daniel.

Apocryphal Supplements

In the Greek OT, two stories are added following Daniel 12: the story of Susanna (13:1-64), and the story of Bel and the Dragon (14:1-42). Both stories underscore Daniel's wisdom. Such a conclusion has the effect of putting Daniel more securely with the wisdom literature.

Susanna is the story of the beautiful, virtuous wife of Joakim. She is framed by two lecherous judges because she refuses their adulterous proposal. Susanna would be executed for adultery if it were not for Daniel's intervention. His cross-examination of Susanna's accusers leads to the disclosure of their perjury and to their death by stoning. Note the ironic wordplay in 13:54-55, 58-59 (cf. notes on 5:25).

In the stories of Bel and the Dragon (snake), Daniel is able by clever moves to demonstrate the weakness of the idol Bel and of the serpent that King Cyrus of Persia is worshiping. Daniel is a wise strategist and exposes them as nothing in comparison to the living God. These additions to Daniel are likely fictitious. *[Supplements to Daniel, p. 297.]*

THE TEXT IN BIBLICAL CONTEXT

Resurrection

In the OT, all people go to the grave. The OT tells of persons raised from the dead: the widow's son at Zarephath (1 Kings 17:17-24); the Shunammite's son (2 Kings 4:32-37); and a man whose body was put in Elisha's grave (2 Kings 13:21).

Often in the OT, dying is compared to lying down and sleeping. This forms a basis for speaking of resurrection as awaking and rising (Dan. 12:2, 13). A frequent refrain in the OT to indicate death is to say that one sleeps with the ancestors, as did David (1 Kings 11:21), Solomon (11:43), Rehoboam (14:31), Asa (15:24), and Ahab (22:40). This means they joined their forebears in the earthly tomb. Yet this reunion is never mentioned jointly with reference to Sheol. Both the good (Jacob, Gen. 37:35) and the evil (Numbers 16:30) go down to Sheol (grave, pit, underworld). After this life, a shadowy existence in Sheol is suggested, but few details are given (ABD, 2:102-104). Even the wisdom literature says "the dead know nothing" (Ecc. 9:4-6, 10; Job 7:9; 14:21). Yet sometimes the dead were consulted, though it was forbidden by the Torah (Deut. 18:11; 1 Sam. 28; 2 Kings 21:6; Isa. 8:19).

Generally, the Israelites hoped for a long life on the earth (Exod. 20:12) rather than for a future resurrection. The ideal was to live to "a good old age," like Gideon (Judg. 8:32). Yet Hebrews 11:19 says that Abraham, pondering the outcome of Isaac's shortened life if he were sacrificed and the threat to God's promise of descendants for him, "considered the fact that God is able even to raise someone from the dead." The OT proclaims the Lord's (Yahweh's) power, which no force can check. God masters life and death. This supplies roots for faith in the resurrection. Hannah sings, "The Lord kills and brings to life; he brings down to Sheol and raises up" (1 Sam. 2:6; cf. Deut. 32:39). In mercy the Creator of the world can give life again (2 Macc. 7:23). Isaiah writes, "Your dead shall live, their bodies shall rise" (Isa. 26:19). Here the Hebrew text is difficult, but the verse likely promises resurrection for those who died as martyrs for the sake of the name of the God of Israel (ABD, 5:682).

Ezekiel's vision of dry bones (Ezek. 37–38) appears to prefigure some kind of a resurrection. No doubt the scene is meant originally in a corporate sense, that the bones are the exiles and the miracle is the reestablishment of Judah on its "own soil" (37:12-14). Likewise, Hosea 6:1-3 expresses hope for the repentance and restoration of Israel, the northern kingdom; 1 Corinthians 15:4 sees a fulfillment of this in Christ's resurrection. These OT texts indirectly anticipate the doctrine of the resurrection.

The passage in Daniel 12:2-3 is the most explicit reference to resurrection in the OT. Details about a general or a particular resurrection are left unexplored. It is not even claimed that all are raised, but it says that Jews ("the many") are raised to receive everlasting life or contempt, and the wise to receive special honor (see notes above). Here the concept of resurrection provides hope and encourages endurance among those suffering and even dying because of being faithful to God's covenant. The martyred righteous are cut short before they can live the usual God-given life span. This does not square with God's compassion and steadfast love, keeping covenant (Dan. 9; 2 Macc. 7). Those who deny their faith and become renegades will be raised to face judgment. Belief in resurrection goes with faith in God's righteous judgments and his vindication for the faithful. God's justice is affirmed throughout the OT and must eventually become manifest. The resurrection allows justice to happen even if it has not been seen earlier. Thus belief in the resurrection is based on *Yahweh's power, justice, and love* (Dan. 9:4-19; ABD, 5:684).

Many interpreters claim that during the exile or the time of Antiochus IV, there was no clearly developed doctrine of the resurrection. But L. J. Greenspoon challenges such a conclusion. He describes the range of meanings given to such terms as *life* and *death* and proposes that the concept of resurrection is found in Israel's early history, connected with Yahweh as Divine Warrior. He concludes that Daniel 12 draws from Isaiah 26:14 and 19. Here again, the first meaning is the return of the exiles and the restoration of Israel to "worship the Lord on the holy mountain at Jerusalem" (27:12-13). Yet Isaiah 26 indirectly anticipates the doctrine of the resurrection. Though seeming to be dead, the exiles will be gathered and raised up by God, who gives the breath of life (Gen. 2:7; Ps. 104:29-30).

Greenspoon examines the settings of other OT texts and places them en route to the clarion statement in Daniel 12:2-3. Ecclesiastes calls mortals to enjoy life because no one survives after death. The "dust returns to the earth as it was, and the breath returns to God who gave it" (2:24; 3:21-22; 12:7). Job 14:12 says there is no hope for mortals to live again. The translation and meaning of Job 19:25-27 is difficult. Here Job does affirm faith in a Redeemer-Vindicator, who will see that his justice is recognized before God. Three times he claims that he will see God. The NRSV rendering allows the possibility of a resurrected Job. Yet the emphasis is upon his vindication and seeing God (reinforced in Job 38–42).

As noted above, Ezekiel 37:1-14 envisions Israel reestablished in its own land. Isaiah 52:13—53:12 celebrates the Servant's redemptive suffering and subsequent exaltation. This refers first of all to God's people, the covenant community. The exiles, suffering while scattered among the nations, will be raised up and restore all people to God, to the astonishment of onlooking rulers. Yet a righteous remnant seems to be in the picture, and Christians believe the prophecy is best fulfilled in the servant ministry, death, and resurrection of Jesus Christ (Mark 10:33-45; Acts 3:13; 4:25-30; 8:32-35; Matt. 8:17; 1 Pet. 2:24-25). The stories of Elijah and Elisha in 1 and 2 Kings have already been mentioned. In completing his survey, Greenspoon (319) claims that "a concept of the bodily resurrection of the dead is expressed in biblical material that ranges in date of composition from the ninth to the second centuries B.C."

The OT explains that the hope of the righteous is to be with God (as in Ps. 73:23-25; cf. Ps. 16:9-10). This testifies to the nearness of God even through ordeals and thus provides a foundation for later confidence that not even death can separate us from God's love (Rom. 8:34-39; cf. 2 Cor. 5:8). The NT offers more doctrinal development. Its theology builds on the resurrection of Jesus Christ, who is "the first fruits" for the coming "resurrection of the dead." Those who belong to Christ will be raised at his coming and experience bliss and fellowship with him (1 Cor. 15:20-23). Whoever believes in Christ, confesses with lips and life that Jesus is Lord, and believes "that God raised him from the dead"—this one "will be saved" and not "put to shame" in the judgment that goes with the resurrection (Rom. 10:8-13; 1 Tim. 2:10-13; Mark 8:38). Unbelievers will be condemned and separated from God (Luke 16:19-31, wicked in torment; John 5:28-29; 2 Cor. 5:10; cf. Rev. 20:13).

In Daniel, the heavenly messenger's words parallel Ezekiel's vision of the valley of dry bones. There is hope for the people of God in the reestablishment of Israel: "Thus says the Lord God: I am going to open your graves, and bring you up from your graves, O my people; and I will bring you back to the land of Israel" (Ezek. 37:12-14). Gabriel may also be echoing prayers for the Lord's help, in which the oppressed call for deliverance from death, and for judgment upon oppressors (see Ps. 69–70). God sent this messenger (Dan. 10:11) to promise renewed life to the faithful, and shame and contempt for the unfaithful. Here the book of Daniel goes further than any other OT passage to indicate that many individuals are raised to experience *everlasting life* beyond this mortal life span, especially after being cut short by martyrdom (11:33). There is to be joy for the righteous and glory for *the wise, who understand* and *lead many to righteousness* (12:2-3, 10).

Revelation 21:1—22:5 provides a NT commentary on Daniel 12. It describes the resurrected community, gathered around "the throne of God and of the Lamb." This passage in Daniel also provides background for Luke 14:12-14 and Matthew 13:43: "Then the righteous will shine like the sun in the kingdom of their Father."

In the OT, the existence after death is not clearly defined. Sheol, the underworld, is a joyless, shadowy place for good and evil alike. But in Daniel, the concept of the resurrection of many of the dead is definitely set forth. Between the writing of Daniel and the days of Jesus, more and more was said about the resurrection (2 Macc. 7:23; 1 En. 22–27; 92–105). Some texts affirm immortality for the righteous (4 Macc.; Wisd. of Sol. 1–6; Jub. 23:31 [as joyful spirits]). Reward and punishment regularly goes along with resurrection (Ps. of Sol. 3, 13–15; 2 Bar. 49-51; 2 Esdras 7; cf. 1QS 3:13—4:26). There was no consensus, however. The Sadducees, basing themselves on the Torah (Pentateuch), denied that there was a resurrection in either angelic form or spirit form. However, the Pharisees, Jesus, and his followers strongly embraced belief in the resurrection (Matt. 22:23-33; Acts 23:7-8; Viviano).

According to the NT, the resurrection of Jesus Christ carries with it the promise of resurrection of believers. Jesus teaches, "I am the resurrection and the life. Those who believe in me, even though they die, will live" (John 11:25). Jesus speaks of raising believers at the last day (John 6:39-51).

A most startling emphasis on the resurrection came in the early church. The resurrection of Jesus Christ became a central point of proclamation by the apostles (as in Acts 2:22-32; Rom. 1:4). This brought them into conflict with the Sadducees because they claimed that "in Jesus there is the resurrection of the dead" (Acts 4:2). These believers were completely convinced of Jesus' resurrection and willingly suffered and died for this belief. They also insisted that those believing in Jesus belong to him and would be raised to be with him (1 Cor. 15:12-29; 1 Thess. 4:13-18). The present work of the Spirit in believers' lives is a "guarantee" that they will share in the resurrection life given by that same Spirit if they *persevere* in faithfulness even through suffering (2 Cor. 5:1-10; Rom. 8:16-25; cf. Dan.

12:12). Moreover, a resurrection of the unrighteous dead was also assumed (Heb. 9:27; Rev. 20:12-15).

The NT teaches that all will rise and face judgment, those in Christ and those without him. The resurrection of believers is to life eternal. Relatively little is said about those without Christ (cf. Rev. 20). In John 5:29, Jesus speaks of the "resurrection of life" and also of "the resurrection of condemnation" (cf. Acts 24:15). These Scriptures echo the words of the heavenly messenger: *Many of those who sleep in the dust of the earth shall awake, some to everlasting life, and some to shame and everlasting contempt* (Dan. 12:2). In these words we find an early and fleeting glimpse into the promise of resurrection life in the Christian gospel. The book of Daniel points to the truth enunciated by Paul, "If for this life only we have hoped in Christ, we are of all people most to be pitied" (1 Cor. 15:19).

THE TEXT IN THE LIFE OF THE CHURCH

Prayer and Spiritual Warfare

Daniel has been mourning, fasting, and praying for three weeks about the future of his people when he receives a true word about *a great conflict* (10:1-12). For him, prayer is not just a "two-way transaction" but "also involves the great socio-spiritual forces that preside over so much of reality" (Wink, 1992:309). With the book of Daniel, we have the first revelation of how these powers block answers to prayer. The angel prince of Persia opposes Gabriel's coming to Daniel until Michael, Israel's guardian angel, draws the angel of Persia into diversionary battle so the messenger angel can slip through to deliver the vision of the future for God's people.

Daniel represents Israel, struggling to resist anything that would detract from fidelity to Yahweh, to recognize all the "counterfeits for the rule of God" (Aukerman: 49-51). For three weeks Daniel contends with unseen spiritual powers, perhaps with Babylonian spirituality and his training in practices considered an abomination to Israel (see notes on Dan. 1:3-7). His prayers are heard on the first day the words leave his lips, but God *seems* not to answer. Meanwhile a fierce battle is being waged in the heavens between the angels of two nations. "The angel of Persia does not want the nation he guards to lose such a talented subject people" and for twenty-one days is able to frustrate Yahweh (Wink, 1992:310). Finally Israel's guardian angel intervenes so the messenger angel can get through.

This tells us something about our own prayers. Wink makes an interesting suggestion. For years we have been praying for peace while the "angel of the United States" and the "angel of the Soviet Union" have been locked in deadly military competition. It seemed futile, with spiritual inflexibility on both sides. Yet God was working through the demonstrations and prayers for peace, and through churches and pastors in eastern Europe. Eventually a nuclear weapons reduction treaty was negotiated. Later the Soviet regime fell apart and the United States found that it could not afford the arms race.

The spiritual powers (angels) resist the sovereignty of God over history, but they can prevail only for a time. God is limited by our freedom, and also by the freedom of institutions and systems, which often frustrate his will for a while. These powers hinder and delay God's work and healing in his world, but God is not mocked. Our intercessions help God to undermine the powers of the Domination System, whose brutality is often a sign of desperation. Their time is short. God will prevail, whether it takes twenty-one days, years, or centuries (Wink, 1992:310-313).

Thus Daniel can release us to more energized, assertive, expressive, and persistent praying. God will prevail, and our prayers can help overcome obstacles to God's reign. Martyrdom and the cross may work to purify the faithful (Dan. 11:35) and stir up God's mercy and resurrection power (2 Macc. 7:23). Immense evil forces are arrayed against God, but in faith and in prayer, we affirm God's miracle-working power (Wink, 1992:317; Dan. 9:15). Truly believers struggle "against the rulers, against the authorities, against the cosmic powers of this present darkness, against the spiritual forces of evil in the heavenly places" (Eph. 6:12). But, praying "in the Spirit at all times," believers "stand firm" and "proclaim the gospel of peace," clad in God's armor and taking "the sword of the Spirit, which is the word of God" (Eph. 6:13-18).

Awaiting the Last Day

In the church today there seems to be a great desire to know the sequence of international events at the end of time. The Gulf War (1991) provided an unusually rich opportunity for such speculation, especially since Iraq is in the area of ancient Babylon and Saddam Hussein was seen by some as a modern Nebuchadnezzar. Thus far, predictions about international events made on the basis of biblical materials have been, for the most part, unreliable. Now it appears that with the collapse of the Soviet Union, North American prophecy experts will have to identify a new set of antagonists to fit their predictive schemes.

Many have tried to use the book of Daniel as a timetable or a crystal ball for discerning future events. Often this overshadows the abiding message of the book: the call to faithfulness and endurance in times of persecution, and the affirmation of the rule of God. Some find it easy to project end-time world crises by using Daniel's phrases: *what shall be hereafter* (2:45), *at the end of days* (10:14), and *the time of the end* (11:35, 40; 12:4, 9, 12). However, these phrases are best applied chiefly to the termination of ancient crises, as explained in the notes. This language does hint at even greater things, that after the people are delivered from Antiochus, God's everlasting kingdom would come in, and God would be king over all the earth (Dan. 2:44; 7:14, 18, 27; cf. Zech. 12–14). But this is evocative eschatological language and not spelled out in detail. It is a grand affirmation of faith in God and his rule, which *will* triumph in his world even though the present may look bleak for the faithful.

Today many talk about "the last days" and believe we have entered them in a special or unique way. For the NT writers, however, the last days began with the coming of Jesus and the pouring out of the Holy Spirit at Pentecost. The last days will continue until Jesus returns. Peter saw that the last days began at Pentecost. "In the last days" God would pour out his spirit on all flesh (Acts 2:17). In a similar way, Paul wrote of Christians as those "upon whom the ends of the ages have come" (1 Cor. 10:11, living in the overlap of the old age and the incoming new age).

The preacher in Hebrews said that "in these last days [God] has spoken to us by a Son" (Heb. 1:2). Jesus "has appeared once for all at the end of the age to put away sin by the sacrifice of himself" (Heb. 9:26). At the coming of Jesus, the last days began. F. F. Bruce (1954:68) comments: "The last days began with Christ's first advent and will end with his second advent; they are the days during which the age to come overlaps with the present age." The coming of the Spirit at Pentecost not only inaugurated the last days but also is the guarantee of what is yet to be. Believers experience now the firstfruits of the great harvest at the end (Rom. 8:23).

From the first days of the church, believers were admonished to await the "near" return of the Lord. Peter writes, "The end of all things is near" (1 Pet. 4:7). James agrees: "The coming of the Lord is near" (James 5:8). In Hebrews, the preacher calls believers to assemble and encourage one another "all the more as you see the Day approaching" (Heb. 10:25). Paul observes, "Salvation is nearer to us now than when we first became believers; the night is far gone, the day is near" (Rom. 13:11-12).

In the last days, the church awaits "the last day." Jesus speaks of the last day which will bring resurrection and judgment (John 6:39, 44, 54; 11:24; 12:48). The last day is called "the day" (1 Cor. 3:13; Rom. 2:16), "that day" (1 Thess. 5:4; 2 Tim. 1:12, 18), or "the great Day" (Jude 6). It is also called "the day of the Lord" (1 Thess. 5:2; 2 Pet. 3:10), the "day of God" (2 Pet. 3:12), and "the day of Jesus Christ" (with variation in wording: 1 Cor. 1:8; 2 Cor. 1:14; Phil. 1:6, 10; 2:16). It is "the day of wrath" (Rom. 2:5) and "the day of redemption" (Eph. 4:30).

How long will it be until the last day? God's way of looking at time is different from ours (2 Pet. 3:8). In the meantime, the gospel is to be preached to the whole world (Matt. 24:14). There will be wars and rumors of wars. "This must take place, but the end is still to come" (Mark 13:7). Each day that goes by, God is giving one more day of grace. Time is extended because of the mercy and patience of God. He does not want any to perish "but all to come to repentance" (2 Pet. 3:9).

In stories and visions, the book of Daniel provides the church with illustrations of the lifestyle to which God calls the faithful as he works out his purposes. Daniel and his companions model Peter's instruction to the church for living in the last days. They show "what sort of persons ought you to be in leading lives of holiness and godliness. . . . Strive to be found by him at peace, without spot or blemish" (2 Pet. 3:11, 14).

Resurrection Hope

Martyrs Mirror shows that persecuted believers in the sixteenth century often appealed to stories in the book of Daniel to gain strength for facing their own fiery furnaces and lions' dens. Daniel and the three young men were models of faith and faithfulness for them. Early Anabaptists knew the books of the Maccabees and were impressed with how the Jews endured persecution and martyrdom in the days of Antiochus IV.

They also treasured the promise in Daniel of resurrection for martyrs. Anneken Hendriks in 1571 at fifty-three years of age was betrayed by her neighbor. The bailiff charged her with adopting "the cursed doctrine of the Mennonists" and suspended her by her hands. Though uneducated, she proclaimed her trust in God. They filled her mouth with gunpowder to keep her from testifying any more and threw her alive into the fire at Amsterdam. Braght alludes to Daniel 12:1-3 in his comments: "But the merciful God, who is the comfort of the pious, shall give this faithful witness, for this brief and temporal tribulation, an everlasting reward, when her stopped mouth shall be opened in fullness of joy" (Braght: 872-873).

The stories and visions of Daniel are especially valued by Christians facing tyrannical rulers, who exalt themselves *greater than any god* (Dan. 11:36). Indeed, this is a temptation for any government (as in Rev. 13), and believers need to be on guard, to be *wise,* and to *understand* what belongs to God alone (Mark 12:17; Acts 5:29). Our reliance on God's power, justice, and love leads to a firm resurrection hope as we belong to Christ. Thus we can *persevere* even through *anguish*, to *be purified, cleansed, and refined*. Like Daniel, we go our way in faithful service, rest, and wait for resurrection morning (Dan. 12:13).

Outline of Daniel

Part 1: INTRODUCTION
Daniel 1:1-21 (in Hebrew)

Faithfulness in an Alien World	**1:1-21**
Historical Introduction	1:1-2
The National Crisis	1:1
How the Sacred Vessels Arrived in Babylon	1:2
Nebuchadnezzar's Plan for the Captives	1:3-5
Qualifications and Education	1:3-4
The Food and drink	1:5
Ashpenaz's Selection	1:6-7
Daniel's Decision and Proposal	1:8-16
Rejecting the King's Food	1:8
The Test	1:9-14
Results of the Test	1:15-16
Negotiating the Training	1:17-20
Historical Note	1:21

Part 2: A TRACT TO THE NATIONS
Daniel 2:1—7:28 (2:4b—7:28 in Aramaic)

God the Revealer: Nebuchadnezzar's Dream	**2:1-49**
A Case of Royal Insomnia	2:1-13
Nebuchadnezzar's Dream	2:1-2
Nebuchadnezzar and the Chaldeans	2:3-11

- The Conclusion of the Letter — 4:34-37
  - Nebuchadnezzar's Praise and Restoration — 4:34-36
  - Nebuchadnezzar's Testimony — 4:37

The God to Be Honored: Belshazzar's Feast — 5:1-30

- Belshazzar's Banquet — 5:1-9
  - Eating, Drinking, and Gross Irreverence — 5:1-4
  - Mysterious Writing, Failure, and Fear — 5:5-9
- The Queen's Counsel — 5:10-12
- Belshazzar Seeks Daniel's Help — 5:13-16
- Daniel's Sobering Response — 5:17-28
  - Daniel Rejects Rewards — 5:17
  - Daniel Recalls Nebuchadnezzar's Glory — 5:18-21
  - Daniel Indicts Belshazzar — 5:22-23
  - Daniel Interprets the Writing — 5:24-28
- The Interpretation Confirmed — 5:29-31
  - Daniel Rewarded and Elevated — 5:29
  - Belshazzar Slain — 5:30
  - Darius the Mede Receives the Kingdom — 5:31

The Living God: Rescue from the Lions' Den — 6:1-28

- Darius Organizes His Kingdom — 6:1-5
  - Daniel's New Position — 6:1-3
  - Daniel's Vulnerability — 6:4-5
- Collusion to Remove Daniel — 6:6-9
  - The Appeal to Darius's Vanity — 6:6-7
  - Darius's Prayer Law — 6:8-9
- Daniel Prays to His God — 6:10
- Daniel Disgraced — 6:11-18
  - Daniel Charged Before the King — 6:11-14
  - Daniel Thrown to the Lions — 6:15-18
- Daniel Delivered — 6:19-24
  - Conversation at Dawn — 6:19-22
  - Released from the Pit — 6:23
  - Fate of Conspirators — 6:24
- The New Decree — 6:25-27
- Daniel's Renewed Success — 6:28

The Rule of God, His Angels, and His People: Daniel's Dream — 7:1-28

- Introduction — 7:1

Description of Daniel's Dream	7:2-14
Four Great Beasts (on Earth)	7:2-8
The Ancient One (in the Heavenly Court)	7:9-10
The Beasts Judged (on Earth)	7:11-12
One Like a Son of Man (in the Heavenly Court)	7:13-14
The Interpretation of the Dream	7:15-27
Daniel's Condition and Request	7:15-16
A General Interpretation	7:17-18
Daniel Asks About the Fourth Beast	7:19-22
A Detailed Interpretation	7:23-27
Postscript	7:28

Part 3: READING SCRIPTURES AND RECEIVING VISIONS
Daniel 8:1—12:13 (in Hebrew)

Daniel's Vision of the Ram and the Goat	**8:1-27**
Introduction	8:1
The Vision	8:2-14
In Susa	8:2
A Charging Ram	8:3-4
A Flying Goat	8:5-8
Emergence of the Evil Little Horn	8:9-12
Concerned Holy Ones	8:13-14
The Vision Interpreted	8:15-26
Gabriel Appears	8:15-17a
The Time of the End	8:17b-22
A Dreadful King	8:23-26
Postscript: Daniel's Response	8:27

The Meaning of Jeremiah's Prophecy	**9:1-27**
Introduction	9:1-2
Date	9:1
Meditation on Scripture	9:2
Daniel's Intercessory Prayer	9:13-19
Preparation for Prayer	9:3-4a
"If They . . . Repent" (1 Kings 8:47-48)	9:4b-14
"And Plead" (1 Kings 8:47, 49)	9:15-19
Heaven's Response: A Vision	9:20-27
Gabriel's Arrival	9:20-23

Gabriel's Interpretation of Seventy Years — 9[illegible]
  Sevenfold Chastisement — 9[illegible]
  First Seven Weeks of Years — 9[illegible]
  Next Sixty-two Weeks of Years — 9:25b
  Final Week of Years — 9:26-27

Daniel's Vision of the Future — 10:1—12:13

Introduction — 10:1—11:1
  The Promise of a Vision — 10:1
  Daniel's Preparation — 10:2-3
  The Arrival of the Heavenly Messenger (Gabriel) — 10:4—11:1
    Time, Place, and Appearance — 10:4-6
    Daniel's Reaction to the Sight and Sound — 10:7-9
    The Heavenly Messenger Responds to Daniel — 10:10—11:1
The Message — 11:2—12:4
  Persian Kings — 11:2
  A Warrior King — 11:3-4
  Turning Tides Between South and North — 11:5-20
    A Powerful Prince — 11:5
    An Alliance Between South and North — 11:6
    North Invaded by South — 11:7-8
    South Invaded by North — 11:9
    North Continues Harassment of South — 11:10
    Resistance of Southern King — 11:11-12
    Invasion by Northern King — 11:13-15
    Triumph and Fall of the North — 11:16-19
    Northern King's Tribute Collector — 11:20
  The Dreadful King of the North — 11:21-45
    His Rise to Power — 11:21-24
    His First Invasion of the South — 11:25-28
    His Second Invasion of the South — 11:29-35
    His Defiance of the God of Gods — 11:36-39
    His Final Southern Campaign and End Predicted — 11:40-45
  Deliverance of the Faithful — 12:1-4
Conclusion — 12:5-13
  How Long? — 12:5-6
  The Messenger's Response — 12:7
  Daniel Requests Further Explanation — 12:8
  Final Words of the Messenger — 12:9-13

Apocryphal Supplements — (13–14)

Essays

OUTLINE

ABOMINATION THAT DESOLATES This phrase has a number of variations. In Daniel 9:27 it is *abomination that desolates*, in Hebrew a plural noun and singular participle. In 11:31 it is *abomination that makes desolate*, in Hebrew a singular definite noun and a participle; and in 12:11 it is *the abomination that desolates*, in Hebrew with a singular noun and participle.

The Greek name for the Olympian Zeus when rendered into Semitic language becomes "baal shamem" (2 Macc. 6:2). Literally, this means "Lord of Heaven." The Jews in their hatred for this title substituted *šiqquṣ* for *baal* and *šomem* as a pun for the word *šamem*. *Šiqquṣ* was a word used almost exclusively for idolatry and idolatrous practices, and thus meant "a detested thing" or "abomination." *Šomem* had two meanings: "to be appalled" in the sense of overwhelming dread or amazement, and "to be desolate" in the sense of no longer inhabited.

Antiochus IV Epiphanes likely thought he was purifying and restoring the ancient Jewish religion (Goldstein, 1976:125-160). He installed an altar to Zeus in the Jerusalem temple (2 Macc. 6:2; 1 Macc. 1:54, a "desolating sacrilege"), perhaps with meteorites to be worshiped (Goldstein, 1976:145-152). In referring to this, the faithful Jews refused to use the Gentile phrase, "Lord of Heaven," and instead substituted "the detested thing which appalls or devastates." For the Jews, the altar of Zeus had emptied the temple not only of true worshipers but also of God himself. Jesus and Paul know of such desolating sacrilege, foreign worship in the temple of God (Mark 13:14; Matt. 24:15; 2 Thess. 2:4).

ALEXANDER THE GREAT Alexander of Macedonia (356-323 B.C.) was the son of Philip II of Macedon. His tutor was Aristotle, whose influence on the brilliant young prince can only be surmised. Alexander came to his father's throne in 336 B.C.and two years later began an invasion of the Persian empire. His purpose was to "liberate" Greek cities in Asia Minor. But, once on his way, there was no stopping. He defeated the Persians at the river Granicus (334 B.C.) and at Issus (333 B.C.) and then turned south to Egypt. Next he proceeded northeast to Mesopotamia, where he finished off the Persian empire as King Darius III fled (331 B.C.). In 327 B.C. he continued eastward through Babylon and on to India (Pakistan) and the Indus River. His army refused to go further into India, so they turned back.

In June 323 B.C. Alexander died at Babylon. One of his generals took his body to Egypt, where it lay for centuries in Alexandria, founded by the king in 331 B.C. While still living, Alexander apparently requested that the Greeks worship him, and the ruler-cult tradition was carried on in Syria, Egypt, and later for Roman emperors. Hence, Antiochus IV Epiphanes had precedents to follow in exalting himself as though a god.

Alexander's conquest began a new era in history, the *Hellenistic* age, when Greek language, philosophy, theology, religions, art, customs, and commodities penetrated the inhabited world of western Asia. In exchange, Asiatic ideas entered the West and influenced the development of civilization from the fourth century B.C. onward. An assessment of Alexander the Great has been given by the historian W. W. Tarn (1948): "He was one of the supreme fertilizing forces of history. He lifted the civilized world out of one groove and set it in another; he started a new epoch; nothing could again be as it had been. . . . Particularism was replaced by the idea of the 'inhabited world,' the common posession of civilized men. . . . Greek culture, heretofore practically confined to Greeks, spread throughout the world; and for the use of its inhabitants, in place of the many dialects of Greece, there grew up the form of Greek known as the *koine*, the common speech" (quoted by Porteous: 123). As early as the third century B.C., the OT was translated into this common Greek for many Greek-speaking Jews in Egypt and elsewhere. This text was widely used in the early church. The best known of these versions is the Septuagint.

Upon Alexander's death, his newly acquired empire was broken up into provinces ruled by his generals: (1) Macedonia and Greece under Antipater and Cassander; (2) Thrace under Lysimachus; (3) Syria under Seleucus I; and (4) Egypt and Palestine under Ptolemy I (cf. the four horns of Dan. 8:8). Antigonus, who received what is now called Turkey, attempted to maintain the unity of the empire. He was defeated and lost his life at the hands of the other four generals at Ipsus in 301 B.C. Additional splitting occurred. However, three dynasties finally became established in Macedonia, Egypt, and Syria. These Greek kingdoms lasted for centuries, until the rise of Rome. *[Ptolemies, below. Seleucids, below.]*

ANTICHRIST The antichrist is a satanic or satanic-human figure that, many believe, will appear before the second coming of Jesus Christ. The antichrist is supposed to be the last persecutor of Christians and will be defeated by Jesus Christ upon his return. The origins of this concept are obscure. As Jesus Christ was God incarnate, so the antichrist is considered to be an incarnation of Satan.

One of the earliest Christian references is found in Mark 13. There Jesus predicted that before the coming of the Son of Man in clouds, there would be "many" false Christs and false prophets. The false Christs (not just one) will perform signs and wonders and will lead many astray. In 2 Thess. 2:3-12,

Paul speaks of the "lawless one" who will appear and oppose every god and object of worship. He will take a seat in the temple of God, declaring himself to be God. This lawless one will perform signs and wonders and deceive those who refuse the truth. When Jesus comes, he will destroy the lawless one with "the breath of his mouth" (likely exposing evil with the proclaimed gospel; cf. Rev. 19:11-16).

In 1 John, the antichrist is the spirit of heresy. Whoever denies the incarnation is an antichrist (2:18-23).

The antichrist motif is also present in Revelation (9:1-11, 13-19; 13:1-18; 16:12-16; 17:13-14; 20:7-10). The two beasts in chapter 13 are given power by the dragon (the devil) and portray roles of antichrist. The first beast draws on the four beasts of Daniel 7 and has ten horns, seven heads, and a mortal wound in one of the heads. The first beast is interpreted as the antichrist, Satan incarnate in the Roman empire persecuting the saints. The second beast, the false prophet (19:20), has two horns like a lamb. As a false Christ, it performs miracles and demands the worship of the first beast (emperor worship; cf. 16:12-16). In chapter 17, the scarlet beast (the Roman empire, especially Nero in 17:8) is a consort of the woman, mother of whores ("Babylon," Rome). Chapter 18 is a prophetic dirge over the fallen city of Rome. The two beasts raise armies for a final battle. Christ returns with his heavenly armies, and the beasts are defeated and thrown into the lake of fire. Their followers are struck down with the sword coming from Christ's mouth—likely the preaching of the gospel and Word of God (Rev. 19).

Among early Christians, the first beast likely symbolized the Roman empire and its emperors. The whore signified Rome. The antichrist motif and the false prophet, however, are mysterious. The antichrist tradition has continued through the centuries. It even worked its way into Islam as ad-Dajjal, a Jewish false messiah, who will be slain by Jesus.

Since the days of the apostles, attempts have been made to identify the antichrist with world leaders, with empires, and with power structures. Using the number 666, Irenaeus (second century A.D.) identified the antichrist with a specific emperor rather than the empire itself. In the pre-Reformation and Reformation period, the Roman church was seen as Babylon and the papacy as antichrist. In turn, the Reformers were also labeled as antichrists. In more recent history, many have labeled national leaders, especially in times of war, as antichrists, fearing that the world was in its final conflict. Some named Napoleon, Kaiser Wilhelm, and Hitler as antichrists.

The dreadful king of Daniel has become a prototype for the antichrist. *[Antiochus IV Epiphanes, below.]* This cruel king oppressed and persecuted the Jews and attempted to destroy their worship. Depicted as the little horn (7:8), this contemptible person (11:21) exalted himself against God (11:36) but was brought to an inglorious end (11:45).

Many believe that in the future there will be an antichrist who will be destroyed by Jesus Christ at his coming: Theologically, this person would claim to be God. Politically, this person would claim to rule the whole world. His power would come from Satan. He would arrogantly attempt to be a satanic substitute for Jesus Christ.

Whether by a dreadful king of the past or by antichrists of the future, the faithful understand and believe that, as God broke arrogant rulers of the past "not by human hands" (Dan. 8:25), so Jesus Christ will overcome any antichrist of the future.

ANTIOCHUS IV EPIPHANES (175-164 B.C.) The earliest Seleucids desired friendship with the Jews. Antiochus III (233-187 B.C.) replaced this with intolerance and even hostility to the Jews, and following kings stayed in his track. *[Seleucids, below.]* Antiochus IV Epiphanes tried harder than any other to eliminate Jewish religious practices and impose Greek ideas and culture on Jewish communities. *[Hellenism, below.]* "Then the king [Antiochus] wrote to his whole kingdom that all should be one people, and that all should give up their particular customs" (1 Macc. 1:41).

Antiochus, ruling from Antioch in Syria for 11 years, intended to solidify his rule over a diversified set of peoples by spreading Greek culture. Antiochus himself was proud, extravagant, and severe. Immediately he backed Jews who wanted to Hellenize. Joshua was the younger brother of the orthodox Jewish high priest Onias III and had his name changed to Jason to show his readiness to adopt Greek ways. Strife developed between Jewish factions, between Jewish loyalists and Jewish Hellenists, and between persons outbidding one another for positions.

The pious Onias III had gone to Antioch to appeal to Seleucus IV to curb the schemes of his enemy Simon. At that time, Seleucus IV died and Antiochus IV came into power. He accepted a bribe from Jason and had him installed as high priest in place of Onias III, with the agreement that Jason would promote Hellenism (2 Macc. 4:1-17). The old royal policy was that Jews should observe the Torah. Now the new royal policy was that they should follow the Greek way of life. Repeatedly in his reign, the king sought to secure his rule over Palestine. At times he let his troops plunder Judea and lavished wealth on his favorites (see notes on Dan. 11:21-24). Antiochus with a Syrian army was in Jerusalem in 172 B.C., welcomed by Jason (2 Macc. 4:21-22). Later that year Menelaus offered a larger bribe than Jason and so became high priest and pushed Hellenization even harder (2 Macc. 4:24). Soon afterward, Menelaus had Onias III, the earlier priest, killed (2 Macc. 4:30-34). Then Antiochus invaded Egypt and in the conflict elephants were used along with chariots. While there, a false rumor arose that he was dead. Jason, pro-Egyptian, began massacring Jews of both factions (pro-Judaism, pro-Hellenism). When the news reached Antiochus, he took it to mean that Judea was in revolt. In rage, he marched on Jerusalem, pillaged the temple, and put thousands to death (169 B.C.; 1 Macc. 1:16-28; 2 Macc. 5:1-23; see notes on Dan. 11:25-28).

About a year later, while returning from a second invasion of Egypt which the Romans forced him to abandon (see notes on Dan. 11:30), Antiochus once more moved toward Jerusalem (168-167 B.C.). He dispatched Apollonius with a detachment of 22,000 men to the city. The army deliberately paraded in Jerusalem on the Sabbath, when Jews loyal to the law did not yet fight. By royal decree, all that smacked of Judaism was to be destroyed. The temple was profaned, sacred books were burned, and many were killed. Judas Maccabeus and a few other escaped to the wilderness (2 Macc. 5:24-26). *[Maccabees, below.]* Jewish-type worship was forbidden and pagan religious rites were introduced. The Jews were directed to sacrifice swine (1 Macc. 1:44-49). Soon afterward came the ultimate insult to the Jewish way of worship. The king had an altar to Zeus erected within the Jerusalem temple (2 Macc. 6:1-2; 1 Macc. 1:54). *[Abomination That Desolates, above.]*

Another decree in 167 B.C. forbade circumcision, even Sabbath observance and the reading of the law. Jews were forced to eat unclean food (1 Macc. 1:56-64). Antiochus so wanted to get rid of every semblance of

Jewish faith that he was massacring those faithful to the Torah. People fled into the wilderness. Many compromised. Active resistance flared at Modein, not far from Jerusalem (1 Macc. 2; likely in 166 B.C.). *[Maccabees, below.]* After some three years, Jews "zealous for the law" (1 Macc. 1:27) overcame the forces of Antiochus but did not yet oust them from the citadel in Jerusalem. They cleansed the temple, rededicated the altar, and restored the daily sacrifices (164 B.C.; 1 Macc. 3-4). Antiochus heard of Nicanor's defeat and died soon afterward in 164 B.C. in Persia after an unsuccessful attempt to plunder a Persian temple (1 Macc. 6:1-16; 2 Macc. 9; Polybius, *History* 31.11; Josephus, *Ant.* 12.9; Appian, *Syr.* 66; 2 Macc. 1:13-17 likely confuses Antiochus IV with Antiochus III: ABD, 4:1020).

For the Jews, Antiochus represented the embodiment of evil. He called himself Antiochus Epiphanes ([god] manifest); the people lampooned him as Antiochus Epimanes (madman). The Jewish point of view of these events is found in 1-2 Maccabees.

The interpretation followed in this commentary is that much of the material in Daniel 7-11 must be read with Antiochus Epiphanes in mind (see notes on Dan. 7-11). His evil behavior and severe persecution of the people of God provide a prototype for any satanic figure(s) called antichrist(s).

APOCALYPTIC LITERATURE The apocalyptic style grew out of prophecy, though some have tried to make the case that its roots are in wisdom literature. The prophets of Israel were men of action. They were eloquent preachers and critiqued the politics of Israel and Judah. The prophets pleaded for the rule of God over his people. They addressed specific sins of the people and were rarely misunderstood. Their bluntness and forthrightness opened them to rejection and persecution. The prophets predicted the judgment of God upon the sin and rebellion of the people. For the prophets, the nations were often God's agents in bringing judgment or deliverance to Israel (as in Jer. 21; Isa. 44-45). Yet occasionally the prophets also rebuked surrounding nations and called them to submit to God's rule (as in Amos 1-2; Isa. 19).

The apocalypticists used the written word. Reaching beyond Palestine, they developed visions for a worldwide cosmic mission of God and his people. Instead of a focus on Davidic messianism, they saw the whole world as God's domain. For them, the nations were God's enemies en masse. Instead of blunt speech, their message was couched in visions so puzzling to both writer and reader that angels were needed to explain the message.

Most baffling is the symbolism of apocalyptic writing. In it, common things of life have symbolic meaning, such as birds and animals. The lion suggests royalty; the ox, strength; the eagle, speed; the horns of an animal, power. Parts of the body have symbolic value: hand suggests power; legs, stability; white hair, age or majesty; mouth, oracle either divine or demonic; eyes, insight and knowledge. Clothing has meaning: a long robe means priesthood; a crown means status. Colors also have symbolic value: white means purity or victory; blood red signifies suffering or martyrdom, while scarlet suggests decadent luxury. Above all, numbers indicate more than numerical value: four points to the corners of God's created world; seven and forty suggest perfection and completion.

This tendency to see symbolism in animals and birds, for example, continues into the present. Hawks are advocates of military solutions to world problems. Doves suggest peaceful means. A chicken suggests cowardice. A pig is a glutton. The owl represents wisdom. A rabbit suggests excessive reproduction.

Apocalyptic writing was an exilic and postexilic development that broadened the prophetic message. Although Palestine, *the beautiful land* (Dan. 11:41), might be in the spotlight in earlier material, the whole world becomes the stage for the apocalypticist. Instead of the prophet's concern chiefly about the struggle between evil and good *within* the Jewish community, the concern shifts to worldwide conflict. For the apocalypticists, this battle rages in heaven and is played out on earth. They looked for God to take direct action in history and to transform it into a new order. From the heavens the eternal kingdom of God would break into the present.

The OT has apocalyptic (or more accurately, proto-apocalyptic) passages in Isaiah (24–27), Joel, and Zechariah (9; 14). Ezekiel and Daniel lead in the development of this form. Apocalyptic visions flourished in the intertestamental period, in apocryphal (2 Esdras) and in pseudepigraphical writings (such as 1 Enoch and 2 Baruch). The NT offers apocalyptic passages in Mark 13, Matthew 24, and Luke 21; in 1 and 2 Thessalonians; and supremely in Revelation. In apocalyptic materials, secrets of heaven, earth, and the future are revealed from above in veiled, symbolic terms. For detailed discussions, consult works by Russell (1964), Collins (1984), Morris (1972), and Hanson (1975). For the texts and orientation, consult an annotated Apocrypha for 2 Esdras and Charlesworth for Pseudepigrapha. The veiled nature of apocalyptic writing continually tempts believers to use these materials to predict the future, especially in relation to the end-time and the return of Jesus Christ.

BABYLON/CHALDEA Two civilizations flourished in Mesopotamia from the third millennium B.C. to the last centuries before the time of Christ. They were named for the capital cities, Asshur and Babylon. The Babylonian and Assyrian civilizations were largely contemporaneous with that of Egypt. Assyria and Babylonia were in the area of today's Iraq. Babylonia lay in the region between the Tigris and Euphrates rivers, from Baghdad south to the Persian Gulf. Assyria occupied territories north and to the east of the Tigris.

The earliest references to Babylon can be traced back to 2200 B.C. The name in Akkadian is *bab-ilim*. In the Bible it was Babel, "gate of God." A late form of the name Babylon, "gate of the gods," became *babulon* in Greek, leading to the modern name Babylon.

In the early history of Babylon, the area was dominated by shifting alliances of unstable political states until the rise of Hammurabi (1792-1750 B.C.). Under Hammurabi, Babylon became a major power. By the end of his reign, he dominated all Mesopotamia. He called himself "King of the Four Quarters of the World." Hammurabi built a reputation as a great king and legal mind. His famous law code was discovered at Susa in A.D. 1901. Hammurabi was the most successful king of the dynasty that made Babylon the leading city in western Asia until the early centuries following Christ.

The book of Daniel deals with a far later period in the history of Babylon. A series of dynasties followed the first dynasty of Hammurabi until the coming of the Chaldean dynasty, the Neo-Babylonian empire (626-539 B.C.). Nabopolassar in 626 B.C. led attacks on Nippur and the Assyrians to free the Babylonians from their rule. When he defeated the Assyrians in a battle near Babylon, the Babylonians in elation crowned him king in 625 B.C. He spent the next ten years making his position secure, and then marched up the Euphrates to seize territory under Assyrian control. A new power emerged in western Iran, the Medes, who helped to pound at the Assyrians. In 614 B.C. the Median Cyaxares marched on Asshur and it fell. Nabopolassar, in order to take part of the spoil, met Cyaxares near Asshur. Peace was cemented when Nebuchadnezzar, Nabopolassar's son, married Amyitis, a granddaughter of the Median king. Then the allies besieged and eventually captured the city of Nineveh in 612 B.C.

Nabopolassar undertook additional campaigns against Assyria. The Assyrian king Assur-uballit II (611-609) was trying to rule from Haran (Gen. 11:31) but had to flee to Syria in 610 B.C. He awaited help from his ally Pharaoh Neco II of Egypt, who was advancing toward Syria. On the way, he defeated Josiah (609 B.C.; 2 Kings 23:29-30) and made Judah a vassal of Egypt. Neco moved on to Carchemish (on the northern Euphrates 60 miles west of Haran) to assist the Assyrian army. In the spring of 605 B.C., the crown prince Nebuchadnezzar attacked and defeated the Assyrian-Egyptian alliance at Carchemish (Jer. 46). The victory celebration was cut short by the death of Nabopolassar, and Nebuchadnezzar went home to be crowned. *[Kings of Judah, below.]*

The period of Nebuchadnezzar and those that followed is called the (New) Neo-Babylonian or Chaldean empire. The name *Chaldea* is derived from the name of a region of swamps and lakes in the lower courses of the Tigris and Euphrates rivers from which the families of these kings came. *[Nebuchadnezzar, below.]*

During the reign of Nebuchadnezzar, the city of Babylon received worldwide recognition for its architecture. He built fortifications, walls, palaces, and famed "Hanging Gardens." There were gates and temples and magnificent boulevards for processionals and festivals. In addition, private homes of many sizes and styles had ingenious structural devices and stunning decorations.

The contributions of Babylon to the world have been numerous and far-reaching. Writing itself appeared there in the fourth millennium B.C., in cuneiform (wedge-shaped). This was carried through the Middle East as far west as Ebla in the third millennium B.C., and even into Palestine in the second millennium B.C. Thereafter cuneiform was mostly superseded, but Assyria did bring some of it into Palestine in the eighth-seventh centuries B.C. for legal and administrative matters (ABD, 1:1212-1218). Writing led to the development of literature from legal texts to school curriculum, philosophical works concerned with moral and ethical problems, drama, poetry, and proverbs and maxims.

Divination was a discipline in which the Babylonians tried to communicate with the gods. The Babylonians were advanced in the practice of medicine. Ancient medical texts list symptoms with instructions for medication. It is in the field of mathematics that the Babylonians excelled. In the old Babylonian period, there were tables for multiplying, dividing, squares and square roots, based on a sexagesimal system. They developed astronomical data and calendars and astrology. The more we become aware of these contributions of the Babylonians, the more exciting the interpretation of Daniel becomes. On one hand, we discover the impact of Babylonian culture and learning on the book; and on the other, an awareness of Babylonian culture, learning, and history sheds light on how to interpret many passages.

CHRONOLOGY

Major Events

627-587 B.C.	Jeremiah prophesies
612	Nineveh and Assyrians defeated by Medes and Babylonians
605	Egypt defeated at Carchemish by Nebuchadnezzar
604-603	Nebuchadnezzar establishing rule over Syria-Palestine
603-601	Judah pays taxes to Babylonia
601-600	Nebuchadnezzar rebuffed by Egypt; Judah sides with Egypt
699	Nebuchadnezzar sends bands against Jerusalem
598-597	Jerusalem besieged by Nebuchadnezzar; Jehoiakim dies; Jehoiachin reigns three months; Zedekiah appointed *First* major deportation; many taken into exile (2 Kings 24:6-17)
587/586	Fall of Jerusalem; temple destroyed; *Second* major deportation (2 Kings 25:1-12; Jer. 52:4-15)
582	*Third* deportation (Jer. 52:30)
562	Evil-merodach (Amel-marduk) succeeds Nebuchadnezzar
559	Cyrus begins reign in Persia
554-539	Belshazzar rules Babylon under Nabonidus (556-539)
550	Cyrus conquers the Medes to form Medo-Persian empire
539	Babylon falls to Gubaru (Darius the Mede) and Cyrus
538	Cyrus allows Jews to return (Isa. 45:13; Ezra 1)
520-516	Jerusalem temple rebuilt; rededicated 70 years after its fall (see notes on Dan. 9:2; Ezra 6:15)
336	Alexander the Great becomes king in Macedonia
334-331	Persian empire falls before Alexander
323	Death of Alexander the Great

Kings of the South—Egypt	Kings of the North—Syria
Ptolemy I Soter 323-282 B.C. (Dan. 11:5) (rules Palestine and Phoenicia) (takes some Jews to Alexandria)	Seleucus I Nicator 312-281 B.C. (11:5) Antiochus I Soter (Savior) 281-261
Ptolemy II Philadelphus 282-246 (11:6) (time of translating Septuagint)	Antiochus II Theos 261-246 (11:6)
Ptolemy III Euergetes 246-222 (11:7-9)	Seleucus II Callinicus 246-225 (11:7-9) Seleucus III Soter 225-223 (11:10)
Ptolemy IV Philopator 222-204 (11:10-12) (cf. 3 Maccabees)	Antiochus III the Great 223-187 (11:10-19; vassal of Rome, 190/188 B.C.)
Ptolemy V Epiphanes 204-180 (11:14-17)	Seleucus IV Philopator 187-175 (11:20)
Ptolemy VI Philometor 180-145 (11:25-28) (appeals to Rome for help, 168 B.C.)	Antiochus IV Epiphanes (God Manifest) 175-164 (11:21-45; cf. 1-2 Macc.)

Domination of Jews by World Powers

609-605 B.C.	Judah a vassal of Egypt after Josiah's death
604-587/586	Judah a vassal of Babylon after battle of Carchemish
601-598/597	Judah revolts against Babylon; sides with Egypt
597-587	Babylon in control; many Jews deported to Babylon
587/586-539	Jerusalem burned; Jews in exile, under Babylonian rule
539-334	Jews under (Medo-)Persian rule
334-323	Jews under Alexander the Great, Greek rule
322-198	Jews under Egypt (Ptolemies, Hellenistic)
198-164/142	Jews under Syria (Seleucids, Hellenistic)
167/166-164	Jewish guerrilla resistance, led by Maccabees

164-142	Jerusalem liberated except for Syrian citadel Temple cleansed, religious freedom (1 Macc. 4:41-61) Continued struggle for complete political freedom
142-63	Independence, Hasmonean rulers (1 Macc. 13:41)
63 B.C.-A.D. 325	Jews under Rome

CYRUS THE PERSIAN/DARIUS THE MEDE Cyrus II the Great is generally considered the one responsible for the establishment of the Achaemenian (or Persian) empire. This name is traced to Cyrus's ancestor, the family founder Achaemenes. Cyrus became king of Persia in 559 B.C.

Cyrus was the son of a Persian king, Camybses I (585-559 B.C.). Legend says that his mother was the daughter of a Median king, Astyages, and that he was raised by a shepherd and later revolted against his maternal grandfather and overlord. Cyrus was born around 590-589 B.C. He conquered Babylon in 539 B.C., when he was about 50 years of age.

Cyrus began his reign over the Persians around 559 B.C. In 550 B.C., Cyrus defeated the Medes and incorporated them into the Medo-Persian empire (Dan. 5:27; 6:8; Esther 1). Cyrus was helped by the defection of Astyages' soldiers. Next Cyrus marched against Lydia. Its capital was Sardis, near the west coast of what is now called Turkey. This campaign can be dated around 547-546 B.C. Then Cyrus turned his attention to the east. In anticipation of the growing Persian threat, Nabonidus returned to Babylon, bringing the gods from the Babylonian countryside to the city.

According to ancient records, the Medes and Persians chose to attack Babylon during a festival (October 539 B.C.), when the Babylonians drank and reveled all night long (Belshazzar's feast, Dan. 5). Gubaru/Ugbaru (Gaubaruwa; Greek: Gobyras; ABD, 2:39; ANET: 306; see below), governor of Gutium in Media, led the troops of Cyrus into the city of Babylon without a battle. One report says they entered through the riverbed of the diverted Euphrates. Two weeks later Cyrus entered the city. Because of the incompetent reign of Nabonidus and his son Belshazzar, the Babylonians welcomed Cyrus as a liberator and threw green twigs in his path. Cyrus claimed that Marduk chose him to restore the true worship of that god after Nabonidus had "interrupted" it. Cyrus worshiped Marduk and quickly moved the images back to their permanent sanctuaries in the sacred cities. He complimented himself for abolishing the yoke of forced labor for inhabitants of Babylon, the kind of oppression noted in Dan. 4:27 (ANET: 315-316).

In the book of Daniel are several references to Darius: (1) *Darius the Mede received the kingdom* (5:31—6:28). (2) *In the first year of Darius the son of Ahasuerus, by birth a Mede* (9:1). The Greek form of Ahasuerus is Xerxes, which many believe was an ancient royal title. (3) *In the first year of Darius the Mede* (11:1). Note that this Darius never seems to get beyond his first year of reigning in Babylon.

There are several references to Cyrus: (1) *And Daniel continued until the first year of King Cyrus* (1:21). (2) *So this Daniel prospered during the reign of Darius and the reign of Cyrus the Persian* (6:28). (3) *In the third year of Cyrus king of Persia a word was revealed to Daniel* (10:1).

A Median king Darius is unknown to historians, though the name is known for later Persian kings. Furthermore, there is no time chronologically for a king or kingdom between Nabonidus/Belshazzar (the last Babylonian kings) and Cyrus, who conquered the Medes and then invaded Babylon in 539 B.C.

There are several theories as to the identity of Darius the Mede. First and most plausible, Darius the Mede is identified with Gubaru (Ugbaru, Gobyras), governor of Gutium, in Media. He was about sixty-two years of age when he led the army of Cyrus into Babylon without a battle (5:31). Two weeks later, they were there to help the city welcome Cyrus. Cyrus appointed Gubaru "governor of Babylon and the region beyond the river," a vice-regent over Mesopotamia. Gubaru was appointing governors until his death eight months later (hence, Daniel always has him in his first year). Darius may have been a shortened version of a Persian throne name (*Darayarahu:* "He who holds firm to the good"). Even though the Medes were quickly eclipsed by the Persians (Dan. 8:3), having a Mede as the first king over Babylon after the collapse of the Babylonian empire fits a popular ancient conception that there was a succession of four world empires: Assyria (replaced by Babylon in the scheme of Daniel; ABD, 2:30), Media, Persia, Greece (cf. notes on Dan. 2, 7, 8). It also fits prophecy that Median troops would overcome Babylon (Isa. 13:17-19; 21:2, 9; Jer. 51:1, 27-28; ABD, 2:38-39; ANET: 306).

Second, some propose that Darius and Cyrus are the same person, and that Daniel 6:28 should be translated, "Daniel prospered during the reign of Darius, *that is*, the reign of Cyrus the Persian." In this view Darius the Mede was a throne name for Cyrus. Some support for this view is found in a few ancient versions of Daniel in which 11:1 reads the *first year of Cyrus*. Further, Cyrus was related to the Medes and was also called "King of the Medes." Yet the best calculations have him in his early fifties when he became king of Babylon (cf. Dan. 5:31, *sixty-two*). According to inscriptions, he appointed many subordinate officials, as Daniel 6:1 suggests, but he might have done some of that through Gubaru (see above).

There is no agreement among scholars about the various theories. Some scholars reject all of them. However it is settled, it is clear that Darius the Mede and Cyrus the Persian are closely associated or the same person in the initial Medo-Persian rule over Babylon.

Cyrus was known for his clemency to subdued peoples. He abolished the yoke of forced labor (ANET: 316) and demonstrated his leniency by allowing captive Jews to return to Jerusalem and to rebuild the temple (2 Chron. 36:22; Ezra 1:1-8). In Isaiah 44:28—45:1, the Lord calls Cyrus his "shepherd" and "his anointed" (Hebrew: *mašiaḥ*, or messiah).

Cyrus disappeared during combat in Central Asia and was succeeded by his son Cambyses II (530-522 B.C.), who took Egypt. The Persian empire became the largest the world had yet seen. It ruled the entire East as far as India.

DANIEL: DATE AND AUTHORSHIP Who wrote the book of Daniel and when? Among scholars there is much debate. The nature of the book makes it almost impossible to determine date and authorship with finality. The series of stories about Daniel and his friends suggest one set of answers (Dan. 1-6). The visions attributed to Daniel suggest other answers (Dan. 7-12).

The *stories* reflect historical events and experiences. But they are not history as history writing is understood today. At times details of the stories deviate from what is known about kings such as Nebuchadnezzar or about empires such as Babylon and Persia. To seek to identify authors or dates of writing through details of the stories may lead to false conclusions. Some details in Daniel's interpretation of Nebuchadnezzar's dream (Dan. 2:36-45) do seem to call for a date in the Maccabean period, at least for the final form of the story. One can see how every story meets a need of the Jews in the stress of the Maccabean period, but none of the stories *requires* that setting (Rowley in ABD, 2:30). In general, the stories suggest an early date, pre-Maccabean, perhaps even in some form stemming from the sixth century B.C., the time of exile.

The *visions* lead scholars to designate Daniel as an apocalypse. *[Apocalyptic Literature, above.]* This genre provides clues of another sort to determine date and authorship. The rise of apocalyptic writing—its forms, the nature of religious faith, allusions to events in the past, its view of things above, of things to come, of humans, and of other worldly beings—all these contribute to determining date and authorship. Apocalyptic writing reached its zenith between 200 B.C. and 200 A.D. This suggests a later date such as the time of oppression under Antiochus IV Epiphanes (175-164 B.C.), in the second century B.C.

The stories reflect a Babylonian background. The visions, though attributed to a Daniel in Babylon, are concerned with *the beautiful land* (the Jewish homeland), with Jerusalem and the temple, and with dreadful events that would befall the people at the hands of a violent oppressor.

The six edifying stories revolve around Daniel and his companions. Their style and content do not demand that Daniel be regarded as their author. The stories are given from a third-person perspective. They could have been transmitted orally across the generations, then compiled in the second century and adapted to meet the crisis of faith in Maccabean times. As far as the stories are concerned, that Daniel's name is on the book need mean no more about their authorship than does the name *Esther* or *Ruth* on those books.

The four visions create a different problem. Daniel 7 says that Daniel *wrote down the dream*. That vision and those that follow are, for the most part, written in first person: *I saw in my vision* (7:2). *A vision appeared to me* (8:2). *While I was speaking in prayer, the man Gabriel . . . came to me* (9:20-21). *I, Daniel, alone saw the vision* (10:7). Though it is characteristic of apocalyptic literature to be attributed to prominent personalities of the past, some interpreters believe such material should be interpreted literally, not allowing for this trait known so well in the Pseudepigrapha.

The visions purport to trace future history from Daniel's time to the second century B.C. Hence, some interpreters believe that the visions must be attributed to the Daniel of the sixth century in order to safeguard the possibility of divinely inspired, predictive prophecy (Yamauchi). Yet it is possible to match many details in the visions with details in history right up to 165-164 B.C. (see notes on Dan. 11:40-45). From there the visions become less precise and more evocative, predicting the downfall of Antiochus IV (who died in late 164 B.C.) and expressing general confidence in the triumph of God's everlasting kingdom.

Jesus alludes to Daniel 9:27 as spoken "by the prophet Daniel" (Matt. 24:15). This leads those who follow a literal interpretation to attribute the material to Daniel the man rather than to the book that carries his name.

One problem related to a late date for the book of Daniel is its acceptance into the Jewish canon. There would be insufficient time, some claim, for materials written so late to be circulated, venerated, and accepted as Scripture, assuming that the canon was finalized near the time of Jesus, who calls Daniel a prophet and speaks of "the law of Moses, the prophets, and the psalms" (Luke 24:44). The Psalms formed the opening and longest part of the third division of the Hebrew Scriptures, the Writings, in which the book of Daniel is found. The rabbinical discussions at Jabneh in about A.D. 90 about writings that "soiled the hands" was about books already canonized up to two centuries earlier and not a canonization decision (ABD, 1:841). Writings were not necessarily immediately given the authority of Scripture. The process of incorporating books into a canon is still conjectural, however. The fact that fragments from Daniel have been found at Qumran (200 B.C.—A.D. 100), gives further evidence of Daniel being highly regarded, whether or not then as part of the canon.

In this commentary it is assumed that materials in Daniel, especially the stories, are of early origin. The collection of stories and the visions were brought together in the second century to meet the crises facing the faithful in the days of Antiochus IV Epiphanes.

Thus the stories and visions seem to call for differing views of authorship. In the Aramaic part, the stories may have been arranged in their unique way (Dan. 2 paralleling the vision of Dan. 7; Dan. 3 paralleling Dan. 6; and Dan. 4 paralleling Dan. 5) when the other visions, written in Hebrew (Dan. 8, 9, 10-12), were assembled. Daniel 1 was probably prepared last to unify the whole and to provide a Hebrew *inclusio* or bracket for the whole.

The stories dealing with life in the court during the exile present the view that if Daniel and his friends were faithful and experienced the faithfulness of God, others could do so as well. The visions reflect another situation in which God's people are powerless and persecuted by foreign rulers. The people are divided, some supporting and others opposing the foreign oppressors and their actions to impose foreign ways and religions upon them. The people are confused, unable to understand why God does not intervene when his temple, his worship, and his people are attacked.

More interpreters are coming to the opinion that the authors, if they appear in the book, were *the wise* and discerning referred to in 11:32-35; 12:3, 10; and 1:4. The wise identified themselves with Daniel and his friends. As teachers, their task was to make many understand, to teach, not to fight. They knew that in so doing some would die, but in the resurrection they would be singled out to *shine like the brightness of the sky, . . . like the stars forever and ever* (12:3).

The wise are not to be identified with those Hasideans (Hasidim, likely forerunners of the Pharisees and perhaps also of the Essenes) who joined the Maccabees in violent action against renegade Jews and the Syrians (1 Macc. 2:39-48; 7:12-18; 2 Macc. 14:6; ABD, 3:68-69). However, the wise would fit as leaders of those who would rather die (and many did die) than be "defiled by food," "profane the holy covenant" and "the sabbath day," or "do what the king commands." They hid in caves and apparently took an absolute stand not to fight back (1 Macc. 1:62-64; 2:29-40; but see 2 Macc. 6:11, not on the Sabbath). The wise disparaged the *little help* of the militaristic Maccabees, who rallied Jews to fight even on the Sabbath (Dan. 11:34; 1 Macc. 2:39-41). The wise called fellow Jews to trust in God to deliver them *not by human hands* (Dan. 8:25). Even though this way would entail tremendous suffering and the death of many, the wise said the experience would *purify* the people. They counseled perseverance and hope in God to overcome evil rulers, establish his reign, and raise up martyrs to share in God's everlasting kingdom (11:33-35; 12:2-3, 10-13; cf. 2 Macc. 7; 14:46; and miracles of deliverance in 2 Macc.). This bold faith is an example for believers in all ages.

HELLENISM This term refers to devotion to Greek thought, customs, and religion or imitating the same. It includes an emphasis on reason, the pursuit of knowledge, the arts, moderation, civic responsibility, and bodily development. Typically it also included an attempt to identify other gods with the Olympian pantheon. Alexander the Great (356-323 B.C.) was considered to be an exponent of Hellenism. The Hellenistic influence let loose in Palestine presented a severe challenge to Judaism. By the second century B.C., Jerusalem was divided into pro-Hellenists ("renegades") and anti-Hellenists (keeping the Mosaic covenant; 1 Macc. 1:11-15).

The issue came to a crisis when Antiochus IV Epiphanes (175-164 B.C.) impressed upon the Jews detested Greek customs, practices, and religion—with the death penalty for disobeying his decree. This was part of his general policy to have the people in his empire united in language, religion, culture, and dress (1 Macc. 1:41-64; 2 Macc. 4-7). Antiochus tried to eradicate observance of the Torah. He wanted to establish in Jerusalem the worship of the Olympian Zeus as patron of the Seleucid dynasty and empire (ABD, 5:15). This led to the Maccabean revolt under Mattathias and his sons against Antiochus (beginning in 167 B.C.). *[Antiochus IV Epiphanes, above.] [Maccabees, below.]*

KINGS OF JUDAH The final years of the kingdom of Judah were turbulent. The southern kingdom of Judah, established following the reign of Solomon in the tenth century, lasted 335 years. The final years were politically unstable; two of the last four kings each reigned only three months.

Josiah began to reign in 640 B.C. at eight years of age (2 Kings 22:1). According to the Chronicler, he sought the God of David in the eighth year of his reign (age sixteen) and began to purge Judah and Jerusalem of the high places of foreign worship in his twelfth year (2 Chron. 34:1-7). In his eighteenth year (622-621 B.C.), he began to repair the temple. The high priest found the "book of the law" in the temple, which led to a great spiritual revival (likely an earlier form of Deuteronomy; 2 Kings 22–23). At this time the Assyrian empire began to totter. Pharaoh Neco (also Nechoh, Necoh), when going to the aid of Assyria, seized Judean provinces near Egypt and attempted to attach them to his domain. Josiah went "to meet" Neco at Megiddo (2 Kings 23:29), either to fight him (2 Chron. 35:20-27) or more likely to welcome him as an ally and open the pass for him. But Neco himself wanted to control Megiddo and his path for retreat (if necessary, as it was in 605 B.C.) rather than let it in the hands of an ally who might change sides (ABD, 3:1017). In any case, there Josiah was slain or mortally wounded (609 B.C.; 2 Kings 23:29; 2 Chron. 35:23-24).

Jehoahaz, son of Josiah, was the people's choice for the throne after Josiah's death. But Neco now had full control of Palestine, with Judah as a vassal state. Three months later, on his way back from trying unsuccessfully to wrest Haran from the Babylonians, Neco deposed Jehoahaz and carried him away to Egypt (2 Kings 23:30-34). There Jehoahaz, also called Shallum, died (Jer. 22:10-12; Ezek. 19:4). Neco placed Jehoiakim (Jehoahaz's brother) on the throne (609 B.C.).

Jehoiakim was given that name and placed on the throne by Neco. First named Eliakim, he was another son of Josiah and ruled eleven years until he died (609-598 B.C.; 2 Kings 23:34—24:6). The religious abuses removed by Josiah returned under Jehoiakim. Jehoiakim was the king whom Jeremiah addressed in his famous letter dictated to Baruch. In utter contempt, Jehoikim cut Jeremiah's letter in little pieces, burnt the scroll, and persecuted the prophet (Jer. 36).

Judah had to pay heavy taxes to Egypt. But the supremacy of Egypt over Palestine was doomed when Nebuchadnezzar defeated Neco at Carchemish (605 B.C.), followed by another victory at Hamath. Nebuchadnezzar's father died, and he had to rush home to be crowned king. In each of his next four regnal years, Nebuchadnezzar was campaigning in the west. Probably in 604-603, soon after Ashkelon fell to him, Jehoiakim and Jerusalem also submitted to the Babylonians after Judah's fasting (Jer. 36:9) in November 604 B.C. because of Nebuchadnezzar's advance against nearby Ashkelon (Jer. 47). Thus 604 B.C. is the earliest date for Daniel's deportation to Babylon, but 597 B.C. is more likely (see below).

Jehoiakim paid taxes to Nebuchadnezzar for "three years," 603-601 B.C. (2 Kings 24:1; cf. notes on Dan. 1:1). Then in 601-600 B.C. Nebuchadnezzar tried to invade Egypt but was rebuffed, with heavy losses on both sides. This sign of Babylonian weakness encouraged Jehoiakim to rebel, withhold taxes in 600 B.C., and favor Egypt and Neco, who had elevated him to the throne. Nebuchadnezzar sent Babylonian units already in Palestine against Judah (2 Kings 24:2). Failing in this, Nebuchadnezzar sent his army (598-597 B.C.), and Jerusalem was taken in March 597 B.C. after a short seige. Jehoiakim died before the city fell and before Nebuchadnezzar himself arrived (2 Kings 24:6-12). However, the Chronicler says Nebuchadnezzar bound Jehoiakim to take him to Babylon—but drops further reporting (2 Chron. 36:6). Josephus (*Ant.* 10.6.3) reports that Nebuchadnezzar killed Jehoiakim and threw his body before the walls of Jerusalem, without burial (thus fulfilling Jer. 22:13-19; 36:30; ADB, 3:664-665).

Jehoiachin, son of Jehoiakim, became king of Judah in 598 B.C. while Nebuchadnezzar was on his way to punish Jehoiakim. Jehoiachin ruled three months. When Nebuchadnezzar arrived, Jehoiachin surrendered. According to 2 Kings 24:8-16 and 2 Chronicles 36:10, Nebuchadnezzar took Jehoiachin to Babylon along with treasures from God's house and many captives, likely including Daniel and Ezekiel. This was in the eighth year of Nebuchadnezzar's reign (597 B.C.). Jehoichin was in prison in Babylon until the death of Nebuchadnezzar. Then Evil-merodach freed him, gave him a stipend and an honored seat, and let him dine in the king's presence every day (2 Kings 25:27-30). Jeremiah called Jehoiachin "Jeconiah" (Jer. 24:1; 27:20; 28:4; 29:2) and "Coniah" (22:24-28; 37:1).

Zedekiah was placed on the throne by Nebuchadnezzar and thus named as a sign of vassalage (597 B.C.). Earlier named Mattaniah, he was the last king of Judah and the third son of Josiah to be enthroned. Zedekiah held office until everything fell before the Babylonians in 587-586 B.C. He ruled the remnant left behind after the deportation of Jehoiachin along with thousands of leaders and artisans. Though Zedekiah promised allegiance to Babylon (Ezek. 17:13-19), he and his associates plotted against Babylon and leaned toward Egypt, which had promised support. Jeremiah (21) saw the folly of this action and warned against it.

In Zedekiah's ninth year (589 B.C), encouraged by negotiations with Egypt, he rebelled against Babylon and withheld tribute. Nebuchadnezzar sent an army against the rebels, which laid seige to the city (2 Kings 24:20—25:3). The inhabitants of Jerusalem held on for a year and a half. In desperation, Zedekiah promised to free Hebrew slaves and appealed to Egypt, which advanced and drew the Babylonians off for a while, so those freed were again enslaved (Jer. 34; 37:5). But Judah's hope in Egypt and the belief that God would defend his city and temple were dashed. When the wall was breached, Zedekiah attempted to flee but was captured. His children were slain before him, then he was blinded, with that horrible sight as his last. He was carried captive to Babylon. In 587-586 B.C. the city of Jerusalem was burned and the residue of the people were taken captive. The kingdom of Judah had come to an end (2 Kings 25:4-11).

MACCABEES This is the name given to the Jewish family that led the armed revolt against Syria at the time of Antiochus IV Epiphanes and furnished a dynasty of priests and rulers of the state that emerged. *[Antiochus IV Epiphanes, above.]* The dynasty is also known as the Hasmonaeans, a name derived from a mythical family ancestor Hasmonaeus.

The revolt came as a result of the policies of Antiochus IV Epiphanes which were quite unacceptable to devout Jews. After about a year of severe persecution, the revolt began when Mattathias killed a royal officer and a Jew about to offer a heathen sacrifice. He leveled the altar and then fled with his five sons to the hills, where they were joined by others "zealous for the law" like Phineas (167 B.C.; 1 Macc. 2; Num. 25). After some months of vigorous fighting, Mattathias died. The revolt was left to his five sons. Two sons, Eleazar and John, were killed.

Judas called Maccabee became the leader (166-160 B.C.), and from him comes the name Maccabees. Maccabee means "hammer," a nickname likely given because he would hit his enemies like a hammer hitting a nail (ABD, 4:454). Judas was a warrior with the goal of defending and enforcing observance of the covenant law and reestablishing an independent Jewish state. Judas successfully defeated the Syrian generals Apollonius and Seron. This cut down the revenues Antiochus was receiving from Palestine, and in desperation he set out to raise funds in Persia, where he died. Meanwhile, to quell the revolt in Judea, Antiochus sent Lysias with three generals, Ptolemy, Nicanor, and Gorgias. Judas called the men of Galilee together and at Emmaus defeated Gorgias (165-164 B.C). In 164 B.C. Judas defeated Lysias at Bethzur. In December 164 B.C. Judas cleansed the temple of Gentile abominations and reestablished worship with a great new Feast of Dedication (1 Macc. 3–4). The Syrians and renegade Jews still held the citadel in Jerusalem and struggled to keep a toehold of political control.

Judas waged war against his enemies east of Jordan, while another brother brought the Jews scattered in Galilee to Judea for safety.

Lysias returned with a large army and defeated Judas. Lysias, however, did not attempt to disrupt Jewish worship.

After the death of Antiochus IV Epiphanes (164 B.C.; 1 Macc. 6; 2 Macc. 9), his successor Demetrius I sent Nicanor to put an end to the rebellion. He was defeated by Judas. Nicanor threatened in turn to burn the temple if Judas was not turned over to him. This aroused great support for Judas and led to the slaying of Nicanor. Judas then made a treaty of friendship with Rome as though Judea were a sovereign state. The Roman senate sent word to Demetrius I to stop fighting the Jews. Before the message arrived, however, Judas was defeated by the Syrian general Baccides and killed (1 Macc. 7:26—9:22).

Jonathan undertook leadership of the revolt in 160 B.C. In a battle to avenge the death of his brother John, Jonathan was defeated. Jonathan continued until 142 B.C., when he was succeeded by Simon, another son of Mattathias. After a quarter century of struggle and warfare, the Jews achieved political freedom from the yoke of the Gentiles in 142 B.C. (1 Macc. 13:41-

42). In 140 B.C. Simon became high priest while serving also as military commander and civil governor of the Jews. Simon met a violent death in 134 B.C., and was succeeded by his son John Hyrcanus (134-104 B.C.), who brought the Jewish state to it highest point of influence and prosperity. The Hasmonaean period extended to 63 B.C., when Pompey invaded Palestine and Roman rule began.

The stories of the Maccabees are told in the books of 1, 2, and 4 Maccabees. These books are from the Greek OT, and 1–2 Maccabees appear in Bibles that include the Apocrypha. In deference to Eastern Orthodox churches, the NRSV Apocrypha also prints 3 Maccabees (about struggles of Egyptian Jews half a century prior to Antiochus IV) and 4 Maccabees (an expansion of 2 Macc. 6:12—7:42, interpreted by Greek philosophy, with emphasis on immortality of the soul instead of resurrection). Scholars consider parts, such as 1 Maccabees, to be relatively reliable, but embellishments appear especially in other books. However, even history is told with a bias.

First Maccabees is written to praise the Maccabees for their freedom fighting, show parallels between them and OT leaders, and legitimize the Hasmonean dynasty as priests and kings. It criticizes pious folks who are massacred because they refuse to fight, bound by their religion to obey the Torah and not to rebel, and not even to defend themselves on the Sabbath (1:54-64; 2:29-38; cf. 2 Macc. 6:11). Such people are portrayed as foolish for trusting the words of Seleucid agents (1 Macc. 7:5-30). The Jews are delivered by the Maccabean exploits, without prophecy or miracles from heaven. This book does not mention the reward of resurrection—probably due to Mattathias, who discouraged unresisting martyrdom as the only pious course. Mattathias honors the stories of the three young men in the furnace and Daniel in the lions' den (2:59-60), but 1 Maccabees says nothing of the visions, probably regarding them as forgery (Dan. 7-12). The book even takes pains to correct the sequence or content of events predicted in Daniel 11 (Goldstein, 1976:42-54). Salvation comes from obeying the law *and* the Hasmonaeans (1 Macc. 5:62).

Second Maccabees tells the story of the Maccabean brothers but shows that they were "at best ineffective and at worst tainted by treason and sin" (Goldstein, 1976:33). Miracles of deliverance abound. Martyrs are praised. There is affirmation of resurrection for martyrs. God is acknowledged as creating all from nothing (2 Macc. 7; 12:42-45; 14:46). Victories come from divine favor won by the martyrs and by prayer. Even Judas says he trusts God rather than arms (8:18). The book has two parallel sections, each recounting a threat to the temple, martyrdom, triumph "with the Almighty as their ally" (8:24), and then the first celebration of a new festival: the Feast of Dedication (2 Macc. 1–10), and the Day of Nicanor (11–15). Onias III is a model and helps to show that covenants with Gentiles can be beneficial as long as the Jewish law is not neglected. In several ways, 2 Maccabees (rather than 1 Maccabees) is more compatible with Daniel in valuing prayer, in trusting God to deliver, and to some degree in practicing nonresistance (2 Macc. 6:11-17), leading to martyrdom, and resurrection (Goldstein, 1976:4-36; ABD, 4:440-450).

NABONIDUS When Nebuchadnezzar died in 562 B.C., he was succeeded by his son Evil-merodach. Evil-merodach (Amel-marduk) treated the exiled king of Judah, Jehoiachin, well, kindly allowing him to eat at his table (2 Kings 25:27-30). Evil-merodach was killed in a revolution (560 B.C.) and was succeeded by Nergal-sharezer (Neriglissar), who was married to Nebuchadnezzar's daughter (Jer. 39:3, 13). He died in 556 B.C. and was succeeded by a young son Labashi-marduk, who was removed after three months, when Nabonidus assumed the throne. Nabonidus ruled from 556 to 539 B.C., when the Medo-Persian invaders were victorious.

Nabonidus, whose name means "the god Nabu is to be revered," was a strange ruler. Not of Nebuchadnezzar's family, he was concerned with history and the restoration of ancient shrines. Nabonidus entrusted the kingship to Belshazzar, his son in 554 B.C. (ANET: 313; for the "problem" of Belshazzar as Nebuchadnezzar's son, see notes on Dan. 5:2, 11, 18). The mother of Nabonidus was high priestess in the temple of Sin at Haran and introduced him to Nabopolassar and Nebuchadnezzar. Nabonidus claimed that Sin ordered him to live at Tema in northwest Arabia for ten years. This was also a good place from which to control trade routes between Arabia and Mesopotamia and to stay out of the way of the growing Persian power (ABD, 4:973-976). The clergy of Babylon had many complaints about Nabonidus mixing up the rites, introducing the worship of strange gods like Nanna and Sin, living at Tema, using forced labor to build fortifications and a palace there, and neglecting his responsibilities, leaving them in the hands of his son. The Persians insisted that Nabonidus was trying to replace Marduk with Sin and that their conquest restored the ancient worship of Marduk (ANET: 312-316).

While in Tema, Nabonidus experienced a seven-year illness. Many believe this illness is that ascribed to Nebuchadnezzar in Daniel 4. Among the texts found at Qumran is the Prayer of Nabonidus (4QprNab), likely dated from the late second or early first century B.C., and telling a story about Nabonidus which is similar to Daniel 4 about Nebuchadnezzar. A chief difference is that Nebuchadnezzar was cured by God when he recognized God's sovereignty, but in the Qumram fragment, a Jewish exorcist healed Nabonidus by forgiving his sins and teaching him the truth about God.

This is the text (Vermes: 274):

> The words of the prayer uttered by Nabunai king of Babylon, [the great] king, [when he was afflicted] with an evil ulcer in Teiman by decree of the [Most High God].
>
> I was afflicted [with an evil ulcer] for seven years . . . and an exorcist par-doned my sins. He was a Jew from among the [children of the exile of Judah, and he said], "Recount this in writing to [glorify and exalt] the name of the [Most High God." And I wrote this]:
>
> "I was afflicted with an [evil] ulcer in Teiman [by decree of the Most High God]. For seven years [I] prayed to the gods of silver and gold, [bronze and iron], wood and stone and clay, because [I believed] that they were gods. . . ."

Did the writer of Daniel 4 choose to combine the image of Nebuchadnezzar, destroyer of Jerusalem and architect of the exile, with events in the extension of his reign, under Nabonidus? When Nabonidus returned to Babylon in 543 B.C., Cyrus of Persia had conquered Media, and Babylonia was open to invasion. There are gaps in the record, but Nabonidus was in Babylon to celebrate the New Year festival in 539 B.C. During the celebration, Cyrus was advancing on Babylon. Nabonidus ordered the nation's gods to be brought to Babylon for protection. Shortly thereafter, the army of Cyrus entered Babylon without a battle (for historical documents on the reign of Nabonidus, see ANET: 305-315). It is said that the invaders altered the course of the Euphrates River, which flowed through the city, and entered by the riverbed. In the invasion Belshazzar was killed. (Dan. 5:30). Later Nabonidus was taken prisoner and died in exile.

NEBUCHADNEZZAR OR NEBUCHADREZZER In the Akkadian, Nebuchadnezzar's name *Nabu-kudurri-uṣur* incorporated the name of the deity Nabu. Thus the king's name has the meaning "Nabu, protect my son" or "Nabu, protect my boundary." Nebuchad*r*ezzar is an imitation of Babylonian spelling, as in Jeremiah and Ezekiel. Nebuchad*n*ezzar is a Jewish variant in 2 Kings, 2 Chronicles, and Daniel.

Nebuchadnezzar was the son of Nabopolassar and the father of Evil-merodach (Amel-marduk). He ruled Babylonia 605-562 B.C. Nabopolassar was the founder of the Neo-Babylonian empire. When Nabopolassar rebelled against Assyria (626 B.C), Josiah (640-609 B.C.) attempted to carry out religious reforms and to recapture lost territories. *[Kings of Judah, above.]*

Nabopolassar rebuilt the city of Babylon. In 605 B.C. he sent his son Nebuchadnezzar to meet Pharaoh Neco of Egypt. At Carchemish, a city on the upper Euphrates River, the battle was joined with the historic rout of Egypt and Neco. At that time Nabopolassar died, and Nebuchadnezzar returned home to assume the throne of Babylon. In each of his next four regnal years, Nebuchadnezzar was campaigning west of the Euphrates, collecting tribute and conquering cities. Probably in 604-603, soon after Ashkelon fell to him, Jehoiakim also submitted to the Babylonians (Jer. 36:9, Judah fasted in November 604 B.C. because of Nebuchadnezzar's advance against Ashkelon; cf. Jer. 47). Thus late 604 B.C. is the earliest plausible date for Daniel being carried off to Babylon, but 597 B.C. is more likely (see below).

Jehoiakim paid taxes to Nebuchadnezzar for "three years," 603-601 B.C. (2 Kings 24:1). When Nebuchadnezzar thought his hold on Syria-Palestine was strong enough, he tried to invade Egypt in 601-600 B.C. but was rebuffed, with heavy losses on both sides. This sign of Babylonian weakness encouraged Jehoiakim to rebel, withhold taxes in 600 B.C., and favor Egypt and Neco, who were trying to reassert their claims to Palestine. During this time the prophet Jeremiah warned Jewish leaders against dependence on Egypt. Nebuchadnezzar sent Babylonian units against Judah (2 Kings 24:2). Failing in this, Nebuchadnezzar sent his army (598-597 B.C.), and Jerusalem was taken in March 597 B.C. after a short siege. Captives were taken, likely including Daniel; Zedekiah was installed as king; and heavy tribute was imposed. In the following years, Zedekiah gradually leaned more toward Egypt, until he withheld taxes from Babylonia in 589 B.C. Nebuchadnezzar invaded Judah in 587 B.C. and launched a second siege, which resulted in the destruction of the city of Jerusalem and the temple and the second major deportation of the Jews (586 B.C.).

Nebuchadnezzar was married to Amyitis the daughter of the king of the Medes. This alliance secured the borders of his kingdom to the north and northwest. The tribute Nebuchadnezzar collected went into the building of temples, fortifications, and palaces, with the work done by slave labor brought in from defeated nations.

A major building project of Nebuchadnezzar's was his palace. This was located on the northern edge of the city on the east bank of the Euphrates River. It was in the form of a trapezoid extending 984 feet. The palace contained five major courts. The central court was 170 by 56 feet, with the throne room on its south end. Likely in this great room, Belshazzar entertained his guests.

Little is known about the last thirty years of Nebuchadnezzar's life. The focus of his endeavors seemed to be upon the building of his great city. It is possible that the madness reported in Daniel 4 occurred during this time, but more likely that episode was transplanted from the life of Nabonidus. *[Nabonidus, above.]* Nebuchadnezzar was aware of the growing power of the Medes. A defensive wall was built north of Babylon which extended from Sippor to Opis. It was designed to secure the city from attacks by tribes to the north.

Nebuchadnezzar died in 562 B.C. and was succeeded by his son Evil-merodach (Amel-marduk; 562-560 B.C.).

PTOLEMIES This is the name of the dynasty that ruled Egypt following the breakup of the empire of Alexander the Great (323 B.C.). The Ptolemies ruled until 30 B.C., when defeated by the Romans, who annexed Egypt.

The name comes from Ptolemy I Soter (323-282 B.C.), a general of Alexander the Great who received Egypt after he had been king there from 305 B.C. After many campaigns, Ptolemy I extended his rule to include Palestine and Phoenicia. Little is known about the Jews under the Ptolemies. Jeremiah (44) speaks to the Jewish diaspora there. In 320 B.C. many Jews came to Alexandria as prisoners of war. Under Ptolemy II Philadephus (282-246 B.C.), the Jews began translating the Hebrew Bible into Greek for use in their worship. The fictitious Letter of Aristeas falsely claims that the king asked for it. The best-known Greek version is the Septuagint (LXX). The Jews paid their taxes, and in turn the Ptolemies granted the Jews much autonomy in local affairs.

The control of Judea alternated between the Seleucids and the Ptolemies. Most of the time prior to 198 B.C., it was in the camp of Egypt, but Syria periodically challenged that. Daniel 11:7-9 refers to Ptolemy III Euergetes I (246-222 B.C.) and his invasion of Syria in reprisal for the murder of his sister, the wife of Antiochus II. There is even a report that he sacrificed at the Jerusalem temple as he returned to Egypt (ABD, 5:542). Ptolemy IV Philopator (222-204 B.C.) defeated Antiochus III at Raphia in Gaza in 217 B.C. Daniel 11:11-12 and 3 Maccabees tell of this. During the reign of Ptolemy V Epiphanes (204-180 B.C.), Egypt was defeated at Panium by the Syrians in 200 B.C., and by 198 B.C. it was clear that Palestine was ruled by the Seleucids. *[Seleucids, below.]* Daniel 11 tracks some of the competition between the Seleucids and Ptolemy VI Philometor (180-145 B.C.; see notes on Dan. 11:14-17). He was reigning during the Maccabean revolt and kept trying to reestablish Egyptian power in Asia.

RIDDLES In the biblical world, riddles were common. A riddle was intended to puzzle the hearer. The word *ḥidah* appears in Judges 14:12-19, where Samson posed the riddle:

> "Out of the eater came something to eat.
> Out of the strong came something sweet."

At other times the word *riddle* (Heb. *ḥidah* [s.]; *ḥidot* [pl.]) is used to refer to "hard questions" (1 Kings 10:1). To solve a riddle suggests the ability to make difficult decisions, like Solomon in the case of the two women arguing over a child (1 Kings 3:16-28). The word "riddle" could refer to a "dark saying" or an enigma, such as the riddle of life (Ps. 49:4 [5 in Heb.]). Psalm 49 explores the difficult problem of theodicy, God's ways of dealing with the good and evil. In the case of the dreadful king in Daniel 8:23, *skilled in intrigue* (Heb.: *ḥidot* [pl.]; *riddles*, RSV), there may be the suggestion of involvement in the occult. The *intrigue* may indicate an attempt to invade and wrestle from heaven its secrets (cf. 8:12). It might also hint at the political gamesmanship of Antiochus IV, selling offices to the highest bidder, double-crossing others, and scheming for power and wealth.

At least, ability to handle a "dark saying" suggests intellectual superiority if not heavenly endowment. Daniel could explain riddles (Aram.: *'aidan;* for Heb., *ḥidot;* 5:12). Like Joseph who interpreted puzzling dreams, any such interpreter would need "mantic wisdom," that is, wisdom accessible only through *a spirit of the holy gods*, or heaven (5:11). Only with such mystic wisdom could one understand the enigmatic words on the wall of Belshazzar's banquet hall (5:25-28).

SELEUCIDS This is the name of the dynasty that ruled Syria, Babylonia, and Persia from the breakup of Alexander the Great's empire in 323 B.C. until the rise of the Roman empire in 64 B.C. The name comes from Seleucus I Nicator, a cavalry officer who accompanied Alexander the Great in his military conquests from Macedonia to India (336-323 B.C.). When Alexander's empire was divided, Seleucus received the largest portion that extended from Asia Minor to India. There was much turmoil and conflict, but Seleucus I managed to regain Babylon in 312 B.C. (when the official count of years for his reign starts) and to gain control of Syria and much of Asia Minor in 301 B.C. Seleucia was the eastern capital, and now Seleucus I established a western capital at Antioch. The Seleucid dynasty lasted until Rome defeated the Seleucid empire in 64 B.C. Rome made Syria a Roman province in 63 B.C., the same year Pompey settled a civil war in Judea and put it under the Roman governor of Syria.

The Seleucids of Syria and the Ptolemies of Egypt contested for control of Palestine. Palestine was mostly under Egyptian control from 322-198 B.C. It came more steadily under Seleucid rule in 198 B.C., after Antiochus III the Great was victorious over Egypt in 200 B.C. Antiochus IV Epiphanes, the dreadful king (175-164 B.C.), was a member of the Seleucid dynasty.

The father of Seleucus I Nicator was a Macedonian named Antiochus. Named in his memory were Seleucid kings carrying this name as well as several cities, including the capital in Antioch on the Orontes River in Syria. The Seleucids were noted for their commitment to and propagation of Greek culture and religion to unify their empire. This policy brought them into conflicts with the Jews, which reached its climax under Antiochus IV Epiphanes. *[Antiochus IV Epiphanes, above.]*

SEVENTY WEEKS OF YEARS, DANIEL 9:24-27 Interpreters across the centuries have tried to identify this period of 490 years with known, significant points in history. Some theories regard the 490 years as leading up to Antiochus IV Epiphanes and the rededication of the temple in 164 B.C. Others have seen them reaching to the death of Jesus at the Passover in 32 or 33 A.D. Still others point to the distant future and hold that the termination point is the "Great Tribulation," which is to usher in the millennium.

There is little agreement among those who interpret the chronology strictly in mathematical fashion, as some specifics show. One supposition is that Jeremiah gave *the word . . . to restore and rebuild Jerusalem* (9:25; 605-597 B.C.). He announced that the ruins would yet be rebuilt (Jer. 30:8; 31:11-12, 23-24). A "week" later, 49 years after 605 B.C., Cyrus became king (this would be 556 B.C., but Cyrus actually became king 559 B.C.). The second period ended with the death of the high priest, Onias III in 171 B.C, which was 434 years after Jeremiah's prophecy. By adding these figures of overlapping years (434 + 49) one arrives at 483 years (= 69 weeks of years). The final week is the seven-year period of 171-164 B.C., in which Antiochus Epiphanes inflicted persecution on the Jews.

Alternately, the year of the decree to rebuilt Jerusalem has been figured from the time Nehemiah gained permission to rebuild Jerusalem (445-444 B.C.), to the death of Jesus, the anointed one cut off (32-33 A.D)—a time of about 483 years, or 69 weeks. The seventieth week may then be postponed.

A recent proposal is to begin the count at 551 B.C., the first year of Cyrus (?), when he made a decree. Forty-nine years later, 502 B.C., Nehemiah, identified in this interpretation as "the anointed prince," gained permission to rebuilt Jerusalem. The second anointed one is Hyrcanus, who was removed from being both king and high priest in 68 B.C. In the middle of the last week (68-61 B.C.) Pompey of Rome stopped the sacrifice. In 61 B.C. the 490 years ended, with the loss of Jewish governance to the Romans in 61 B.C. under Julius Caesar (Faulstich: 103-110). Still another of many proposals is that the 490 years stretch from Cyrus's decree to the beginning of the Jewish war against the Romans in A.D. 66 (Lurie).

The divergencies of interpretation turn on (1) some translation issues, (2) the event or time which begins the count of 490 years, (3) whether the numbers of weeks are to be calculated closely or whether they are more representative of time blocks, (4) whether the *anointed one* is intended to mean Jesus the Messiah or another anointed figure in history, and (5) whether the prince (Dan. 9:27) is a malevolent figure or Christ. Here one can favor a particular view and still recognize the force of selected arguments in competing views. The variety of views might be sketched broadly as follows:

Interpretations (cf. Porteous, Young, Baldwin, Goldingay)	***7 wks./49 yrs.***	***62 wks./434 yrs.***	***1 wk./7 yrs.***
Historical	587/586-539 B.C.	539-171 B.C.	171-164 B.C.
Messianic/Symbolic	538-440 (?) B.C.	A.D. 26	A.D. 26-32/33 or 70
Church/Symbolic	587 B.C.-A.D. 32	A.D. 32-end time	Time of antichrist
Dispensational	445-396 B.C.	396 B.C.-A.D. 32/33	Great Tribulation

As for the time to begin the count of years, proposals have ranged from 655 B.C., the supposed announcement by Isaiah of a restoration (Isa. 45:1, 13); to 605 B.C., the rise of Nebuchadnezzar; or 538 B.C., the decree by Cyrus permitting refugees to return to their homeland; or 445 B.C., the permission granted to Nehemiah to rebuild the walls of Jerusalem; or 458 B.C., Artaxerxes' decree to Ezra; and to variations of these.

Does one use solar or lunar calendars in calculating the years? Are the years consecutive? Or is there an uncounted interval, as dispensationalists maintain, between the last two sets of weeks? With that form of calculation, which seems unnatural to many, the ending point of the vision is outside present history. Are the numbers to be treated as historical data or more in keeping with apocalyptic writings? Almost certainly the numbers are to be taken as *representative of time periods.* Instead of thinking of chronology, should one think of "chronography," a stylized way of interpreting historical data (Goldingay: 257). This writer holds to the latter and regards interpretation A in the interpretation chart as most likely.

Thus the 490 years provide a general framework, a "quasi-artificial" scheme (Hartman, 1978:251). This will save the interpreter from either defending Daniel's numbers or criticizing them. Much time and effort has gone into discerning and defending these numbers, usually at the expense of grasping the meaning and thrust of the message. In the Scriptures, many time periods are approximate rather than exact. In Judges, for example, the forty-year periods of oppression or of peace are seldom considered precise periods of time. According to 1 Kings 6:1, Solomon's temple was built 480 years after the Exodus. This would suggest twelve forty-year periods rather than exact chronological information. Even for Jeremiah, seventy years was symbolic of a lifetime, and of completion. Jeremiah's seventy years, when combined with the sevenfold chastisement of Leviticus 26, yields the 490. Thus Gabriel's division of the 490 years simply suggests shorter and longer periods in the sweep of history.

Admittedly, verses 24-27 are perhaps the most difficult of the book. In addition to considerations already given, our interpretation takes account of several factors. There is concern for Jerusalem, the city, the sanctuary, and the abomination of desolation familiar from 8:13. Daniel 9 has a literary connection with the adjacent discussions of Antiochus (Dan. 8 and 10–11). All these tilt toward the view that the seventieth week culminates in the time of Antiochus. This does not foreclose the possibility that the vision may be reapplied and corroborated by events of the first century A.D., such as the crucifixion of Jesus in A.D. 30, or the destruction of Jerusalem in A.D. 70. In prophecy, fulfillments may themselves become prophecies, and there may be secondary fulfillments. Hence, it is not necessarily farfetched to see in Daniel foreshadows of activities of a future antichrist. The prophecy, while pointing to the events of the second century, need not be exhausted by the occurrences of those events.

SUPPLEMENTS TO DANIEL It is known that the book of Daniel circulated in at least two forms. From the manuscripts found at Qumran, it is clear that some stories circulated about Daniel are not found in any modern Bible.

In the Greek version of the OT, the book of Daniel is longer than in the Hebrew version. Most English Bibles are based on the Hebrew version. The four additions in the Greek versions and in the NRSV Apocrypha are: The Prayer of Azariah and the Song of the Three Jews, Susanna, and Bel and the Dragon. The latter two are stories. The chapter and verse references are from the Greek version.

The Prayer of Azariah and the Song of the Three Jews appear in Greek versions of Daniel between 3:23 and 24 (see notes there). In the Greek version of Daniel, two stories (Susanna; Bel and the Dragon) are added after chapter 12 (see notes there). These stories appear in two forms: (1) the Septuagint version (LXX), and (2) the version of Theodotion. These accounts are similar in content but have considerable differences in wording.

The story of Susanna, which follows Daniel 12, does not connect with the visions (Dan. 7–12) nor with the earlier stories (Dan. 1–6). Susanna does not connect chronologically with any part of the book of Daniel except that the setting is in Babylon in the home of a wealthy Jew.

Few advocate the historicity of the story. It is considered a profitable folktale, likely influenced by the story of Joseph and Potiphar's wife. In this story, however, the hero is female. Beside the usual themes of vindication of the innocent and the punishment of the wicked, Susanna's strong faith provided a needed example and also added a woman to the stories of martyrs condemned to death and saved by divine intervention and Daniel's wisdom.

The story of Bel and the Dragon is about the worship practices of Cyrus. When Cyrus worshiped the idol Bel, he noticed that Daniel did not worship. When asked why, Daniel replied that he worshiped the living God and not idols. The king's response was to ask Daniel to observe how much food and drink the idol consumed daily. In a test that followed, Daniel demonstrated that the food was eaten, not by the idol, but by the priests. The enraged king turned Bel and its temple over to Daniel for destruction and killed the priests.

Then the king challenged Daniel to worship the snake that he and other Babylonians worshiped. "You cannot deny that this is a living God," the king said (14:23). Daniel refused to worship and requested permission to prove the snake's mortality. He fed the snake a combination of pitch, fat, and hair. The snake ate the concoction and burst open.

Having killed the sacred snake, the enraged king threw Daniel into the lions' den. For six days the lions refused to eat Daniel. During that time an angel took the prophet Habakkuk, who was carrying a bowl of stew, and carried him by his hair from Judea to Babylon (cf. Ezek. 11:1; Acts 8:39-40) to feed Daniel, then returned him to Judea. On the seventh day the king found Daniel alive. He took Daniel from the den and threw in Daniel's enemies, who were quickly eaten.

The origins of Bel and the Dragon are debated. The detail of Daniel in the lions' den suggests that this story was circulated apart from the book of Daniel (6:16-24). It has been suggested that Bel and the Dragon were priestly anecdotes inspired by Jer. 51:34-35, 44. Another view is that they were parodies ridiculing idols, much like those found in Isaiah 45–46. They were written in the second or first century B.C. to counteract idolatry, especially among Egyptian Jews, since snake worship was long practiced in Egypt. These stories were likely added to the book of Daniel around 135 B.C.

The stories of Bel and the Dragon have motifs found in Daniel 1–6. Daniel is the hero; the king is the protagonist. Daniel's faith gets him into trouble; his faith gets him out of trouble. Daniel is rewarded; his enemies are punished. As a result, Daniel's God is seen as the true God, the living God, the Most High.

THE PRAYER OF AZARIAH AND THE SONG OF THE THREE JEWS
(Additions in the Greek version of Daniel, between 3.23 and 3.24; NRSV)

1 They [Daniel's companions, Hananiah, Mishael, and Azariah; Dan. 1:6-7] walked around in the midst of the flames, singing hymns to God and blessing the Lord. [2]Then Azariah stood still in the fire and prayed aloud:

[3] "Blessed are you, O Lord, God of our ancestors, and worthy of praise;
    and glorious is your name forever!
[4] For you are just in all you have done;
    all your works are true and your ways right,

and all your judgments are true.
[5] You have executed true judgments in all you have brought upon us
and upon Jerusalem, the holy city of our ancestors;
by a true judgment you have brought all this upon us because of our sins.
[6] For we have sinned and broken your law in turning away from you;
in all matters we have sinned grievously.
[7] We have not obeyed your commandments,
we have not kept them or done what you have commanded us for our own good.
[8] So all that you have brought upon us,
and all that you have done to us,
you have done by a true judgment.
[9] You have handed us over to our enemies, lawless and hateful rebels,
and to an unjust king, the most wicked in all the world.
[10] And now we cannot open our mouths;
we, your servants who worship you, have become a shame and a reproach.
[11] For your name's sake do not give us up forever,
and do not annul your covenant.
[12] Do not withdraw your mercy from us,
for the sake of Abraham your beloved
and for the sake of your servant Isaac
and Israel your holy one,
[13] to whom you promised
to multiply their descendants like the stars of heaven
and like the sand on the shore of the sea.
[14] For we, O Lord, have become fewer than any other nation.
and are brought low this day in all the world because of our sins.
[15] In our day we have no ruler, or prophet, or leader,
no burnt offering, or sacrifice, or oblation, or incense,
no place to make an offering before you and to find mercy.
[16] Yet with a contrite heart and a humble spirit may we be accepted,
[17] as though it were with burnt offerings of rams and bulls,
or with tens of thousands of fat lambs;
such may our sacrifice be in your sight today,
and may we unreservedly follow you,
for no shame will come to those who trust in you.
[18] And now with all our heart we follow you;
we fear you and seek your presence.
[19] Do not put us to shame,
but deal with us in your patience and in your abundant mercy.
[20] Deliver us in accordance with your marvelous works,
and bring glory to your name, O Lord.
[21] Let all who do harm to your servants be put to shame;
let them be disgraced and deprived of all power,
and let their strength be broken.
[22] Let them know that you alone are the Lord God,
glorious over the whole world."

23 Now the king's servants who threw them in kept stoking the furnace with naphtha, pitch, tow, and brushwood. [24]And the flames poured out above the furnace forty-nine cubits, [25]and spread out and burned those Chaldeans who were caught near the furnace. [26]But the angel of the Lord came down into the furnace to be with Azariah and his companions, and drove the fiery flame out of the furnace, [27]and made the inside of the furnace as though a moist wind were whistling through it. The fire did not touch them at all and caused them no pain or distress.

28 Then the three with one voice praised and glorified and blessed God in the furnace [with this Song]:

[29] "Blessed are you, O Lord, God of our ancestors,
and to be praised and highly exalted forever;
30 And blessed is your glorious, holy name,
and to be highly praised and highly exalted forever.
[31] Blessed are you in the temple of your holy glory,
and to be extolled and highly glorified forever.
[32] Blessed are you who look into the depths from your throne on the cherubim,
and to be praised and highly exalted forever.
[33] Blessed are you on the throne of your kingdom,
and to be extolled and highly exalted forever.
[34] Blessed are you in the firmament of heaven,
and to be sung and glorified forever.

[35] "Bless the Lord, all you works of the Lord;
sing praise to him and highly exalt him forever.
[36] Bless the Lord, you heavens;
sing praise to him and highly exalt him forever.
[37] Bless the Lord, you angels of the Lord;
sing praise to him and highly exalt him forever.
[38] Bless the Lord, all you waters above the heavens;
sing praise to him and highly exalt him forever.
[39] Bless the Lord, all you powers of the Lord;
sing praise to him and highly exalt him forever.
[40] Bless the Lord, sun and moon;
sing praise to him and highly exalt him forever.
[41] Bless the Lord, stars of heaven;
sing praise to him and highly exalt him forever.

[42] "Bless the Lord, all rain and dew;
sing praise to him and highly exalt him forever.
[43] Bless the Lord, all you winds;
sing praise to him and highly exalt him forever.
[44] Bless the Lord, fire and heat;
sing praise to him and highly exalt him forever.
[45] Bless the Lord, winter cold and summer heat;
sing praise to him and highly exalt him forever.
[46] Bless the Lord, dews and falling snow;
sing praise to him and highly exalt him forever.
[47] Bless the Lord, nights and days;
sing praise to him and highly exalt him forever.
[48] Bless the Lord, light and darkness;
sing praise to him and highly exalt him forever.

[49] Bless the Lord, ice and cold;
sing praise to him and highly exalt him forever.
[50] Bless the Lord, frosts and snows;
sing praise to him and highly exalt him forever.
[51] Bless the Lord, lightnings and clouds;
sing praise to him and highly exalt him forever.

[52] "Let the earth bless the Lord;
let it sing praise to him and highly exalt him forever.
[53] Bless the Lord, mountains and hills;
sing praise to him and highly exalt him forever.
[54] Bless the Lord, all that grows in the ground;
sing praise to him and highly exalt him forever.
[55] Bless the Lord, seas and rivers;
sing praise to him and highly exalt him forever.
[56] Bless the Lord, you springs;
sing praise to him and highly exalt him forever.
[57] Bless the Lord, you whales and all that swim in the waters;
sing praise to him and highly exalt him forever.
[58] Bless the Lord, all birds of the air;
sing praise to him and highly exalt him forever.
[59] Bless the Lord, all wild animals and cattle;
sing praise to him and highly exalt him forever.

[60] "Bless the Lord, all people on earth;
sing praise to him and highly exalt him forever.
[61] Bless the Lord, O Israel;
sing praise to him and highly exalt him forever.
[62] Bless the Lord, you priests of the Lord;
sing praise to him and highly exalt him forever.
[63] Bless the Lord, you servants of the Lord;
sing praise to him and highly exalt him forever.
[64] Bless the Lord, spirits and souls of the righteous;
sing praise to him and highly exalt him forever.
[65] Bless the Lord, you who are holy and humble in heart;
sing praise to him and highly exalt him forever.

[66] "Bless the Lord, Hananiah, Azariah, and Mishael;
sing praise to him and highly exalt him forever.
For he has rescued us from Hades and saved us from the power of death,
and delivered us from the midst of the burning fiery furnace;
from the midst of the fire he has delivered us.
[67] Give thanks to the Lord, for he is good,
for his mercy endures forever.
[68] All who worship the Lord, bless the God of gods
sing praise to him and give thanks to him,
for his mercy endures forever."

SUSANNA (chap. 13 of the Greek Version of Daniel; NRSV)

1 There was a man living in Babylon whose name was Joakim. [2]he married the daughter of Hilkiah, named Susanna, a very beautiful woman and one who feared the Lord. [3]Her parents were righteous, and had trained their daughter according to the law of Moses. [4]Joakim was very rich, and had

a fine garden adjoining his house; the Jews used to come to him because he was the most honored of them all.

5 That year two elders from the people were appointed as judges. Concerning them the Lord had said: "Wickedness came forth from Babylon, from elders who were judges, who were supposed to govern the people." [6]These men were frequently at Joakim's house, and all who had a case to be tried came to them there.

7 When the people left at noon, Susanna would go into her husband's garden to walk. [8]Every day the two elders used to see her, going in and walking about, and they began to lust for her. [9]They suppressed their consciences and turned away their eyes from looking to Heaven or remembering their duty to administer justice. [10]Both were overwhelmed with passion for her, but they did not tell each other of their distress, [11]for they were ashamed to disclose their lustful desire to seduce her. [12]Day after day they watched eagerly to see her.

13 One day they said to each other, "Let us go home, for it is time for lunch. So they both left and parted from each other. [14]But turning back, they met again; and when each pressed the other for the reason, they confessed their lust. Then together they arranged for a time when they could find her alone.

15 Once, while they were watching for an opportune day, she went in as before with only two maids, and wished to bathe in the garden, for it was a hot day. [16]No one was there except the two elders, who had hidden themselves and were watching her. [17]She said to her maids, "Bring me olive oil and ointments, and shut the garden doors so that I can bathe." [18]They did as she told them: they shut the doors of the garden and went out by the side doors to bring what they had been commanded; they did not see the elders, because they were hiding.

19 When the maids had gone out, the two elders got up and ran to her. [20]They said, "Look, the garden doors are shut, and no one can see us. We are burning with desire for you; so give your consent, and lie with us. [21]If you refuse, we will testify against you that a young man was with you, and this was why you sent your maids away."

22 Susanna groaned and said, "I am completely trapped. For if I do this, it will mean death for me; if I do not, I cannot escape your hands. [23]I choose not to do it; I will fall into your hands, rather than sin in the sight of the Lord."

24 Then Susanna cried out with a loud voice, and the two elders shouted against her. [25]And one of them ran and opened the garden doors. [26]When the people in the house heard the shouting in the garden, they rushed in at the side door to see what had happened to her. [27]And when the elders told their story, the servants felt very much ashamed, for nothing like this had ever been said about Susanna.

28 The next day, when the people gathered at the house of her husband Joakim, the two elders came, full of their wicked plot to have Susanna put to death. In the presence of the people they said, [29]"Send for Susanna daughter of Hilkiah, the wife of Joakim." [30]So they sent for her. And she came with her parents her children, and all her relatives.

31 Now Susanna was a woman of great refinement and beautiful in appearance. [32]As she was veiled, the scoundrels ordered her to be unveiled, so they might feast their eyes on her beauty. [33]Those who were with her and all who saw her were weeping.

34 Then the two elders stood up before the people and laid their hands

on her head. [35]Through her tears she looked up toward Heaven, for her heart trusted the Lord. [36]The elders said, "While we were walking in the garden alone, this woman came in with two maids, shut the garden doors, and dismissed the maids. [37]Then a young man, who was hiding there, came to her and lay with her. [38]We were in a corner of the garden, and when we saw this wickedness we ran to them. [39]Although we saw them embracing, we could not hold the man, because he was stronger than we, and he opened the doors and got away. [40]We did, however, seize this woman and asked who the young man was, [41]but she would not tell us. These things we testify."

Because they were elders of the people and judges, the assembly believed them and condemned her to death.

31 Then Susanna cried out with a loud voice, and said, "O eternal God, you know what is secret and are aware of all things before they come to be; [43]you know that these men have given false evidence against me. And now I am to die, though I have done none of the wicked things that they have charged against me!"

44 The Lord heard her cry. [45]Just as she was being led off to execution, God stirred up the holy spirit of a young lad named Daniel, [46]and he shouted with a loud voice, "I want no part in shedding this woman's blood!"

47 All the people turned to him and asked, "What is this you are saying?" [48]Taking his stand among them he said, "Are you such fools, O Israelites, as to condemn a daughter of Israel without examination and without learning the facts? [49]Return to court, for these men have given false evidence against her."

50 So all the people hurried back. And the rest of the elders said to him, "Come, sit among us and inform us, for God has given you the standing of an elder." [51]Daniel said to them, "Separate them far from each other, and I will examine them."

52 When they were separated from each other, he summoned one of them and said to him, "You old relic of wicked days, your sins have now come home, which you have committed in the past, [53]pronouncing unjust judgments, condemning the innocent and acquitting the guilty, though the Lord said, 'You shall not put an innocent and righteous person to death.' [54]Now then, if you really saw this woman, tell me this: Under what tree did you see them being intimate with each other?" He answered, "Under a mastic [*schinon*] tree." [55]And Daniel said, "Very well! This lie has cost you your head, for the angel of God has received the sentence from God and will immediately cut [*schisei*] you in two." [The Greek words for *mastic tree* and *cut* are similar, thus forming an ironic wordplay. Cf. notes on Dan. 5:25.]

56 Then, putting him to one side, he ordered them to bring the other. And he said to him, "You offspring of Canaan and not of Judah, beauty has beguiled you and lust has perverted your heart. [57]This is how you have been treating the daughters of Israel, and they were intimate with you through fear; but a daughter of Judah would not tolerate your wickedness. [58]Now then, tell me: Under what tree did you catch them being intimate with each other?" He answered, "Under an evergreen oak [*prinon*]." [59]Daniel said to him, "Very well! This lie has cost you also your head, for the angel of God is waiting with his sword to split [*katapris*ē] you in two, so as to destroy both." [The Greek words for *evergreen oak* and *split* are similar, thus forming an ironic wordplay. Cf. notes on Dan. 5:25.]

60 Then the whole assembly raised a great shout and blessed God, who saves those who hope in him. [61]And they took action against the two elders,

because out of their own mouths Daniel had convicted them of bearing false witness; they did to them as they had wickedly planned to do to their neighbors. [62]Acting in accordance with the law of Moses, they put them to death. Thus innocent blood was spared that day.

63 Hilkiah and his wife praised God for their daughter Susanna, and so did her husband Joakim and all her relatives, because she was found innocent of a shameful deed. [64]And from that day onward Daniel had a great reputation among the people.

BEL AND THE DRAGON (chap. 14 of the Greek Version of Daniel; NRSV)

1 When King Astyrages was laid to rest with his ancestors, Cyrus the Persian succeeded to his kingdom. [2]Daniel was a companion of the king, and was the most honored of all his friends.

3 Now the Babylonians had an idol called Bel, and every day they provided for it twelve bushels of choice flour and forty sheep and six measures [a little more than fifty gallons] of wine. [4]The king revered it and went every day to worship it. But Daniel worshiped his own God.

So the king said to him, "Why do you not worship Bel?" [5]He answered, "Because I do not revere idols made with hands, but the living God, who created heaven earth and has dominion over all living creatures."

6 The king said to him, "Do you not think that Bel is a living god? Do you not see how much he eats and drinks every day?" [7]And Daniel laughed, and said, "Do not be deceived, O king, for this thing is only clay and bronze outside, and it never ate or drank anything."

8 Then the king was angry and called the priests of Bel and said to them, "If you do not tell me who is eating these provisions, you shall die. [9]But if you prove that Bel is eating them, Daniel shall die, because he has spoken blasphemy against Bel." Daniel said to the king, "Let it be done as you have said."

10 Now there were seventy priests of Bel, besides their wives and children. So the king went with Daniel into the temple of Bel. [11]The priests of Bel said, "See, we are now going outside; you yourself, O king, set out the food and prepare the wine, and shut the door and seal it with your signet. [12]When you return in the morning, if you do not find that Bel has eaten it all, we will die; otherwise Daniel will, who is telling lies about us." [13]They were unconcerned, for beneath the table they had made a hidden entrance, through which they used to go in regularly and consume the provisions. [14]After they had gone out, the king set out the food for Bel. Then Daniel ordered his servants to bring ashes, and they scattered them throughout the whole temple in the presence of the king alone. Then they went out, shut the door and sealed it with the king's signet, and departed. [15]During the night the priests came as usual, with their wives and children, and they ate and drank everything.

16 Early in the morning the king rose and came, and Daniel with him. [17]The king said, "Are the seals unbroken, Daniel?" He answered, "They are unbroken, O king." [18]As soon as the doors were opened, the king looked at the table, and shouted in a loud voice, "You are great, O Bel, and in you there is no deceit at all!"

19 But Daniel laughed and restrained the king from going in. "Look at the floor," he said, "and notice whose footprints these are." [20]The king said, "I see the footprints of men and women and children."

21 Then the king was enraged, and he arrested the priests and their wives

and children. They showed him the secret doors through which they used to enter to consume what was on the table. [22]Therefore the king put them to death, and gave Bel over to Daniel, who destroyed it and its temple.

23 Now in that place there was a great dragon, which the Babylonians revered. [24]The king said to Daniel, "You cannot deny that this is a living god; so worship him." [25]Daniel said, "I worship the Lord my God, for he is the living God. [26]But give me permission, O king, and I will kill the dragon without sword or club." The king said, "I give you permission."

27 Then Daniel took pitch, fat, and hair, and boiled them together and made cakes, which he fed to the dragon. The dragon ate them, and burst open. Then Daniel said, "See what you have been worshiping!"

28 When the Babylonians heard about it, they were very indignant and conspired against the king, saying, "The king has become a Jew; he has destroyed Bel, and killed the dragon, and slaughtered the priests." [29]Going to the king, they said, "Hand Daniel over to us, or else we will kill you and your household." [30]The king saw that they were pressing him hard, and under compulsion he handed Daniel over to them.

31 They threw Daniel into the lions' den, and he was there for six days. [32]There were seven lions in the den, and every day they had been given two human bodies and two sheep; but now they were given nothing, so that they would devour Daniel.

33 Now the prophet Habakkuk was in Judea; he had made a stew and had broken bread into a bowl, and was going into the field to take it to the reapers. [34]But the angel of the Lord said to Habakkuk, "Take the food that you have to Babylon, to Daniel, in the lions' den." [35]Habakkuk said, "Sir, I have never seen Babylon, and I know nothing about the den." [36]Then the angel of the Lord took him by the crown of his head and carried him by his hair; with the speed of the wind [or: by the power of his spirit (cf. Ezek. 11:24; Acts 8:39)] he set him down in Babylon, right over the den.

37 Then Habakkuk shouted, "Daniel, Daniel! Take the food that God has sent you." [38]Daniel said, "You have remembered me, O God, and have not forsaken those who love you." [39]So Daniel got up and ate. And the angel of God immediately returned Habakkuk to his own place.

40 On the seventh day the king came to mourn for Daniel. When he came to the den he looked in, and there sat Daniel! [41]The king shouted with a loud voice, "You are great, O Lord, the God of Daniel, and there is no other besides you!" [42]Then he pulled Daniel out, and threw into the den those who had attempted his destruction, and they were instantly eaten before his eyes.

Palestine
For Daniel
Sidon
Damascus
Mt. Lebanon
Mt. Hermon
Tyre
ARAM
Paneas
Hazor
BASHAN
Acco
GALILEE
Sea of Galilee
Wadi Yarmuk
Mt. Carmel
Mt. Tabor
Mediterranean Sea
GILEAD
Beth-shan
Megiddo
Jezreel
N
W
E
S
Jordan River
SAMARIA
Samaria
Shechem
The Arabah
Aphek
EPHRAIM
Joppa
Shiloh
AMMON
BENJAMIN
Bethel
Rabbath-Ammon
Mizpah
Ai
Gibeon
Ramah
Jericho
Heshbon
Ekron
Anathoth
Jerusalem
Mt. Nebo
Ashdod
Bethlehem
Medeba
Baal-meon
Ashkelon
Lachish
Hebron
Gaza
Dibon
Dead Sea
Aroer
JUDAH
Wadi Arnon
Raphia
MOAB
Beersheba
Kir-heres
Honoraim
Zoar
The Negev
Ije-abarim
Wadi Zered
The Arabah
Bozrah
EDOM

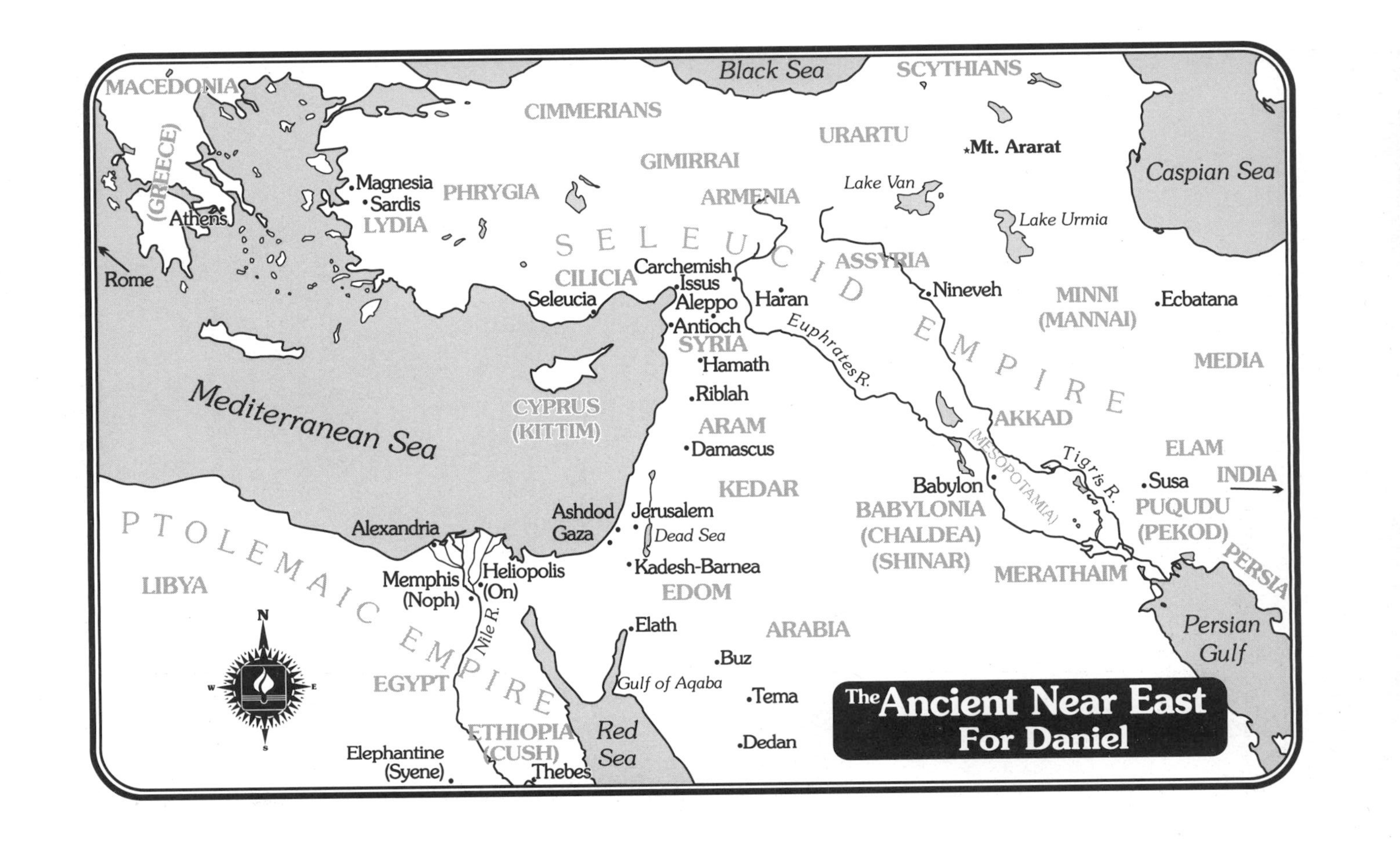
The Ancient Near East
For Daniel
MACEDONIA
(GREECE)
Athens
Rome
Magnesia
Sardis
LYDIA
PHRYGIA
CIMMERIANS
Black Sea
GIMIRRAI
ARMENIA
SCYTHIANS
URARTU
Mt. Ararat
Lake Van
Lake Urmia
Caspian Sea
SELEUCID EMPIRE
CILICIA
Seleucia
Carchemish
Issus
Aleppo
Antioch
Haran
SYRIA
Hamath
Riblah
ASSYRIA
Nineveh
MINNI
(MANNAI)
Ecbatana
MEDIA
Euphrates R.
Mediterranean Sea
CYPRUS
(KITTIM)
ARAM
Damascus
AKKAD
(MESOPOTAMIA)
Tigris R.
ELAM
Babylon
Susa
INDIA
KEDAR
BABYLONIA
(CHALDEA)
(SHINAR)
PUQUDU
(PEKOD)
PERSIA
PTOLEMAIC EMPIRE
Alexandria
Ashdod
Gaza
Jerusalem
Dead Sea
Kadesh-Barnea
EDOM
MERATHAIM
LIBYA
Memphis
(Noph)
Heliopolis
(On)
Nile R.
Elath
ARABIA
Persian
Gulf
N
W
E
S
EGYPT
Buz
Gulf of Aqaba
Tema
ETHIOPIA
(CUSH)
Red
Sea
Dedan
Elephantine
(Syene)
Thebes

Bibliography

ABD
1992 *Anchor Bible Dictionary*. Ed. by D. N. Freedman. 6 vols. New York: Doubleday.
Albright, William Foxwell
1968 *Yahweh and the Gods of Canaan*. Garden City, N.Y.: Doubleday.
Alter, Robert
1981 *The Art of Biblical Narrative*. New York: Basic Books, 1981.
Anderson, Robert A.
1984 *Signs and Wonders: A Commentary on the Book of Daniel*. International Theological Commentary. Grand Rapids: Eerdmans.
ANET
1950 *Ancient Near Eastern Texts Relating to the Old Testament*. Ed. by James B. Pritchard. Princeton: University Press.
Archer, Gleason L., Jr.
1985 "Daniel." In *The Expositor's Bible Commentary*, vol. 7. Ed. by Frank E. Gaebelein. Grand Rapids: Zondervan.
Aukerman, Dale
1993 *Reckoning with Apocalypse: Terminal Politics and Christian Hope*. New York: Crossroad.
Baldwin, Joyce G.
1978 *Daniel: An Introduction and Commentary*. Tyndale Old Testament Commentaries. Madison, Wis.: InterVarsity Press.
Barr, J.
1960 "Daniel." In *Peake's Commentary on the Bible*. OT ed. by H. H. Rowley. Nashville: Nelson.
Beale, G. K.
1984 *The Use of Daniel in Jewish Apocalyptic Literature and in the Revelation of St. John*. Lanham, Md.: University Press of America.
Bender, H. S.
1944 *The Anabaptist Vision*, Scottdale, Pa.: Herald Press.
Braght, Thieleman J. van
1938 *Martyrs Mirror*. Trans. from the original Dutch ed. of 1660 by J. F. Sohm. Etchings by Jan Luyken. Scottdale, Pa.: Herald Press.
Bruce, F. F.
1954 *The Book of Acts*. The New International Commentary on the

New Testament. Ed. by F. F. Bruce. Grand Rapids: Eerdmans.
1963 *Israel and the Nations*. Grand Rapids: Eerdmans.
1969 *The New Testament Development of Old Testament Themes*. Grand Rapids: Eerdmans.

Brueggeman, Walter
1978 *The Prophetic Imagination*. Philadelphia: Fortress Press.

Charles, R. H., ed.
1913 *The Apocrypha and Pseudepigrapha of the Old Testament*. 2 vols. Oxford: Clarendon Press.

Charlesworth, James H., ed.
1983-85 *The Old Testament Pseudepigrapha*. 2 vols. New York: Doubleday.

Collins, John J.
1977 *The Apocalyptic Vision of the Book of Daniel*. Missoula, Mont.: Scholars Press.
1984 *Daniel: With an Introduction to Apocalyptic Literature*. Grand Rapids: Eerdmans.

Davidson, B.
1956 *The Analytical Hebrew and Chaldee Lexicon*. London: Bagster and Sons.

Ewert, David
1980 *And Then Comes the End*. Scottdale, Pa.: Herald Press.

Faulstich, E. W.
1988 *History, Harmony & Daniel: A New Computerized Evaluation*. Spencer, Iowa: Chronology Books.

Fewell, Danna, N.
1991 *Circle of Sovereignty*. Nashville: Abingdon.

Friedman, Edwin H.
1985 *Generation to Generation: Family Process in Church and Synagogue*. New York: The Guilford Press.

Fritsch, Charles T.
1955 " 'God Was with Him': A Theological Study of the Joseph Narrative." *Interpretation* 9 (no. 1): 21-34.

Gammie, John G.
1983 *Daniel*. Knox Preaching Guides. Ed. by John H. Hayes. Atlanta: John Knox.

Gardner, Richard B.
1991 *Matthew*. Believers Church Bible Commentary. Scottdale, Pa.: Herald Press.

Goldingay, John E.
1989 *Daniel*. Word Biblical Commentary, vol. 30. Ed. by D. A. Hubbard et al. Dallas, Tex.: Word Books.

Goldstein, Jonathan A.
1976-1983 *I Maccabees. II Maccabees*. The Anchor Bible, vols. 41-41A. Ed. by W. F. Albright and D. N. Freedman. Garden City, N.Y.: Doubleday.

Greenspoon, L. J.
1981 "The Origin of the Idea of Resurrection." In *Traditions in Transformation*. Ed. by B. Halpern and J. D. Levenson. Winona Lake: Eisenbrauns.

Hammer, Raymond
1976 *The Book of Daniel*. New York: Cambridge University Press.

Hanson, Paul
1975 *The Dawn of Apocalyptic: The Historical and Sociological Roots of Jewish Apocalyptic Eschatology*. Philadelphia: Fortress.
Hartman, Louis F.
1968 "Daniel." In *The Jerome Bible Commentary*. Ed. by R. E. Brown et al. Englewood Cliffs, N.J.: Prentice Hall, Inc.
Hartman, Louis F., and Dilella, Alexander
1978 *The Book of Daniel*. The Anchor Bible, vol. 23. Ed. by W. F. Albright and D. N. Freedman. Garden City, N.Y.: Doubleday.
IDB
1962, 1976 *The Interpreter's Dictionary of the Bible*. Vols. 1-4, ed. by G. A. Buttrick, 1962; Suppl. vol., ed. by K. Crim, 1976. Nashville: Abingdon.
Josephus, Flavius (A.D. 37-100)
1987 *The Works of Josephus*. Translated by William Whiston. Peabody, Mass.: Hendrickson Publishers.
Knight, George A. F.
1971 "The Book of Daniel." In *The Interpreter's One-Volume Commentary on the Bible*. Ed. by C. M. Layman. Nashville: Abingdon.
Koch, Klaus
1984 *The Prophets*. Vol. II: *The Babylonian and Persian Periods*. Trans. by M. Kohl. Philadelphia: Fortress.
Larkin, Clarence
1919 *The Book of Revelation*. Philadelphia: Author.
1918 *The Second Coming of Christ*. Philadelphia: Author.
Lehman, Chester K.
1950 *The Fulfillment of Prophecy*. Scottdale, Pa.: Mennonite Publishing House.
Lucas, E. C.
1989 "The Origin of Daniel's Four Empires Schema Re-examined." *Tyndale Bulletin* 40 (no. 2): 185-202.
Lurie, D. H.
1990 "A New Interpretation of Daniel's 'Sevens' and the Chronology of the Seventy 'Sevens.' " *Journal of the Evangelical Theological Society* 33:303-309.
Martens, Elmer A.
1986 *Jeremiah*. Believers Church Bible Commentary. OT ed. by E. A. Martens. Scottdale, Pa.: Herald Press.
Mauro, Philip
1970 *The Seventy Weeks and the Great Tribulation*. Swengel, Pa.: Reiner Publications.
Menno Simons
1956 *The Complete Writings of Menno Simons*. C. 1496-1561. Trans. from the Dutch by L. Verduin. Ed. by J. C. Wenger. Scottdale, Pa.: Herald Press.
Mickelsen, A. Berkeley
1984 *Daniel and Revelation: Riddles or Realities?* Nashville: Nelson.
Montgomery, James A.
1979 *A Critical and Exegetical Commentary on the Book of Daniel*. Edinburgh: T. & T. Clark.
Moore, Carey A.
1977 *Daniel, Esther, and Jeremiah: The Additions*. The Anchor Bible,

vol. 44. Ed. by W. F. Albright and D. N. Freedman. Garden City, N.Y.: Doubleday.

Morris, Leon
1972 *Apocalyptic*. Grand Rapids: Eerdmans.

NOAB
1991 *The New Oxford Annotated Bible with the Apocryphal/ Deuterocanonical Books, NRSV.* Ed. by B. M. Metzger and R. E. Murphy. New York: Oxford University Press.

Oates, Joan
1986 *Babylon*. Rev. ed. New York: Thames and Hudson.

Owens, John Joseph
1971 *Daniel*. The Broadman Bible Commentary, vol. 6. Ed. by C. J. Allen. Nashville: Broadman.

Payne, J. Barton
1978 "The Goal of Daniel's Seventy Weeks." *Journal of the Evangelical Theological Society* 21 (no. 2, June 1978): 97-115.

Porteous, Norman W.
1965 *Daniel*. Philadelphia: Westminster.

Prophecy Conference
1953 *Prophecy Conference*. Report of Conference Held at Elkhart, Ind., Apr. 3-5, 1952. Scottdale, Pa.: Mennonite Publishing House.

Pritchard, J. B. *See* ANET.

Reid, Stephen Breck
1989 *Enoch and Daniel*. Berkeley, Calif.: Bibal.

Roop, Eugene F.
1987 *Genesis*. Believers Church Bible Commentary. OT ed. by E. A. Martens. Scottdale, Pa.: Herald Press.

Russell, D. S.
1964 *The Method and Message of Jewish Apocalyptic 200 B.C.-A.D.100*. Philadelphia: Westminster.
1981 *Daniel*. Philadelphia: Westminster.

Simons, Menno
See Menno Simons.

Sources
1985 *The Sources of Swiss Anabaptism*. Ed. by L. Harder. Classics of the Radical Reformation. Scottdale, Pa.: Herald Press.

Stauffer, Ethelbert
1945 "The Anabaptist Theology of Martyrdom." *The Mennonite Quarterly Review* 19 (no. 3, 1945): 179-214.

Stauffer, J. L.
1949 *Studies in the Book of Daniel*. Scottdale, Pa.: Herald Press.

Talmon, Shemaryahu
1987 "Daniel." In *The Literary Guide to the Bible*. Ed. by R. Alter and F. Kermode. Cambridge, Mass.: Belknap Press of Harvard Univ. Press.

Tatford, Frederick A.
1953 *Daniel and His Prophecy*. London: Oliphants. 1980 reprint, Minneapolis: Klock & Klock.

TDNT
1964-76 *Theological Dictionary of the New Testament*. 10 vols. Ed. by G. Kittel and G. Friedrich; tr. and ed. by G. W. Bromiley. Grand Rapids: Eerdmans.

TDOT
1977-90 *Theological Dictionary of the Old Testament.* Vols. 1-6. Ed. by G. J. Botterweck and H. Ringgren. Grand Rapids: Eerdmans.

Thomson, J. E. H.
1983 "Daniel." In *The Pulpit Commentary*. Ed. by H. D. M. Spence and J. S. Excell. Reprint, Grand Rapids: Eerdmans.

Towner, W. Sibley
1984 *Daniel.* A Bible Commentary for Teaching and Preaching. Ed. by J. L. Mays et al. Atlanta: John Knox.

Viviano, Benedict T., and Justin Taylor
1992 "Sadducees, Angels, and Resurrection (Acts 23:8-9)." *Journal of Biblical Literature* 111:496-498.

Vermes, G.
1987 *The Dead Sea Scrolls in English*. 3d ed. London: Penguin Books.

Wallace, Ronald S.
1979 *The Lord Is King: The Message of Daniel*. Downers Grove, Ill.: InterVarsity Press.

Walvoord, John F.
1971 *Daniel: The Key to Prophetic Revelation*. Chicago: Moody.

Wink, Walter
1984 *Naming the Powers: The Language of Power in the New Testament.* The Powers, vol. 1. Phildaelphia: Fortress.
1986 *Unmasking the Powers: The Invisible Forces That Determine Human Existence.* The Powers, vol. 2. Philadelphia: Fortress.
1992 *Engaging the Powers: Discernment and Resistance in a World of Domination.* The Powers, vol. 3. Minneapolis: Fortress.

Wood, Leon
1973 *A Commentary on Daniel*. Grand Rapids: Zondervan.

Yamauchi, Edwin M.
1990 *Persia and the Bible*. Grand Rapids: Baker Book House.

Young, E. J.
1949 *The Prophecy of Daniel*. Grand Rapids: Eerdmans.

Selected Resources

Anderson, Robert A. *Signs and Wonders.* International Theological Commentary. Grand Rapids: Eerdmans, 1984. Brief, well-written commentary on Daniel.

Baldwin, Joyce G. *Daniel: An Introduction and Commentary.* Tyndale Old Testament Commentaries. Madison, Wis.: Inter-Varsity Press, 1978. Masterful, carefully written. Excellent for personal study.

Bruce, F. F. *Israel and the Nations.* Grand Rapids: Eerdmans, 1969. Helpful background materials for the study of Daniel.

_______________. *New Testament Development of Old Testament Themes.* Grand Rapids: Eerdmans, 1969. Masterful chapters on "Rule of God," "People of God," and "Servant Messiah."

Ewert, David. *And Then Comes the End.* Scottdale, Pa.: Herald Press, 1980. Study of the end-times, based on the New Testament, but rooted in Old Testament themes.

Goldingay, John E. *Daniel.* Word Biblical Commentary, vol. 30. Dallas: Word Books, 1989. Excellent for person or group that wants to go more deeply into the interpretation of Daniel.

Wallace, Ronald S. *The Lord Is King: The Message of Daniel.* The Bible Speaks Today. Downers Grove: InterVarsity Press, 1979. Readable. Takes the text seriously, expounds it, and relates it to life today. Sees in Antiochus IV Epiphanes a foreshadowing of an antichrist in the last days.

Walvoord, John F. *Daniel: The Key to Prophetic Revelation.* Chicago: Moody, 1971. An example of commentaries written from the viewpoint that Daniel provides an outline of the program of God from Babylon to the second advent of Christ.

Index of Ancient Texts

(Other Than Daniel)

The Author

Paul M. Lederach, Souderton, Pennsylvania, was ordained to the ministry in the Franconia Mennonite Conference at Norristown, Pa., in 1944. Since then, he has served in a variety of pastoral and churchwide responsibilities and now is chair of the overseers for that same conference.

While connected with the Mennonite Publishing House (1952-78) at Scottdale, Pa., he was an editor of the pioneer Mennonite graded Sunday school project, the *Herald Graded Sunday School Series* (1953-61), a cooperative venture with the General Conference Mennonite Church. He served as director of the Curriculum Development and Service Department (1961-69) and as administrator of the Congregational Literature Division (1970-73). From 1973 to 1978 he was the executive director of the *Foundation Series*, the second graded Sunday school curriculum project, this time involving five cooperating denominations.

Lederach served as president of the Mennonite Board of Education (1964-71) and presently represents the Franconia Mennonite Conference on the General Board of the Mennonite Church. While living in Scottdale, he was active in the Allegheny Mennonite Conference, serving in executive positions and as an overseer. Returning to Franconia Conference in 1987, he served as pastor of the Franconia Mennonite Church before assuming his present position in 1991.

Paul received a B.A. from Goshen (Ind.) College, a Th.B. from

Goshen Biblical Seminary, an M.R.E. from Eastern Baptist Theological Seminary (Philadelphia), and a D.Ed. from Southwestern Baptist Theological Seminary (Fort Worth). He has written many books published by Herald Press, such as *Reshaping the Teaching Ministry, Mennonite Youth, Teaching in the Congregation,* and *A Third Way*.

Paul and Mary (Slagell) his wife, an elementary public school teacher, are the parents of four children: Judith (Styer), James, Deborah (Gunden), and Rebecca (Allebach). All are married and are members of congregations in the Anabaptist-Mennonite tradition. Paul and Mary have traveled widely in North America, Europe, Africa, and Asia in personal and church-related activities, including a teaching assignment at Union Biblical Seminary, Pune, India. They are members of the Norristown New Life Mennonite Church.